Techniques in
HOME WINEMAKING

The Comprehensive Guide to
Making Château-Style Wines

Daniel Pambianchi

Véhicule Press

Cover design by J.W. Stewart
Typeset by Pathology Images Inc.
Printed by Marquis Printing Inc.
Technical Editing by Tim Vandergrift

LIBRARY AND ARCHIVES CANADA CATALOGUING IN PUBLICATION

Pambianchi, Daniel
Techniques in home winemaking : the comprehensive
guide to making château-style wines
/ Daniel Pambianchi. — Newly-rev. and expanded ed.
Includes index.

ISBN 978-1-55065-236-9

1. Wine and wine making—Amateurs' manuals. I. Title.
TP548.2.P346 2008   641.8'72   C2008-901567-3

Published by Véhicule Press
P.O.B. 125, Place du Parc Station
Montreal, Quebec H2X 4A3

www.vehiculepress.com

U.S. Distribution: Independent Publishers Group, Chicago, IL
Canadian Distribution: LiTDistCo, Georgetown, ON

Printed in Canada
on 100% post-consumer recycled paper

TECHNIQUES IN HOME WINEMAKING

DISCLAIMER

Additives, reagents and other products and chemicals referenced in this book have applications in winemaking. With care and caution, these can be safely used in home winemaking although some may be unsafe or may pose a health hazard if not used in the recommended concentrations or if used by unskilled winemakers.

Commercial winemaking regulations may prohibit or limit the use of such chemicals or products, and vary from one country or winemaking region to another. Some commercial wineries also shun the use of additives or similar products because they simply deem these as unnatural and unconventional, going against traditional winemaking methods. For home winemaking use, chemicals approved for enological applications should be used with great care, and recommended concentrations should be strictly followed. Generic substitutes for enological chemicals should not be used.

Neither the author, editors, or the publisher assumes any responsibility for the use or misuse of information contained in this book.

References to winemaking supplies from various sources are included to illustrate typical use of these supplies from companies whose products are the most prevalent in the home winemaking market. The use of these references and all trademarks and copyrighted material from cited manufacturers, suppliers, wholesalers, retailers, distributors or other constitute neither sponsorship nor affiliation of these companies with the author, editors and publisher, or with this book. Companies have not paid any promotional fees to have their names and/or products listed here.

TABLE OF CONTENTS

FOREWORD

The journey from grape to glass is filled with many key decisions for any winemaker. Every step of the way a winemaker has to pick from among a host of different techniques to create their dream wine. Luckily for hobby winemakers, Daniel Pambianchi is around as a guide through the often-confusing world of winemaking. In every issue of *WineMaker Magazine* since 2000 Daniel has helped hobby winemakers better understand how to make better wine with his "Techniques" column. From testing the fresh grapes before crush all the way to bottling, Daniel has covered the full spectrum of techniques you need in a clear, easy-to-understand way over the years. Daniel has a real skill in breaking down complex information into laymen's language that at the same time doesn't water down the subject. In fact, *WineMaker Magazine's* readers have always given Daniel high marks in annual surveys and mention his skill of making all techniques and winemaking science, no matter how advanced and difficult, simple and comprehensible. Just like *WineMaker* readers have found out when reading Daniel's articles, you will get straightforward, practical techniques and learn skills you can put to use in your home winery in the pages that follow.

In the years since the first edition of *Techniques in Home Winemaking* was published Daniel has tirelessly added to his winemaking knowledge. He continues to write his "Techniques" column in the magazine as well as judging our annual wine competition. Behind the scenes at the magazine, he acts as our Technical Editor reviewing every article we publish for technical accuracy and keeping up on new trends and information in the winemaking world. Outside of the magazine, he has taken his award-winning home winemaking hobby to the next level by now becoming an award-winning professional winemaker. His Maleta Estate Winery in Niagara-on-the-Lake, Ontario is garnering critical praise as Daniel continues to discover new techniques in winemaking and to offer advice from which one can benefit by reading his book. This new edition of his *Techniques in Home Winemaking* incorporates this wealth of knowledge and all the latest information and experience that Daniel has to share.

In our offices at *WineMaker Magazine* and winemaker-mag.com, earlier editions of Daniel's *Techniques in Home Winemaking* are dog-eared and show the wear and tear of constant use as we refer back again and again to answer some winemaking question we might have when working on a story. I'm thrilled now with this new edition I can get my hands on some fresh copies with plenty of fresh new content to replace those worn out earlier editions. Enjoy Daniel's book as it helps you enjoy the fun and satisfying world of hobby winemaking.

Brad Ring
Publisher, *WineMaker Magazine*

ACKNOWLEDGMENTS

This third edition would not have been possible without the continued, tremendous support of Simon Dardick and Nancy Marrelli, publishers of Véhicule Press, and Irving Dardick (Pathology Images Inc.) for "piecing" together my work, and the many individuals, manufacturers, suppliers and retailers who have provided product information and feedback, many of whom have reviewed parts of the manuscript. New and updated information is also largely based on my articles that have been published over the years in *WineMaker Magazine*, and so I am thankful to all my readers who have taken the time to share their experiences and provide invaluable feedback.

Without a doubt, however, my experience of running a commercial winery, Maleta Winery in Niagara-on-the-Lake, Ontario, Canada, alongside our talented consulting winemaker, Arthur Harder, has been the source of the wealth of new information in this updated edition. Arthur's international winemaking experience and astute know-how have provided much inspiration for this work.

I am also grateful to Brad Ring, publisher of *WineMaker Magazine*, for his support and generosity, and for allowing me to reuse published material. And a big, heartfelt thank-you goes out to Tim Vandergrift, Technical Services Manager at Winexpert, Inc., for his technical review of this book, and Don Martin for his wonderful work on the illustrations.

Most importantly, I wish to thank my wife, Dalia, and my two wonderful sons, Justin and Eric for their patience throughout this project, and the many friends who have provided feedback on my wines and shared their stories over the years. In the end, this is what winemaking is all about – enjoying good wine with friends and family.

PREFACE

The subject of wine comprises three major areas: Viticulture, enology, and wine appreciation. Viticulture and enology are the sciences and practices of grape growing and winemaking, respectively. Wine appreciation includes tasting – for the purpose of evaluating wine and to convey that assessment to wine enthusiasts – and drinking. This book specifically deals with the science and practice of winemaking, or enology. Consult Appendix E for a list of references available for further reading on viticulture and wine appreciation.

The objectives of this book, then, are to introduce winemaking techniques and products – updated to reflect what is currently available on the market – to novice home winemakers while providing serious and advanced amateur winemakers with proven and practical techniques to produce premium-quality wines that are virtually indistinguishable from their professional counterparts. On occasions, when experimenting or when the year's crop has produced low or average quality grapes, home winemakers will have to make use of techniques and products described herein to "correct" the wine. Correction is required to achieve balance among aromas, flavors, body, taste and color in the finished wine. Ultimately, wine is best enjoyed when it is well balanced.

Techniques and products include the use of various winemaking equipment, enological chemicals and ingredients, and vinification (the conversion of grape juice into wine by fermentation) techniques and procedures. The ability to produce a good to superior wine under adverse conditions depends on one's knowledge and experience of these techniques and products. Experienced winemakers will know how to vinify must (grape juice) into wine through the various stages such that the probability of faults in the finished wine is greatly reduced. Home winemakers are encouraged to experiment to decide which techniques produce a desired wine style.

How to use this book

This book can first be read to learn about the science, principles and practices of home winemaking, and wine analysis. It can then serve as a reference textbook for analytical procedures, to determine quantities of ingredients to be added, to review specific advice on winemaking procedures, and to determine the root cause when encountering problems.

Chapters are presented in a logical order by first providing an introduction to winemaking and necessary winemaking equipment. A thorough discussion of must and wine analysis serves as a foundation to understanding winemaking and vinification procedures. A solid working knowledge of sugar and alcohol measurements, acidity, pH, sulfur dioxide levels and phenolic compounds is necessary to be able to produce the highest quality wine according to one's desired wine style. Detailed descriptions of winemaking procedures are then presented in the general order that these are performed from fermentation to aging and bottling.

When used as a reference textbook, readers can consult any chapter or section as these have been laid out independently of one another. This also allows winemakers to pick and choose procedures according to the desired wine style. For example, the section on malolactic fermentation can be skipped entirely if this type of fermentation is not desired. Likewise, the chapter on oak barrels may be skipped if not oak-aging wine although alternatives to barrels are discussed.

Specifically:

Chapter 1 provides an overview of winemaking and winemaking terminology, the various wine types and styles that home winemakers can produce, and the available grape juice varieties. Pros and cons of winemaking from grapes, juice and concentrate are discussed. Winemaking flowcharts are presented to illustrate the complete processes from grape crushing to fermentation to bottling.

Chapter 2 describes all the necessary equipment for home winemaking and instructions on its proper use for producing premium wines. The importance of cleaning and sanitizing all equipment and of maintaining a sanitized environment throughout the winemaking cycle is also explained.

Chapters 3 deals with the analysis and control of musts and wines – specifically, sugar and alcohol, acidity and pH, sulfur dioxide, and phenolic components – which are key in producing the best wines. This chapter explains the significance of measuring and controlling these components and their role in winemaking.

Chapter 4 discusses vinification and winemaking procedures essential to producing premium wines, from crushing and destemming – or, must preparation, in the case of juice or concentrate – to stabilization. Other procedures include maceration, micro-oxygenation, delestage, pressing, and alcoholic and malolactic fermentations.

Chapter 5 details clarification procedures, namely, racking, fining and filtration. These are discussed separately so that winemakers can decide which method(s) to adopt to produce a desired wine style. Clarification by fining and/or by filtration remain much-debated topics. This chapter provides pros and cons of each process to allow winemakers to make their own choice.

Chapter 6 describes physical, chemical and microbial stabilization processes and products key to ensuring that wines remain stable once bottled, and how to screen for spoilage organisms that may affect the quality of wine. The all-important topic on stabilizing filtration – better known as membrane filtration, or (though inappropriate) sterile filtration – is described in detail.

Chapter 7 provides guidelines on the traditional art and process of blending wines. The practice of blending wines has existed since the early days of winemaking and is still used in modern winemaking in spite of the popularity of varietals (wines from single grape varieties). Blending allows winemakers to take advantage of the individual grape variety characteristics to produce more complex, interesting wines and to achieve balance among components, namely, sweetness, acidity, alcohol, body, aromas, and flavors.

Chapter 8 describes the use, conditioning or preparation and maintenance of oak barrels in winemaking, and how to ferment and age wine in barrels. Barrel spoilage problems, their treatments and preventive measures are also discussed. Alternatives to oak barrels for imparting oak aromas are presented. And if you are a handy person skilled in woodworking, you will enjoy the section on barrel reconditioning and extending the life of your barrels.

Chapter 9 describes the necessary equipment required for bottling wine as well as various techniques used to increase bottling efficiency.

Chapters 10, 11, 12 and 13 provide step-by-step instructions on the production of Pinot Noir wine from grapes, sparkling wine, Port and Icewines, respectively, making use of techniques introduced in earlier chapters.

Chapter 14 provides a comprehensive guide and quick reference chart for troubleshooting the most common vinification problems that home winemakers may come across, and techniques used to resolve them. This is undoubtedly one of the most important chapters because things don't always proceed according to plans.

Chapter 15 outlines the proper design and construction of a small home winery and cellar that will serve your winemaking and cellaring needs. Planning and building instructions will help you set up that perfect environment for your wines.

Appendix A lists conversion factors between Metric, US and Imperial systems for relevant measurements.

Appendix B provides a handy conversion table for converting between Specific Gravity, Brix % sugar (wt/vol) and potential alcohol, as well as tables to correct hydrometer readings taken at different temperatures than the instrument's calibration temperature.

Appendix C provides a winemaking log chart that can be used to record all winemaking and vinification activities. Keeping records of a wine's progress and treatments is key to successful winemaking.

Appendix D provides a summary chart of winemaking ingredients and chemicals, and concentrations presented throughout this book. It can be used as a quick-reference guide.

Appendix E lists some recommended reading to learn more about grapes, winery technology, the chemistry of vinification, analytical methods in winemaking and oak barrel maintenance.

The following table can be used as a guideline to determine which sections of this book are recommended for you based on your level of expertise, knowledge and skills.

Sections	Beginner	Intermediate	Advanced
1.1–1.7	✓	✓	✓
2.1–2.6	✓	✓	✓
3.1	✓	✓	✓
3.2–3.5		✓	✓
4.1–4.2	✓	✓	✓
4.3		✓	✓
4.4–4.5			✓
4.6–4.7	✓	✓	✓
4.8		✓	✓
4.9	✓	✓	✓
4.10			✓
5.1–5.3	✓	✓	✓
6.1		✓	✓
6.2	6.2.4	6.2.4	✓
7.1–7.2	✓	✓	✓
7.3–7.4		✓	✓
8.1–8.2	✓	✓	✓
8.3–8.4		✓	✓
8.5	✓	✓	✓
8.6–8.7		✓	✓
8.8			✓
9.1–9.7	✓	✓	✓
10.1–10.4		✓	✓
11.1–11.4			✓
11.5–11.6		✓	✓
12.1–12.3	✓	✓	✓
13.1–13.2			✓
14.1–14.19	✓	✓	✓
15.1–15.3		✓	✓

ABOUT UNITS OF MEASURES

Winemaking in most parts of the world is greatly influenced by European methods and processes. Therefore, the use of the Metric system (also known as the International System of Units or *Système International d'Unités* (SI) in French) for units of measures has proliferated to most winemaking countries. In the U.S., the Metric system is also widely used in laboratory analysis, but the U.S. system is most often used for winemaking equipment manufactured there. For example, French oak barrels sold in the U.S. are described in liters and American barrels are described in gallons.

Readers are advised to exercise caution with the use of units of measures when obtaining winemaking "recipes" from books and other sources to ensure proper dosage. Many U.S. and Imperial units use the same terms but their quantities are quite different – a U.S. gallon is smaller than an Imperial gallon.

This book provides all measurements primarily using the Metric system as well as the U.S. system for U.S.-manufactured equipment. Fahrenheit conversions are provided since this is the primary unit used in the U.S.

The most often used unit of measurement in laboratory analysis is concentration, the amount of a solid present in a liquid. Concentrations are expressed in grams per liter, abbreviated as g/L, or in grams per hectoliter (100 liters), abbreviated as g/hL or in milligrams per liter, abbreviated as mg/L. Other concentration units used in the industry are percentages – weight to volume (w/v) or volume to volume (v/v) – and parts per million, abbreviated ppm. The ppm unit signifies a volume-to-volume ratio for liquids dissolved in liquids or a weight-to-volume ratio for solids dissolved in liquids. For liquids to be dissolved in liquids, one ppm is equivalent to 1 mL per 1,000 L using the Metric system. Using the U.S. system, 1,000 ppm is equivalent to 0.13 fl oz/gal.

For solids to be dissolved in liquids, one ppm is equivalent to 1 mg/L using the Metric system. In the U.S. system, 1,000 ppm is equivalent to 0.01 lb/gal. These assume a density of solids of 1 g per mL and 1¼ oz per fl oz, respectively. Weight measurements are greatly simplified with these conversion factors since it is easier to measure small volumes as opposed to small weights.

For acidity measurements, concentrations are expressed both in g/L or as a percentage of weight to volume where 1 g/L represents a 0.1% acid concentration. For example, a 0.65% acid solution represents 6.5 g of acid dissolved in 1 L of liquid. This book uses g/L for acid concentrations and can be easily converted to a weight-to-volume percentage by dividing the g/L value by 10.

For sulfur dioxide (SO_2) measurements, concentrations are expressed in mg/L although the industry-accepted measurement is ppm. It can be assumed that 5 mL (1 tsp) of sulfite powder weighs approximately 5 g – an acceptable approximation. SO_2 measurements in ppm can then be easily converted to an approximate mg/L value one for one. For example, 50 ppm is approximately equivalent to 50 mg/L.

For sugar concentrations, Brix is the standard unit of use in commercial winemaking while in home winemaking, Specific Gravity is very often used. Given the wide use of both units, this book provides measurements using both units. Residual sugar concentrations are still expressed in g/L.

In some cases, cup, teaspoon or tablespoon-equivalent measurements are provided, as these are standard and practical kitchen measures.

Appendix A provides the list of conversion factors for Metric, U.S. and Imperial systems.

Although specific measurements are given for each product described, readers should always follow manufacturers' recommended measurements as ingredients and chemicals may be sold with different concentrations or may have different compositions.

1
INTRODUCTION

Home winemaking has gained tremendous popularity as a hobby in recent years. Although the cost per bottle of homemade wine is very low compared to commercial wine, the increase in popularity is really attributed to the pleasure and pride of producing one's own wine. The quality of homemade wines can also match or surpass that of commercial wines, whether using grapes, fresh juice or even kits, particularly with the availability of premium and ultra-premium wine kits.

With the availability of high quality four- and six-week wine kits, more and more novice and serious enophiles are now becoming home winemakers. Kits can produce very good to excellent quality wines easily, quickly and economically. Access to winemaking materials previously not available to home winemakers, coupled with improvements in wine production technology and techniques, are also key contributing success factors.

1.1 WINEMAKING TERMINOLOGY

Let's start with a high-level review of basic winemaking and related terminology to establish a common framework of reference.

Winemaking refers to the set of processes, from juice extraction to bottling, for producing wines from fruits such as grapes. Some processes may be skipped for different winemaking styles or may be not be required altogether, for example, when making wine from kits. The specific process of fermentation, converting fruit juice into wine, is referred to as vinification.

The major steps in winemaking include crushing and pressing of the grapes, maceration, alcoholic fermentation, malolactic fermentation, clarification including racking, fining and filtration, stabilization, aging, blending and bottling. These operations are performed differently and optionally in the production of white, rosé, red and sparkling wines, or to create different styles of wine. Certain operations may not be required at all depending on the type of juice used. For example, crushing and pressing are not required unless making wine from grapes.

When grapes are first crushed and pressed before fermentation, the extracted juice is referred to as the must, and as a result of pressing, it contains some solids such as pulp. Must, the technically correct word, is often referred to as juice or grape juice. Juice also refers to commercially available fresh juice that has been separated from grape particles. Once fermentation of the must has begun and alcohol is present, the must is referred to as wine. When starting with fresh grape juice or concentrated juice, crushing, pressing and maceration operations are not required.

When grapes are crushed and/or pressed, all grape remainders – skins, seeds and stems – are referred to as the pomace. The process of leaving the must in contact with the pomace for color, flavor and tannin extraction is referred to as maceration. Maceration is always used in the production of red wines, but seldom in white winemaking. During maceration and fermentation, the pomace will start to form a cap that will rise to the top of the container and float on the must.

Alcoholic fermentation is the chemical process of converting fermentable sugars into alcohol and carbon dioxide under the action of yeast. Fermentable sugars include glucose and fructose that occur naturally in grapes, and dextrose (corn sugar) or sucrose (beet or cane sugar) that are added by the winemaker. The process of adding sugar to the must or wine to increase the potential alcohol content and/or to sweeten a wine is referred to as chaptalization. Although it is possible to make many different types of fruit wines by alcoholic fermentation, this book deals only with wine production from grape derivatives.

Although wines undergo a single alcoholic fermentation in the production of still (non-sparkling) wines, it is common in home winemaking to refer to primary and secondary fermentations to describe arbitrary phases relative to the amount of fermentable sugars still present in the must; it is usually related to fermentation vigor. The transition from the vigorous primary fermentation to the lesser active secondary fermentation signals the need to transfer the wine to another container, usually recommended in kit winemaking. Most literature refers to both fermentations as one, i.e., the alcoholic fermentation, and helps avoid confusion when referring to malolactic fermentation, quite often referred to as the secondary fermentation. Malolactic fermentation is a non-alcoholic fermentation under the action of bacteria – as opposed to yeast in alcoholic fermentation – that transforms the sharper malic acid in wines into the more supple lactic acid and carbon dioxide. Second (not secondary) fermentation refers to the bottle fermentation process in the production of sparkling wines. Bottle fermentation is simply an alcoholic fermentation carried out in the bottle to retain the carbon dioxide gas in the wine.

Clarification is the process of removing particles still in suspension in the wine or that have settled at the bottom of a container affecting clarity and limpidity. Clarification can be achieved by racking, by fining, using natural products or chemicals, commonly referred to as fining agents, or by mechanical filtration.

Racking is the process of separating wine from its sediment that has settled at the bottom of the container. Sediment resulting from yeast activity during alcoholic fermentation is referred to as lees. The settling action of suspended particles as sediment is referred to as sedimentation. Fining agents are added to a wine to coagulate particles in suspension and cause them to sediment. A subsequent racking is required when fining to separate the sedimented particles, or lees. Filtration is the process of passing wine through a filter medium by mechanical means to separate particles in suspension. Filtration does not involve sedimentation.

Stabilization is the process of readying the wine for consumption or aging to ensure that clarity, freshness and balance of the wine are maintained. Stabilization also protects the wine from microbial spoilage, re-fermentation, premature oxidation, and crystallization of tartaric acid while the wine is aging and once bottled. Stabilization is a necessary step before bottling or bulk aging of wine for an extended period of time.

Recently, consumers have become more aware of the presence and the role of sulfite in wines. Sulfite plays a key role as an antioxidant and preservative in wines. Sulfur dioxide (SO_2), a component of sulfite, is both an enological ingredient and a natural by-product of fermentation, albeit in small quantities. Sulfite, commonly added to wines to prevent microbial spoilage, is also used to sanitize winemaking equipment.

Bottle or bulk aging refers to the maturation phases of winemaking necessary for wine to develop its character, structure, and to increase its complexity. Both aging methods will improve wine;

however, bulk aging in oak barrels will impart special aromas and taste as the wine will extract favorable compounds from the wood. The aging period can vary from several months to several years depending on the quality of juice or grapes used, grape varieties, vinification methods, stabilization and preservation techniques, and aging process, just to name a few factors.

Blending, considered an art in winemaking circles, is the process of mixing different wines or batches to achieve a desired style, or to improve balance of organoleptic (color, taste, smell and mouthfeel) qualities. The final blend should exhibit the desired organoleptic qualities inherited from the various blending wines.

Bottling is the final winemaking operation where wine is transferred from bulk containers to bottles for further aging or for drinking. Bottled wine should be properly sealed with appropriate closures, such as corks, to protect it from the elements.

1.2 THE PHILOSOPHY OF MAKING CHÂTEAU-STYLE WINES

There is no denying that good, premium-quality wine can only be made from the best raw material, i.e., grapes, juice or concentrate. You cannot make premium-quality wine from poor grapes or juice. The best you can hope for is decent, drinkable wine, and not memorable, hedonistic, age-worthy wine. Section 1.4 provides some insight on choosing the raw material.

In producing premium-quality wines, winemakers follow the evolution of their wines from fermentation to bottling and aging, and nurture them to ensure good structure, great complexity, and organoleptic balance of all components. Beyond this, wines must express the winemaker's individual character. Different winemaking and vinification techniques are used to achieve this individuality, often dictated by the winemaker's beliefs in quality, process experience and preference of wine style. As winemaking is not an exact science but rather a subjective art, techniques will vary greatly depending on the desired style and quality of wine. Processing and blending techniques are often well-guarded secrets within premium wineries.

There are essentially two opposing mind-sets within the winemaking industry. First, there are the traditionalists, or minimalists, who process their wines with minimal or no additives such as sulfites, and limited clarification without filtration. Their primary objective is to produce the best quality age-worthy wines, and they spare no expense achieving this goal. Traditional wine production requires careful and constant monitoring and control to prevent spoilage throughout the long winemaking period. Modern commercial wineries, on the other hand, which have short-term financial objectives and constraints, often use additives and processes for quick commercialization of young, ready-to-drink wines.

For home winemaking, it is recommended to adopt a philosophy that lies between these two approaches. The risk of spoilage or oxidation will be reduced while maintaining a high level of quality. In this case, home winemakers will have more control over expected results and can usually recover from faults when they are detected early.

Readers are advised to follow the procedures described in this book and to experiment within the prescribed bounds to establish a personal preference of wine style.

References 13 [Olney] and 14 [Olney] in Appendix E provide a history and insight into winemaking philosophies at the Domaine de la Romanée-Conti (Burgundy) and Château d'Yquem (Sauternes), respectively. Their wines are testament to their wineries' obsession with making only the best wines, and how high consumer demand and small supply fuel the sometime insane wine prices.

1.3 WINE STYLES

Wine styles can be categorized according to presence of carbon dioxide gas, color, sweetness and alcohol level.

Wines are first classified according to the presence of carbon dioxide, characterized by fizziness or abundant bubbles. Still wines have no carbon dioxide whereas sparkling wines are characterized by the presence of carbon dioxide. Sparkling wines are produced by conducting a second fermentation in the bottle or in a closed vat, or by carbonating the wine. The second fermentation is achieved by the addition of fermentable sugar and yeast. Bottle fermentation is the preferred method to produce the best-quality sparkling wine, and is used in the Champagne region of France to produce the world-famous bubbly known as Champagne, as well as Spanish *cava*, and Californian bubbly. Another well-known bubbly is the vat-fermented Asti Spumante from the Piedmont region of Italy. The carbonation method is not used in the production of premium sparkling wines, a practice normally not allowed in commercial winemaking, but is an excellent alternative in home winemaking.

All wines are classified according to color – white, red or rosé. White wines are produced from white grapes or white-juice red grapes, referred to as *blanc de blancs* and *blanc de noirs* wines, respectively. Red wines are produced from red-juice or white-juice red grapes where the juice is macerated with the grape skins to extract the red color. Rosé wine, often referred to as blush wine in North America, is first produced as red wine, with only a short maceration period to extract a little red color, and then vinified as white wine.

Wines are also classified according to the level of sweetness. When the must is allowed to ferment until the amount of residual sugar is below a certain level, usually not detectable by taste, the wine is said to be dry. Most commercial table wines are dry. Beyond this minimum level, the wines become off-dry, semi-sweet or sweet depending on the amount of residual sugar, and are great for accompanying desserts or served on their own as apéritif with hors-d'œuvres or as dessert. White wines make the best sweet wines although it is possible to produce sweet red wines, such as Port, the famous fortified wine from Portugal.

The last classification includes fortified wines where alcohol, usually a distilled spirit such as brandy, is added to increase the alcohol content of the finished wine. Sherry and Port are two popular types of fortified wines.

The types of wine can be blended to produce different styles such as a semi-sweet bubbly rosé or a Port-style wine.

1.4 GRAPES, FRESH JUICE, RECONSTITUTED JUICE, OR CONCENTRATE?

Home winemakers now have a plethora of choices of so-called raw material for types of must: grapes, fresh grape juice, reconstituted juice, or concentrated grape juice – essentially juice with some or all water content removed. Refer to Figure 1-1.

The choice of must type depends on the desired style, quality, and aging potential, which depend on the concentration of total dissolved solids (TDS) – also known as total soluble solids (TSS) – in the raw material. TDS refers to the concentration of all solutes in the must, mainly sugar (glucose and fructose) but also acids and a host of other organic and inorganic substances. In general, the higher the TDS concentration in the raw material, the higher the potential for making age-worthy wine, i.e., wines from low TDS concentration musts are usually meant for early-drinking.

The choice of must type also depends on time and effort that one is prepared to invest, as well as cost and availability of winemaking equipment. Each type of must has pros and cons relative to these factors.

Note: "Kit" is the more common term generally used to refer to either concentrate or a blend of concentrate and juice as the raw material because these are packaged and sold along with all required ingredients to make a batch of wine; however, it can be confusing as reconstituted juice, for example, can also be purchased as a kit that includes the necessary ingredients and/or equipment to start mak-

Figure 1-1: Kit, reconstituted juice, fresh juice, or grapes?

ing a first batch of wine. In this book, the term "concentrated grape juice" is used to refer to either concentrate or a blend of concentrate and juice, unless a distinction is necessary.

1.4.1 WINE FROM GRAPES

Winemaking from grapes is the traditional method and the serious alternative to juice or concentrate. Through careful and elaborate winemaking techniques, wines of outstanding quality can be produced from grapes. This method is also the most prone to errors and disappointing results if constant care is not exercised throughout the winemaking process.

The main advantage of using grapes over other types of musts is that both the length and the temperature of the maceration period (and, hence, extraction of color, flavors and tannins) are under the control of the winemaker, who can balance the organoleptic qualities to a desired style and type of wine. Wines produced from grapes should be processed minimally to reduce removal of key compounds essential for the wine's evolution. In general, these wines are the most age-worthy owing to their higher concentration of TDS in the raw material as compared to wines produced from juice or concentrate.

The disadvantages are that grapes are subject to vintage variations and therefore consistency of style and quality from one vintage to another cannot be guaranteed. Winemaking from grapes can also require a significant cost investment for modest productions, it is more time-consuming, and tends to be messier.

For home winemaking, California is a popular source of grapes packaged in 16.3-kg (36-lb) cases although grapes from other states and countries are available through special order. One can expect to pay a premium price for special orders. Home winemakers' challenge, however, is how to certify authenticity and quality of grapes.

33

Note: In this book, "grape variety" or "variety" refer to specific varieties of grapes used in winemaking whereas "varietal" refers to wine made from a single grape variety. For example, a Chardonnay is a varietal made from 100% Chardonnay grapes or juice.

Certifying grapes

There is undeniable truth to the adage that "great wine is made in the vineyard". Of course wine is not physically made in the vineyard, but rather, great wine requires excellent grapes – the raw material – and then, great winemaking. And excellent grapes require perfect growing conditions from vineyard location and soil chemistry to microclimate to viticultural practices, i.e., how the vines are trained, irrigated, etc. – the complex interaction of all these is what the French call *terroir*.

Terroir plays a major role in defining the quality of grapes, specifically, acid-sugar balance, pH, berry size and color, spectrum and intensity of flavors, and overall healthiness of the grapes; however, with the plethora of purveyors of grapes and grape varieties from the world over, not to mention clones within the same varieties, and home winemakers' lack of knowledge of grape quality, it can be a daunting task choosing quality grapes, or even the expected variety.

A winemaker's first task then is to assess quality based on these criteria, a task that requires much experience. Assessing quality can be quite challenging and overwhelming for novice winemakers, particularly that grapes from different terroirs can quite possibly have very different profiles.

The bulk of California shipping grapes come from Lodi where, for example, Cabernet Sauvignon does not have typical Bordeaux character; it is much more fruit-driven and less varietal, and could probably be mistaken for a Syrah (Shiraz) or Zinfandel from that area. And then there is the challenge of distinguishing one variety from another; many varieties can look the same to the untrained eye.

So what is a home winemaker to do?

Do your homework

Undoubtedly the single most important step in ensuring authentic, quality grapes is to develop a relationship with reputable suppliers that have quick turnover of inventory to guarantee freshness of grapes. Whether working directly with a grower, a middleman, or a purveyor of grapes, develop a strong relationship while establishing provenance and quality of grapes. Provenance includes grower and vineyard location, which provide many clues on grape quality.

Here are some important questions to ask before buying grapes: Where is the vineyard located? Is it in a warm- or cool-climate region? How reputable is the grower or vineyard? How and when were the grapes packed and shipped? What should I expect to pay for specific grape varieties from this supplier?

Cool-climate grapes will tend to have higher acidity, lower sugar concentration and, quite possibly, different flavor profile and character. Grape chemistry and physiology also depend greatly on how grapes were grown and harvested, information typically not available to buyers. For example, some growers harvest for quantity, not quality, because they get paid "by weight", and quality suffers as it is inversely proportional to quantity. Quality greatly declines when grapes are harvested at high yields because water content in berries dilutes sugar, acidity, color and flavors, and would result in a lighter, "thinner" wine.

Grapes packed in cases or bushels "in house", as opposed to in the vineyard, will usually look healthier having gone through a triage to weed out leaves and green or spoiled bunches before being shipped. For cost-saving and expediency reasons, field-packed grapes do not go such triage and will tend to have undesirable elements that need to be sorted out prior to crushing.

Ideally, grapes should be handled minimally and delivered to the crusher as soon as possible after harvest. Grape chemistry, physiology and flavors are always compromised during excessive handling or delayed shipping.

Research the market price in your area for each grape variety to make sure you are getting what you pay for. If the price of Cabernet Sauvignon grapes is expected to be in the US$1 per pound range in your market (premium grapes from premium vineyards typically cost much more), Cabernet Sauvignon grapes selling at almost half the price are almost definitely not genuine.

The next tip is to properly research grape varieties you are considering buying so that, if you want Cabernet Sauvignon, you get Cabernet Sauvignon and not a blend of inferior varieties. For each variety, study the physiology of the grape bunch, berry and leaf, and its expected chemistry and flavor profile. Consult the many books and internet-based resources dedicated to ampelography, the science of description and identification of the *Vitis* vine species and its cultivated vine varieties.

Choosing grapes

Once you have found a grower or supplier that can source and deliver your desired grape varieties, choose grapes with great care.

First, perform a thorough visual examination of the grapes. The grapes should look fresh, clean and healthy. There should be no

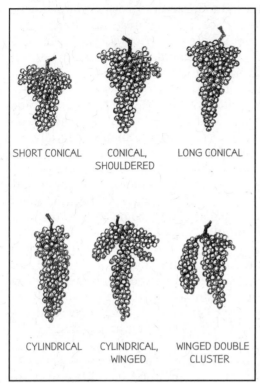

Figure 1-2: Grape cluster shapes[1]

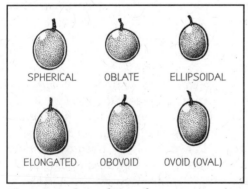

Figure 1-3: Grape berry shapes[1]

shriveled, spoiled or rotten berries or bunches; reject any batch that does not look healthy. Stems should look green, but not overly green, which could otherwise impart unpleasant, harsh tannins to wine. Whitish residue from vineyard sprays, such as sulfur-based products, should never be excessive, which could otherwise cause hydrogen sulfide problems (rotten-egg smell) in the wine.

Examine a sample of whole grape cluster for shape and size to ensure that they are typical of the variety. Shape can be short or long conical, possibly shouldered, cylindrical, perhaps winged, or winged double cluster. Size can range from small to very large. Figure 1-2 illustrates some common grape cluster shapes.

Then, take a sample berry, wipe the residues and examine its color, shape and size, and thickness of the grape skin. If the color does not look right for the variety, then it may not be what has been declared. Shape can be spherical (round), oblate, ellipsoidal, perhaps elongated, obovoid, or ovoid (oval). Figure 1-3 illustrates some common grape berry shapes. Some grape varieties, such as Pinot Noir, have thin skin and will therefore yield a lighter colored wine because there is less color to extract during maceration.

[1]Adapted from Bettiga, Larry J., Golino, D.A., McGourty, G., Smith, R.J., Verdegaal, E., WINE GRAPE VARIETIES IN CALIFORNIA. California: University of California, Division of Agriculture and Natural Resources, Publication 3419. 2003.

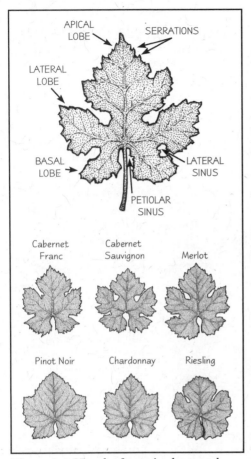

Figure 1-4: Vine leaf terminology and common leaf shapes[1]

Ideally, there should be no leaves with grapes when shipped or picked up from a local market; however, if there is at least one leaf, examine its morphology – shape, size, number of lobes, shape and size of serrations, etc. – to get some clues about variety. Each vine species within a genus is characterized by common traits, particularly when it comes to leaf shape, illustrated in Figure 1-4, which is easiest to examine, albeit not always obvious. For example, *V. vinifera* varieties typically have a five-lobe leaf, but to the untrained eye, that simple count is not always easy. Then, each variety within a species is characterized by a specific petiolar sinus, lateral sinus, and shape of serrations.

Leaf morphology alone cannot provide a definitive answer on variety as it can vary even for leaves from the same vine. This is also very difficult to assess by an untrained eye, so study hard and long.

At this point, bunch, berry and leaf morphologies for any variety should be easily described and compared to data from grape variety handbooks. For example, the following would be typical descriptions for Pinot Noir, Cabernet Sauvignon, and Chardonnay varieties. A picture of grape bunches and leaves for each are provided in Figure 1-5, 1-6 and 1-7, respectively.

Pinot Noir
Grape bunch: small; conical
Berry: small; spherical
Skin: very thin; light colored
Leaf: deep petiolar sinus; shallow lateral sinuses

[1]See footnote, page 36

Cabernet Sauvignon

Grape bunch: small to medium; cylindrical to conical
  with shoulders
Berry: small; spherical
Skin: thick; blue-black
Leaf: very deeply 5-lobed; large serrations

Chardonnay

Grape bunch: small to medium; cylindrical, often winged
Berry: small; spherical
Skin: yellow to amber when ripe
Leaf: more or less entire with shallow lateral sinuses;
  short, broad teeth

Figure 1-5: Pinot Noir cluster

Figure 1-6: Cabernet Sauvignon cluster

As a second step, quantitatively assess sugar content in grapes, if possible. The sugar level determines a wine's potential alcohol level. Ideally, you should also measure acidity and pH, at a minimum, but this is seldom practical. Some growers may provide such data. Growers or purveyors usually don't like it when winemakers show up with a hydrometer to test sugar content because that means crushing a whole cluster or more of grapes – both messy and a waste. Rather, the best (and most discreet) method to determine sugar content is using a refractometer where only a couple of drops of juice are required, and the reading is instantaneous. Section 3.1 provides

Figure 1-7: Chardonnay cluster

detailed instructions on using a refractometer for measuring sugar content in juice.

The last and most critical step is the gustatory test, i.e., how do the grapes taste? There is a direct correlation among the grapes' and wine's flavor profile, complexity and intensity. Taste a couple of berries while chewing them slowly and (discreetly) spit out the seeds, and let the juice cover the tongue as much as possible. Evaluate flavors, their intensity and complexity along with sweetness and acid balance, and tannin quality. The importance of this assessment cannot be overstated – flavor is as important as sugar and acidity when determining when to pick or buy grapes.

Availability

Depending on harvest conditions, Northern Hemisphere grapes are usually available early September through late October or as late as November. Early to mid-October is the best time to buy grapes for winemaking, as these would have reached an optimum sugar level, without being rotted, and good flavor balance. Establish a good relationship with a reliable supplier who can provide updates on harvest conditions and who can inform you when grapes will be arriving (presumably at an optimum sugar level).

1.4.2 Wine from fresh grape juice

Fresh (non-concentrated) grape juice is typically sold in 20- or 23-L pails, or 100-L containers. It is available as fresh cold-stored juice, but increasingly, consumers should be aware that this cold-stored juice is often frozen to prolong its shelf life especially when shipped from Europe. As the juice is not pasteurized or stabilized against spontaneous fermentation, fresh juice should always be stored in a cold refrigerator.

Fresh grape juice is simply cold-pressed juice, which is then packaged for sale. In an effort to provide a higher-quality product with year-over-year consistency, producers most often make adjustments to the must. For example, fresh grape juice can contain additives such as sugar or grape concentrate to adjust the sugar level, and sulfite (also referred to as sulfur dioxide or SO_2) as a preservative, and one or more acids to achieve a desired acidity level.

Avid home winemakers often expect not to find any additives in fresh grape juice. They prefer to make any required adjustments themselves. It is therefore wise to read carefully the small print on the container and to question the supplier closely to avoid any disappointment. The addition of acid and sulfur dioxide is not a bad thing in itself, but a winemaker should monitor the sugar, acidity, and free sulfur dioxide (SO_2) levels before adding any more of these substances. Refer to chapter 3 for a complete discussion on the effects of sugar, acids, pH, sulfur dioxide, and phenols, and how to measure and control these substances and parameters.

To make wine from fresh grape juice, the juice is first brought back up to fermentation temperature, and then allowed to ferment by adding yeast or letting the producer-added or indigenous yeast in the juice take its course, though the use of indigenous yeast is not recommended because results are unpredictable. Since fresh juice is not sterilized, it still contains indigenous yeast capable of starting fermentation without addition of other yeast.

The advantage of grape juice is that there is no need for crushing and pressing, and this reduces production time and effort, and minimizes the investment in winemaking equipment. White wines made from fresh juice have some very real benefits over fresh-crushed grapes owing to the fragility of the latter when shipped long distances and to the fact that the processing time is greatly reduced. White wines are most susceptible to oxidation, and therefore, time from harvest to vinification should be minimized.

One important disadvantage of fresh grape juice, especially for red wines, is that it does not allow any further control over the extraction of color, the level of tannin, flavor, and structure and complexity. Since there is no maceration involved, the grape juice is not allowed to extract the important compounds from grape skins, resulting in lower TDS concentration.

Some alternative solutions in overcoming these drawbacks are now available. Purveyors of fresh grape juice or wine kits now provide juice with crushed grape skins in 20-L pails or in so-called "crushed grapes in a kit" format that can make wine in six weeks. The latter is produced by crushing and pressing grapes to extract first-run juice that will be used for the kit wine. Skins and grapes are flash-frozen and then stored frozen without the addition of any preservative until they are packaged into 2-kg (4.4-lb) shelf-stable packs and sold with the kit.

These are excellent ideas enabling home winemakers to have crushed grapes without the investment in equipment and time. Red wines can now be vinified by maceration to extract color, tannins and flavor compounds to achieve a desired wine style.

Fresh juice, like grapes, is also subject to vintage variations and therefore consistency of style and quality from one vintage to another cannot be guaranteed. It is also only available during the fall season following harvest. Some winemaking supply shops may carry fresh Southern Hemisphere (e.g., Chilean) grape juice during the Northern Hemisphere Spring. The selection of grape varieties is also more limited or more difficult to find than concentrates.

1.4.3 WINE FROM RECONSTITUTED GRAPE JUICE

Reconstituted grape juice is a popular choice among home winemakers as it requires no water to be added (unlike concentrates). The juice is essentially reconstituted concentrate, (i.e., water is added by the producer), which has been sterilized by pasteurization to eradicate wild yeasts. Liquid-invert sugar and acid – tartaric acid or a blend of acids – may have also been added to achieve optimum balance for a desired style of wine. Sulfite is also added to stabilize the juice and to prolong its shelf life, and allow storage at room temperature.

To make wine, yeast is added to start fermentation, and wine can be bottled within two months. Liquid-invert sugar, which consists of glucose and fructose, will ferment more favorably than sucrose when yeast activity starts. The composition of wine relative to fermentable sugars is discussed in section 1.6, and the use of sucrose and dextrose in chaptalization is discussed in section 3.1.3.

Reconstituted grape juice kits are also available complete with instructions to ensure problem-free winemaking. Kits are packaged with a fining agent, usually bentonite, and isinglass or gelatin, to clarify the wine, yeast and yeast nutrients (diammonium phosphate to favor a good fermentation), sulfite (to preserve the wine), and potassium sorbate (a stabilizing agent) to prevent re-fermentation once the wine is bottled.

As with fresh grape juice, the disadvantage of reconstituted juice is that it does not allow any further control over the color of the wine, the level of tannins, flavor, and structure and complexity. The grape juice is not allowed to extract the important compounds from grape skins. Wines produced from reconstituted juices also do not age as well owing to the lower TDS concentration.

1.4.4 WINE FROM CONCENTRATE

Today, 4- and 6-week wine kits using a blend of concentrate and grape juice are very popular among wine hobbyists, especially beginners, and are available in a wide array of styles for every palate.

To make wine from concentrate, the concentrate is first reconstituted by adding water to bring the total must volume to 19 or 23 L, depending on the kit, and then yeast is added to start fermentation.

The advantages of kits are that they require minimum investment in winemaking equipment, minimum time and effort to produce good quality, early-drinking wines, and they are available throughout the year. These kits also provide consistency of style and quality from batch to batch and are therefore ideal for reproducing similar batches and styles of wine. Many different types and styles of wine are now available which are otherwise not available as grape juice or grapes, such as Bordeaux, Chablis, Port and Icewine. With international wine production regulations now restricting the labeling of musts and wines to reflect their true appellation of origin, home winemakers need to inquire or confirm the contents of the concentrate. For example, concentrates from California or other parts of the world can no longer be labeled Bordeaux-style unless they are truly from that region. Alternatively, different styles can be created with additives often supplied with kits.

With the quality of concentrates constantly improving, this winemaking alternative has become a favorite among wine aficionados. For beginners, wine kits are ideal since the risk of failure is minimized because all ingredients are pre-packaged in pre-measured quantities and because the concentrate is balanced and ready for making wine; they usually require little or no correction for sugar, alcohol and acidity balance. Concentrated grape juice is also sold separately without the necessary enological ingredients. These are recommended for experienced winemakers only, as ingredients need to be selected separately and measured accurately.

Concentrate is processed to remove some of the water content, pasteurized to eradicate any wild yeast, and then sulfite is added to make it stable and to extend its shelf life. Storing the concentrate in cold storage or in a freezer can further extend the shelf life. It is best to use the concentrate as soon as purchased, especially if no "Best before" date is provided. The concentrate may also contain liquid-invert sugar to achieve a desired sugar level in preparation for fermentation. Liquid-invert sugar, which consists of glucose and fructose, will ferment more favorably than sucrose when yeast activity starts. Tartaric acid or a blend of other acids may have been added to adjust the acid level for a balanced wine, and possibly some enological tannin depending on the type and style of wine to be produced. Refer to the sidebar on **How Wine Kits Are Made** for more information on the manufacturing process behind kits.

Wine kits comprise of concentrate packaged in aluminum or plastic bags in a variety of volumes, and come complete with instructions for problem-free winemaking. The kits are usually packaged with a fining agent, yeast and yeast nutrients, sulfite, and a stabilizing agent to prevent re-fermentation once the wine is bottled. Depending on the type of wine being produced, some kits may also contain other ingredients or additives such as enological tannin, dried elderberries and banana flakes, and oak chips to impart special aromas to the wine and to add complexity.

Four main types of kits are available:
- Concentrate-only
- Concentrate and fresh juice
- Premium
- Ultra-premium

Concentrate-only kits
Concentrate-only raw material is usually packaged in inexpensive four-week kits for making light, early-drinking wines. The concentrate has the lowest TDS concentration of all types of raw material, and therefore, wine from four-week kits are meant for quick fermentation and bottling, meant to be drunk early, i.e., soon after bottling. The small volume of concentrate, e.g., 7.5 L, is reconstituted by adding water up to the 20- or 23-L level, as per the kit's instructions.

Concentrate and fresh juice kits
Four-week kits containing a blend of concentrate and fresh juice as the raw material are also available for making wine with more body than their concentrate-only counterparts. The addition of fresh juice increases the TDS concentration and, as such, although these wines can be enjoyed in four weeks, they will undoubtedly improve with a few months of cellaring.

Premium kits
Premium, six-week kits comprise of concentrate plus varietal grape juice, and are larger in volume, e.g., 15 L, and therefore require less water to reconstitute the juice to the 20- or 23-L level. They have a higher TDS concentration than their concentrate-only and concentrate-and-fresh-juice counterparts. As a result, premium-kit wines have better aging potential and should be cellared for

How Wine Kits Are Made

Wine kits contain concentrate, juice and other staples like acid and sulfite. The process that brings these together to make a kit is fascinating.

First, manufacturers contract to purchase grapes from growers by specifying conditions at harvest (acid, pH, sugar content, and color) and organoleptic qualities (flavor and aroma). When the grapes are ripe they are harvested and taken to a winery, where they are sulfited and crushed.

White grapes are pressed and the juice is pumped into a settling tank. Enzymes are added to break down pectin and gums, which would make clearing difficult after fermentation. Then bentonite is added to the juice and re-circulated. After several hours the circulation is shut off and the tank is crash-chilled below freezing. This helps precipitate grape solids, and prevents spoilage. When the tank is settled and the juice almost clear, it is roughly filtered, the sulfite is adjusted, and it is either pumped into tanker trucks for shipment to the kit facility or into a vacuum concentrator.

Red grapes are crushed, sulfited and pumped through a chiller to a maceration tank, where special pectinoglycolytic enzymes are added. These break down the cellulose membrane of the grape skins, extracting color, aroma and flavor. The tank is chilled to near-freezing to prevent the must from fermenting. After two to three days the red must is pumped off, pressed and settled. The pressed grape skins then undergo secondary processing to extract further skin components, which can then be added back to the juice.

Vacuum concentrators work like the reverse of a pressure cooker. By lowering the pressure inside the tank, water can be made to boil at less than 50° C (120° F). At temperatures this low, browning and caramelization are prevented and water comes off as vapor, leaving behind concentrated grape juice. Because some aromatic compounds can be carried away in this vapor, there is a fractional distillation apparatus on the concentrator to recover these essences, which are returned to the concentrate after processing.

The juices and concentrates are then shipped to the kit facility. There they are pumped into nitrogen-purged tanks, tested for quality and stability, and held at very low temperatures. This both speeds up the formation of wine diamonds (crystals of potassium bitartrate from the tartaric acid naturally occurring in the wine) and preserves the liquids.

(continued next page)

How Wine Kits Are Made (*continued*)

After the quality control checks are passed, the juices and concentrates are blended in giant tanks. When the formulation is approved, the must is pumped through the pasteurizer. The pasteurizer is a heat exchanger that rapidly heats and then cools the must, killing yeast and spoilage organisms, but not caramelizing the must. From there it goes into the bag filler, which purges the sterile bags with a double flush of nitrogen and then fills each bag.

The bags are then capped and loaded into the kit boxes, after which the additives are placed on top. The boxes are shrink-wrapped and packed on a skid for a quality-assurance microbiological hold. This hold can last from three days to a week, while the product is examined for bacterial or yeast activity. If it passes, it is shipped to the warehouse, and from there to dealers, and finally, into the hands of the customer.

by Tim Vandergrift

---

a few months to a year before drinking to allow the amalgam of aromas, flavors and taste to develop to their peak potential.

Owing to the varietal grape juice added to the concentrate, wines from premium kits are much more typical of the intended style and tend to be fuller-bodied.

Ultra-premium kits
Ultra-premium kits are similar to premium, six-week kits but contain a higher ratio of varietal grape juice, and are larger in volume, e.g., 16 L. The juice can be from specific, premium wine regions, often down to single vineyards, and therefore is most expressive of that region's style.

Ultra-premium kits have the highest TDS concentration of all raw materials found in kits, and therefore, the wines are fuller bodied with the longest aging potential. Wines must be cellared for at least a year or more to allow the wine to develop to its intended style and to express its full potential. They can often surpass the quality of wines made from fresh juice and even grapes.

1.5 GRAPE VARIETIES

All grape varieties referenced in this book are from the European *Vitis vinifera* (*V. vinifera*) species only because they are globally the most important in winemaking, although they can be very finicky to grow in cold or hot climates, or under poor weather conditions. In spite of the challenges, they are the undisputed choice for producing premium-quality wines. These varieties include the likes of

Chardonnay, Sauvignon Blanc, Cabernet Sauvignon, Merlot, and Pinot Noir.

Alicante Bouschet, a hybrid (a cross between different species) of *vinifera* and non-*vinifera* species, is not classified as a *vinifera* variety in ampelography; however, owing to its wide use as a *teinturier* (French term for a deep-colored blending wine used to improve color in red wines) in France, it is often recognized as a *vinifera* variety.

Countless other grape varieties from North American species, such as *Vitis labrusca* (*V. labrusca*) and *V. riparia*, and from American or French hybrids that can make very good wine are available throughout the US and Canada. Many are winter-hardy varieties that are grown where weather conditions would not allow *V. vinifera* varieties to survive. Given the harsh climatic conditions where some varieties are grown, grapes often do not achieve a desired balance between sugar and acidity, and consequently, the juice must be adjusted when making wine. Some interesting varieties to consider that produce very good wine include Catawba, Niagara, Seyval Blanc, and Vignoles in whites, and Baco Noir, Chambourcin, de Chaunac, Maréchal Foch, and Norton in reds, only to name a few.

While it is possible to get *V. vinifera* varieties from California regions such as Napa and Sonoma as well as from other New World vine-growing regions such as Washington, Oregon, New York (Finger Lakes, Long Island), Virginia, Ontario (Niagara), British Columbia (Okanagan Valley, Vancouver Island), most North American fruit available to home winemakers still comes from California's Central Valley. Such grapes can be decent but may have a high sugar content with weaker concentration of flavors because of the too-high vine yields (over-cropping) common to the region resulting from overzealous use of irrigation, unremitting sunshine, and growers' general business need to harvest for quantity over quality. Over-cropping also produces diluted, light-colored wines with less complexity. Special orders of premium grapes from selected growers from other parts of California are available, albeit at higher prices.

In the following sections, typical characteristics of California white- and red-wine *V. vinifera* varieties are listed to help home winemakers make the proper selection based on desired wine type and style to be produced. Grapes bought from, say, cool-climate regions (e.g., Riesling from Niagara instead of the Central San Joaquin Valley) will have a totally different make-up and, hence, a different flavor profile. For a discussion on grape varieties grown in California and worldwide, consult references 3 [Bettiga et al.] and 21 [Robinson], respectively, in Appendix E. For a discussion on grape varieties specifically grown in cool climates, consult reference 10 [Jackson et al.].

Of the grape varieties listed, many produce poor or average quality wines on their own because of inadequate color, low acidity or high pH, lack of fruitiness, low tannin level and/or low alcohol content. Winemakers are encouraged to experiment with blending wines from different grape varieties to balance the organoleptic elements. Many well-known blends such as Cabernet Sauvignon, Merlot and Cabernet Franc in Bordeaux, or Sauvignon Blanc and Sémillon in Sauternes, produce exceptional wines. In the Châteauneuf-du-Pape appellation, wineries are allowed to blend up to 13 different grape varieties. It should be noted, however, that grape varieties exhibit different characteristics depending on where these have been grown. Chapter 7 provides some guidelines on blending wine.

Table 1-1 and Table 1-2 list the characteristics of common California white and red grape varieties, respectively, and provide some general guidelines to achieve desired styles. The best way to learn about different varieties is to experiment, to blend different wines, and to determine your preference.

Consult your local grape suppliers to see which grape varieties are available in your area. Many of the listed varieties are very difficult to find and are often not available as vineyards typically sell their premium harvest to commercial wineries.

Note: Some data presented in Tables 1-1 and 1-2 are subjective, particularly on quality of grape varieties, and can depend on provenance of the grapes, viticultural practices, grower reputation, and a winemaker's experience and stylistic preferences. The data are to be used as general guidelines only.

1.5.1 WHITE GRAPE VARIETIES FROM CALIFORNIA

Table 1-1 lists popular California *V. vinifera* white wine grape varieties and their typical characteristics, which can be used to determine the type and style of wine to be produced.

When selecting white grape varieties, characteristics to be considered include:
- Acidity level (low, moderate, high)
- Affinity for oak (not recommended, poor, good, very good, excellent)
- Aging potential (poor, good, very good, excellent)
- Overall quality of the grape variety (poor, average, good, very good, excellent)

1.5.2 RED GRAPE VARIETIES FROM CALIFORNIA

Table 1-2 lists popular California *V. vinifera* red wine grape varieties and their typical characteristics, which can be used to determine the type and style of wine to be produced.

When selecting red grape varieties, characteristics to be considered include:
- Depth of color (light, medium, deep)
- Tannin level (low, moderate, high)
- Acidity level (low, moderate, high)
- Affinity for oak (not recommended, poor, good, very good, excellent)
- Aging potential (poor, good, very good, excellent)
- Overall quality of the grape variety (poor, average, good, very good, excellent)

Note that although many red grape varieties have white juice – and as such can produce white (*blanc de noirs*) wines – only those types and styles worthy of white-wine quality are identified. For example, although Pinot Noir is used to make superb, highly sought red wine, it is also used to make Champagne and other white bubblies. Grape varieties suitable for rosé and sparkling wine production are also identified.

1.6 THE COMPOSITION OF WINE

The key to producing well-balanced wines is a good understanding of the components of wines and how to analyze and control them.

Table 1-3 lists the key ingredients of enological significance found in grape juice (must) and wine that comprise total dissolved solids (TDS). Typical concentration ranges are provided for healthy, normal juice and dry table wine.

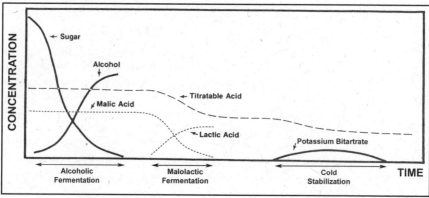

Figure 1-8: Relationship between sugar, alcohol and acids during vinification and winemaking

Figure 1-8 illustrates the relationship between sugar, alcohol and acids, and changes in their concentrations resulting from vinification and winemaking. An understanding of this relationship will prove useful in predicting and adjusting vinification results.

When grape juice is fermented, fermentable sugars (glucose and fructose) are converted into ethanol (ethyl alcohol). The alcohol produced is proportional to the amount of sugar fermented. A by-product of fermentation is glycerol, which affects a wine's perceived sweetness. Glycerol does not affect viscosity – as is often believed – as evaluated from the wine's tears streaming down a glass. When juice is converted into wine, the water content also increases.

The naturally occurring (organic fixed) acids are reduced and transformed to give wine its required freshness. These acids are often referred to as a grouping termed titratable acid, a term used to quantify total acidity in wines. Of these acids, tartaric acid is the most significant – it is the strongest and is present in both grape juice and wine. The second most significant acid is malic acid, which is converted into lactic acid in malolactic-fermented wines. Malic acid is found in many fruits, such as Granny Smith apples, and is often described as having a sharp taste and sensation. Lactic acid is found, for example, in sour milk or milk by-products, such as yogurts. When malic acid is reduced by malolactic fermentation, titratable acid is also reduced.

Malolactic fermentation (MLF) is used mostly in the production of red wines, but also in some whites, such as Chardonnay, to add complexity and reduce acidity for improved balance. Malolactic fermentation is discussed in section 4.8.

Grape juice may also contain a very small amount of citric acid – an acid found in citrus fruits such as lemons – which is usually reduced completely during vinification.

Titratable acid is also reduced when the wine is stabilized under cold temperature. During cold stabilization, tartaric acid is precipitated as potassium salt and then separated from the wine by racking. Acids and titratable acid are discussed in detail in section 3.2.

The complex transformation of grape acids is further complicated by the presence of minerals and elements in the (vineyard) soil, namely potassium, which affect the acid balance and the wine's ability to protect itself from spoilage microorganisms. These have a direct impact on quality and longevity of the wine. A wine's pH value, which measures the active acidity, gives an accurate indication of chemical stability and protection against spoilage. The precise significance of pH, and how to measure and control it, is explained in section 3.3. *Text continued on page 54*

Table 1-1
California *V. vinifera* white grape varieties

Grape variety	Types & styles	Main characteristics	Acidity	Affinity for oak	Aging potential	Quality
Chardonnay	Dry Sparkling	High alcohol Fruity aroma Buttery texture	Moderate	Excellent	Very good	Excellent
Chenin Blanc	Dry Sweet Sparkling	High sugar content High acidity	High	Poor	Excellent (for sweet wines)	Very good
Colombard	Dry	Low alcohol	High	Poor	Poor	Average
Gewürztraminer	Dry Sweet Icewine Sparkling	High alcohol Spicy aroma and taste Deep color	Low	Good	Good	Good
Muscat	Dry Fortified Sweet Sparkling	High sugar content Grapey aroma	Moderate	Good	Poor	Good
Palomino	Dry Icewine Fortified	Low sugar content Oxidizes quickly	Low	Not recommended	Poor	Average

Table 1-1, continued

Grape variety	Types & styles	Main characteristics	Acidity	Affinity for oak	Aging potential	Quality
Pinot Blanc	Dry Sparkling	High alcohol	Low	Poor	Poor	Good
Pinot Grigio (Pinot Gris)	Dry	Low acidity Multi-colored berries	Low	Good	Poor	Very good
Riesling	Dry Sweet Icewine Sparkling	Petrol aroma Mineral notes Citrus flavors	High	Not recommended	Excellent	Excellent
Sauvignon Blanc	Dry Sweet	Grassy aroma	High	Good	Good	Very good
Sémillon	Dry Sweet	Grassy aroma Deep color	Moderate	Good	Excellent (for sweet wines)	Very good
Thompson Seedless (Sultana)	Dry Sparkling	High sugar content	Moderate	Not recommended	Poor	Poor
Trebbiano (Ugni Blanc)	Dry	Low alcohol	High	Poor	Poor	Average
Viognier	Dry	High alcohol Deep color Fruity aroma	Low	Not recommended	Poor	Excellent

Table 1-2
California *V. vinifera* red grape varieties

Grape variety	Types & styles	Main characteristics	Depth of color	Tannin	Acidity	Affinity for oak	Aging potential	Quality
Alicante Bouschet	Dry Fortified	Red juice	Deep	Moderate	High	Poor	Poor	Average
Barbera	Dry	High acidity	Deep	Low	High	Good	Good	Average
Cabernet Franc	Dry Rosé	Low alcohol Cedar and green vegetal aromas	Medium	Low	Low	Good	Good	Good
Cabernet Sauvignon	Dry	Blackcurrant and cedar aromas	Deep	High	Moderate	Excellent	Excellent	Excellent
Carignan	Dry	Bitterness	Deep	High	High	Not recommended	Good	Average
Carnelian	Dry Rosé	Blackcurrant Fruity aroma	Deep	Moderate	Moderate	Not recommended	Good	Average
Gamay Noir	Dry Rosé	Light Fruity aroma High acidity	Light	Low	Moderate	Very good	Good	Very good
Grenache	Dry Rosé	High alcohol Peppery flavor	Light	Low	Moderate	Not recommended	Poor	Good
Merlot	Dry	Fruity aroma	Medium	Moderate	Low	Very good	Very good	Excellent

Table 1-2; continued

Grape variety	Types & styles	Main characteristics	Depth of color	Tannin	Acidity	Affinity for oak	Aging potential	Quality
Mission	Dry Fortified Sweet	Low alcohol	Light	Low	Low	Not recommended	Poor	Poor
Nebbiolo	Dry	High alcohol Tar aroma	Deep	High	High	Very good	Very good	Excellent
Petite Sirah	Dry	Tough astringency Fruity aroma	Deep	High	Moderate	Very good	Very good	Good
Pinot Noir	Dry Sparkling (white)	Fruity aroma Berry aroma	Medium	Low	Low	Very good[2]	Good	Excellent
Ruby Cabernet	Dry	Astringency	Deep	High	Moderate	Good	Good	Average
Sangiovese	Dry	High alcohol	Medium	High	High	Very good	Very good	Good
Syrah (Shiraz)	Dry Fortified (white, rosé)	High alcohol Black pepper aroma	Deep	High	Moderate	Very good	Very good	Excellent
Valdepeñas (Tempranillo)	Dry	Low alcohol	Medium	Moderate	Low	Very good[2]	Good	Average
Zinfandel	Dry Sweet (rosé)	Blackberry aroma	Medium	Moderate	Moderate	Good	Good	Excellent

[2]The use of new oak should be avoided with this grape variety when using Central Valley grapes.

Table 1-3
Key ingredients in grape juice and wine as an approximate
percentage of total volume

Key Ingredients	Grape Juice	Wine
Water	70–75%	84–87%
Sugars	20–25% Fermentable sugars glucose fructose	<0.2% (dry wines) Non-fermentable sugars
Alcohol (Ethanol)	0%	11–14%
Glycerol	0%	Approximately 1%
(Fixed) Acids	0.6–0.9% tartaric malic citric	0.4–0.7% tartaric malic[2] lactic[2]
Phenols: Tannin and color pigments	<0.15%	<0.03% (white wines–no color pigments) <0.2% (red wines)

[2]Malic acid will not be present in totally malolactic-fermented wines. Lactic acid will be present in either partially or totally malolactic-fermented wines. Refer to section 4.8.

Other compounds, such as tannins, flavors and color pigments, are extracted from the grape skins, seeds and stems, and play a determining role in the structure, complexity, and ultimately, the quality of the wine. Refer to Figure 1-9 for a cross-section of a grape.

Tannins, flavor compounds and color pigments belong to a group of substances known in enological science as phenolics. The concentrations of these phenolic substances are significantly different between red and white wines. In the production of red wine, the must is allowed to macerate with the grape skins, seeds and, optionally, the stems. Tannin, flavor and color pigment extractions are carried out until the desired concentrations are achieved. The astringency of the tannins and the alcohol level need to be properly balanced. For example, a highly tannic red wine will be unbalanced, and probably undrinkable, at an alcohol level of 10.0% alc./vol. Conversely, a highly alcoholic red wine will seem overly hot if paired with little tannin concentration. In the production of white wine, there is minimal or no maceration. The color of white wine is obtained strictly from the juice. High concentrations of tannin are also not desirable as they impart an astringent sensation that does not marry well with white wines owing to their higher acidity, which exacerbates the astringent sensation because whites are served at colder temperatures.

As can be seen, ingredients in juice undergo complex transformations when fermented into wine. Many vinification parameters must be monitored and controlled throughout this process. The quality of the wine is therefore highly dependent on the winemaker's ability to achieve a balance among the many components. A wine's chemical balance of alcohol, sugar, acidity, tannins, flavors and color will determine its organoleptic balance and the overall quality of the wine.

1.7 WINEMAKING PROCESS

Different processes are used for winemaking from grapes, fresh juice, reconstituted juice and concentrate. Differences in winemaking procedures of the different types of musts are highlighted in the following sections and summarized in Table 1-4. Each winemaking and vinification stage for each process is discussed in more detail in subsequent chapters.

This book presents all the winemaking methods and techniques using grapes so that home winemakers can make informed decisions throughout the winemaking process. Many of these methods and techniques will need to be adapted for wines from grape juice or concentrate, or may not be required at all.

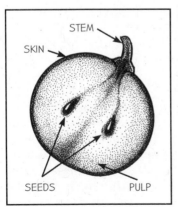

Figure 1-9: Cross-section of a grape berry

1.7.1 WINEMAKING FROM GRAPES

Figure 1-10 and Figure 1-11 illustrate the white and red winemaking processes, respectively, using grapes to extract juice for fermentation. The major differences between these two processes are as follows:

1. In white winemaking, grapes are pressed either as whole bunches with the stems or immediately following the crushing/destemming operation. There is usually no maceration of the juice with the grape solids.

55

2. Malolactic fermentation in white wines is inhibited except for a few select grape varieties, such as Chardonnay.
3. Bulk aging of white wines is done in glass or stainless steel containers. Only very few types of varietals benefit from oak barrel aging, particularly in white wines.

Rosé wine is produced by one of three methods. The first method uses red grapes and involves a short maceration period of the must with grape solids, without fermentation, to extract a little color. The second method involves pressing red-juice red grapes. Both methods then use white vinification processing where the light-red juice is transferred to a glass vessel and is readied for fermentation. The third method uses a blend of white wine with a very small portion of red wine.

Carbonic maceration, or *macération carbonique* in French, is another popular technique used by commercial wineries in the production of young, fruity red wines. Whole grape bunches are put into a fermentor and go through an intra-cellular fermentation. Fermentation is initiated within the berries, with or without the addition of yeast (spontaneous fermentation can start from wild indigenous yeast), by injecting carbon dioxide in the closed fermentor. This fermentation process produces soft, less tannic, early drinking wines with up-front fruit. They are not meant for aging and should be drunk within a few months from production.

Carbonic maceration is used extensively in the Beaujolais region of France in the production of Beaujolais Nouveau, and also used by North American wineries. Pinot Noir and Gamay grape varieties are the most popular and most used in nouveau wines vinified using this technique. Although more difficult to conduct carbonic maceration in home winemaking, a partial carbonic maceration is possible where a portion of the grapes are crushed and destemmed, and the rest are whole-cluster fermented. Figure 1-12 illustrates the red winemaking process from grapes using partial carbonic maceration and is described in section 4.7.4.

1.7.2 WINEMAKING FROM FRESH GRAPE JUICE

Figure 1-13 and Figure 1-14 illustrate the white and red winemaking processes, respectively, using fresh grape juice. The major differences between winemaking from grapes and from fresh juice is that the latter does not involve crushing, destemming, or pressing operations, and no maceration is required as the juice has already been separated from the grape solids. The remainder of the processes is identical to grape winemaking.

Table 1-4
Summary of winemaking procedures for different types of musts

Type of must	Grapes	Fresh juice	Reconstituted Juice	Concentrate	Refer to section
Crushing/ Destemming	Yes	No	No	No	4.2
Maceration	For reds only	No	No	No	4.3
Macro- & Micro-Aeration	For reds only	For reds only	No	No	4.4
Delestage	For reds only	No	No	No	4.5
Pressing	Yes	No	No	No	4.6
Alcoholic Fermentation	Yes	Yes	Yes	Yes	4.7
Malolactic Fermentation	Yes	Yes	No	No	4.8
Fining	Optional	Optional	*	*	5.2
Filtration	Optional	Optional	*	*	5.3
Stabilization	Yes	Yes	Yes	Yes	6
Oak Aging	Yes	Yes	No	No	8.4

*As per manufacturer's instructions

1.7.3 WINEMAKING FROM RECONSTITUTED GRAPE JUICE

Figure 1-13 and Figure 1-14 illustrate the winemaking process using reconstituted grape juice for white and red winemaking, respectively. As with fresh juice, this process does not involve crushing, destemming, or pressing operations, or any maceration as the juice has already been separated from the grape solids. The major differences from fresh juice winemaking are as follows:

1. Malolactic fermentation is improbable, as the juice has been completely sterilized, and is not recommended.
2. Aging in bulk is done in glass or stainless steel containers. Wines from this type of juice do not benefit from extended or oak-barrel aging.

Text continued on page 61

Figure 1-10: White winemaking from grapes – process flowchart

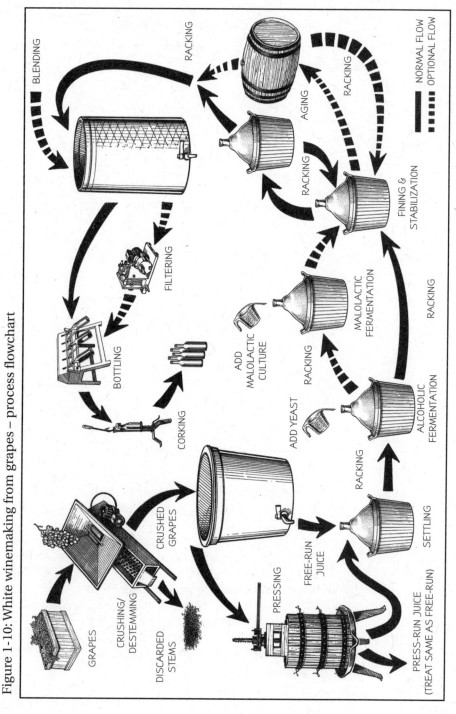

Figure 1-11: Red winemaking from grapes – process flowchart

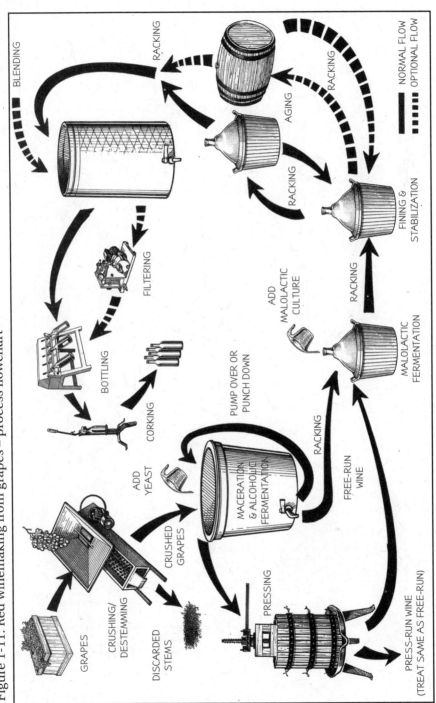

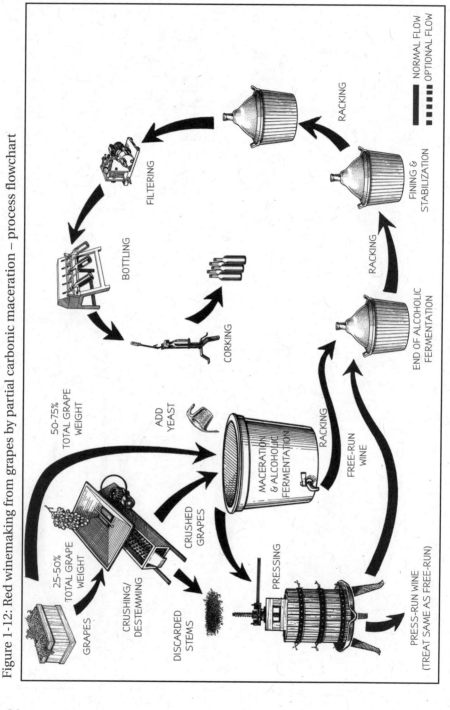

Figure 1-12: Red winemaking from grapes by partial carbonic maceration – process flowchart

Reconstituted juice can be fermented in a plastic pail, properly protected with a plastic lid, being less prone to oxidation during the vigorous stage of fermentation when lots of carbon dioxide is being given off, forming a protective layer over the fermenting wine.

1.7.4 WINEMAKING FROM CONCENTRATE

Figure 1-15 illustrates the winemaking process using concentrate and applies to both white and red winemaking. It requires the addition of water to the concentrate to reconstitute the juice before fermentation, and is then vinified in the same manner as reconstituted juice. Use distilled water if water in your area is hard, has high iron content, or has organic contamination, all of which could affect the quality of the wine.

When possible, add purified water when reconstituting the juice. Distilled water is recommended because it is chlorine-free, which could otherwise impart off-flavors to wine. Tap water should be avoided as it contains impurities and chlorine that may affect vinification or the quality of the finished wine.

Concentrated juice can be fermented in a plastic pail, properly protected with a plastic lid, since it is less prone to oxidation during the vigorous stage of fermentation when lots of carbon dioxide is being given off, forming a protective layer over the fermenting wine.

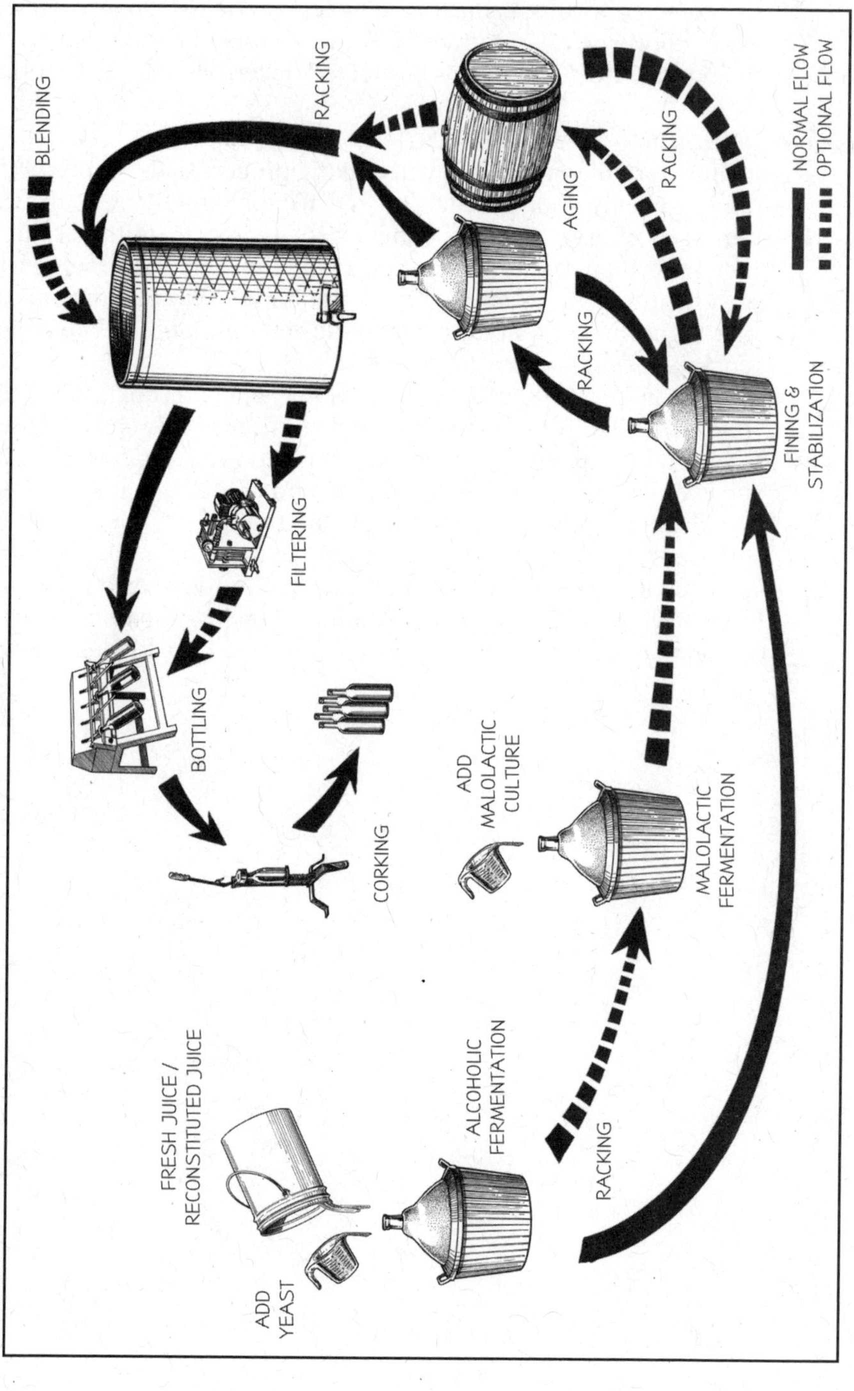

Figure 1-13: White winemaking from fresh grape juice or reconstituted juice – process flowchart

Figure 1-14: Red winemaking from fresh grape juice or reconstituted juice – process flowchart

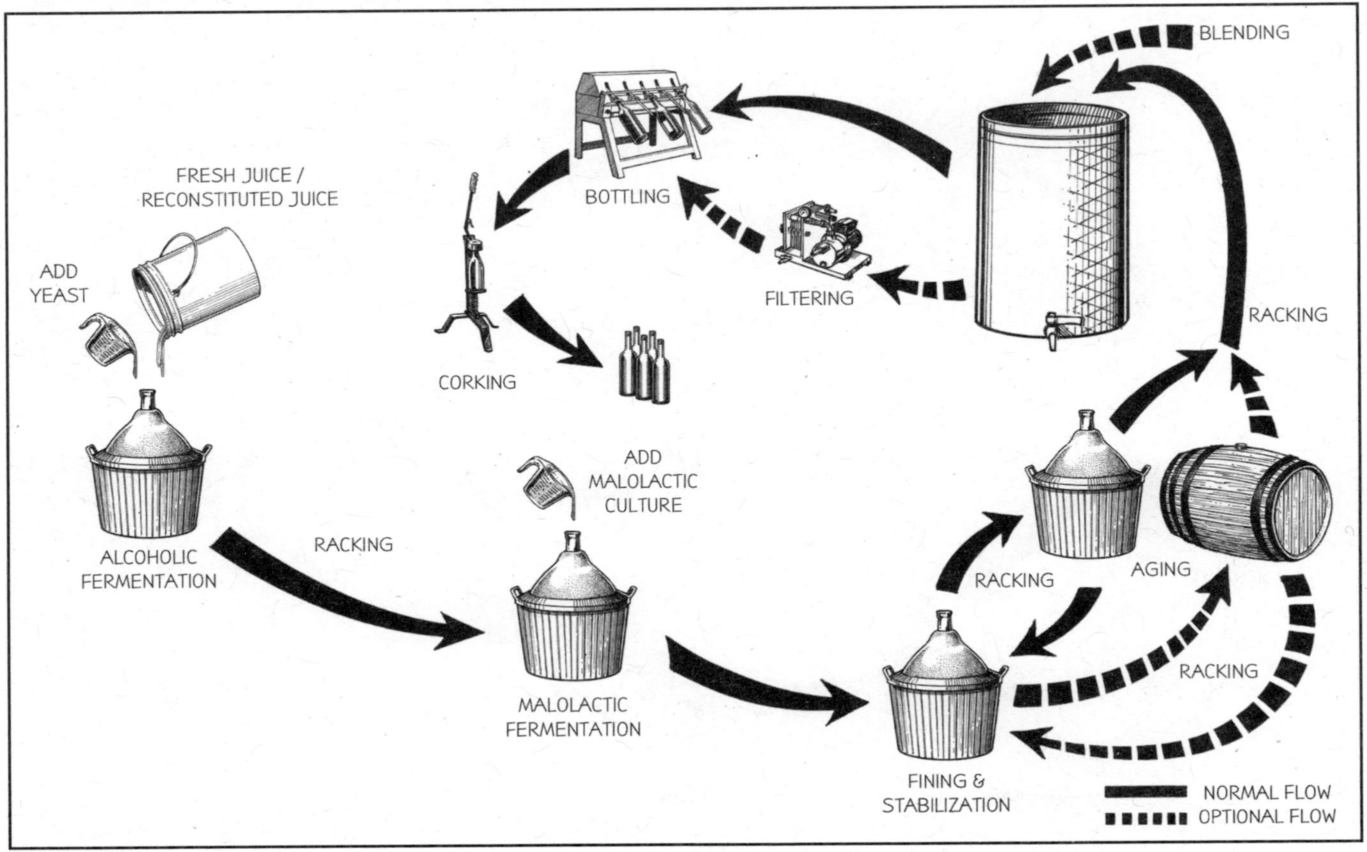

- BLENDING
- RACKING
- RACKING
- AGING
- RACKING
- RACKING
- NORMAL FLOW
- OPTIONAL FLOW
- FILTERING
- BOTTLING
- CORKING
- ADD MALOLACTIC CULTURE
- MALOLACTIC FERMENTATION
- FINING & STABILIZATION
- RACKING
- FRESH JUICE / RECONSTITUTED JUICE
- ADD YEAST
- ALCOHOLIC FERMENTATION
- RACKING

Figure 1-15: Winemaking from concentrated grape juice – process flowchart

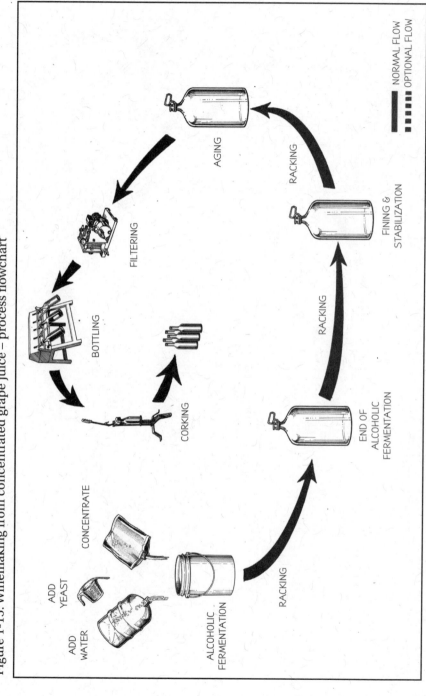

2
WINEMAKING EQUIPMENT AND SANITATION

Winemaking has become a popular hobby with its relatively low cost compared to commercial wines. Winemaking equipment and products that greatly facilitate the production of premium-quality wines are now available to home winemakers. Low-cost, high-quality wines require a small to modest investment, one that will last a lifetime. Depending on the type of raw material (must) chosen – grapes, fresh juice, reconstituted juice, or concentrate – some equipment may not be required.

This chapter provides information on selecting and using essential winemaking equipment to make great wines as well as on cleaning and sanitizing equipment to avoid the pitfalls of microbial spoilage.

2.1 CRUSHER AND DESTEMMER

The crusher is an indispensable tool for serious winemakers and is strictly used for winemaking from grapes. Its purpose is to break the skin of grapes and to allow the juice to flow out so that it can combine and interact with yeast to start fermentation. The crushing operation is optional for white winemaking where the juice can be extracted by pressing whole-cluster grapes without crushing, although more difficult to perform. Crushing is necessary, howev-

Figure 2-1: Hand-cranked, double-roll crusher

er, for red winemaking to allow the juice to macerate with the grape skins for tannin and color extraction, except in the case of the carbonic maceration technique.

The crusher consists of a funnel-shaped hopper to receive the grapes and one or two aluminum crushing rolls that rotate in opposite directions, and is available with a number of options to meet various needs and budgets. For small-scale winemaking, the basic hand-cranked, single-roll or double-roll model, such as the one shown in Figure 2-1, will serve the purpose. Double-roll models are typically equipped with an agitator designed to ease movement of the grapes through the rolls. To ease and to speed up the crushing process, power-driven crushers are available equipped with a motor.

A choice of stainless steel or enamel-paint model is available. The stainless steel model is costlier but will not rust therefore ensuring that the must and wine are not affected by rust. Wine that has been in contact with rust can become spoiled and undrinkable.

For serious amateur winemakers, power-driven crushers are also available equipped with a built-in destemmer that removes all stems following crushing. The destemmer is attached to the crusher's exit chute and consists of a rotating screw-fork in a perforated semi-cylindrical drum. As the grapes are crushed, they are channeled and driven through the drum that causes the crushed grapes and juice to fall below into a container. The stems are ejected at the other end for disposal. The perforated drum can be removed when destemming is not required. Figure 2-2 illustrates a power-driven crusher/destemmer with the protective cover removed to expose the destemming mechanism. Other power-driven crusher models are equipped with an auger inside the hopper to mechanically feed the grapes through the rolls – a very practical safety feature.

Stands for crusher/destemmers, such as the one shown in Figure 2-2, are also available to channel crushed and destemmed grapes into a pail when grapes need to be dumped into another container.

Grapes can be separated from the stems before or after crushing depending on the desired wine style. Section 4.2 discusses the effects of destemming before or after crushing. At the present time,

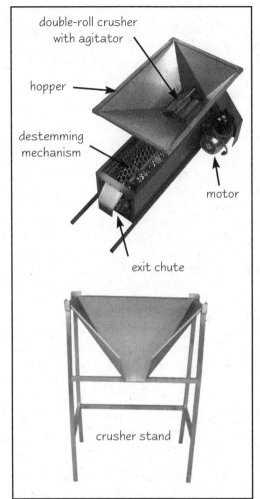

double-roll crusher
with agitator

hopper

destemming
mechanism

motor

exit chute

crusher stand

Figure 2-2: Power-driven crusher/
destemmer and stand with grape chute

there is no affordable, commercially available tool for home winemakers to destem grape bunches before crushing; such equipment, geared for commercial winemaking, is very expensive. A hand destemmer can be built from a wire mesh in a wooden frame, with openings large enough to allow grapes to pass through without the stems. This can be a labor-intensive task, however, for larger volumes of grapes.

The crusher or crusher/destemmer operation is very simple. The apparatus is positioned over a container capable of receiving all the grapes. The grapes are then dropped gently into the hopper where the crushing rolls can be started manually or with a motor. Remove any vine leaves that may still be in grape bunches before crushing. Vine leaves can impart undesirable flavors to the wine and can affect its quality.

2.2 WINEPRESS

The winepress, or simply press, is not an absolute requirement for red winemaking, although very useful, but it is essential for making white wine. It is strictly used for winemaking from grapes. Its purpose is to press the crushed grapes, or grape bunches if not previously crushed, to extract as much juice as desired.

There are two common types of winepresses for home winemaking: the iconic and very popular basket press, also known as a ratchet press, and the bladder press. Both are known as vertical presses to distinguish them from the horizontal types common in commercial wineries.

67

2.2.1 BASKET PRESS

The basket press, shown in Figure 2-3, consists of a sturdy three-legged paint or stainless steel grade tray with a spout to drain juice or wine, a hardwood-stave or stainless steel basket, a double-ratchet mechanism mounted on a vertical screw, and wooden pressure discs and blocks. The pressure mechanism operates like a ratchet and can be made to rotate in either direction to exert or release pressure. Direction of rotation is controlled with two metal inserts, known as pawls, within the pressure mechanism. Although more expensive, the newer types of presses with stainless steel baskets are more effective since the holes in the baskets are much smaller than the gap between wood staves.

Basket press models and sizes are usually identified by the basket diameter times the height in inches, e.g., 14×18, or, as often done on imported models, by a number representing the inner diameter of the basket, in centimeters. For example, a No. 45 press has a 45-cm (diameter) basket. Basket presses are available in sizes from 10 to 28 inches in diameter by 12 to 34 inches high. The commonly available Italian models range from No. 15 to 70 in increments of 5, and a size No. 80. Table 2-1 lists commonly available models along with capacity information. A press size No. 45, 50, or 18×24, 20×26 are recommended for serious winemakers with modest productions. Presses smaller than No. 30 or 12×14 are mainly used for fruit wines other than from grapes.

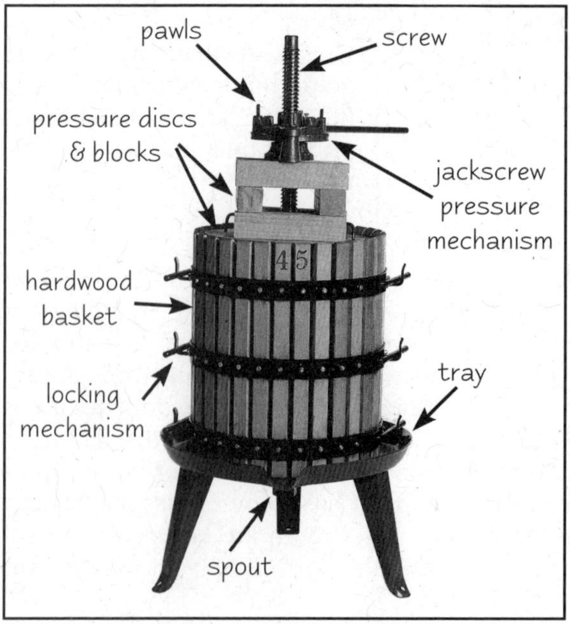

Although the basket press is a heavy-duty tool, it must be operated carefully to avoid damage. With the basket centered on the tray, fill the press with crushed or uncrushed grapes without overfilling it. Place the pressure discs over the grapes and exert pressure to level them. For crushed grapes, place a pail under the spout when loading the grapes as juice starts to run. Place the pressure blocks on top of the discs and install the pressure mechanism.

Figure 2-3: No. 45 vertical winepress

Table 2-1
Basket press models and approximate capacities

No.	Basket Diameter x Height (cm)	Basket Diameter x Height (inches)	Capacity (Metric)		Capacity (US)	
			liters	kg	gallons	lbs
25	25 x 30	10 x 12	15	25	4	54
30	30 x 35	12 x 14	25	40	7	89
35	35 x 45	14 x 18	42	68	11	149
40	40 x 50	16 x 20	61	98	16	216
45	45 x 60	18 x 24	96	155	25	340
50	50 x 65	20 x 26	129	208	34	458
55	55 x 70	22 x 28	155	273	41	600

Exert pressure on the grapes until you feel a little resistance while collecting the free running juice. Wait a few minutes to allow the flow of juice to subdue. Do not rush this operation as it can otherwise damage the press. The free running juice is referred to as free-run juice and will produce free-run wine, or *vin de goutte* in French. Repeat the process until you feel considerable resistance when exerting pressure. Continue pressing as much as possible, ensuring a few minutes wait between each press cycle. Juice extracted from this pressing is referred to as press-run juice and will produce press-run wine, or *vin de presse* in French. Use free-run juice for making your best wine since press-run juice can be much more astringent. The quality of free-run juice decreases as pressure increases. The yield of free-run juice will however be much smaller. Section 4.6 discusses the effects of pressing grapes with stems and vinification of free-run and press-run juices.

For some types of grapes with slippery skins, for example, Muscat, leave or add some stems to the grapes when pressing; otherwise, the pomace might cause the press basket to lift making the pressing operation very tedious. Alternatively, you can use pressing aids, such as cellulose or rice hulls, to facilitate pressing and juice or wine drainage, particularly with grape varieties with slippery skins. The use of pressing aids is discussed in section 4.6.

2.2.2 BLADDER PRESS

The bladder press, shown in Figure 2-4, is relatively new to home winemaking, and although it is considerably more expensive than its ratchet counterpart, it greatly simplifies pressing by using water pressure, increases efficiency resulting in considerable time savings, extracts more juice, and applies gentler pressure resulting in less harsh tannin extraction.

The bladder press consists of a sturdy three-legged tray with a spout to drain juice or wine, a hardwood-stave or stainless steel basket with a metal cover, a rubber bladder mounted vertically up the center of the press, and the piping, valves and gauge to control the flow of water in and out of the bladder. Stainless steel basket models are equipped with a large, cylindrical fiberglass splashguard or other protective device mounted over and around the basket, as juice will tend to splash out under the heavy bladder pressure. You will

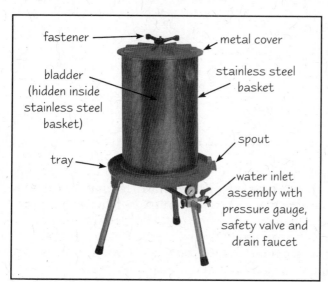

Figure 2-4: 160-L bladder press

also need a nylon sack mounted on the inside circumference of the basket to keep large solid grape particles in the basket. Large volume presses are mounted on wheels for easy moving, and may also have a tilt mechanism to allow the basket to be tilted to a horizontal position for easy removal of the cake (pressed grape solids).

Bladder presses are available in various sizes such as 40, 80, 160 and 300 liters. Table 2-2 provides approximate press capacities for models available on the market.

To extract juice or wine, first place a pail under the tray spout, then prepare the press by installing and securing the basket into place (don't forget the nylon sack), and load the grapes inside the basket. Secure the metal cover over the bladder and basket, place the splashguard over and around the basket, and finally, connect the water supply to the water inlet of the press using a garden hose attachment. Slowly open the water line to start filling the bladder

Table 2-2
Bladder press models and approximate capacities

No.	Basket Diameter x Height (cm)	Basket Diameter x Height (inches)	Capacity (Metric)		Capacity (US)	
			liters	kg	gallons	lbs
27	27 x 40	10 x 15	19	31	5	68
34	34 x 50	13 x 19	42	68	11	149
40	40 x 50	16 x 20	61	98	16	216
42	42 x 60	17 x 23	79	127	21	280
45	45 x 60	18 x 22	86	138	23	304
50	50 x 65	20 x 26	124	200	33	439
54	54 x 70	21 x 28	159	278	42	612
70	70 x 85	28 x 34	323	522	85	1148

and exerting pressure on the grapes. The water inlet is equipped with a safety valve that activates when the specified maximum pressure is reached. The flow of water at the source can then be left open, without the need for flow control, until the pressing completes. If the press is not equipped with a safety valve, monitor the pressure on the gauge and be sure not to exceed the maximum rated pressure to avoid rupturing the bladder.

Note: When making both white and red wines using a wooden basket-style press, first press white grapes so as not to contaminate the wood with the red pigment that would still be present in the basket's staves. Since whites are pressed on arrival, and reds are pressed after or late in the alcoholic fermentation phase, one usually presses the whites first quite naturally. Therefore this should not be a problem.

Total juice or wine yield for basket presses can be roughly estimated to be 50 L (13 gal) of free-run juice and 20 L (5 gal) of press-run juice, usually more for bladder presses, for every 100 kg (220 lbs) of grapes. These quantities and proportions will depend on the grape variety, berry physiology, and extent of pressing.

2.3 VESSELS FOR FERMENTING, STORING, AND AGING WINE

Various types of vessels of different materials are used in home winemaking. The most popular ones are glass demijohns and car-

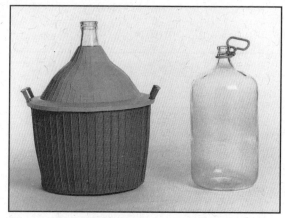

Figure 2-5: 54-L demijohn and 23-L carboy

boys, non-glass food-grade containers, food-grade plastic and cement vats, oak barrels, and stainless steel tanks. Open-top vats are used for maceration of grapes in must and cannot be used for storing and aging wine. Glass demijohns and carboys, oak barrels, and stainless steel tanks can be used for fermenting must as well as storing and aging wine. When containers are used for fermentation, they are referred to as fermentors.

Except for oak barrels, which react favorably with wine, all other containers must be inert so that they do not impart any off-flavors, or worse, spoil the wine. Avoid plastic containers that are not food-grade as toxic chemicals can leach into wine once in contact.

Section 2.6 describes how to clean and sanitize containers, in addition to instructions provided in the following sections.

2.3.1 DEMIJOHNS AND CARBOYS

Glass demijohns and carboys are practical containers for home winemaking. They are inert, fairly inexpensive, and are available in a variety of sizes, shapes and colors. Color is not an important factor if the wine will be stored for a short time away from light. If wine is intended to be stored for a long time, for example, longer than 6 months, or if the wine is exposed to light, it is highly recommended that tinted-glass containers be used. They are available in brown or green tints to reduce the negative effects of UV light and to slow down maturation. Clear glass vessels have the advantage of allowing unobstructed visual inspection of the wine, facilitating the monitoring of sediment and the racking operation. Figure 2-5 illustrates a demijohn and carboy.

Demijohns are available in sizes of 5, 10, 15, 20, 25, 34 and 54 L, in clear, brown- or green-tinted glass. They usually come enclosed in a protective plastic cover or straw wickerwork with carrying handles. Straw-covered demijohns are not recommended, as the wickerwork will deteriorate over time and are much more difficult to clean. Clear-glass carboys are available in sizes of 18.9, 20 and 23 L, and occasionally as 25 L.

Special carrying handles that fit around the neck of carboys and secured with a wing nut are available to easily move carboys around. The 23-L (6-gal) carboy shown in Figure 2-5 also illustrates a carboy-carrying handle.

You should always have available different demijohn and carboy sizes, depending on the volume of wine you produce, to ensure wine is always topped up in containers. Topping up is required when fermentation subdues. As the amount of carbon dioxide produced decreases, a small amount of air space will be needed in the properly locked container. A number of 3.8-L (1-gal) glass containers as well as standard 750-mL and 1.5-L bottles are useful to have on hand to hold small amounts of wine to top up larger containers. Section 5.1.2 discusses the practice of topping up containers.

For conducting fermentation, choose a container sufficiently large to allow for expansion of fermenting wine. For the vigorous phase of fermentation, fill the container to approximately 75% capacity. When racking the wine to a secondary fermentor to complete fermentation, fermentation will still be quite vigorous but expansion will be limited. You should still only fill containers to approximately 90% capacity. When the fermentor is properly protected from air, the air cannot react with the wine as carbon dioxide will fill the empty space and protect the wine.

2.3.2 NON-GLASS FOOD-GRADE CONTAINERS

Two popular non-glass food-grade containers are the V Vessel, sometimes used in brew-your-own (BYO) operations, and polyethylene tere-phthalate plastic containers, better known as PET carboys.

The V Vessel System

The V Vessel, shown in Figure 2-6, is a newer type of fermentor now available to home winemakers, which eliminates the need for cumbersome racking from carboy to carboy.

It consists of an inverted teardrop-looking, food-grade plastic container with a valve and a ball-shaped collection capsule assembly for "racking" the wine, including a female coupler with a barbed adapter and tube for siphoning wine, and a hole at

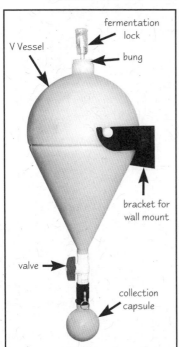

V Vessel

fermentation lock

bung

bracket for wall mount

valve

collection capsule

Figure 2-6: The V Vessel System

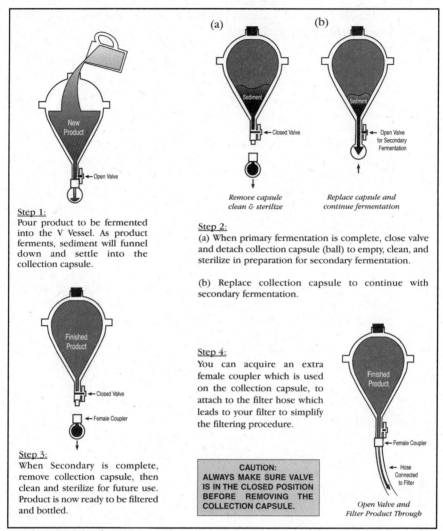

(a) **(b)**

Sediment

Sediment

←Closed Valve

←Open Valve
for Secondary
Fermentation

*Remove capsule
clean & sterilize*

*Replace capsule and
continue fermentation*

New
Product

←Open Valve

Step 1:
Pour product to be fermented into the V Vessel. As product ferments, sediment will funnel down and settle into the collection capsule.

Step 2:
(a) When primary fermentation is complete, close valve and detach collection capsule (ball) to empty, clean, and sterilize in preparation for secondary fermentation.

(b) Replace collection capsule to continue with secondary fermentation.

Finished
Product

←Closed Valve

←Female Coupler

Step 3:
When Secondary is complete, remove collection capsule, then clean and sterilize for future use. Product is now ready to be filtered and bottled.

Step 4:
You can acquire an extra female coupler which is used on the collection capsule, to attach to the filter hose which leads to your filter to simplify the filtering procedure.

> **CAUTION:**
> **ALWAYS MAKE SURE VALVE IS IN THE CLOSED POSITION BEFORE REMOVING THE COLLECTION CAPSULE.**

Finished
Product

←Female Coupler

← Hose
Connected
to Filter

*Open Valve and
Filter Product Through*

Figure 2-7: V Vessel operation

the top for inserting a fermentation lock and bung. The 23-L capacity V Vessel can be mounted on a supplied freestanding bracket or on a wall using the supplied wall bracket.

Its operation, illustrated in Figure 2-7, is very simple. Pour juice or concentrate into the vessel from the top, and turn the valve to the open position to let the juice enter the collection capsule. As wine ferments, sediments will travel to the bottom and into the collection capsule. When the primary fermentation is complete, close the valve and detach the collection capsule to remove the sediment. Empty and rinse the capsule, and then place it back on the valve assembly to continue with the secondary fermentation. Re-open the valve and repeat the sediment removal procedure following completion of the secondary fermentation.

When the wine is ready for bottling, you can bottle right from the V Vessel with no need for any racking.

PET Carboys

FDA-approved polyethylene tere-phthalate (PET) plastic containers, such as the Better Bottle PET carboy shown in Figure 2-8, are not new, but they are a recent addition to home winemaking tools.

The main advantage of PET-type carboys is that they are unbreakable, and therefore safer around the home winery, are very light making them very easy to move around, and are very easy to wash and sanitize.

Better Bottle carboys are available in plain or ported 3-, 5- and 6-gal formats, i.e., 11.4-, 18.9- and 22.7-L formats. Ported carboys have a port (hole) at the bottom that can be fitted with a special valve to make such operations as racking a cinch. The 3-gal format has a handle incorporated in the container; handles that attach to the neck of the carboy are available for the 5- and 6-gal formats.

Better Bottle carboys also come with a whole host of valves and racking adapters, closures and fittings, shown in Figure 2-8, that greatly simplify, for example, racking, wine transfer and bottling by eliminating the need for siphons. The reduced exposure to air also greatly reduces the potential of oxidation of the wine. Of special interest is the Better Bottle DryTrap air lock, which, unlike standard fermentation locks, does not use any water or sulfite

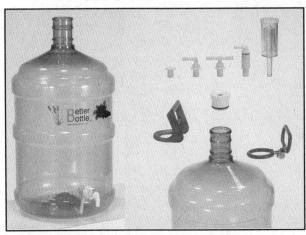

Figure 2-8: 20-L Better Bottle PET carboy and accessories

solution, therefore it does not dry out and does not cause a backflow problem. See section 2.4 for more information on fermentation locks, and section 5.1 for instructions on how to rack using PET carboys and accessories.

2.3.3 PLASTIC AND CEMENT VATS

Food-grade plastic and cement vats are used for macerating grapes in juice. While both types of vats can be cleaned easily, plastic vats can be moved easily as opposed to their cement counterparts. Cement vats are still popular in home winemaking and commercial winemaking. Proprietor-made Beaujolais and Bordeaux wines as well as those from Italy, Spain and Portugal are still produced in cement vats.

Choose a container as wide as possible so that the crusher rests on it and, when using a destemmer, the stems are discarded away from the container. It is important to have a wide container to maximize the surface area of grape juice in contact with the cap therefore maximizing the effects of maceration. For example, a deeper color is obtained in a shorter maceration period. Figure 2-9 illustrates a 350-L (92-gal) plastic vat with a capacity of over 300 kg (660 lbs) of crushed grapes used for macerating red wine juice.

Containers that can be sealed to protect wine from air are required as fermentors to complete fermentation following maceration or to store and age wine.

Food-grade plastic vats come in many different sizes depending on your needs. They can be bulky and cumbersome for storage when not in use. Therefore, when determining capacity needs, consider your future requirements if you intend to increase production, and to allow for volume expansion of the must during fermentation. Do not use plastic containers for storing or aging wine for a prolonged time; plastic is a permeable material and will cause wine to oxidize.

Figure 2-9: A 350-L, food-grade plastic vat for macerating red wine juice

Warning: Only use non-toxic, food-grade plastic to avoid spoiling the wine, or even worse, harming people drinking your wine. If in doubt, select plastic vats specifically designed for winemaking. Avoid recycled containers that were previously used to store olives or unknown substances.

To clean a cement vat, first strip it of any tartrate deposit, easily accomplished with a light scrubbing using a plastic-bristle brush, and then clean it using a caustic soda solution. After cleaning, brush on a layer of tartaric solution before using the vat.

2.3.4 OAK BARRELS

The use of oak barrels in home winemaking has not been a common practice. The most common reason heard is that the use of oak barrels is too risky and should be left to experienced professional winemakers. With very little know-how and routine supervision and maintenance, the use of oak barrels can be made to be risk-free and fun in home winemaking. The quality of the finished wine is well worth the additional investment in time and money.

Ideally, you should purchase new oak barrels to reduce any potential problems with used barrels. You can reuse new barrels multiple times for several years therefore justifying the investment. Old wooden barrels can be troublesome, as they need to be prepared, cleaned and sanitized carefully before use. Lastly, never store or age white wine in oak barrels previously used for red wine. White wine will absorb red pigments from the wood and will become a reddish color.

Chapter 8 presents a full discussion on barrel types and uses as well as alternatives to barrels, maintenance and preparation of oak barrels for fermenting and aging wine, and barrel reconditioning.

2.3.5 STAINLESS STEEL TANKS

The availability and affordability of stainless steel tanks coupled with the wide assortment of types, volumes and features have made these an excellent alternative to demijohns and carboys in home winemaking for fermenting wine and for high-capacity, short- and long-term wine storage.

The two major types of stainless steel tanks are closed-top and open-top, floating-lid, the most affordable ones manufactured from AISI (American Iron and Steel Institute) 304 stainless steel. The choice of one type versus the other will depend on your budget and winemaking style. For example, do you prefer to punch down the cap (mass of grape solids above the juice during red wine fermentation) instead of pump-over in red winemaking? Do you need to chill wine? Do you have inert gas available for protecting wine during aging or do you prefer not to leave any headspace?

Closed-top tanks have a fixed volume – although partial fill is possible by protecting wine with inert gas – with access to the wine through a top manhole (usually called a manway in winemaking parlance). Open-top, floating-lid tanks, more commonly referred to as simply floating-lid tanks or variable-capacity tanks (VCT), are used for variable volumes and provide easy access to wine for such operations as cap punching, undoubtedly their greatest advantage.

Tank prices can vary greatly depending on size, configuration and features. Size, alloy composition and thickness are factors that impact price the most.

Estimate your winemaking capacity for the foreseeable future and choose an adequate tank size to fit your needs and budget, keeping in mind extra headspace required for expansion during fermentation. When choosing a tank size, give proper consideration to the ratio of tank diameter versus tank height. During maceration (see Section 4.3) where optimum extraction of color, tannins and flavor compounds is critical in red winemaking, it is most desirable to have tanks with a large diameter-to-height ratio for increased surface area exposure of grape solids to juice or wine, as opposed to tall and skinny, small diameter-to-height ratio tanks.

Alloy composition provides an indication of the stainless steel's corrosiveness. Standard inert (does not react with wine) alloys available are AISI 304 and AISI 316. The 304 alloy is considerably

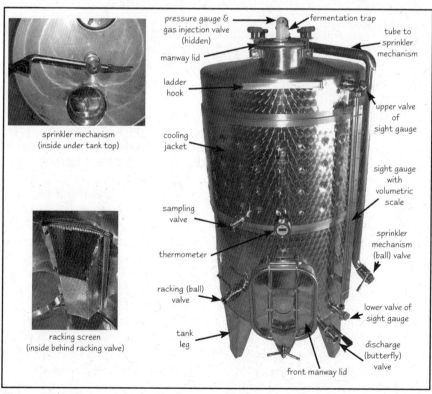

Figure 2-10 (Counterclockwise from top left): Sprinkler mechanism, racking screen, closed-top tank

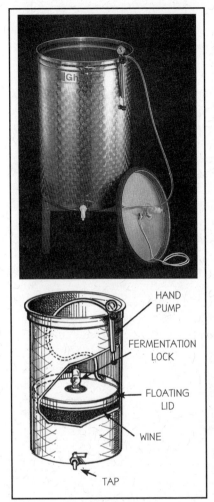

HAND PUMP

FERMENTATION LOCK

FLOATING LID

WINE

TAP

Figure 2-11: Top, A variable-capacity, floating-lid tank (VCT); Bottom, operation of a VCT

less expensive but is more susceptible to pitting from sulfur dioxide (SO_2) than the 316 alloy, which contains molybdenum providing a higher degree of resistance to SO_2, salts and strong, corrosive acids. AISI 316 tanks are commonly found in commercial wineries whereas nearly all tanks for home winemaking are AISI 304 because they are more affordable for hobbyists. Small, closed-top tanks may still include an AISI 316 top even though the rest of the tank is AISI 304; this is because the top section of the tank has a higher concentration of diffused SO_2 gas. All other parts that will come into contact with wine should also be stainless steel; other metals such as brass or copper will impart metallic flavors to wine.

Steel thickness can range between 0.6–1.2 mm, or $\frac{3}{128}$ to $\frac{3}{64}$ inch. The smaller the thickness, the more prone the tanks are to dents from accidental hitting; therefore, opt for a heavier gauge tank, budget and availability permitting. Note that steel thickness is usually described as a gauge number; the lower the gauge, the thicker the steel.

Following is a list of various features that can be installed on stainless steel tanks to create different combinations of a particular tank configuration. Specific feature combinations may not be possible on a particular configuration or tank size. Figures 2-10 and 2-11 depict typical features of a closed-top tank and a floating-lid tank, respectively. Figure 2-11 also illustrates how a floating-lid tank provides variable capacity.

A closed-top tank is equipped with a small manway at the top for access to the wine. The manway lid has a silicone gasket to provide an airtight seal, and is usually equipped with a marble-operated fermentation trap to let gas escape during fermentation. The trap can be removed and replaced with a solid rubber stopper when fermentation is complete so as to avoid letting air in the tank; marbles inside the trap can move and let air in, such as when the tank is accidentally banged. The lid can also be fitted with a simple ball valve and pressure gauge, useful if you intend to inject gas into the tank to protect the wine.

Warning: The marble-operated fermentation traps found on tanks are ***not*** *oxygen barriers; they must be replaced with a fermentation lock (see Section 2.4,) or, with a solid bung (see Section 2.5.1) when fermentation is complete.*

An open-top tank has a stainless steel lid with an inflatable membrane around the circumference that transforms the tank into a variable-capacity container. The lid is placed inside the tank, on top of the wine, and allowed to float. The membrane is then inflated using the supplied hand air pump to seal the tank and protect the wine from air. The hand air pump is connected to the membrane via a polyethylene tube. A pressure gauge indicates the membrane pressure, which can be adjusted at any time to maintain an airtight seal. The pump has a release valve to deflate the membrane when the lid is to be removed. Always respect the manufacturer's recommended maximum air pressure in the membrane to avoid damaging it. Some retailers suggest that you purchase an extra membrane … just in case. The membrane creates a perfect seal on the inner circumference of the tank to protect the wine. As with closed-top lids, the floating lid also uses a marble-operated fermentation trap. During fermentation, the lid can be placed high above the wine surface to allow for expansion or cap formation, or placed directly on the wine surface when aging. The lid is secured with a rope to ease removal when the lid is low down in the

Figure 2-12: A large VCT tank equipped with a lid hoisting attachment

tank. Unfortunately, this is also an annoyance because the rope is fastened through a single eyelet on the center of the lid causing it to tilt sideways upon removal, and often dropping into the wine. A newer type of lid on the market uses three eyelets that keep the lid balanced. The larger volume tanks – over 2000 liters (529 gallons), as the one shown in Figure 2-12 – have a lid hoisting attachment fixed to the side that reaches toward the center of the tank.

Useful tip: When inflating the lid to seal the tank, inflate the membrane partially until the lid can be pulled up without it falling back down. Lift the lid a little, an inch or so, and then pump the membrane up to the recommended pressure. This avoids having wine pouring out from the fermentation trap due to the lid's downward pressure on the wine if it is not raised.

Warning: When emptying variable-capacity tanks during such operations as racking or bottling, deflate the membrane on the lid before drawing wine from the tank; otherwise, the tank will implode.

A bottom manway and lid with a silicone gasket – the lid is usually round, oval or rectangular in shape and approximately 12 inches in width – provides easy access to the inside of the tank for cleaning and for removing grape solids once fermentation and maceration are completed.

A racking ball valve sitting a few inches above the bottom of the tank is used to rack wine out of the tank. If you intend to work with grape solids, the tank should be equipped with an interior screen (see Figure 2-10) to avoid racking grape solids. Choose a model with a removable screen, which makes cleaning a simple task. In general, small tanks only have a one-inch ball valve at the bottom of the tank for racking, sampling, filtering, and bottling.

A discharge butterfly valve sitting at the lowest point at the bottom of the tank is used for discharging liquid or solids when washing or emptying the tank. A butterfly valve is used (instead of a ball valve) because it will not clog when solids are discharged. The valve can be located either at the center of a conical-bottom tank or at the side of a 5% or 10% sloped-bottom tank for effective discharging.

If you intend to work with grape solids or large tank volumes, all valves should be a minimum of at least 1½ inch to avoid clogging equipment and to have better flow rate when moving wine. Tri-Clover fittings and clamps, shown in Figure 2-13, are the standard for connecting hoses, valves and other equipment. Some Italian equipment uses the more-difficult-to-handle Garolla

Figure 2-13: Tri-Clover & Garolla clamps

clamp, shown in Figure 2-13. Other fitting types, such as threaded fittings, are also available but spare parts seem harder to find. Be sure to always use a silicone or Teflon gasket between valves and hose fittings to avoid leakage.

A small, half-inch sampling valve usually located midway on the tank's side will prove useful for sampling your wine during fermentation or aging.

A thermometer is essential for monitoring fermentation temperature or temperature of wine being chilled. The thermometer is equipped with a temperature-sensitive probe inserted into the tank's thermometer well, which protrudes inside the tank towards the center. Choose a probe that will extend close to the center of the tank to get as an accurate temperature reading as possible; temperature of wine towards the center and closer to the tank wall can differ greatly.

A cooling jacket is used to control wine temperature, for example, to reduce the rapid rising temperature during red wine fermentation, to maintain a cool temperature during aging, or to chill wine for cold stabilization. It is simply a shell surrounding the exterior circumference of the tank, towards the top, which allows a refrigerant, such as water or glycol, to circulate in and out of the jacket to cool wine. If you have ever visited a commercial winery and noticed frost or ice on tanks, that is the result of the cooling jacket's effect. The cooling jacket is dimpled to increase flow turbulence of the refrigerant, which increases heat transfer. Standard, brass ball valves are used at the inlet and outlets of the cooling jacket to connect to the refrigeration system.

Some manufacturers provide alternate solutions for chilling wine, such as cooling by evaporation, as refrigeration in home winemaking is not always possible or affordable. In evaporation cooling, instead of a cooling jacket, the tank is equipped with a pipe leading to the top of the tank that connects to a water supply line at the bottom and to a cooling ring at the top. Cold water is run to the top and allowed to drip on the tank sidewalls for the cooling

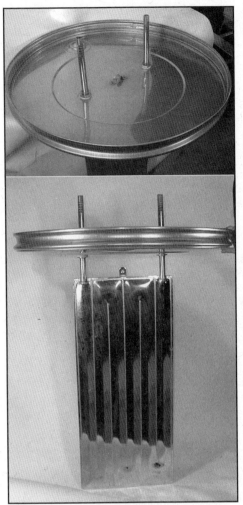

Figure 2-14: Immersion plate installed on the lid of a floating-lid tank

effect. This technique, also known as skin cooling, is not as effective because an abundant amount of ice cold water is required, which must also be constantly chilled, and because of the high thermal loss to the surrounding environment.

Section 6.1.1 provides more information and instructions on the use of cooling jackets for cold stabilization applications.

Open-top tanks offer advantages, and greater flexibility and efficiency when it comes to cooling. A device known as an immersion plate, or more specifically known as a cooling plate when used for cooling applications, shown in Figure 2-14, often mounted on a floating lid, that is inserted in the wine greatly improves cooling efficiency. A cooling plate allows cold water to be circulated in and out and draw heat out of the wine. By positioning the cooling plate at the center and along the depth of the wine, wine can be cooled quite efficiently.

A volumetric, clear-glass gauge is used for monitoring total wine volume in the tank. The sight gauge should be equipped with small, top and bottom valves to control flow of wine into the gauge and to simplify cleaning (water is more easily moved in and out of the gauge when equipped with valves). See below on how to calculate volume of wine in your tank if it is not equipped with a calibrated sight gauge.

Large-volume tanks are usually equipped with a three-legged stand while small tanks are generally sold with an optional stand. Tall tanks also have a ladder hook for securing an aluminum ladder for access to the top. On small tanks, it is recommended to forego this feature and opt for a safer, easy-to-use, light work ladder.

The most popular exterior finish is the marble finish; a polished, mirror finish is often available upon request. This is simply a matter of personal preference and price.

When buying a tank, first choose your cellar location carefully – tanks can be very heavy even when empty – as you will not be able to move it around, and be sure that you buy a tank size that will fit through your cellar door.

You will also need to buy a good supply of FDA-approved, food-grade, suction/discharge hoses as well as stainless steel hose barb (serrated) fittings and Tri-Clover clamps. Ensure that valve and hose barb fitting dimensions match and fit the hose diameter. For 1½-in valves and fittings, you will need a 1½-in ID (inner diameter) hose. A heavy-duty hose, such as Kuri Tec's Tigerflex (Food Transfer) FT-150 clear PVC hose, is recommended for winemaking applications. Kuri Tec specifically lists their WSTF-coded hoses for winemaking applications; these have an exposed outer PVC helix for added durability (hoses tend to be dragged quite a bit on concrete floors); however, the added costs may not be warranted.

Instructions on the use of stainless steel tanks in specific winemaking applications are provided in relevant sections throughout this book. Section 2.6.4 provides instructions on maintaining, cleaning and sanitizing tanks.

Prior to the start of winemaking season, it is recommended to fill each tank partially – just above the highest welded joint in the tank – with water and let it sit overnight to test for any leaks from pinholes that might have developed in and around welded joints. Optionally, add food dye to the water to make detecting leaks visually easier. Do not let the water sit in the tank for more than 12–24 hours to prevent spoilage organisms from forming.

Similarly, check for leaks in the cooling jacket, if so equipped, by connecting a water supply, such as a garage hose, to the jacket's inlet with the outlet valve closed. Cooling jackets are rated for a maximum pressure (ask the manufacturer if not indicated in the tank's specifications); so it is a good idea to install a pressure gauge inline with your water supply hose. Shut the water supply when you are nearing the maximum rated pressure, and check for any pressure drop and water leaks.

If you store away your tanks during the off-season, daub all silicone gaskets with food-grade grease that can be easily wiped off and rinsed prior to use to protect them from the elements and from drying out. If a gasket shows any sign of wear and tear, such as dryness or small cracks, replace it with a new one to avoid potential leakage problems.

How much wine is in the tank?

You should always know how much juice or wine is in a tank, particularly when trying to figure out how much of an additive is needed for the volume of must or wine. The amount of yeast, nutrients, acid, fining agent, and other ingredients and chemicals to be added to wine are all calculated based on volume of wine. If a tank is not equipped with a sight gauge, the volume can be easily calculated as follows.

First, measure the inside diameter (in centimeters) of the tank with a measuring tape as well as the wine depth inside the tank, in centimeters (cm). For a quick approximation, eyeball the wine level from the outside of the tank by looking at the wine level inside the tank, and mark that level on the side of the tank. For a more accurate determination, use a long (sanitized) stainless steel or plastic rod, dip it vertically straight into the wine until it touches the bottom of the tank. Use your thumb to mark the wine level on the rod. Retrieve the rod and use a measuring tape to determine the wine depth, i.e., measure the length from the bottom of the rod to the thumb mark.

If you are measuring using inches, divide each measurement in inches by 0.39.

Finally, calculate the approximate volume in liters by plugging the tank diameter and wine depth values, in cm, in the following equation:

$$\text{Volume (L)} = \frac{\pi r^2 h}{1000}$$

Where π is approximately 3.14
      r = the radius of the tank = ½ of the diameter of the tank
      h = the depth of the tank

Or use the following simplified equation:

Volume (L) = (0.0007854 × tank diameter × tank diameter × wine depth)

In gallons, simply divide the above result by 3.79.

For example, if the tank diameter is 70 cm (27¼ in) and the wine depth is 60 cm (23½ in), then the volume is 0.0007854 × 70 × 70 × 60, or approximately 231 L, or 61 gal.

2.4 FERMENTATION LOCKS

The fermentation lock is an essential device in winemaking to protect must or wine from the elements while allowing carbon dioxide gas to escape from a closed fermentor during fermentation without letting any air in. Air is wine's worst enemy and will cause spoilage if in contact with the wine for any significant period of time.

There are various types of fermentation locks available. A favorite among winemakers is the S-shaped fermentation lock that produces a symphonic sound during the vigorous phase of fermentation. The advantage of the S-shaped fermentation lock is that it prevents water or sulfite solution from flowing back into the wine under cellar temperature fluctuations. Temperature changes will cause sulfite solution to be forced in or out of the fermentation lock. In the straight-cylinder fermentation lock model, water or sulfite solution will contaminate the wine under such conditions. An advantage of the straight-cylinder fermentation lock is its ease of cleaning. Figure 2-15 illustrates two types of fermentation locks fitted with silicone rubber bungs.

Note: Some literature advises using water instead of a sulfite solution in fermentation locks as the latter is believed to cause a little hydrogen sulfide (H_2S) to form. H_2S is responsible for imparting a rotten-egg smell.

Always have a good supply of fermentation locks in stock; you do not want to be caught short when your local supply store is closed.

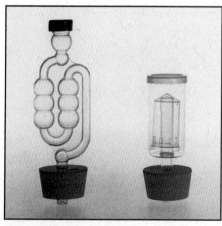

Figure 2-15: Fermentation locks and silicone rubber bungs

To use a fermentation lock, first attach a silicone rubber bung with a hole to the lock, then add water or a sulfite solution (refer to section 2.6.3) up to the level indicated on the fermentation lock, and insert it firmly in the opening of the wine container. The bottom tube of the fermentation lock should protrude from the bung by approximately 0.5 to 1 cm, and the tube should be approximately 2 cm above wine level. The top portion of the lock, where the carbon dioxide gas escapes, should be protected with a lid to prevent dust and flies from entering the lock. The lid is designed to let the carbon dioxide gas escape freely. Some cotton wool can be put into the opening instead of the lid. Replace the water or sulfite solution every 3 to 4 weeks, as it can become contaminated, including the sulfite solution as it loses effectiveness when exposed to air for a prolonged time.

Do not allow the wine to enter the fermentation lock as it could come in contact with contaminated water or sulfite solution in the lock, or it can become exposed to air. This can be avoided by monitoring the wine level in each container to ensure that it does not rise with temperature fluctuations in the fermentation area or cellar.

2.5 MISCELLANEOUS EQUIPMENT

There are many other miscellaneous devices that will prove very useful and indispensable for home winemaking. These include bungs, siphoning tubes, special sieve and faucet attachments for plastic fermentors, floating thermometers, vinometer, various size funnels, long-handled spoons and stirrer, gravy baster or winethief, cleaning brushes and measuring spoons. A portable balance will also come in handy for measuring chemicals to remove guesswork when using baking measuring spoons.

Other miscellaneous equipment, such as hydrometer, refractometer, pH meter, and sugar, acid and sulfite analysis kits are described in Chapter 3 as these pertain to the analysis and control of musts and wines. Filtering and sparkling winemaking equipment are described in sections 5.3 and chapter 11, respectively.

2.5.1 BUNGS

You should have a good supply of both no-hole and single-hole bungs (stoppers) of varying sizes for demijohns, carboys and smaller containers. Silicone rubber bungs provide a better airtight seal and are preferred over cork stoppers. They are the most efficient and reliable for providing an airtight seal as the bung material adjusts to the shape of the opening when inserted, and are preferred over cork stoppers, which do not guarantee a good seal because their stiffer materials do not adjust to the shape of the opening. Bungs should fit snugly and should be sufficiently inserted into the mouth opening of the container to ease later removal.

There is a plethora of bung types designed for every personal preference and container type.

The most popular type is the beige-colored rubber bung, available in half-size increments ranging from a No. 2 to a No. 14, with or without a hole, to accommodate standard 750-mL bottles up to 54-L demijohns and large oak barrels. You will need to stock various sizes depending on the types of containers you use because the short taper on these bungs cannot adapt to different opening diameters.

To provide a good seal, this type of bung should be inserted at least halfway down the taper while leaving sufficient grip for removing the bung. Bungs inserted too deep can become very difficult to remove, especially when the seal dries out over time. If a bung becomes stuck, use a flathead screwdriver to pry the bung progressively, just above the opening, around its circumference until it can be pulled out by hand. Use caution when doing this on glass containers so as not to chip the glass. Use the thumb of your other hand as a lever and do not let the screwdriver touch the glass.

Another type is the cup-shaped Buon Vino bung having features that provide a number of benefits. First, Buon Vino bungs come in three sizes only – small, medium and large – to fit containers ranging from 12 L to 54 L, and also available with or without a hole. The bungs have a longer taper, which means they can fit openings of various diameters, and you therefore need to stock fewer of these.

Buon Vino bungs have a lip that prevents them from falling into the container if over-inserted and that greatly helps removal of the bung. Another feature is the cup-shaped design that can hold a small amount of liquid in the event the fermentation lock overflows due to excessive release of fermentation gas or sudden temperature changes. This is particularly interesting in oak barrel applications where you need to avoid liquid spilling around the bung area, which could become a breeding ground for molds and bacteria.

Barrel Builders is another supplier of high-quality, silicone bungs used mainly for large barrels since they mostly cater to commercial wineries. Barrel Builders bungs are available only in a standard large size – they do fit 54-L demijohns – and three types: solid, recessed and EasyGrip.

The solid type is a standard bung with a longer taper while the recessed type is similar to the solid bung but has a small recess or cavity in the bottom portion. The recess in the bung bottom makes these bungs more flexible and better adapted where a tighter fit is desired.

The EasyGrip type is a solid bung with a shorter taper and a lip to allow a closer fit to the stave (one of the long pieces of wood of the barrel) and easier removal, and are particularly practical when barrels need to be rolled around. Long-tapered bungs make barrel rolling much harder because they stick out more.

Ferm-Rite has developed the Breathing Bung designed to act as a one-way valve. No need for a fermentation lock on these bungs – it's a clever design! The Breathing Bung consists of two parts, both

Figure 2-16: Bungs - Silicone/rubber, Buon Vino's, Barrel Builders', Ferm-Rite's and BestBung

made of silicone material: a bung with 5 holes and a "breathing flap". The breathing flap is simply a thin flap with a stem. The stem is fitted into the center bung hole and lowered until the flap rests flatly over the remaining four holes. During fermentation, gas escapes through the holes and under the flap. The pressure causes the flap to lift and release gas, and then falls back over the holes when pressure decreases to prevent air from entering the container. Breathing Bungs are available in two sizes: regular and carboy. The regular size fits large barrels and 54-L demijohns, while the carboy size fits standard home winemaking carboys.

If you work with large, 225-L (59-gal) oak barrels, another type of bung specifically designed for barrel fermentation is the BestBung. It is lightly inserted into a barrel bung hole, and during active fermentation, the bung rises slightly to let gas out of the barrel. As fermentation slows down and pressure inside the barrel has equalized, the bung lowers into the bung hole and eventually seals the barrel.

Figure 2-16 shows the various types of bungs described above. Table 2-3 can be used as a quick reference to determine the proper bung type and size based on the type and size of container.

Note: Barrels from different manufacturers have different bung hole diameters. Measure the diameter of the hole before heading out to your supplier to buy bungs for your barrels.

Bored vs. solid bung
The decision of bored versus solid (no hole) bungs is really one trying to solve the fermentation lock backflow problem, i.e., when should you replace the bung/lock with a solid bung. Water or sulfite solution in the fermentation lock will tend to shift inwards or outwards as temperature or atmospheric pressure change. If contaminated liquid in the lock backflows into the container, it can contaminate and spoil the wine.

Table 2-3
Recommended bung sizes for glass containers and barrels

Type of container		Recommended bung size
Metric volumes	US volumes	
750-mL bottle	Standard wine bottle	#4 or #4½
4-L jug	1-gal jug	#6 or #6½
12, 18.9, 20, 23-L carboys	3, 5, 6-gal carboys	#7 Buon Vino Small Ferm-Rite Carboy
Small 57-L barrel	Small 15-gal barrel	#9 Buon Vino Medium
10, 15, 20, 25, 34-L demijohns	2.5 to 9-gal demijohns	#9½ Buon Vino Medium
Large 227-L barrel	Large 60-gal barrel	#10½ or #11 Buon Vino Large Ferm-Rite Regular Barrel Builders – all types BestBung
54-L demijohn	14-gal demijohn	#11 or #11½ Buon Vino Large Ferm-Rite Regular Barrel Builders – all types

You can forego the fermentation lock and insert a solid bung when you are preparing wine for final stabilization, i.e., when fermentation has totally completed and there is no residual gas.

Caution: Never use a solid bung on containers with fermenting wine or if the wine still has residual gas.

Insert the solid bung tightly to ensure it does not pop out during temperature or pressure fluctuations. Be sure to leave a small headspace of approximately 2 cm (¾ in) to allow for expansion and contraction of wine volume.

It is a good idea to also invest in a borer to make holes in solid rubber bungs in the event you run out of bored bungs. Bung borers will make a smoother hole than by using a drill bit, which tends to bore a rather rough hole. You want to make sure that air does not leak in through the bored hole between the bung and fermentation lock.

Bung care

Bungs will last many years when properly cared for. Before use, simply rinse bungs under warm water and sanitize using a sulfite solution as you would with any other equipment. Moistening the bung circumference with sulfite solution will greatly ease insertion into the opening of glass containers. Insert the bung by rotating it slightly when applying downward pressure. Without the rotation, the bung will tend to slip back up. Use a rubber mallet to drive solid bungs in barrel bungholes – it's the easiest method to avoid finger pain.

When removing bungs to taste, test or transfer wine, rinse the bungs using a sulfite solution to eliminate any potential mold or any deposit that may have formed.

2.5.2 SIPHONS

Home winemaking siphoning equipment consists of a solid clear-glass J-tube with an end cap, or antidregs tip, and a clear, food grade, flexible plastic (polyvinyl) tubing available in various lengths. Popular plastic tube diameters are 6 mm (¼ in), 10 mm (⅜ in), 13 mm (½ in), 19 mm (¾ in), and 26 mm (1 in). The 6- and 10-mm tubings are the standard size for small-capacity winemaking equipment and filtration systems. The 10-mm tubing should be used for quicker transfer of wine from one container to another. The 13, 19, and 26-mm tubings are used on larger-scale home winemaking equipment and filtration systems.

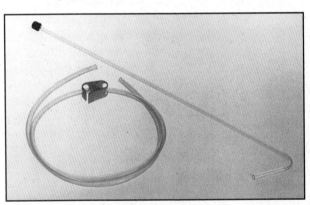

Figure 2-17: J-tube with an antidregs tip and plastic tubing used for siphoning wine

The antidregs tip is attached at the bottom of the J-tube and is used to prevent sediment from entering the tube when siphoning wine during the various winemaking operations. Figure 2-17 illustrates a J-tube with an antidregs tip and plastic tubing for siphoning.

Figure 2-18: Top, special faucet and sieve; Bottom, setup in a plastic fermentor

To siphon or rack wine from one container to another, place the container with the sediment at a higher level than the second container. A height difference of 1 m (3 ft) between the containers will cause a good siphoning action. Insert the J-tube, antidregs tip and plastic tubing assembly in the container with sediment. Start the flow of wine into the lower container by creating suction using your mouth from the end of the tubing. Containers with wine and sediment should not be displaced for a few days before racking. The siphoning will be a lot more efficient and the racked wine will be clearer with less waste if the sediment is not disturbed. This is especially true if the wine has been fined recently.

2.5.3 SPECIAL SIEVE AND FAUCET

Although it is possible to siphon red wine from the plastic fermentor, following maceration, to a demijohn or a carboy, this will prove to be a tedious task as the siphoning tube will clog easily with grape skins, seeds and other solids. Also, it is not practical to place the heavy fermentor higher to achieve an effective siphoning action. The best solution involves using a special plastic sieve and faucet that allow drainage of wine from the fermentor without clogging. The special sieve will filter large grape particles allowing the must or wine to flow freely. The faucet, which has a 26-mm (1-in) or 32-mm (1¼-in) diameter, can be opened or closed easily to control the flow of wine.

The sieve is mounted from the inside of the plastic fermentor and is held in place by both a bracket and the faucet that are mounted through a hole in the fermentor. Figure 2-18 shows the special sieve and faucet, and the setup in a plastic fermentor.

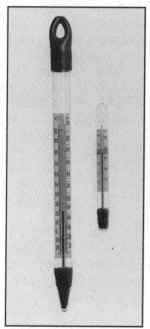

Figure 2-19: Floating thermometers

2.5.4 FLOATING THERMOMETER

A floating thermometer is necessary to ensure that the temperature of the must remains within the recommended temperature range before adding yeast to start fermentation. It is also used to monitor the temperature of the must and wine to ensure a proper and consistent fermentation environment. Figure 2-19 illustrates two sizes of floating thermometers for winemaking purpose. The smaller thermometer is most practical when used in clear juice or wine. The larger thermometer is mainly used during the maceration stage or in larger productions. In the former, the grape solids would bury the smaller thermometer making it hard to locate. The larger thermometer is sufficiently long to penetrate through the cap to measure the must temperature.

2.5.5 VINOMETER

A vinometer is an inexpensive and practical device for a quick but approximate determination of an unknown alcohol content in a finished dry wine. It is particularly useful in the event that potential alcohol before fermentation was not determined and therefore the alcohol content cannot be calculated. Figure 2-20 illustrates two vinometer models. This instrument is not intended for alcohol determination of sweet wines because the high sugar content will yield false readings.

To determine the approximate alcohol content, pour a small amount of dry wine in the vinometer opening. When the wine fills up the tiny tube inside, invert the vinometer. The wine will flow out and will stop due to capillary action. Read the alcohol content from the vinometer scale at that point.

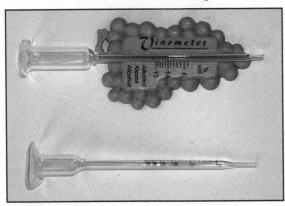

Figure 2-20: Top, Vinoferm's Precision Vinometer; Bottom, standard vinometer

The major drawback of the vinometer is its poor accuracy, and the higher the alcohol content, the greater the inaccuracy. To reduce the margin of inaccuracy, particularly in high-alcohol wines as well as in sweet wines, dilute the wine sample with an equal volume of water. Perform the test, take a reading and then multiply the alcohol content reading by 2.

Figure 2-21: Plastic funnel with a removable sieve, and large-hole sieve

Vinoferm's Precision Vinometer, shown in Figure 2-20, is more accurate as it uses a 4–15% alc./vol. scale as opposed to the 0–25% alc./vol. scale on the previous model, and is equipped with a reflective blue background that greatly simplifies readings for white wines.

An ebulliometer, discussed in section 3.1.4 is required for accurate alcohol determination.

2.5.6 OTHER MISCELLANEOUS EQUIPMENT

Here is some other miscellaneous equipment that will prove very useful in any home winemaker's toolkit.

Double cheesecloth and a good plastic strainer will come in handy for separating grape juice from pulp and other unwanted solids when, for example, transferring red wine from the one fermentor to another. Do not use metal strainers unless they are stainless steel.

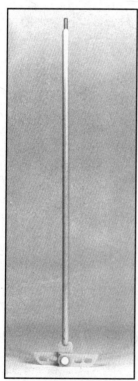

Figure 2-22: Stirring stem

Plastic funnels, one small and one large, with a built-in removable plastic sieve are useful for transferring must and wine from one fermentor to another. Figure 2-21 illustrates a plastic funnel with a removal sieve and a sieve to separate juice from large grape particles.

A long-handled plastic spoon is required to stir must and wine for various winemaking operations in carboys. For larger containers, a stirrer – the type equipped with two stirring paddles that move to a horizontal position when spun rapidly using an electric drill, shown in Figure 2-22 – is recommended to ease stirring. The apparatus is inserted into a container to stir wine.

A gravy baster and/or wine-thief are also practical for withdrawing small samples of wine from containers. Small and large polyester brushes with metal handles are useful for cleaning tough stains and sediment from glass containers. A set of measuring spoons from ⅛ tsp (0.625 mL)

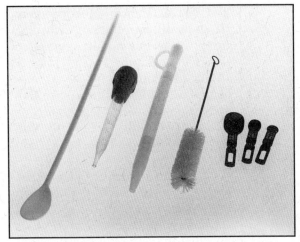

Figure 2-23: Miscellaneous winemaking equipment (left to right); long-handled stirring spoon, gravy baster, plastic wine thief, large polyester cleaning brush, and set of measuring spoons

to 1 tbsp (15 mL) is indispensable for measuring the many powdered chemicals used in winemaking.

Measuring spoons commonly used for baking are very handy for quick, approximate measurements of chemicals. When the weight of a chemical can be related to its volume in teaspoon or tablespoon measurements – such as the tables often provided in the appendix of winemaking books – these spoons are very practical. The only problem is that their margin of error may be significant, and this is an important drawback when working with chemicals to be added in accurate amounts.

Figure 2-23 illustrates miscellaneous winemaking equipment. Figure 2-24 illustrates a small and larger wine-thief.

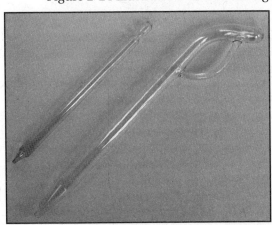

Figure 2-24: Wine thieves

And if you need to move carboys and demijohns around in the cellar, a winch-operated lift, such as the one shown in Figure 2-25, will prove most useful, particularly to lift containers higher for either racking or storage on a high shelf. The lift is equipped with fixed casters at the rear and swivel casters at the front for easy maneuverability, even in the smallest cellar.

2.5.7 MISCELLANEOUS LABORATORY EQUIPMENT

Your home winery will most likely be equipped with some basic laboratory equipment for analytical determination of various parameters such as sugar, acidity and sulfite. The investment in

Figure 2-25: Winch-operated lift

and sophistication of equipment depends on your budget, skills and extent of desired quality control on your winemaking.

In addition to equipment presented in the above sections and in specific relevant sections, your wine laboratory should include the following additional equipment that will prove very useful.

A measuring balance, such as the Ohaus SC4010 model depicted in Figure 2-26, will prove to be an excellent investment over time. A portable model operating on either battery or AC power is most practical. They are available in many capacities; 400-g, 600-g or 1200-g balances will meet most winemakers' needs. Some models also provide measurements in various units including grams and ounces. The most important consideration in choosing a balance is its readability, or accuracy. A balance with reading in 0.1 g increments is quite sufficient. Higher accuracy balances will commend higher prices. 1-g increment balances might be fine for most measurements; however, in the long run, the 0.1-g will prove to be a better investment.

An assortment of measuring equipment and glassware such as graduated cylinders, beakers, flasks, burets, pipets and test tubes, shown in Figure 2-27, will prove indispensable for measuring test samples, reagents and other solutions. Following is a recommended list of syringes and glassware.

- eyedropper
- 1-mL, 5-mL, 10-mL and 20-mL syringes
- 20-mL and 100-mL graduated cylinders
- 100-mL and 250-mL beakers
- 100-mL and 250-mL Erlenmeyer flasks and rubber stoppers
- 25-mL buret with stopcock
- 5-mL, 10-mL and 25-mL pipets
- 10-mL test tubes

2.6 CLEANING AND SANITIZING

Cleaning and sanitizing procedures are seldom discussed in literature; they are considered menial but necessary tasks that all winemakers wish they could do away with. The reality is that cleaning and sanitizing are vital to good winemaking, if not critical. They can make the difference between sound wine and spoiled wine. So there is no debating; cleaning and sanitizing of winemaking equipment are a must before any juice or wine makes contact with equipment and containers including bottles. These procedures are critical in preventing microbial spoilage in wines.

A word of caution though! Winemaking literature often refers to sterilization as opposed to sanitization. Sterilization refers to the process of eradicating all living microorganisms by using advanced technology and methodologies, typically only seen in pharmaceutical and state-of-the-art laboratories. In wine-

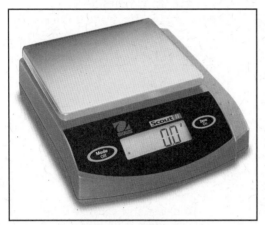

Figure 2-26: A Ohaus SC4010 balance with a 400-g capacity and 0.1-g accuracy

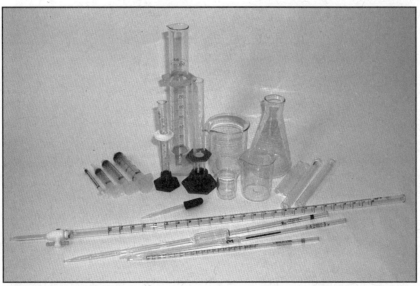

Figure 2-27: Miscellaneous lab equipment and glassware such as graduated cylinders, beakers, flasks, burets, pipets and test tubes

Soft and hard water

It is best to use soft water for cleaning winemaking equipment, i.e., water with a low mineral content. Hard water causes scaling, or the formation of limescale when minerals precipitate, and requires much more cleaning agent compared to soft water to clean effectively. You can quickly determine if your water is hard. Pour a small amount of liquid soap – not detergent – in some water in a flask or closed container and shake vigorously, or alternatively, rub your hands with a bar of soap under running water. The soap should foam easily; otherwise, the water is hard. Use an alternative source of water or a water softener if your water is hard.

making, an acceptable level of sterilization is possible using a hot-water treatment at 80° C (176° F) for 20 minutes for most equipment, although some equipment cannot withstand such a treatment. In home winemaking, it is too difficult, not economical, and impractical to achieve and maintain such a temperature for that long. It is also not a requirement since we are mainly interested in eradicating living microorganisms to an acceptably low level such that any remaining microorganisms will not adversely affect the wine. In other words, sanitization is a limited form of sterilization and is perfectly acceptable to achieve microbial stability in wine. Microbial stability is further discussed in section 6.2.

To clean and sanitize equipment and containers – or anything that will come into contact with wine – first rinse the equipment thoroughly with plenty of clean and fresh soft water (see sidebar). Use hot water at a temperature between 50°–70° C (122°–158° F) on heat-tolerant equipment, such as tanks, vats and glass containers, in conjunction with a pressure washer, if available, for a more effective rinsing. For pumps, hoses, connectors and fittings, simply let cool (not hot) water circulate through the equipment by running the pump for at least 10 minutes. Using an appropriate cleaning agent for each type of material, thoroughly clean all equipment and then rinse with plenty of cool water. Lastly, sanitize all equipment using a suitable sanitizing agent to eradicate microorganisms that could otherwise spoil wine followed by a thorough cool water rinse. Drain the equipment well so that there is no residual water. At the end of the cleaning and sanitizing operations, the equipment should be free of any solids, precipitates and odors.

Caustic (alkaline) chemicals, such as sodium carbonate and sodium percarbonate, are the most common and most effective cleaning agent for winemaking equipment. Other products including chlorine and specialized formulations are also available. Avoid using soaps and detergents on winemaking equipment; these will leave a soap film and residues that could be difficult to rinse away and could therefore affect the taste of wine. For sanitizing, sulfite is the industry standard because it is very effective in eradicating or suppressing unwanted microorganisms to an acceptable level. In addition to cleaning and sanitizing agents, you will need plenty of water for rinsing, and more rinsing.

2.6.1 CAUSTIC CHEMICALS

Sodium carbonate, a white powder commonly known as soda ash, is a caustic cleaner that can be used as a substitute for soap on plastic materials. It also has two other useful properties: it dissolves tartrates and neutralizes acetic acid. For these reasons, manufacturers often recommend soda ash for cleaning oak barrels; however, this should be avoided as essential oak flavor will be leached out and potentially affect the taste of wine. Refer to section 8.6 for a description on the proper care and maintenance of oak barrels.

Use soda ash at a rate of 8–12 g/L of water. Soda ash does not dissolve easily; so first dissolve the powder in hot water and then dilute the solution to the required concentration by adding cool water. Use the solution to thoroughly clean equipment, leaving the solution in contact with the surface for at least 10 minutes. After the soda ash treatment, rinse the equipment thoroughly with plenty of water followed by a thorough sulfur-citric rinse (see section 2.6.3 below), and lastly another water rinse.

Sodium percarbonate or sodium carbonate peroxide, both synonyms for sodium carbonate peroxyhydrate and commonly referred to as percarbonate, is a granular-form caustic cleaning agent produced from sodium carbonate through chemical bonding with hydrogen peroxide. Hydrogen peroxide is an effective disinfectant and bleaching agent. Sodium percarbonate can therefore be used to disinfect and bleach winemaking equipment including oak barrels and stainless steel tanks. It is the recommended alternative to soda ash for cleaning oak barrels and to remove excess tannin, and particularly in treating barrels affected by spoilage organisms.

Use sodium percarbonate, such as Aseptox (One Step) or ProxyClean, at a rate of 1–3 g/L of water by first dissolving the powder in some hot water and then adding cool water to bring the solution to the required concentration. Store sodium percarbonate solution in a properly stoppered glass container, as hydrogen peroxide tends to break down quickly.

Caution: *Always wear protective clothing and eyewear when working with caustic chemicals.*

2.6.2 CHLORINE

Chlorine bleach (sodium hypochlorite solution) is very effective in cleaning stubborn stains on glass carboys and demijohns, and in decolorizing equipment when switching from red to white winemaking. Its major drawback is that it is the main cause of 2,4,6-trichloroanisole, more commonly known as TCA (see below), the compound responsible for the moldy, musty smell in so-called "corked" wines. For this reason, chlorine-based cleaning agents are not recommended. If you have to deal with stubborn stains and want to use chlorine bleach, do so outdoors well away from any winemaking equipment or area. Chlorine powder particles can easily become airborne, find their way into your home winery, and contaminate equipment, which could then spread out of control throughout the whole area. Trying to eradicate a TCA infection could prove to be a formidable challenge if not impossible.

Prepare a chlorine solution by dissolving (deep pink colored) chlorine crystals at a rate of 1 g/L of **lukewarm** water. Fill containers that need to be cleaned with the chlorine solution and let stand for at least 10 minutes, or more to fight tough stains. Thoroughly rinse the containers with plenty of water. Then, rinse the containers with a sulfur-citric solution (see section 2.6.3 below) followed by a thorough water rinse. There should be absolutely no trace of chlorine or chlorine smell after the water rinse; otherwise, wine will inherit an off-odor and/or off-flavor.

Avoid using chlorine bleach on plastic winemaking equipment and oak barrels, which could otherwise impart a bad flavor to wine. To clean such equipment, use a sulfur-citric solution followed by a thorough water rinse. Refer to section 2.6.3 for instructions on preparing a sulfur-citric solution. Also, do not use chlorine bleach on stainless steel tanks, instead use a caustic solution, and follow the instructions in section 2.6.4.

Caution: Always wear protective clothing and eyewear when working with chlorine-based products.

Warning: Never mix chlorine bleach with alkaline compounds or solutions as it would produce dangerous chlorine gas.

Chlorine and 2,4,6-trichloroanisole (TCA)
TCA, or 2,4,6-trichloroanisole, is a compound that produces a moldy, musty smell and is the result of a chemical reaction between phenolic compounds, present in both oak wood and wines, and mold or chlorine, and which can be detected at

extremely low concentrations, in the parts per trillion (ppt) range. Although TCA poses no health hazards, it is a serious wine fault as the wine becomes devoid of its complex flavors and aromas that we seek out so much. In the worst case, it can propagate to contaminate an entire cellar or winery making it almost impossible to eradicate.

You can be at risk if you use poorly processed natural corks or corks containing some percentage of natural raw material, such as agglomerates or hybrid corks, or if you use chlorine around your wine cellar.

Natural corks are produced from the bark of oak trees, which inherently have a high phenolic content. However, mold can also grow on oak trees and cause TCA to form well before the bark is harvested for cork production, and can therefore infect a perfectly healthy wine once bottled and corked.

In the past, unbeknownst to them, cork producers further compounded the problem when they were trying to eradicate molds and bacteria during the cork production process. The practice was to bleach and disinfect corks with a chlorine solution, but this in fact increased the risk of TCA forming. Although any chlorine residue was to be neutralized with oxalic acid, only a miniscule amount of TCA, as little as 1 ppt, is needed to contaminate a wine. This underlines the challenge of totally eradicating this foul-smelling compound, although many people can only detect it at much higher levels, e.g., 10 ppt. As an illustrative example of the impact of TCA, "one half-tablespoon of pure TCA could destroy all of the wine produced in the United States"[1]. Nowadays, cork producers process and wash corks using hydrogen peroxide or, to a lesser extent, potassium metabisulfite, which have greatly reduced the risk of TCA taint.

Contamination in bottled wine is a result of the wine coming into contact with an infected cork while the bottle is stored on its side to keep the cork moist. If a bottle is stored upright, the cork could dry out and then contract and would no longer provide a good seal. Air would be allowed in and cause the wine to oxidize and eventually spoil.

Unfortunately, TCA contamination is not limited to corks produced from natural material. It can find its roots just about anywhere in the winery where the mold can grow, such as oak barrels, cardboard cases, or empty bottles, or where chlorine vapor from chlorine-based cleaning agents may find its way on equipment or into barrels. This is cause for concern and can be disheartening to winemakers trying to zero in on the source of

[1]Sogg, Daniel. ARE YOU READY FOR THE NEW CORK. Wine Spectator Online (www.winespectator.com). November 15, 1998.

contamination. Detecting TCA contamination in the cellar is not easy, let alone trying to eradicate the problem.

You can greatly reduce the risk of TCA contamination in your home cellar or winemaking area through good cellar hygiene practice, namely, by maintaining a clean workspace, and following proper cleaning and sanitizing procedures. If you use any equipment, such as oak barrels, where mold likes to grow, you need to be doubly careful and prevent contamination. And so, use chlorine only when absolutely necessary.

2.6.3 SULFITE

Potassium and sodium metabisulfite, also shortened to metabisulfite, bisulfite or more commonly to sulfite, are the most widely used and most effective sanitizing agents for winemaking applications. Sulfite can only be used to sanitize – they are not cleaning agents.

As a sanitizing agent, a 1% effective SO_2 solution[2] is very effective. To prepare a 1% sulfite solution from sulfite powder, dissolve approximately 17 g of powder in 500 mL of lukewarm water and stir vigorously, and then add cool water to the 1 L level. Use the solution within a few months as it loses effectiveness over time being sure to properly stopper the container. Sanitize equipment with the sulfite solution for approximately 10 minutes.

You can add citric acid to the sulfite solution to increase its sanitizing effectiveness. Dissolve equal volumes of critic acid crystals and sulfite powder in water to prepare an effective sulfur-citric sanitizing solution. Let the entire surface of equipment make contact for a few minutes with the sulfite solution and then rinse thoroughly with water.

Warning: *Prepare and use a sulfite solution in a well-ventilated area.*

2.6.4 MAINTAINING, CLEANING AND SANITIZING TANKS

Always clean stainless steel tanks thoroughly before and after use. Remember though … do **not** use sulfite or bleaching products on stainless steel; these products will pit the surface of the tank and will shorten its life. Instead, use a caustic sodium percarbonate solution, or a sodium carbonate solution if the former is not available.

To clean and sanitize a stainless steel tank, first rinse the entire inside surface of the tank thoroughly with hot water. Repeat using a sodium percarbonate solution followed by a citric acid treat-

[2]Sulfite is approximately 57% SO_2. See section 3.4 for more information.

ment. Use the maximum rate of 3 g/L (approximately 1 tbsp per gallon) to prepare the sodium percarbonate solution. Prepare the citric acid solution by dissolving 10 g/L (approximately 3 tbsp per gallon) of lukewarm water. Use just enough solution of each to thoroughly rinse the entire inside surface of the tank, and then complete the cleaning with a thorough hot water rinse and let the tank cool down. Use a pump for greater cleaning efficiency; this will also clean the pump and hoses.

Be sure to clean all surfaces and parts that will come in contact with wine including valves, volumetric sight gauge, lid, sprinkler system, and racking screen, making sure to pay particular attention to nooks and crannies where foreign matter and microbes can be difficult to reach. Open and close valves during the cleaning process to properly clean the entire surface inside valves and other parts.

Once the tank is clean and has cooled down, wine can be transferred to the tank.

3

ANALYSIS AND CONTROL
OF MUSTS AND WINES

Key enological ingredients found in grapes include fermentable sugars, (fixed and volatile) acids and phenols (namely, tannins, flavor compounds and color pigments). Refer to Table 1-3 on page 54 for more information on key ingredients found in grape juice and wine. During vinification of must into wine, these ingredients undergo transformations and become present in the finished wine in different concentrations from their initial amounts. The relative concentration of each ingredient will determine the structure of a wine.

A wine's structure is primarily determined by the alcohol content, the amount of residual sugar, acidity and pH levels, tannin level, and color intensity. These components must be present in balanced concentrations for the desired type and style of wine to be produced. For example, an age-worthy, full-bodied dry red wine should have between 12.5% and 14.0% alc./vol. with a residual sugar content less than 2.0 g/L, good acidity with a low pH, a relatively high tannin level and a deep color. Chapter 7 provides more details of balance in wines and also provides guidelines for common styles of wines.

A wine's quality is judged based on the balance of these components. It is crucial, therefore, to be able to monitor and control the sugar content, acidity and pH levels, tannin level, and color intensity during vinification. Various instruments and chemical analysis procedures exist for the monitoring and control of sugar, acid and pH. No such commercially available home winemaking tool exists for the determination of the tannin level. Winemakers rely on their tasting experience to adjust the tannin level. Similarly, no inexpensive analytical tool is available for the determination of color intensity; spectrometers are available but are very expensive. In home winemaking, color is monitored and adjusted by visual inspection.

The must and finished wine should also be monitored and controlled to ensure they have an adequate amount of sulfite, necessary for preserving and aging wine, without exceeding recommended thresholds, which could otherwise cause the wine to be considered faulty and possibly undrinkable.

3.1 SUGAR/ALCOHOL ANALYSIS AND CONTROL

Fermentable sugar is an essential component in the production of wine. During alcoholic fermentation, yeast feeds on the sugar naturally occurring in grape juice and any sugar added by the winemaker, and converts it to ethyl alcohol (ethanol) and carbon dioxide. The amount of sugar present before fermentation determines the **potential** alcohol content, i.e., the maximum amount of alcohol that could be produced if all the sugar was to be fermented. The actual alcohol content is established by the actual amount of sugar fermented, and any leftover sugar plus any unfermentable sugars – those that yeast cannot convert to alcohol, e.g., pentose, and exist only in very small concentrations – contribute to what is known as residual sugar (RS), which is partly responsible for sweetness in wine.

3.1.1 UNDERSTANDING SUGAR AND ALCOHOL

Glucose and fructose are the main fermentable sugars in grape juice. Although each type of sugar exists in approximately equal concentrations, fructose is roughly twice as sweet as glucose. Glucose is also fermented at a faster rate, which means that a wine fermented to dryness will have less residual glucose than fructose. Any glucose and fructose remaining in the wine at the end of fermentation contribute to residual sugar. And if two wines have the same residual sugar concentration, the one with more fructose will taste sweeter.

Cane (table) sugar, which consists of sucrose, is another source of glucose and fructose that can be added to juice to increase the

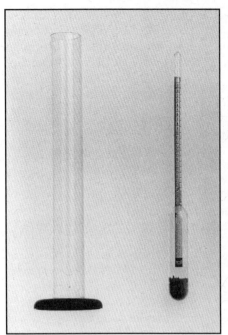

Figure 3-1: The hydrometer

potential alcohol content of wine. Enzymes present in wine naturally invert sucrose in cane sugar, which "split" sucrose into glucose and fructose. Alternatively, winemakers often use corn sugar (or dextrose, which is another name for glucose) because yeast ferments it at a higher rate, and therefore reduces the risk of fermentation problems and ending up with a sweet wine that is meant to be dry.

Clearly, determining, monitoring and controlling the amount of sugar in must and wine at key intervals and stages of vinification is critical to ensure a proper rate of fermentation, in order to avoid fermentation problems, and achieving the desired style of wine, i.e., dry, off-dry, medium-sweet, or sweet.

The hydrometer, depicted in Figure 3-1, is the winemaker's most essential tool for measuring the concentration of fermentable sugars in the must and the potential alcohol level of the wine. The hydrometer operates on Archimedes' Principle of buoyancy and provides the relative density or concentration of a liquid compared to the density of another liquid, usually water. Several hydrometer scales have been developed to measure sugar concentration. The most common scales used in North America are Brix degrees, usually abbreviated B° and often referred to as degrees Brix (°B) or simply Brix, and Specific Gravity, abbreviated SG. Brix is used in commercial winemaking though common also in home winemaking, but Specific Gravity seems to be most popular in home winemaking. Other common scales include Balling, which is basically the same as the Brix scale but calibrated at a different temperature, and Baumé and Öechsle, which are used mainly in Europe. Both Brix and Specific Gravity scales are used from here on in this book.

Brix is a (approximate) measure of the amount of sugar, in grams, in 100 g of must at 20° C (68° F). For example, a Brix reading of 23 B° denotes a must consisting of 23 g of sugar in 100 g of must at 20° C (68° F), or 23 percent sugar **by weight** and abbreviated as 23% wt/wt. Since it is most common to deal with volume units when it comes to must and wine, or any liquid solution in general,

107

A word of caution about sugar measurements

In chemistry terms, must and wine are very complex solutions with a vast number of soluble matter and compounds. Trying to segregate and to quantify precisely the amount of sugar in must or wine, exclusive of all other solubles not contributing to sugar and alcohol concentrations, is highly complex, if not impossible. And although scientists and enologists understand the chemical reaction of sugar fermentation into alcohol, actual results are different than theoretically expected because each grape variety, fermentation environmental conditions, and a whole host of other factors all affect the end results in analytically complex fashion. Therefore, there will be discrepancies between theoretical or expected results and actual results when measuring sugar and alcohol.

Historically, researchers have made various and differing assumptions in trying to quantify sugar concentration in simple and practical fashion, hence the reason for the many density scales in use today. This also explains why winemaking literature has different density tables – Brix, SG and alcohol values do not seem to be consistent.

What is important is that the assumptions are fair, measurements are approximate, and final results are acceptable. You have to accept this and you should not lose sight of the objective – making good wine.

the amount of sugar, in grams, in a liter of must or wine is a more practical measure. For example, 23 g/L of sugar, or 2.3% **weight by volume** and abbreviated as 2.3% wt/vol, means that there is 23 g of sugar in 1 liter of must or wine, or 2.3 g in 100 mL. As similar volumes of different solutions, such as must and wine, have different weights, % wt/wt and % wt/vol are also different, and you should always confirm which units are used when dealing with sugar percentages.

Brix measurements have been standardized at a temperature of 20° C (68° F) although Brix measurements using an older temperature standard of 15.5° C (60° F) are still very much in use. A Brix measurement for the same must or wine will be different at the two temperature standards, therefore, be sure to know which standard is being used when working with sugar concentrations.

Specific Gravity (SG) is a measure of must or wine density relative to the unit density (1.000) of water and must be specified for a given temperature as the density of aqueous solutions changes with temperature. For example, a must with an SG of 1.092 at 20° C (68° F) denotes that its density due to sugar is 1.092 times the density of water when measured at 20° C (68° F), or its weight due to sugar is 1.092 times the weight of water for the same volume. SG measurements also are stated using 20° C (68° F) as a reference to align with standardized Brix measurements although 15.5° C (60° F) is still commonly used. When converting SG to/from Brix, ensure that both are at the same temperature reference, otherwise the readings will represent different sugar concentrations.

When purchasing a hydrometer, check its calibration temperature – most are calibrated at 15.5° C (60° F) or 20° C (68° F), although the former is the most prevalent on the market – and be sure to consistently use Brix or SG measurements at the same temperature as your hydrometer.

Appendix B provides a useful cross-reference table to convert sugar concentration measurements between SG, Brix and potential alcohol, and tables to correct Brix/SG measurements to compensate for different calibration temperatures.

A wine is said to be dry when, for all practical purposes, most or all of the fermentable sugar has been fermented, and there is an almost imperceptible amount of residual sugar. Alcohol has a lower density (SG) than water, and so, in a dry wine, the SG falls below 1.000 and the Brix can be a negative value.

Since consumers are not familiar with Brix or Specific Gravity measurements, the amount of sugar left in the finished (bottled) wine, or residual sugar (RS), is usually expressed in g/L or as a percentage wt/vol. For example, a dry wine with 2.0 g/L (0.2%) of residual sugar contains 2.0 g in 1 L of wine – in a standard 750-mL bottle that would be 1.5 g of sugar.

Although the hydrometer does not provide an accurate reading of the sugar level, it is the most practical and most widely used winemaking instrument. Hydrometer readings are affected by both the presence of alcohol and particles in suspension. The margin of error is small and is within acceptable tolerance.

Another very useful tool to measure the sugar content in unfermented musts and other juices is the hand-held refractometer. It measures sugar content, in Brix degrees (B°), by measuring the refractive index of juices; however, it cannot be used with musts that have begun fermenting because the presence of alcohol alters the refractive index and gives false readings.

The refractometer is a relatively expensive instrument but will prove indispensable when the sugar content and the potential alcohol level need to be determined before harvesting or when buying grapes. It is very practical as it only requires a drop or two of juice to read the sugar content. Figure 3-2 illustrates a hand-held refractometer and its method of use.

Before using a refractometer, ensure that it is properly calibrated to avoid false readings. Open the lid and wipe the window of any dust that might otherwise invalidate readings. With an eyedropper, place one or two drops of **distilled** water on the window and close

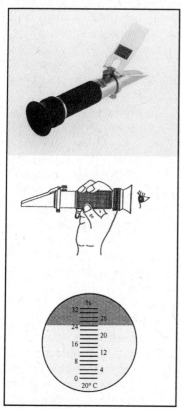

Figure 3-2 (from top): A refractometer, using a refractometer, and how to read a measurement

the lid, making sure that there are no bubbles in the sample and that the whole window is covered with water. Ensure that the water sample **and** the refractometer are as close as possible to the refractometer calibration temperature, usually 20° C (68° F). Wait 30 seconds and then look into the eyepiece while holding the refractometer pointed to a strong light source to get a reading. If the reading is not 0 B°, turn the calibration screw until the reading reaches 0 B°. The refractometer is now calibrated and ready for measuring a juice sample, following the same instructions as the water sample.

Pick berries from inside the cluster as well as from the outer edge, measure the Brix, and repeat several times with berries from different parts of various clusters as each berry will have a different Brix. Berries on the inside, having had less exposure to the sun, will have a lower Brix than berries on the outside. Compute the average to get a fairly good approximation of expected sugar concentration and use the table in Appendix B to determine the potential alcohol level. Ideally, Brix should lie between 22.0 and 26.0 for wine with a desired alcohol level of 11.5% to 13.5% alc./vol.

Potential alcohol is most commonly expressed as a percentage of alcohol by volume, i.e., alcohol volume to wine volume, abbreviated as % alc./vol. or very often as % alc. v/v, % alc., or ABV (Alcohol By Volume). For example, a 12.5% alc./vol. wine contains 125 mL of alcohol in 1 L of wine, or approximately 94 mL in a standard 750-mL bottle of wine. As % alc. may also refer to the alcohol content as a percentage by weight (% alc. wt/wt), it is important to know which one is being used as the two measurements are significantly different. This book always uses % alcohol, volume to volume, or % alc./vol.

You can also compute the **theoretical** amount of potential alcohol of a must from your hydrometer reading. The computation is based on the expected chemical reaction and can be calculated by the following equation:

% alc./vol. = B° × 0.55 − 0.63
    with B° measured at 20° C (68° F)

It has been established by analytical tests that the **actual** amount of alcohol produced is somewhat different from the theoretical value arising from the complex concentration of sugars and other solids that impact fermentation. Therefore, it should be understood that potential alcohol values are always an approximation, and this is perfectly acceptable. It is not uncommon for wine labeling laws to allow a certain tolerance when specifying alcohol content, for example, ±1% alc./vol. A wine labeled as containing 12.5% alc./vol. could be measured to be anywhere between 11.5% and 13.5%. In this book, the theoretical value is always used, unless stated otherwise and supported by ebulliometric analysis (refer to section 3.1.4).

Appendix B provides a useful cross-reference table to convert between sugar concentration measurements and potential % alc./vol.

3.1.2 MEASURING SUGAR AND POTENTIAL ALCOHOL CONTENTS

The hydrometer is most useful in monitoring fermentation progress and completion. Measure the sugar concentration at crushing, or pressing for white wine production, and throughout the fermentation period. For musts from concentrate or juice, take the first reading before yeast inoculation. If fermentation stops or slows down due to an undetermined cause, hydrometer readings can help you identify the problem. Section 14.1 discusses techniques to deal with fermentation problems.

Get into the habit of plotting Brix/SG readings on a graph, at least once a day, and compare your curve to the typical, normal fermentation curve for a dry wine shown in Figure 3-3. The fermentation curve illustrates the rate of conversion of sugar into alcohol from yeast inoculation to end of fermentation, and its slope can increase or decrease when temperature rises or falls, respectively. For the first 24–48 hours, there is no significant activity, as the yeast is only getting ready to go work and has not yet started fermenting sugar. Once fermentation starts, sugar is converted at a high rate over the next 5–7 or more days, depending on a number of factors, of which temperature is the most critical. As the amount of fermentable sugars reduces and the alcohol content increases, yeast activity subsides considerably until it stops completely.

Before measuring the sugar content, the must or wine sample should be as clear as possible to obtain a more precise reading. Filter out grape particles and pulp, which would otherwise affect

111

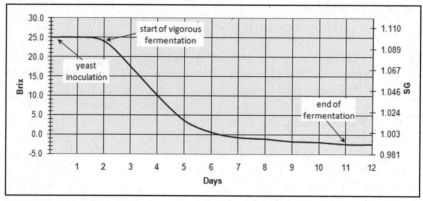

Figure 3-3: Typical curve for a normal fermentation at 20° C (68° F)

the hydrometer reading, using cheesecloth, or let the sample settle overnight in a large graduated cylinder, carefully pour the clear sample without disturbing the sediment into a measuring cylinder, and then take a Brix (SG) reading. A sojourn in the fridge will speed this process up, but be sure to bring the sample back up to your hydrometer's calibration temperature before measuring, unless temperature corrections are made.

The sugar content reading will be slightly inaccurate if the measurement temperature is above or below the calibration temperature. You can compensate the reading by adjusting up or down according to the tables provided in Appendix B; however, if you do not adjust the reading, the margin of error is small for all practical purposes. Use your hydrometer's calibration temperature, i.e., either 15.5° C (60° F) or 20° C (68° F), to determine which correction table to use. For example, a Brix reading of 20.0 B° measured at 25° C (77° F) using a hydrometer calibrated at 15.5° C (60° F) should be corrected to 20.5 B° (20.0 + 0.5). Similarly, if you are using SG as the unit of measure, an SG reading of 1.083 at 25° C (70° F) should be corrected to 1.085. From these examples, the adjustment figures represent a 0.2% alc./vol. correction – hardly anything to worry about.

To measure the Brix or SG, fill the cylindrical tube to within 3 cm of the top and then insert the hydrometer in the tube. You may need to stir the must

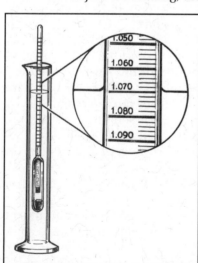

Figure 3-4: Measuring the sugar content using a hydrometer

or wine by spinning the hydrometer in combination with some heat to remove carbon dioxide and air bubbles to ensure a proper reading. Read the hydrometer scale at eye level as shown in Figure 3-4.

To determine the **actual** alcohol content of wine, subtract the hydrometer reading at end of fermentation from the potential alcohol reading at the start. For example:

	B°	SG	% alc./vol.
Initial reading	22.9	1.096	12.0
Final reading	–2.6	0.990	0.0
Final % alc./vol.			12.0

Table 3-1 lists suggested initial and final sugar concentrations, recommended alcohol content, and percentage residual sugar (RS) for different types of wines. A wine is considered dry when fermentation is complete and the Brix (SG) reading has stabilized at –2.6 B° (0.990) for at least two weeks.

As a general guideline, the amount of residual sugar in dry wine should be less than 2.0 g/L, and for off-dry, medium-sweet and sweet wines, the amount of residual sugar should be in the range 2–10 g/L, 10–50 g/L and 50–200 g/L or more, respectively.

A wine termed as "dry" always contains a small amount of sugar, which drinkers may or may not perceive. Although sweetness due to residual sugar may not be detected, glycerol (a minor by-product of alcoholic fermentation, also referred to as glycerine) and ethyl alcohol also contribute sweetness, confusing sensation with actual residual sugar content.

You can use CLINITEST Reagent Tablets, shown in Figure 3-5, used for urine testing and available from drug stores, to quickly and easily test wines for residual (reducing) sugar content. Tablets use a "standardized self-heating method for quantitative determination of sugar by copper reduction, i.e., they contain copper sulfate that reacts with reducing substances in wine converting cupric sulfate to cuprous oxide. This results in a color which varies with the amount of reducing substances present."[1] The resulting color is then simply matched against a set of predetermined concentration colors provided with the tablets. Be sure to confirm the method used for the color chart provided with the tablets; it can use a 2-drop or 5-drop method. The following procedure[2] has been

[1]http://www.vinquiry.com/pdf/ClinitestReducingSugar2001.pdf
[2]Adapted from Vinquiry's instructions at http://www.vinquiry.com/pdf/ClinitestReducingSugar2001.pdf

Table 3-1
Suggested sugar concentrations for various types of wines

	Type of wine				
	Dry white	Dry red	Off-dry	Medium -sweet	Dessert (sweet)
Initial B°	20.0–24.0	22.0–26.0	18.5–23.0	18.5–23.0	32.0–38.0+
Initial SG	1.083–1.101	1.092–1.110	1.075–1.095	1.075–1.095	1.135–1.153+
Final B°	–2.6	–2.6	2.0	4.0	15.0
Final SG	0.990	0.990	1.008	1.015	1.060
% alc./vol.	10.4–12.6	11.3–14.1	9.0–11.5	8.3–11.1	10.6–13.1
Residual Sugar (g/L)	<2.0	<2.0	2.0–10	10–50	50–200+

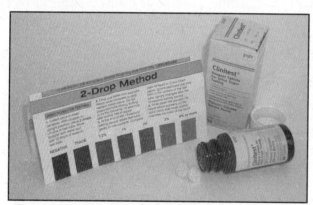

Figure 3-5: CLINITEST Reagent Tablets for sugar content analysis

adapted for wine testing using 10 drops of sample and the 2-drop color chart.

To measure RS, place 10 drops (0.5 mL) of wine sample in a test tube and then drop in a reagent tablet. The sample will boil and heat up. Watch the reaction closely with the color chart in hand. Do **not** shake the test tube during the reaction or for 15 seconds after the boiling has stopped. After the wait period, shake the test tube gently and compare the color of the sample against the color chart.

If the color matches one of the colors on the chart without "passing through" the orange shade of 10 g/L and without turning brownish, then the RS content is simply read from the matched color.

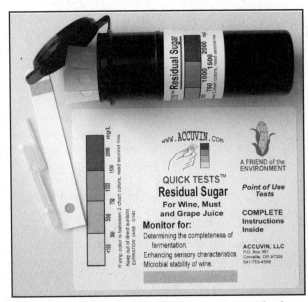

Figure 3-6: ACCUVIN QUICK TESTS AV-Residual Sugar kit

If the color "passes through" the 10 g/L orange color and becomes brownish, then the RS content is greater than 10 g/L, and the sample will need to be diluted and retested. If so, place 2 drops (0.1 mL) of the wine sample and 8 drops (0.4 mL) of water in a test tube, then drop in a reagent tablet, observe the color change, and match the color against the color chart. If there is a match, then the RS is simply 5 times the reading from the chart. For example, if the diluted sample results in a measurement of 4.0 g/L, then the actual RS content in the wine is 5 × 4.0 g/L, or 20 g/L.

Note: Phenolic substances, including anthocyanins (color pigment in reds) and tannins from grapes and/or oak barrels, as well as ascorbic acid will interfere with CLINITEST tests and cause a false reading. Therefore, the test is most accurate in unoaked white wines.

Caution: CLINITEST Reagent Tablets are poisonous and highly corrosive, and must be handled very carefully.

Another product available on the market to measure the amount of residual sugar in musts and wines is ACCUVIN's QUICK TESTS AV–Residual Sugar kit, shown in Figure 3-6. The kit includes test strips in a black tube that protects strips from light and moisture for up to one year, sampler bulbs for obtaining test samples, and a color chart. The test is simple and takes only minutes to perform, and can measure RS up to 2 g/L with an accuracy of ±0.5 g/L. To determine RS, simply transfer the test sample on the absorbent layer on the test strip using a sampler bulb, wait 2 minutes for the color to develop, and then compare the color of the dot on the reverse side of the strip against the color chart provided. Be sure to compare colors under incandescent or natural lighting, not fluorescent lighting. For musts or wines where RS is expected to be greater than 2 g/L, dilute the sample in water in a 1:20 ratio, perform the test, and adjust the result by a factor of 20. For example, if after dilution you obtain a result of 1 g/L, then the actual RS is 20 g/L.

3.1.3 CHAPTALIZATION – CORRECTING THE SUGAR CONTENT

Chaptalization is the practice of adding sugar to musts or wines to increase the alcohol content and/or to produce a sweet wine. It is a shunned procedure among traditional-minded winemakers; however, chaptalization is perfectly acceptable and is widely used in cooler-climate winemaking regions of the world, such as Burgundy, where grapes may not always reach the desired sugar level.

When chaptalizing must with only a relatively small amount of sugar, say, 10–20% of the original Brix (SG), add fermentable sugar at the onset of fermentation when the must is richer in yeast content, therefore favoring fermentation of the added sugar. If more is needed, add sugar in stages to avoid shocking the yeast, which could cause fermentation to stop. Successive chaptalization also has the benefit of prolonging maceration and fermentation periods, which will produce a richer, more complex fuller-bodied wine with greater color and flavor.

When required to chaptalize musts produced from grapes where the exact volume of juice cannot be measured accurately until after pressing, first estimate the total volume to be chaptalized in order to add a reasonably approximate amount of sugar. A simple estimation rule is to assume a yield of approximately 50 L (13 gal) of free-run juice plus 20 L (5 gal) of press-run juice for every 100 kg (220 lbs) of grapes. This estimation depends on the grape variety (certain varieties, such as Cabernet Sauvignon, have a smaller yield than others), the amount of pressure exerted during the pressing operation, and vintage quality. A wet vintage will produce grapes with a high water content therefore increasing yield.

Appendix B provides a conversion for Brix (SG) to percent sugar, weight to volume. This will help you in measuring the amount of additional fermentable sugar needed to achieve a desired final alcohol level. As a rule of thumb, adding 17 g of fermentable sugar – dextrose (corn sugar) or sucrose (beet or cane sugar) – per liter will raise the alcohol content by 1% alc./vol, or 9.2 g/L will raise the Brix by 1 B°.

To chaptalize, first dissolve sugar in a small quantity of warm must, let it cool down, and then add the syrupy must into fermentor. Be sure that the fermentor is no more than three quarters full and that the syrupy must is cool; otherwise, the resident yeast population (necessary for a successful fermentation) in the fermentor will be shocked and cause a stuck fermentation. When fermentation begins and becomes vigorous, add the sugar progressively in stages all the while ensuring that fermentation continues without any problems especially since chaptalization will raise the fermentation temperature, and too high a temperature can cause fermentation to become stuck. Also, over-chaptalization may inhibit start of fermentation, as the yeast cannot start activity with excessive sugar. Expect a lot of foaming when chaptalizing fermenting wine; so be sure to fill containers no more than three-quarters to avoid over-foaming, not to mention a messy floor. You will also need to recalculate total production capacity, as each kg of sugar added will increase the must/wine volume by approximately 0.7 L.

To determine the final, actual % alc./vol. when chaptalizing in stages, you will need to re-measure the potential % alc./vol and recalculate the amount of alcohol produced before each sugar addition. Here is an example of final % alc./vol. determination when chaptalizing in stages.

	B°	SG	Potential % alc./vol.	Actual change in % alc./vol.
Initial reading	20.0	1.083	10.4	
				} 2.8
Second reading	15.0	1.061	7.6	
First chaptalization	17.5	1.072	9.0	
				} 1.4
Reading	15.0	1.061	7.6	
Second chaptalization	15.3	1.062	7.8	
				} 7.8
Final reading	−2.6	0.990	0.0	

The final alcohol content of the chaptalized wine would therefore be 2.8 + 1.4 + 7.8 = 12.0% alc./vol. The non-chaptalized must would have resulted in a wine with 10.4% alc./vol. if fermented to dryness.

To sweeten a wine by chaptalization, add non-fermentable sugar once the wine has been cleared and stabilized. Never add fermentable sugar to a finished wine to produce a sweet wine as it may ferment in the bottle and cause it to explode. Instead, use a wine sweetener-conditioner (made from concentrated grape juice or liquid-invert sugar) and add at a rate of 12–25 mL/L of clear, stable, ready-to-bottle wine. This super-sweet syrup, which reduces the aging time of the wine, also contains potassium sorbate (refer to section 6.2.4) to prevent renewed fermentation. A sweetener-conditioner made from concentrated grape juice gives better results as the juice content enhances the flavor and aromas of wine. This is not the case with the sweetener-conditioner made from liquid-invert sugar.

If you do add fermentable sugar to sweeten wine, the wine must be adequately stabilized to protect it from renewed fermentation while aging in bulk, or worse yet, after it has been bottled. Residual sugar in non-stabilized wine is an open invitation to latent yeast and bacteria to restart fermentation if/when environmental conditions become favorable. The wine could potentially spoil and become undrinkable, and the increasing bottle pressure can become dangerously explosive. Refer to section 6 for details on how to stabilize wine.

An alternative method to chaptalization for sweetening wines is to stop fermentation so that the finished wine has naturally occurring residual sugar. This method is described in section 4.7.5.

3.1.4 MEASURING ACTUAL ALCOHOL CONTENT IN DRY WINE

Accurately measuring alcohol content in wine is not trivial for home winemakers. An approximation can be readily measured using a vinometer, discussed in section 2.5.5.

Various other procedures and apparatus, such as distillation, gas chromatography, dichromate oxidation, and enzymatic analysis, are available for high-accuracy alcohol content determination; however, these are very expensive, and used in laboratories providing specialized services where such investments are economically justifiable, and so are beyond the scope of amateur winemaking. Of these, ebulliometry is the standard procedure used in determining alcohol content in wines as it is relatively quick and simple to perform, it provides reliable accuracy, and, although quite expensive, it is still considerably cheaper than its alternatives. The procedure is simple enough for amateurs interested in accurately measuring alcohol content.

The alcohol content is determined by measuring the difference in boiling points between wine and water using an ebulliometer, also known as an ebullioscope, shown in Figure 3-7, and then cross-referencing the wine's boiling point to alcohol content on an ebulliometric disc provided with the ebulliometer.

The most popular and most basic ebulliometer is the BATF-approved DuJardin-Salleron nickel-plated, single-boiler model, which includes all accessories and a nicely crafted, foam-padded, wooden carrying case. It uses an alcohol lamp as the heat source to measure boiling points (in Celsius only) and can measure alcohol

Figure 3-7: An ebulliometer

content in the range 0–17% alc./vol. A less-expensive model is the Malligand brass model. Electric and electronic models are also available but are very expensive.

To determine the alcohol content of wine using a DuJardin-Salleron ebulliometer, first determine the precise boiling point of distilled water to establish a reference point, for example, 100.10° C, and align this value on the disc with the zero-mark on the alcohol content scale on the ebulliometric disc. When multiple samples are to be measured, perform as many as possible at the same time to avoid having to re-calibrate the boiling point of water, which can fluctuate with changes in atmospheric pressure. Be sure to let the thermometer stabilize before taking a final reading.

Next, determine the boiling point of the wine sample and use the ebulliometric disc to map the boiling point to alcohol content. Be sure that the reference boiling point of water is still zeroed on the disc. For example, if the boiling point of the wine sample is 91.50° C, the alcohol content corresponding to this boiling point is 11.90% alc./vol.

Note that the higher the alcohol content in a wine sample, the lower its boiling point will be. For wine samples with alcohol contents outside the ebulliometer's range, carefully dilute the sample with water to a known ratio and then adjust the measurement by the ratio. For example, if you dilute a wine sample with the same volume of water and the alcohol content of the diluted sample measures 10.30% (92.40° C), then the actual alcohol content is $10.30 \times 2 = 20.60\%$ alc./vol.

Ebulliometry provides accurate results for dry wines – those having residual sugar (RS) content less than 2 g/L. For wines slightly sweeter than 2 g/L RS, use the dilution technique to obtain a good approximation. For sweet dessert wines, ebulliometry does not provide satisfactory results, and advance laboratory techniques (distillation) are required.

3.2 ACID ANALYSIS AND CONTROL

The concentration of all acids, or total acidity, is an important consideration in wine balance; acidity must be balanced with the sweetness and astringency (from tannins) for each wine style. For example, a dry (no perceptible sweetness) Chardonnay requires less acidity than a syrupy-sweet Sauternes or an Icewine. Similarly, a tannic red wine will also be better balanced with less acidity than a light, fruity red.

Acidity is also essential in preserving wine and provides the backbone in age-worthy wines. But excessive acidity – considered a serious wine fault – will result in a green, tart or acidulous and unbalanced wine, and it will diminish the drinking pleasure. Too little acidity, on the other hand, will cause the wine to be flabby, thin or flat.

The need for balance is essential because acidity, sweetness and astringency are detected by three of the five primary taste areas on our tongue; the fourth, although not relevant in wine tasting, is saltiness, and the fifth is umami, the "new" basic flavor found in savory or "brothy" foods.

Winemakers must therefore strike a balance among these components, and that requires the ability to quantify and control acidity throughout all stages of winemaking. This also provides a better understanding of the effects of acidity on a wine's evolution and ultimately its sensory evaluation when drinking wine.

3.2.1 UNDERSTANDING ACIDITY

Grapes contain many different naturally occurring (fixed organic) acids, three of which are of enological significance: tartaric, malic and citric acids. Lactic acid is only present in trace amounts in grapes, but it will become important in wine.

Total acidity is relatively high when grapes start to ripen and then subsides during ripening on the vines as the hard malic acid decreases. Grapes are harvested when the acidity level, established by the viticulturist and winemaker, is typically between 6–9 g/L, at times higher, particularly in cool-climate viticultural winegrowing areas or with certain grape varieties that have inherently high acidity. The decision on the timing of harvest must take into account the acid concentration in grapes, and weighed along with sugar content, typically in the range 21–26 B° (SG between 1.088–1.110), and flavor development. The amount of sun exposure and rainfall during grape ripening and harvest affect the acid concentration as well as concentration of sugars, aromas, and eventually flavors in the final wine. The result can be an unbalanced wine if grapes are not harvested at an acid level balanced with sugar and flavors.

During vinification and winemaking, the acids change as grape juice is transformed into wine, namely, tartaric and malic acid concentrations decrease while lactic acid is possibly formed. There are other acids in wine, but they exist in trace amounts only – including citric acid. Therefore, the three acids of enological significance in wines are tartaric, malic and lactic.

Tartaric acid is the most significant and the strongest of these acids in both grapes and wine, and is responsible for making a wine lively and fresh.

Malic acid imparts a sharp, green-apple sensation. Many winemakers find malic acid undesirable in red wine and thus convert it to lactic acid, a much softer acid, by a secondary fermentation known as malolactic fermentation (MLF), discussed in detail in section 4.8. Each acid has a specific isomer (a compound that contains the same number of atoms of the same element as another compound but differs in structural arrangement and properties) that is of specific enological significance, and each is identified as L-malic acid and L-lactic acid. This complex chemistry would not be required knowledge except for the fact that an isomer of lactic acid, D-lactic acid specifically, is indicative of lactic acid bacteria spoilage, and therefore needs to be monitored and avoided (refer to section 6.2.3 for more details). In this book, "malic" and "lactic" are always used to refer to the L isomer of each acid, and "D-lactic" is used to refer specifically to lactic acid resulting from lactic acid bacteria spoilage.

Although citric acid in very small amounts can add a little zing to white wine, it is generally undesirable in higher amounts since its sour taste does not complement wines well, and also interferes with vinification processes such as MLF.

Acetic acid is another important acid in winemaking only because it is dreaded and afflicts too many good wines with volatile acidity (VA). Acetic acid is the main component of VA, and is produced only in small quantity during the alcoholic fermentation phase if controlled properly using a low-VA producing yeast strain (refer to section 4.7.1), but can spoil a wine if it is not kept in check. A very small amount of VA is still believed to be necessary to appreciate the wine's bouquet.

VA is caused by a group of spoilage bacteria, known as *Acetobacter aceti* (*A. aceti*), or simply *Acetobacter* or acetic acid bacteria, which feed on alcohol to produce acetic acid. The usual culprit of the bacterium is the dreaded fruit fly, commonly pervasive around

Table 3-2

Recommended TA and pH ranges for different types
of must and wine

Type of wine	TA range for must (g/L)	TA range for wine (g/L)	pH range for must and wine
Dry white	7.0 – 9.0	5.0 – 7.5	3.1 – 3.4
Dry red	6.0 – 8.0	4.0 – 5.5	3.3 – 3.6
Sweet white	7.5 – 9.0	5.5 – 7.5	3.1 – 3.2

winemaking season. Being volatile, VA is organoleptically detectable by smell when the threshold starts exceeding 1 g/L. It imparts the familiar sour taste and smell of vinegar. A very small concentration of ethyl acetate can also develop, which is detectable as an off-putting aroma of nail polish remover at higher concentrations.

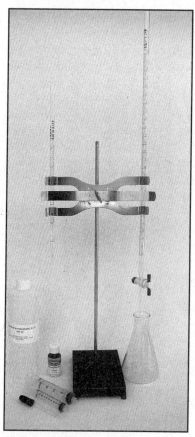

Figure 3-8: Acid titration kit

Acetobacter is always present in wine but only thrives in the presence of oxygen to cause spoilage, i.e., prolonged exposure to air will cause *Acetobacter* spoilage. It is usually the result of poor or defective winemaking equipment, excessive manipulation of wine during transfers or other cellar operations, or simply, careless winemaking, such as a poor topping regimen. MLF will also increase the amount of acetic acid by transforming any citric acid present. For this reason, wines to be malolactic-fermented should have a low citric acid component.

Home winemakers need not be overly concerned with measuring VA since a qualitative analysis is sufficient and because it requires extensive laboratory equipment and experience to perform the measurement. A wine affected by excessive acetic acid (a condition known as acetification) should be discarded. Never blend wine affected by acetic acid as an attempt to improve it – it will not! If you want to monitor VA to avoid problems before it is too late, the laboratory procedure for measuring VA is outlined in section 3.2.4, if you are so inclined.

Total titratable acidity (TA) is used to quantify a wine's acidity, including VA, and it represents the concentration of all organic acids in the wine. TA is expressed in grams per liter (g/L) or, quite often, as a percentage of weight to volume (wt/vol). For example, a wine with a TA of 7.0 g/L is said to contain 0.7% total acidity.

Since all acids are factored into the TA measurement and not all have the same chemical properties, a reference point is used to qualify the measurement. In North America, tartaric acid is used as the reference whereas Europe uses sulfuric acid. This means that, in North America, the TA value represents acid concentration as if it were all tartaric acid. Multiply this value by 0.65 to convert it to TA expressed as sulfuric acid. In this book, all TA measurements are expressed as tartaric acid equivalent. In the example above, a TA of 7.0 g/L then represents 7.0 g of equivalent tartaric acid in 1 L of must or wine.

Table 3-2 lists recommended TA ranges for different types of musts and wines.

Note: "Total acidity" and "total titratable acidity" are used interchangeably in the winemaking industry and literature although the two have somewhat different meanings. The former also includes potassium and sodium ion concentrations. In this book, total acidity and TA will mean total titratable acidity for brevity and because it is widely used.

3.2.2 MEASURING TOTAL TITRATABLE ACIDITY (TA)

A wine's total titratable acidity (TA) can be measured with one of several kits that use a very simple titration procedure, which involves neutralizing the acid content of a wine sample with a base solution, also referred to as the titrate solution, or simply the titrate. Titrate-method acid testing kits, such as the one shown in Figure 3-8, are the most common and are readily available in any home winemaking shop.

The titration procedure uses a phenolphthalein color indicator solution to determine the point where the acid becomes titrated by the sodium hydroxide (NaOH) solution. NaOH solution is generally available at a concentration of 0.1N or 0.2N, where N stands for Normality, a measurement method in chemistry used to denote the concentration of solutions used in titration. NaOH concentration is often omitted on the product label, so be sure to inquire before performing an acid test; otherwise, results will be off. The kit also includes 10-mL and 20-mL syringes, an eyedropper and a test tube.

To measure TA, transfer 15 mL of must or wine to a test tube. To ensure a proper reading, shake the sample vigorously to remove residual carbon dioxide, if any. Using an eyedropper, add 3 drops of phenolphthalein color indicator solution to the test tube. Using a syringe, carefully measure 10 mL of 0.2N titrate solution.

Add titrate solution to the test tube 0.1 mL at a time until you notice a color change. Shake or stir the test tube while adding titrate solution; this will cause the color to disappear. Continue adding and stirring until the color change is permanent, i.e., it no longer disappears. A **color change** indicates that the solution has been neutralized. The color changes to **pink** for **white wines**. For **red wines**, the color will first turn **grayish green** and then back to a **pinkish** color signifying the end of titration.

At the end of titration, when the color change has occurred, record the amount of titrate solution used, i.e., 10 mL less the amount left. Each mL of 0.2N titrate solution indicates an acid concentration of 1.0 g/L expressed as tartaric acid. For example, if 6.5 mL of 0.2N titrate solution is used, the must or wine has an acid concentration of 6.5 g/L.

An alternate, commonly used method using a 0.1N sodium hydroxide solution to measure TA is to add 100 mL of **distilled** water to a 5 mL sample of must or wine in a glass container, and add 5 drops of phenolphthalein. Similar to the previous procedure, add the titrate solution and stir the sample until the color change is permanent. TA is based on the amount of sodium hydroxide (NaOH) used and (expressed as tartaric acid) is determined as follows:

$$TA \ (g/L) = 1.5 \times mL \ of \ NaOH$$

The generalized equation to determine TA for any volume of must or wine sample and any concentration of NaOH titrate solution is as follows:

$$TA \ (g/L) = \frac{75 \times mL \ of \ NaOH \times N \ NaOH}{mL \ of \ sample}$$

The section "*Standardizing sodium hydroxide with potassium acid phthalate*" at the end of this section describes how to compensate for sodium hydroxide solutions that may have lost some strength.

The color change in red-must or red-wine acid testing may be difficult to notice. A simple trick is to dilute the sample with **distilled** water and viewing it over a bright light. Water addition will not affect the measurement but it will greatly simplify detection of the color change. Additionally, titration can be performed without phenolphthalein until the color changes from red to a greenish blue. Only then is the phenolphthalein added and titration completed until a pink color persists.

Alternatively, you can titrate the sample and monitor the pH using a pH meter; titration is complete when the pH reaches 8.2. This procedure removes the guesswork out of identifying the exact point of color change. Section 3.3 describes the significance of pH in wine analysis and how to use a pH meter.

To measure TA using a pH meter, first calibrate the pH meter using a pH 7.0 buffer solution to ensure an accurate reading. Transfer 15 mL of must or wine to a beaker and fill a 10-mL syringe with a 0.2N NaOH titrate solution. With the pH meter dipped in the sample must or wine, add titrate solution 0.1 mL at a time while continuously swirling the beaker. The pH meter reading will start climbing, and titration is complete when the pH meter reaches 8.2. The number of mL of titrate solution used determines the TA, as in the previous procedure.

Fritz Merkel's SULFACOR (Dr. Stührk'sche Titrierlösung) kit, shown in Figure 3-9, is a simplified version of the acid test kit for TA measurements and is based on a titration developed by Dr. Stührk. The kit includes 250 mL of an ink-blue test solution and a graduated cylinder. The kit can measure total titratable acidity between 0–15 g/L in 0.5 g/L increments. The TA scale is identified as "Säure g/l" on the cylinder. Store the test solution in an airtight container to extend its shelf life.

To measure TA using the Fritz Merkel kit, transfer the must or wine sample to the cylinder and, as in the previous test method, remove any residual carbon dioxide to ensure a proper reading. Bring the sample's meniscus level to the zero mark located at the bottom of the cylinder. Using an eyedropper, add the test solution drop by drop to the sample and shake the cylinder after each drop to stir the sample. Continue adding drops until the sample turns to a **dark greenish** color. View the sample against a

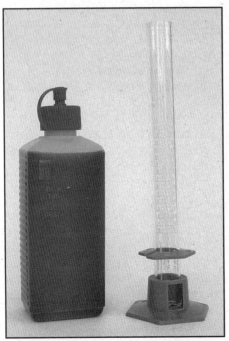

Figure 3-9: Fritz Merkel SULFACOR kit

white background to help you detect the color change. At that point, add single drops of test solution until the sample turns to a **dark blue** color. Cover the top of the cylinder with a stopper and shake the cylinder vigorously. The test is complete when this color change occurs. Take a reading at the meniscus level on the cylinder; this represents the sample's TA in g/L.

Vinoferm's ACIDOMETER, shown in Figure 3-10, is another kit similar to Fritz Merkel's SULFACOR but also includes litmus paper that is used to confirm the titration point, and can measure TA up to 20 g/L. Using an eyedropper, put a drop of the titrated sample on a strip of litmus paper. If there is no color change, the test is complete and accurate, and the reading on the cylinder represents TA in g/L of tartaric acid. If the litmus paper test turns to red, then the titration is not complete and more titrate solution needs to be added to the sample. If the litmus paper test turns to a dark blue color, too much titrate solution was added and the test must be restarted.

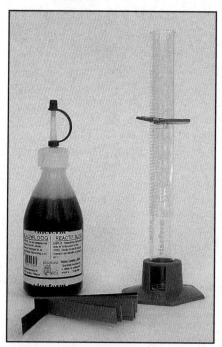

Figure 3-10: Vinoferm
ACIDOMETER kit

With both kits above, the titration point in red must or wine can be difficult to determine, which can be made easier to detect by diluting the sample with an equal volume of water and then multiplying the result by 2. For example, if the reading at the titration point is 3.8, then the actual TA is 7.6 g/L.

Yet another variation of the above kits is ACCUVIN's QUICK TESTS AV–Titratable Acidity kit, shown in Figure 3-11, which can measure TA in the range 4–11 g/L as tartaric acid with an accuracy of ±0.5 g/L. The kit includes vials containing a pre-measured quantity of titrate solution, sampler bulbs for obtaining test samples, and a color chart. To determine TA, simply transfer the test sample to a vial using a sampler bulb, close the vial, shake once or twice, wait 30 seconds for the color to stabilize, and then compare the color against the color chart provided. Use the dilution method for musts or wines with a TA greater than 11 g/L.

Measure TA before start of fermentation, at the end of fermentation, after malolactic fermentation, following any stabilization

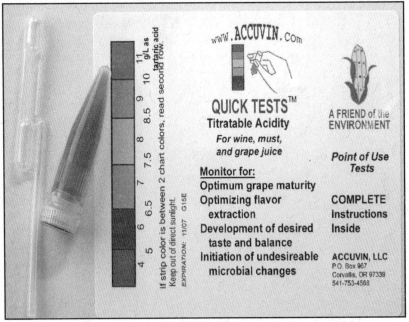

Figure 3-11: ACCUVIN QUICK TESTS AV-Titratable Acidity kit

procedure, and following any acid correction procedure. Measuring during fermentation will not give an accurate reading because carbon dioxide will affect the test unless the gas is removed by a vigorous stirring in combination with some heat.

Measuring malic and lactic acid concentrations

TA provides a measure of total acidity as tartaric acid; however, it does not give any indication of the relative concentrations of the three major components, i.e., tartaric, malic and lactic acids.

Paper chromatography is an analytical test that can be used to determine the presence and a crude approximation of the relative concentration of each acid component in a wine. It is usually only used to determine the presence (or absence) of malic and lactic acids in wines that have undergone malolactic fermentation, discussed in section 4.8. Paper chromatography is described in section 4.8.6.

ACCUVIN has developed two QUICK TESTS kits, AV–Malic Acid and AV–L-Lactic Acid, shown in Figure 3-12, for measuring malic and lactic acid concentrations, respectively.

Each kit includes test strips in a black tube that protects strips from light and moisture for up to one year, sampler bulbs for obtaining test samples, and a color chart. The tests are simple and take only minutes to perform, and provide malic and lactic acid

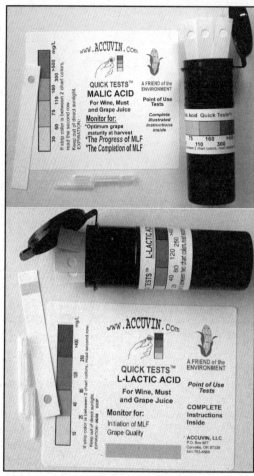

Figure 3-12: ACCUVIN QUICK TESTS
AV-Malic Acid and AV-L-Lactic Acid kits

concentrations in the range 30–500 mg/L (0.03–0.5 g/L) and 10–400 mg/L (0.01–0.4 g/L), respectively. To determine concentration of either acid, simply transfer the test sample on the absorbent layer on the test strip using a sampler bulb, wait 4 minutes for the malic test or 2 minutes for the lactic test for the color to develop, and then compare the color of the dot on the reverse side of the strip against the color chart provided. Be sure to compare colors under incandescent or natural lighting, not fluorescent lighting. For musts or wines where acid concentration is expected to be greater than the test's maximum, dilute the sample in water in a 1:20 ratio, perform the test, and adjust the result by a factor of 20. For example, if after dilution you obtain a result of 120 mg/L, then the actual acid concentration is 2400 mg/L, or 2.4 g/L.

Standardizing sodium hydroxide with potassium acid phthalate
Sodium hydroxide (NaOH) titrate solution should be kept in a properly stoppered bottle to maintain its shelf life. Use the solution within 6–9 months from the date of purchase; otherwise it will lose strength. The phenolphthalein color indicator solution, on the other hand, has a very long shelf life.

You can test the strength of NaOH titrate solution against a standard potassium acid phthalate (KaPh) solution. The test result will help determine if and how to adjust TA results when the titrate solution has lost strength. Alternatively, you can purchase a new container of fresh titrate solution and discard the old one.

You can determine the strength, or Normality (N), of the NaOH solution by titrating a known quantity of potassium acid phthalate (KaPh) solution using 5 drops of phenolphthalein to determine the titration point. Then use the following equation to determine the Normality of the solution:

$$N \text{ NaOH} = \frac{\text{mL of KaPh} \times N \text{ KaPh}}{\text{mL of NaOH}}$$

As with titration for determining TA, add the NaOH solution in 0.1 mL increments while stirring the sample continuously. The pink color will disappear at first and then persist, indicating that the titration point has then been reached. For example, if 5.3 mL of NaOH solution was used to titrate 5 mL of 0.1N KaPh solution, the Normality of the NaOH would be 5×0.1÷5.3 = 0.094 or 0.094N.

Then, you can simply correct a must or wine sample's TA using the following equation:

$$\text{Corrected TA in g/L (expressed as tartaric acid)} = \frac{D \times E}{F}$$

where:

> D = Measured TA in g/L expressed as tartaric acid
> E = Actual Normality of the NaOH solution (determined above)
> F = Theoretical Normality of the NaOH solution

For example, if you determined that the "0.1N" NaOH solution to be 0.094N and the measured TA of the must or wine to be 6.5 g/L, then the corrected TA is 6.5×0.094÷0.1 = 6.1 or 6.1 g/L.

3.2.3 CORRECTING TOTAL TITRATABLE ACIDITY (TA)

The TA of concentrates, reconstituted juice and, often, of fresh grape juice is adjusted during their preparation for commercialization. Generally, home winemakers need not be concerned with TA correction for these musts. It is good practice, however, to always measure TA to ensure a proper balance in the juice and, in the event of a problem, you have all the data to perform a proper root-cause analysis. In the case of musts from grapes and fresh grape juice, you should always measure the TA as it may require adjustments.

The most common methods used to correct the TA in musts and wines include: 1) acidification, i.e., the addition of acid or an acid blend, 2) the blending of musts or wines, 3) deacidification, i.e., the addition of an acid-reducing solution, 4) malolactic fermentation (MLF), 5) cold stabilization, or 6) the addition of water.

Although all methods increase or decrease total acidity (TA), each method acts on different acids and therefore yields different results in the final acid composition (acid type and concentration) of the must or wine. You should select an appropriate acidification or deacidification process based on the desired acid(s) to be increased or decreased. As tartaric acid is the most important and most desired acid in wines, you should always assess carefully the effect of any acid-correcting method on tartaric acid concentration.

Acidification by addition of acid or an acid blend is an effective method, particularly for adjusting musts. It is recommended to add acid before the start of fermentation to allow the acid to evolve with the wine and to contribute to its organoleptic qualities. Acid balance affected by alcoholic fermentation can also be corrected when the wine has been stabilized, particularly if acid reduction is required. The recommended acidification method, however, is to blend a higher-acid wine with the lower-acid one. This method is preferred since it does not use additives and the results are predictable. The only disadvantage is that wines of different TA levels may not always be available when required to perform acid correction. Always use properly stabilized wines for acid correction by blending.

Deacidification is an effective method for acid reduction. The recommended acid reduction methods, however, are to blend a lower-acid wine with the higher-acid one, by malolactic fermentation, or by cold stabilization (refer to section 6.1.1). The addition of water, a technique known quite strangely as amelioration, is not a recommended practice because, although it reduces acidity by dilution of all acid components, it also dilutes aromas, color and other key ingredients necessary for the wine's stability.

Acidification

To increase the TA using the addition method, tartaric acid only or a blend of tartaric and malic acids and possibly citric acid are available. Tartaric acid is the preferred additive, especially if the wine is to undergo malolactic fermentation (MLF) since the malic acid (a different isomer than the previously-mentioned L-malic isomer) found in acid blends does not convert in MLF, and is highly recommended for high pH wines. It is also easier to predict the final TA for tartaric acid only additions; 1 g of acid added to each liter of must or wine increases total acidity (TA) by 1 g/L. Blends become more complicated to predict the final TA because less malic acid and citric acid (if any) than tartaric acid are required to achieve the same TA reduction of 1 g/L. Use a factor of 1.12 and 1.17 for malic acid and citric acid, respectively, to calculate and predict the reduction in TA. For example, in a 3:2:1 tartaric:malic:citric acid blend, adding 1 g of the blend would result in a TA reduction of $(3/6) + (1.12 \times 2/6) + (1.17 \times 1/6) = 1.07$ or roughly 1.1 g/L.

Blends of tartaric/malic/citric acids may also contain a high concentration of citric acid, which has an excessively sour taste and is also partly transformed into the undesirable acetic acid – which contributes to volatile acidity (VA) – and potentially undesirable flavors during malolactic fermentation, and, therefore, are not recommended as wine additives. For premium-quality wines, the use of citric acid is generally not recommended.

When adding tartaric acid, stabilize the wine to prevent acid reduction through precipitation of tartaric acid as tartrate crystals when cold stabilizing. In this case, an effective stabilization method involves the use of metatartaric acid (refer to section 6.1.1), which prevents crystallization of the tartaric acid. Alternatively, the addition of tartaric acid can be over-compensated to balance crystallization during cold stabilization. This latter method is not recommended if you cannot accurately monitor and control acid reduction and cold stabilization.

Add tartaric acid crystals at a rate of 1 g/L of wine to increase total acidity by 1 g/L. First dissolve the crystals in a small volume of wine and then add the tartaric acid solution to the batch of must before the start of fermentation. If you intend to cold stabilize the wine later, increase the rate of addition to 2 g/L.

Blending
To increase or reduce acidity in a wine using the blending method, the TA of both wines to be blended must be known. To determine the required volume of wine, of a specific acidity, to correct another volume of wine with a different TA, the following formula (derived from the Pearson Square, refer to section 7.4) can be used:

$$C = \text{Desired TA} = \frac{(A \times D) + (B \times E)}{(D + E)}$$

where:
A = TA of wine to be corrected
B = TA of wine being used as a blend
D = volume of wine to be corrected
E = volume of wine being used as a blend

You can then determine the required volume E of the blending wine by re-arranging the above equation as follows:

$$E = \frac{D \times (C - A)}{(B - C)}$$

For example, to increase the TA of 20 L (5 gal) of wine from 5.0 to 6.0 g/L using a 7.5-g/L blend wine would require approximately:

$$E = \frac{20 \times (0.60 - 0.50)}{(0.75 - 0.60)} = 13.3 \text{ L of blend wine}$$

This example illustrates the importance of maintaining acidity balance during vinification. Acid correction by blending requires a large volume of blend wine to achieve an incremental TA.

Deacidification

Acid reduction in a finished wine by deacidification is accomplished using a potassium bicarbonate or calcium carbonate solution. Both solutions will first reduce tartaric acid, therefore, care should be taken to prevent reducing the tartaric acid excessively. Potassium bicarbonate is excellent for acid reduction, whereas, calcium carbonate is not recommended as it imparts an unappealing earthy taste to wine. Verify the active ingredient when buying a generic, no-name deacidification solution if you do not want to use calcium carbonate.

Add potassium bicarbonate powder at the rate of 1 g/L of wine for a TA reduction of 1 g/L by first dissolving the powder in a small quantity of **wine** (not water) and then adding the solution to the batch of must or wine. Taste and re-measure a sample before making further potassium bicarbonate additions. This method will cause some precipitation of potassium bitartrate solids – which will further reduce the TA – that will need to be separated by racking after 6–8 weeks of cellaring. The precipitation period will depend on the cellar temperature.

Specially formulated chemicals are also available for reduction of both tartaric and malic acids in musts or wines with a high TA due to malic acid, i.e., low tartaric acid content. Such musts or wines may have an unusually high malic acid content as a result of a poor vintage where grapes did not fully ripen. Two such chemical products, ACIDEX and SIHADEX, can be used to reduce tartaric and malic acids in approximately equal parts by precipitating them in their salt forms – a chemical process known as double salt precipitation. This process involves reduction of both acids in a calculated, pre-measured volume of must or wine, and then blending this volume with the remaining batch. The volume of must or wine to be deacidified is calculated based on the total volume of must or wine, the actual TA, and the desired TA. For example[3], to reduce the TA of 500 L (132 gal) of wine from 12.0 to 7.0 g/L, first

[3]Based on SIHADEX Technical Information, E. BEGEROW GmbH & Co., Germany.

deacidify 278 L (73 gal) using approximately 1.7 kg (3¾ lbs) of SIHADEX, and then blend this volume with the remaining volume. The advantage of these products is that the precipitated solids can be separated from the must or wine within 30 minutes of completing deacidification.

Note: Follow the manufacturers' instructions on the use of ACIDEX and SIHADEX carefully to ensure proper results.

Malolactic fermentation (MLF)

Malolactic fermentation (MLF) is a natural and effective method for reducing TA, which converts the harsher malic acid into the softer lactic acid. It is widely accepted by commercial winemakers, including traditionalists and minimalists, because it is considered a traditional and natural method as opposed to chemical additives.

The only drawback of MLF is in trying to determine an accurate quantitative impact on TA unless the exact amounts of malic acid converted and lactic acid produced can be measured. Use the ACCUVIN QUICK TESTS AV–Malic Acid and AV–L-Lactic Acid kits to assess malic and lactic acid concentrations, respectively. You can assume that roughly half the malic acid will be converted into lactic acid – the other half being converted into carbon dioxide (CO_2) gas – and therefore, TA will be reduced by the same amount. For example, if you determined that a wine with a TA of 7.5 g/L contains approximately 1.0 g/L of malic acid, then roughly 0.5 g/L of lactic acid will result and the final TA will be approximately 7.0 g/L.

Measure the TA before the start of MLF, let the wine undergo the MLF and then measure the TA once this fermentation is completed or stopped. The drop in TA is the change between the value at the start of MLF and at the end. You can then adjust acidity up or down by other methods described here if the TA is still not at the desired level. If the final TA is within the recommended range, it is best not to alter it at this point.

MLF is discussed in depth in section 4.8.

Cold stabilization

Another natural and effective method for decreasing TA in wines is cold stabilization. It is not usually used specifically to decrease TA, but rather to prevent precipitation of tartrate crystals – potassium acid tartrate, the potassium salt of tartaric acid – once the wine is bottled. These are the crystals found at the bottom of a bottle, which had not been cold stabilized and which has been left in the fridge or stored at cold temperatures for too long.

The procedure involves placing the wine in cold storage at a temperature between –4° and 4° C (25° and 40° F) for a minimum of two to three weeks and then racking it. This has the effect of precipitating some tartaric acid as tartrate crystals (potassium bitartrate salt), which decreases TA.

The precise amount of potassium bitartrate that will precipitate is hard to control because of temperature and duration factors, but the maximum amount that can be precipitated is determined by the point at which a wine is considered cold stable. Therefore, it is recommended to cold stabilize the wine, measure the TA, and then adjust accordingly.

Refer to section 6.1.1 for additional information on cold stabilization.

Note: Cold stabilization may increase or decrease a wine's pH depending on the starting pH level before cold stabilization. Refer to section 3.3.3 for more details.

Table 3-3 summarizes the effects on the concentration of each acid component in a wine for each acidification and deacidification method.

3.2.4 MEASURING VOLATILE ACIDITY (VA)

Note: This is a very advanced procedure that requires specialized labware, equipment and chemicals, and laboratory experience; however, it will prove very useful for those wanting to determine VA concentrations quantitatively.

VA is volatile, and as such, it can be easily separated from fixed acids in wine and can be measured quantitatively. Unfortunately, there is no simple method or inexpensive equipment for amateurs to measure VA. Most home winemakers simply monitor VA by smell, but this can often be too late, especially if your detection threshold is high.

For those wanting to measure VA concentration and are skilled in laboratory procedures, VA can be measured using steam distillation analytical methods, specifically, using a Cash still, such as the one illustrated in Figure 3-13, or a Markham still. In addition to the still, other basic glassware and chemicals are required. The procedure involves titrating the distillate (condensed steam) using a standardized NaOH solution, identical to TA determination.

Note that, prior to measuring VA using steam distillation, the sample must be free of carbon dioxide (CO_2) gas and/or sulfur

Table 3-3

Effects of the different acidification and deacidification methods on the different acids in wine

Acidification / deacidification method	Effect on TA (tartaric acid)	Effect on TA (citric acid)	Effect on TA (malic acid)	Effect on TA (lactic acid)
Addition of tartaric acid	increase			
Addition of tartaric/malic/ citric acid blend	increase	increase	increase	
Blending of musts/wines[4]	increase or decrease	increase or decrease	increase or decrease	increase or decrease
Potassium bicarbonate solution	decrease			
ACIDEX or SIHADEX	decrease		decrease	
Malolactic fermentation (MLF)		decrease[5]	decrease	increase
Cold stabilization	decrease			
Addition of water	decrease	decrease	decrease	decrease

[4]Effects on acids depend on acid components present in blending wines.
[5]MLF reduces citric acid and partly transforms it into acetic acid, therefore increasing VA.

dioxide (SO_2) as these will affect results, and so, these must be removed from the wine sample to be analyzed.

You can remove CO_2 by stirring the wine sample vigorously until it dissipates completely. Alternatively, degas the sample using a vacuum pump. Pour a small volume of wine sample in an Erlenmeyer flask and insert a stopper with a hole. Insert a small flexible tube into the stopper and to the vacuum pump inlet. Start the pump and swirl the flask for several minutes. Degassed wine should show no bubbles emanating from the bottom when poured into a test tube.

SO_2 can be "removed" using a 0.3% hydrogen peroxide (H_2O_2) solution during the distillation process (see below).

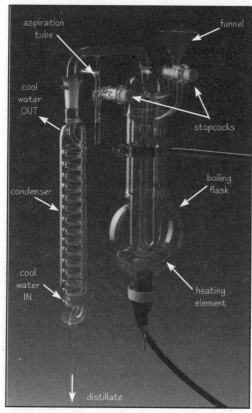

Figure 3-13: A Cash still

Note: Alternatively, for those who are chemically inclined, SO_2 can be compensated in the VA measurement by subtracting the SO_2 acidity equivalent expressed as acetic acid. Consult references 12 [Margalit] or 22 [Zoecklein et al.] for a description of the procedure.

*Note: The following procedure uses a Cash still and has been adapted from references 8 [Iland et al.] and 22 [Zoecklein et al.]. Be sure to use **distilled** water where indicated.*

Rinse all glassware with distilled water and set up the apparatus as per Figure 3-13 or as per your kit's instructions. Start the cool water running through the condenser, making sure that the water feeds into the condenser from the bottom and the water returns from the top of the condenser, and place a 250-mL Erlenmeyer flask under the condenser unit.

Half fill the boiling flask with distilled water by opening the clamp on the tube feeding the outer chamber of the flask. Close the clamp securely when done. Ensure that the heating coil is completely immersed in the water to avoid damage.

Using the funnel at the top of the boiling flask and stopcock, transfer a 10-mL sample of degassed wine and 0.5 mL of 0.3% hydrogen peroxide (H_2O_2) solution into the inner chamber. Rinse the funnel with distilled water and let it flow into the inner chamber, and close the stopcock.

If your unit is equipped with an aspiration device, open the tap to allow water to enter the aspiration tube at the top and exit the aspiration tube at the bottom. The water flow rate should be such that it maintains a steady aspiration pressure, which can be monitored in the glass bubble in the aspiration tube.

Turn on the heater unit and allow the water in the boiling flask to reach moderate boiling.

Steam will form, travel to the condenser, and condense (the distillate) in the Erlenmeyer flask under the condenser unit. Collect 100 mL of the distillate, turn off the heater unit, and remove the flask from under the condenser unit.

Open the funnel stopcock at the top and pour 15 mL of distilled water into the inner chamber to clean the apparatus, and repeat two more times. Open the drain clamp under the boiling flask and let the water flow out to a drain.

Add 3 drops of phenolphthalein indicator to the distillate and titrate, one drop at a time, using **fresh** 0.1N NaOH solution until the distillate remains pink, indicating that the titration endpoint has been reached. This procedure is exactly the same as in TA determination. Record the amount of NaOH used in mL. If the NaOH solution is not fresh, the measurement will be off.

A very small amount of NaOH will be required to titrate VA, and so, you should use a small, 10-mL volumetric burette, which will yield more accurate results.

Determine VA, **expressed as acetic acid**, as follows:

$$\text{VA (g/L)} = \text{mL NaOH} \times 0.60$$

For example, if 1.0 mL NaOH was used to titrate the distillate, then, VA concentration is 0.60 g/L expressed as acetic acid.

If you are using different volumes of wine sample and/or different concentrations of NaOH solution, you can use the following generalized expression:

$$\text{VA (g/L)} = \frac{60 \times \text{mL NaOH} \times N \text{ NaOH}}{\text{mL wine sample}}$$

The expected error of this procedure is ±0.05 g/L, or using our example above, VA could be in the range 0.55–0.65 g/L.

Note: When measuring VA in sweet wines, always perform the analysis <u>before</u> adding any potassium sorbate – used to inhibit renewed fermentation; otherwise, the sorbic acid in potassium sorbate will skew the results.

As a rule of thumb to ensure that wine does not become VA-faulty, VA concentration should not exceed 1.2 g/L in red table wine and should ideally be below 0.7 g/L in healthy, well-balanced wines.

3.2.5 CORRECTING VOLATILE ACIDITY (VA)

There is no "magical" chemical or process to rid wine of volatile acidity (VA) due to acetic acid, although it can be dealt with to some acceptable level depending on the extent of the problem.

Then, the first step in dealing with VA problems is to assess the extent of spoilage caused by *Acetobacter*, the acetic acid spoilage bacteria. Since the bacteria thrive when exposed to air, spoilage starts at the wine surface and works its way down.

If spoilage is in a fairly advanced state, a whitish film will have formed on the surface. Try and remove as much of the film as possible using a clean, absorbent paper towel or with a kitchen baster. Using a wine thief, take a sample from just below the surface, and smell it to assess the intensity of the vinegary smell. Repeat this procedure by taking a sample lower into the wine. When the smell of acetic acid is almost not detectable or is tolerable, you can then rack and dump the wine from the surface down to that point. A small, positive-displacement pump will be helpful for this operation. Sulfite, bottle and drink the wine as soon as possible; do not be tempted to blend it with another wine.

Evidently, when it comes to VA, the old adage that "an ounce of prevention is worth a pound of cure" could not apply more than to *Acetobacter* spoilage.

3.3 pH ANALYSIS AND CONTROL

Lisa Van de Water of the Wine Lab at Napa best summarized the importance of the effects of pH on wines, as reported by Donald E. Gauntner in the American Wine Society Journal, Winter Issue, 1997.

"At **lower pH**, red wines are redder, fresher, fruitier, younger tasting for their age, slower to age, slower to mature, less complex, less full-bodied, much slower to spoil, and easier to maintain free of spoilage in the cellar because the SO_2 is more active at the lower pH."

"**Higher pH** wines, if they are red, are less red (sometimes brown, sometimes purple), less fresh, less fruity, more complex, more full-bodied, faster to age, faster to mature, easier to spoil, and more difficult to manage in the cellar with SO_2."

Clearly, pH plays an important role in determining the quality of a wine. Yet, all too often, home winemakers shy away from understanding the effects of pH on wine and from performing measurements that ensure wines remain trouble-free from vineyard to winery to table.

The relationship between pH and sulfur dioxide (SO_2) is discussed in section 3.4.

**10 tips and best practices in avoiding
high VA and *Acetobacter* spoilage in wine**

1. When making wine from grapes, discard any grape berries or bunches that have deteriorated or shriveled.
2. Choose a yeast strain with low VA production. Yeast strain specifications and performance data is usually available from manufacturers. Refer to section 4.7.1 for a list and specifications of commonly available yeast strains for home winemaking.
3. Protect fermenting wine from fruit flies. For reds, place a heavy tarp over the fermenting vat, and for whites, protect the wine using a bung and fermentation lock on carboys.
4. Ferment wine within recommended temperatures.
5. Minimize the wine's exposure to air during post-ferment cellar operations such as racking and filtering.
6. Keep carboys and barrels topped up properly during storage and aging. Use wine from a previous vintage to top up, if necessary. When no wine is available, flush air out with an inert gas such as CO_2, nitrogen, or argon, and quickly replace the bung on the carboy or barrel.
7. Ensure that bungs or rubber stoppers form airtight seals on carboys and barrels, and check regularly the water level in fermentation locks.
8. If you detect VA by smell, do NOT blend the wine with any other wine.
9. Maintain proper levels of TA, pH and free SO_2 (refer to section 3.4) throughout winemaking, from crush to bottling.
10. Maintain as cool a temperature as possible during wine storage or aging. Ideal temperature is 13° C (55° F).

3.3.1 UNDERSTANDING pH

PH is a close relative of acidity, specifically, total titratable acidity (TA) for wines. TA measures the acid concentration in musts and wines while pH measures the relative strength of those acids. And the pH of wines depends on the pH of the grape juice (must), which in turn depends on such factors as grape variety, type of soil, viticultural practices such as irrigation, climate during grape ripening, and timing of harvest. For example, soils rich in potassium or grapes harvested during heavy rainfalls will tend to have a higher pH.

Two wines with similar TA measurements but different pH will be very different and will evolve differently. A wine with a lower pH may show a redder color (in the case of red wines) with greater stability during aging, and will have more fruit and less complexity

139

and body than a higher pH wine. A lower pH wine will also mature more slowly – and therefore age longer – and will be less susceptible to spoilage. TA on its own is not sufficient to make a complete evaluation of a wine. We also need to understand the relative strength of the acid components, or pH. It is imperative then to always monitor and control a wine's pH to ensure that it does not fall below or rise above critical thresholds.

Technically, pH is the negative logarithm of the effective hydrogen ion concentration or hydrogen ion activity, i.e., $pH = -\log_{10}[H_3O^+]$, and is often referred to as active acidity. Great! But what does it really mean?

Solutions (such as must and wine) can have a pH in the range 0 to 14. A pH of 0 represents a strong acid solution while a pH of 14 represents a strong alkaline solution. Pure water has a theoretical pH of 7, and wines are in the range of 3 to 4. More specifically, the pH level of musts and wines should be within the recommended range shown in Table 3-2 on page 122 for a desired style of wine.

The pH level is closely related to TA and they are interdependent. Adjustment of either parameter will typically affect the other; however, their relationship is a complex one. TA and pH are not proportional although, generally, raising the TA will result in lowering of the pH, and vice versa. There are cases, however, in which one can reduce both the TA and pH, for example. Refer to section 3.3.3 on how to reduce both the TA and pH in wine.

A low-pH wine will taste tart, owing to the higher acid concentration. Conversely, a high-pH wine will taste flat and lack freshness. A high-pH wine also will tend to oxidize faster and therefore will not age as well. It will be more prone to microbial spoilage, thus requiring more sulfite to protect it. As for color, high-pH white wines will tend to brown prematurely and, in the case of red wines, color intensity decreases as the pH increases causing the wine to change from a red to brownish-red color.

The importance of monitoring and controlling the pH level is also illustrated by the fact that a wine with a pH of 3 is ten times stronger (in terms of acidity) than a wine with a pH of 4. Using more representative pH values for wine, a wine with a pH of 3.2 is approximately 25 percent stronger than a wine with a pH of 3.3.

Home winemakers need to be concerned with pH levels that fall outside of the recommended ranges, and take prompt corrective actions. Slight pH variations within the ranges are not as critical, except when adjusting the free sulfur dioxide (SO_2) level, and become important in specific situations, such as MLF, when the pH level definitely should not fall below the prescribed minimum. The interaction between pH and free sulfur dioxide (SO_2) is discussed in section 3.4 while malolactic fermentation (MLF) is discussed in section 4.8.

3.3.2 MEASURING THE pH LEVEL

A crude approximation of a wine's active acidity, or pH, can be measured using pH paper. To determine the pH of musts or wines, a strip of pH paper is immersed in the must or wine and the resulting color of the paper is then matched to a standard set of colors. Each color corresponds to a specific pH level. Inexpensive pH paper, however, provides results with a wide margin of inaccuracy, ±1 pH unit, and is therefore not useful and not a recommended method for precise analysis. The recommended method to measure the pH level accurately is using a pH meter, as the one shown in Figure 3-14, with a resolution of 0.1 and an accuracy of ±0.1 pH unit.

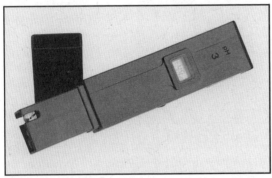

Figure 3-14: A pH meter

Similar to total titratable acidity (TA), measure the pH level before start of fermentation, at the end of fermentation, after MLF has completed, following any stabilization procedure, and following any pH correction procedure. Although not essential, you can also monitor pH during alcoholic fermentation since pH is more accurate than TA measurements during this phase. For this purpose, remove any carbon dioxide gas by a vigorous stirring in combination with some heat to ensure a proper reading. Remember to let the sample cool back down to room temperature before taking a reading.

To measure the pH level using a pH meter, first condition and calibrate the instrument with pre-measured pH solutions according to the manufacturer's instructions. This involves dipping the pH meter probe in a 7.0 pH buffer solution, waiting for the meter to calibrate, and repeating this procedure with a 4.0 pH buffer solution. After calibration, simply immerse the probe in a degassed sample of must or wine to take a measurement. Ensure that the sample is at the calibration temperature of the pH meter, otherwise you will need to adjust the reading as instructed by the manufacturer, or choose a pH meter that has automatic temperature compensation.

Note: Buffer solutions for calibrating pH meters have a limited shelf life. Always use fresh solutions to ensure proper measurements.

Alternatively, you can use ACCUVIN's QUICK TESTS AV–pH kit, shown in Figure 3-15, which provide results in the 3.0–4.0 pH range with an accuracy of ±0.1, which is quite acceptable in home wine-making applications, and is not affected by temperature variations in the sample. Each kit includes test strips, sampler bulbs for obtaining test samples, and a color chart.

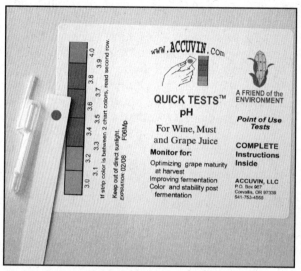

Figure 3-15: ACCUVIN QUICK TESTS AV-pH kit

To determine the pH, simply transfer the test sample on the absorbent layer on the test strip using a sampler bulb, wait 3 minutes for the color to develop, and then compare the color of the dot on the reverse side of the strip against the color chart provided. Be sure to compare colors under incandescent or natural lighting, not fluorescent lighting.

3.3.3 CORRECTING THE PH LEVEL

As with TA, the pH level of concentrates, reconstituted juice and, often, of fresh grape juice is adjusted during their preparation for commercialization. Generally, home winemakers need not be concerned with pH correction for these musts. Still, it is good practice to keep a log of pH measurements to detect potential problems early and, in the event of a problem, you have all the data to perform a proper root-cause analysis. In the case of musts from grapes and fresh grape juice, you should always measure the pH level as it may require adjustments.

The same methods used to correct TA are used to correct pH in musts and wines. These methods include: 1) acidification, i.e., the addition of acid or an acid blend, 2) the blending of musts or wines, 3) deacidification, i.e., the addition of a pH-augmenting solution, 4) malolactic fermentation (MLF), 5) cold stabilization, or 6) amelioration, i.e., the addition of water. Keep in mind that, in general, TA and pH work in opposite directions, i.e., raising the TA decreases the pH, and vice versa. There are exceptions, however, as discussed below.

Although all methods increase or decrease pH, each method acts on different acids and therefore yields different results in the final acid composition (acid type and concentration) of the must or wine. You should select an appropriate pH-adjustment method based on the desired acid to be increased or decreased for a desired pH change. As tartaric acid is the most important and most desired acid in wines, you should always assess carefully the effect of any pH-correcting method on tartaric acid concentration.

Acidification

Tartaric acid addition is an effective method to lower the pH in high-pH wines because it is the strongest acid, it is present in higher concentrations than other acids, and is also easy to control. Tartaric acid addition causes acidity (TA) to increase, which in turn lowers the pH. Acid blends achieve the same results; however, they may contain citric acid, which is not a recommended wine additive since it can have an excessively sour taste and is also partly transformed into the undesirable acetic acid, responsible for the vinegary smell and taste, during alcoholic fermentation and MLF. The addition of an acid blend with no citric acid is recommended.

Add tartaric acid crystals at a rate of 1 g/L of wine to reduce the pH by 0.1 unit, and then make adjustments as necessary. Perform bench trials to determine how the acid addition impacts pH as different grapes have different buffering capacities, meaning that more acid may be needed to obtain the desired pH value. For malic and citric acid additions, assume a pH reduction of approximately 0.08 for each 1 g/L of addition.

First dissolve the crystals in a small volume of juice, and then add the solution to the must, i.e., before the start of fermentation. If the wine will be cold stabilized, increase the rate of addition to 2 g/L.

It is important that the tartaric acid addition be done before the start of fermentation. The pre-fermentation acid addition raises the TA, and hence lowers the pH. During alcoholic fermentation and MLF, TA decreases causing the pH to increase. The pre-fermentation addition reduces the risk of the pH increasing above the range where SO_2 loses effectiveness. There is a risk of shooting the pH too high if tartaric acid is only added after alcoholic fermentation and MLF. Section 3.4 further explains the important relationship between pH and SO_2.

When adding acid blends, use the same rate of addition as tartaric acid, then take a measurement and make adjustments as necessary. Trial and error is required when making adjustments because the ratio of acids in the blends is not usually known; however, since they contain malic and maybe citric acid, the blend will be less acidic than a purely tartaric acid blend. You would then have to increase the rate of addition slightly to achieve similar results.

Blending

Blending is the recommended method for adjusting pH in wines since it is a natural method not involving the use of chemical additives. Its only drawback is that one may not always have the required wines with the needed pH to obtain the desired result.

Given this drawback, the best way to proceed in making any correction is to blend the wine to be corrected with another wine of known pH. If the wine to be corrected requires the pH to be increased, then use a higher-pH wine for blending. Similarly, use a lower-pH wine if the pH needs to be decreased.

Mathematical determination of the resulting pH in a blended wine is complex. An easier method is to calculate the TA of the blended wine using the Pearson Square calculation, outlined in section 7.4, verify the calculation by titration, and then measure the pH. Make any required adjustments to achieve the desired TA/pH.

On rare occasions, a wine will turn out to have both a high TA and a high pH. The TA may be acceptable, but it may be desired to reduce the pH without affecting the TA. The ideal solution would be to blend this wine with another having the same high TA but a low pH. This is quite a challenge since most home winemakers do not have reserves of that many different wines.

Deacidification

The pH in wine can also be increased effectively using potassium bicarbonate or other deacidification formula, such as ACIDEX or SIHADEX.

Potassium bicarbonate raises pH by reducing tartaric acid and is therefore recommended for high-TA, low-pH wines. Dissolve potassium bicarbonate at a rate of 1 g/L of wine for each 0.1 unit increase in pH. For example, for a 20-L (5-gal) batch of wine with a pH of 3.2, 40 g of potassium bicarbonate is required to increase the pH to 3.4.

Other products, such as ACIDEX or SIHADEX, can be used to increase pH by reducing tartaric and malic acids in approximately equal parts by precipitating them in their salt forms – a chemical process known as double-salt precipitation. The advantage of these products is that the precipitated solids can be separated from the wine within 30 minutes. Follow the manufacturer's instructions as each product may have handling differences.

Malolactic fermentation (MLF)

MLF is usually used to soften a wine by converting malic acid into lactic acid and reducing TA. It is not used specifically to increase its pH, although it could. Home winemakers still need to quantitatively assess the change in pH due to MLF.

As with TA, a drawback of this method is that is very difficult to predict and measure the impact on pH. It is simply suggested to measure the pH before MLF, allow the wine to undergo the MLF and then measure the pH once this fermentation is completed or stopped. The increase in pH is the change between the value at the end of MLF and at the start. You can then adjust the pH up or down by other methods described here if it is still not at the desired level. If the final pH is within the recommended range, it is best not to alter it at this point.

MLF is discussed in depth in section 4.8.

Cold stabilization

As with total acidity (TA), cold stabilization is another natural and effective method for increasing pH in wines. The procedure is the same as for reducing TA, described in section 3.2.3.

Note, however, that the cause-and-effect relationship between cold stabilization and pH depends on a wine's starting pH before cold stabilization. Cold stabilization precipitates some tartaric acid as tartrate crystals (potassium bitartrate salt), which decreases acidity (TA). However, potassium contributes to a higher pH, and when it precipitates during cold stabilization, it lowers the pH. This effect actually happens at a pH of 3.65 (use 3.6 when using a pH meter with 0.1 precision) or lower because of the relative concentrations of tartrate and potassium in the wine. At a pH of 3.65 or above, cold stabilization will actually raise the pH.

As a guideline, assume a 0.1 pH unit increase or decrease for every 1 g/L decrease in TA.

The precise amount of potassium bitartrate that will precipitate is hard to control because of temperature and duration factors, but the maximum amount that can be precipitated is determined by the point at which a wine is considered cold stable. Therefore, it is recommended to cold stabilize the wine, measure the TA and pH, and then adjust accordingly.

Refer to section 6.1.1 for additional information on cold stabilization.

Water addition

Adding water to wine is a simple method for increasing pH. By adding **distilled** water (tap water may have a significantly different pH than the theoretical value of 7.0, and may also contain undesirable substances such as chlorine), the acids are effectively diluted thereby reducing TA and increasing the pH. Many home winemakers use this method, although it is not practiced and is not allowed in commercial winemaking. The major disadvantage is that the flavors, aromas and bouquet also get diluted resulting in a "watery" wine with less complexity. Therefore, this method should only be used when small pH changes are required to avoid adding too much water.

Simply insert the pH meter probe in the wine and add distilled water until the desired pH is reached. You should first try this on a small sample to establish expected results. The TA should remain within the recommended range. You should also measure the pH of the water before adding it to the wine to better predict results. The reason is that the pH of water may actually change considerably depending on how it was stored. Distilled water's pH is affected by carbon dioxide in the environment.

Phosphoric acid

The addition of phosphoric acid is another method for reducing the pH level of a high-pH, high-TA wine though its use is not recommended because it affects the taste and texture of wine; it is actually not allowed as an additive in US commercial winemaking. The advantage of phosphoric acid is that it reduces the pH level without significantly altering TA. In home winemaking, use it as a last resort when other pH-reduction techniques are not possible.

Use one or two drops of a 30% solution per liter of wine. After each addition, measure the pH level and taste the wine before any further correction.

Table 3-4 summarizes the effects on a wine's pH for each recommended method of increasing or decreasing pH and the acid causing the change.

3.4 SULFUR DIOXIDE (SO$_2$) ANALYSIS AND CONTROL

One of the first things we all learn in our winemaking adventures is that oxygen (air) is wine's worst enemy, and that wine must be protected, or preserved, with sulfite. Similarly, like many types of food and beverages, sulfite is used in wine to protect against spoilage organisms, namely, "bad" yeasts and bacteria.

Given sulfite's vital role in winemaking, let's review some chemistry concepts to understand how oxidation and spoilage organisms affect wine and what the role of sulfite is in inhibiting these.

3.4.1 OXIDATION, REDUCTION AND MICROBIAL SPOILAGE

Simply stated, oxidation is the result of wine being exposed to air during winemaking, at any time from grape or juice handling to

146

Table 3-4
Effects of the different methods of increasing or decreasing pH
on the different acids in wines

Method to increase / decrease pH	Effect on pH (tartaric acid)	Effect on pH (citric acid)	Effect on pH (malic acid)	Effect on pH (lactic acid)
Addition of tartaric acid	decrease			
Addition of tartaric/malic/ citric acid blend	decrease	decrease	decrease	
Blending of musts/wines[6]	increase or decrease	increase or decrease	increase or decrease	increase or decrease
Potassium bicarbonate solution	increase			
ACIDEX or SIHADEX	increase		increase	
Malolactic fermentation (MLF)		increase[7]	increase	decrease
Cold stabilization[8]	increase or decrease			
Addition of water	increase	increase	increase	increase

[6]Depends on pH of each blending wine. [7]MLF reduces citric acid and partly transforms it into acetic acid, therefore increasing VA. [8]Depends on the pH of the wine at start of cold stabilization.

bottling, and not sufficiently protected with sulfite. The more technical explanation is that free oxygen in air causes an enzymatic reaction with oxidases – the oxidizable enzymes, such as tyrosinase (polyphenoloxidase) – found in grape juice resulting in oxidation of aromatic and pigmentation compounds, as in the case of white wine turning brown prematurely. In such reactions, characterized by the presence of oxygen, oxygen is referred to as an oxidizing agent.

At first, oxidation will manifest itself by the recognizable acetaldehyde smell (a fermentation by-product, albeit in very small quantity) as alcohol oxidizes. The familiar nut-like smell of

147

Sherry or a pungent fruity smell, such as bruised apple, is a telltale sign of oxidation and excessive acetaldehyde. Such wine is often described as being maderized because the aromas and color closely resemble those of the famous wines of Madeira where oxidation is a virtue.

As it progresses, the wine loses precious aromas and takes on a deeper brown color making the wine seem overly tired, or fatigued. In advanced oxidation, oxidative yeasts, such as *Candida mycoderma*, will cause a white film to form on the surface of the wine, as shown in Figure 3-16, and *Acetobacter* will cause acetic acid to develop and impart the familiar sour taste and smell of vinegar. *Acetobacter* is always present in wine but only thrives in the presence of oxygen to cause spoilage.

The enzymatic reaction accelerates as temperature increases, therefore accelerating the effects of oxidation. Must and wine also become more susceptible to oxidative effects as pH increases; low-pH wines are better protected and will tend to age better and longer, and exhibit more aromas and a livelier color.

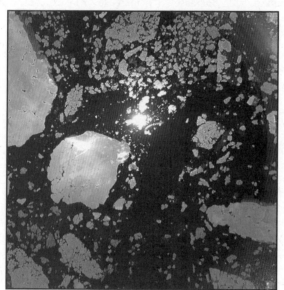

Figure 3-16: *Candida mycoderma* causes a whitisth film to form on the surface of wine

Musts are also more susceptible to oxidation than wine. Fermentation and vinification compounds found in wines, such as alcohol, acidity, tannins, and sulfur dioxide by-product, offer better oxidation protection than musts. The world-renown enologist Émile Peynaud supports this theory in his book KNOWING AND MAKING WINE [reference 16] by stating "musts consume on average 2 milligrams of oxygen per liter per minute whereas wines take 24 hours to consume the same amount". Oxidation susceptibility of must underlines the extra care required during grape and juice handling.

The opposite condition of oxidation is reduction – a condition characterized by the absence of oxygen that can also have a detrimental effect on wine development and quality. Oxidation and reduction are really complementary because, at the molecular level, electrons are transferred from one substance to another causing one substance to oxidize and the other to reduce. The agent that causes reduction is referred to as a reducing agent or as an antioxidizing agent, or simply antioxidant, because it has the ability to bind to oxygen and make it unavailable to other substances in wine that could otherwise become oxidized. And that is precisely the role of sulfite in wine. Ascorbic acid, discussed in more details in section 6.2.4, and phenols are also antioxidants. Red wines are less prone to oxidation effects because of their higher concentration of phenolic compounds that act as antioxidants.

The ability of a substance's oxidation-reduction pair to lose and gain electrons is known as redox potential, but this is well beyond the scope of home winemakers. For more information on redox potential, see reference 22 [Zoecklein et al.].

Microbial spoilage refers to a condition where wine becomes afflicted with microorganisms, or microbes – either indigenous, airborne from the surrounding environment or, even, formed during vinification – that react negatively with other wine components to cause undesirable effects. In winemaking, these spoilage microorganisms belong to two main families: yeasts and bacteria. In layman's terms, we often refer to these as "bad" yeasts or "bad" bacteria to distinguish them from "good" yeasts and bacteria that are at the heart of vinification processes. And sulfite, again, is used to keep spoilage microorganisms in check and preserve wine.

3.4.2 UNDERSTANDING SULFITE AND SO_2

Sulfite is a sulfurous acid salt that is used extensively in the food and beverage industry as an antioxidant and a preservative. Sulfur dioxide (SO_2), a gas formed from burning elemental sulfur (S) and easily detectable as an unpleasant and pungent burnt-match smell, is a major component of sulfite.

Too little SO_2, and the wine is not adequately protected; too much SO_2, and it becomes detectable. The taste or smell of SO_2 is considered a serious wine fault and should never be detectable. It is critical then to keep SO_2 levels to a minimum without the risk of wine spoilage. Excessive sulfite can also seriously jeopardize vinification; for example, it can inhibit yeast activity and cause a stuck alcoholic fermentation.

A small percentage of asthmatic people can be reactive to sulfite, even at low concentrations; hence the requirement to include the "Contains Sulfites" warning on labels of all wines sold in the US.

Clearly, sulfur dioxide concentrations in musts and wines are important enological measurements. Two SO_2-related measurements are used in winemaking: Free SO_2 and bound SO_2. A wine's total SO_2 content is the sum of free and bound SO_2 and is mainly

TECHNIQUES IN HOME WINEMAKING

the result of sulfite addition and of yeast fermentation. All SO_2 concentrations are expressed in mg/L or parts per million (ppm).

Free SO_2, often abbreviated as FSO2, comes mainly from the addition of sulfite but also as a natural by-product of yeast (alcoholic) fermentation, albeit in small quantity, in the order of up to 10 mg/L depending on the yeast type. This by-product is not due to sulfur used by some shippers when packing the grapes; it is also produced in wines fermented from juice. On its own, this small quantity of free SO_2 formed during fermentation is not sufficient to inhibit either cultured or indigenous (wild) yeasts.

Free SO_2 is active, which means that it undergoes chemical transformations altering the total SO_2 composition in wines. The two major transformations include the dissipation of active SO_2 and the combining of SO_2, from free SO_2, with aldehyde compounds to form bound (fixed) SO_2. With every addition of sulfite, some SO_2 becomes active as free SO_2 and some becomes bound, and the sum is total SO_2; however, only free SO_2 has antioxidant and preservative properties.

Over time, due to oxidation and as a result of winemaking operations – such as racking, which favors aeration – free SO_2 becomes bound (and decreases) and the sulfite's antioxidant and preservative effectiveness are diminished. The wine oxidizes as acetaldehyde forms. Acetaldehyde is the most prevalent aldehyde compound responsible for oxidation in wine and is easily detected by its peculiar and unmistakable smell in oxidized wines.

It is critical then to maintain a nominal free SO_2 level throughout vinification and winemaking operations to prevent oxidation and to keep spoilage microorganisms in check. **As a simple rule of thumb, maintain a nominal free SO_2 level of approximately 35 mg/L in red wines, higher for whites, but do not exceed 50 mg/L** unless you are trying to address some specific problems (refer to chapter 14). Be careful to not let a wine's free SO_2 fall below 25 mg/L; otherwise, the wine becomes at higher risk of microbial spoilage. Take frequent measurements and make necessary adjustments to reduce any risk. For kits, there is no need to measure free SO_2 as the manufacturer has provided packets of sulfite to be added as instructed.

Total SO_2 is only detectable at much higher levels than free SO_2, and therefore not as critical. For example, in commercial winemaking, maximum total SO_2 can range between 300–350 mg/L, whereas maximum free SO_2 can be 50 mg/L. In home winemaking, you really only need to monitor free SO_2 concentrations – that's what protects wine – provided sulfite is added judiciously.

SO₂ and pH

Although beyond the scope of this book but for the sake of completeness, you should know that molecular SO_2 is the more specific form of free SO_2 that provides antioxidant and preservative effectiveness. It has been determined that a molecular SO_2 concentration of 0.8 mg/L is deemed to provide adequate protection and is the de facto standard. The effectiveness of molecular SO_2 concentration is however affected by free SO_2 concentration and pH, i.e., to obtain 0.8 mg/L of molecular SO_2, you will need varying amounts of free SO_2 at different pH values. Specifically, at high pH (low acidity), the effectiveness of SO_2 is greatly reduced and wines are therefore not as well protected against oxidation effects and microbial spoilage. This is very important! It is worth repeating. **As pH increases, free SO_2 effectiveness decreases, and therefore, more sulfite is required to protect the wine.**

A very simple rule of thumb can be used to determine the amount of free SO_2 required to adequately protect a wine having a specific pH. **The amount of SO_2 required is approximately [(pH–3.0)×100)] mg/L for red wines; for white wines add 10 to this value.** This calculation assumes that the wine has a pH above 3.0. For example, if a white wine has a pH of 3.4, the amount of free SO_2 should be [(3.4–3.0)×100+10] = 50 mg/L. The same wine, but with a pH of 3.7, would require 80 mg/L to maintain the same level of protection. Clearly, pH cannot be allowed to climb too high.

Alternatively, you can use the graph in Figure 3-17 if you want a more precise value for the amount of free SO_2 required for a given pH value. This graph is for a molecular SO_2 concentration of 0.8 mg/L.

Sulfite becomes detectable at a molecular SO_2 concentration of 2.0 mg/L. Figure 3-18 shows the amount of free SO_2 required for a given pH value at a molecular SO_2 concentration of 2.0 mg/L. For example, at a pH of 3.4, a wine would require approximately 32 mg/L of free SO_2 to be adequately protected, and a maximum of 80 mg/L before it can be detected. Although there is a wide gap between the minimum and maximum values, some people have a much lower detection threshold, so you should always err on the side of caution and add sulfite using 0.8 mg/L of molecular SO_2.

Consult reference 12 [Margalit], 16 [Peynaud] or 22 [Zoecklein et al.] in Appendix E for a thorough discussion of pH and molecular SO_2.

Sources of sulfite

As an additive to musts and wines, sulfite is added as potassium metabisulfite, often abbreviated to KMS, or sodium metabisulfite,

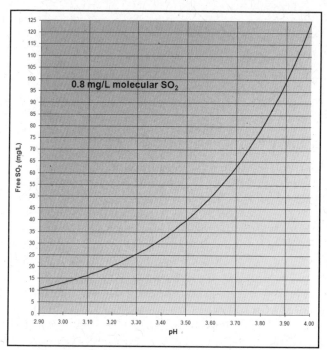

Figure 3-17: Molecular SO₂ concentration of 0.8 mg/L

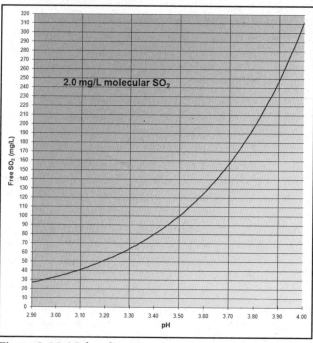

Figure 3-18: Molecular SO₂ concentration of 2.0 mg/L

both often shortened to metabisulfite, bisulfite or simply sulfite. The short-form terminology can cause confusion to those who prefer the use of the potassium form; some people who restrict the amount of sodium in their diets prefer not adding sodium metabisulfite and must be able to distinguish one form from the other.

Potassium metabisulfite (KMS) is available in powder form while sodium metabisulfite is available in either powder or tablet form. Tablets – known as Campden tablets – have the advantage of providing pre-measured quantities of 0.44 g and are most practical when making small quantities of wine. Tablets can be split in half (or quarter) when smaller doses are required. Tablets are costlier and must be crushed before dissolving them in water.

KMS powder is more practical for larger productions because the required quantity is easily measured and it dissolves easily in water.

Approximately half the amount of metabisulfite sourced from potassium or sodium metabisulfite powder or tablet available to home winemakers will actually provide free SO_2. This is a good approximation if the percent free SO_2 provided is not known. Therefore, as an approximation, it can be assumed that from one part of sulfite added to wine, one half will become free SO2. For example, to add 25 mg/L of free SO_2, you will need to add approximately 50 mg/L of sulfite. If a wine's free SO2 concentration is 25 mg/L and the desired level is 50 mg/L, then, you will need 50 mg/L of sulfite.

You can perform a more accurate calculation if you know the percentage of free SO_2 that the source of sulfite provides. Most sources of sulfite contain 57% of SO_2, although some, such as Campden tablets may contain 48%. To calculate the amount of sulfite required, in mg, to achieve a desired free SO_2 level, in mg/L, simply divide the latter by the percent SO_2 content in the sulfite source used.

Using the previous example, to add 25 mg/L of free SO_2, you would need to add 25÷0.57 = 44 mg of sulfite powder containing 57% SO_2 for each liter of wine. For a 20-L (5-gal) batch of wine, you would need 880 mg, or two 0.44-g Campden tablets.

A dilute sulfite solution can also be prepared in advance and then added, as required, to achieve a desired SO_2 level. This method is discussed in section 3.4.4.

Warning: Asthmatic people may react to sulfite, even at low concentrations. Limit or restrict the use of sulfite accordingly.

Warning: Sulfite solution releases overpowering fumes and can cause respiratory problems. Prepare and use the solution in a well-ventilated area.

To use sulfite as a preservative agent, dissolve the required amount of potassium (or sodium) metabisulfite powder or crushed Campden tablets into a small quantity of **warm** water and then stir gently into the must or wine. Do **not** add sulfite powder directly into the must or wine as it may not dissolve properly. If the must is to undergo malolactic fermentation (MLF), reduce the sulfite dosage so as not to exceed the prescribed maximum free SO_2 level, usually less than 10 mg/L or even as low as 5 mg/L. This should take into account the amount of free SO_2 produced during fermentation, typically in the 5–10 mg/L range. Refer to section 4.8 for information on the use of sulfite in MLF.

Efferbaktol and Oenosteryl

Effervescent sulfite tablets, shown in Figure 3-19, are a relatively new source of sulfite now available to home winemakers for easy sulfite additions without the need for weighing or crushing. These tablets contain a blend of potassium metabisulfite and potassium bicarbonate (has negligible effect on pH) and dissolve easily by effervescent action in water, juice or wine, requiring very little stirring in small batches. Two such examples are Efferbaktol and Oenosteryl tablets available in various dosage sizes including 2- and 5-g tablets. Do **not** split tablets to obtain a smaller dosage as potassium metabisulfite and potassium bicarbonate may not be evenly distributed in tablets making additions inaccurate. A 2-g tablet delivers approximately 2 g of SO_2 in one liter of water, juice or wine while a 5-g tablet delivers approximately 5 g. Given these dosage additions, effervescent tablets' primary application is in larger volumes. For example, a 2-g tablet would deliver approximately 100 mg/L of SO_2 in a 20-L (5-gal) carboy or approximately 37 mg/L in a 54-L (14-gal) demijohn.

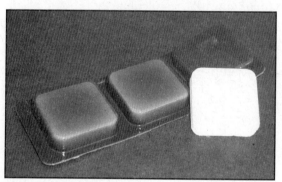

Figure 3-19: Effervescent SO_2 tablets

SO_2 and Lysozyme[4]

Lysozyme, an enzyme isolated from egg whites then purified and freeze dried, and now also available in liquid format, is a relatively new tool in the winemaker's toolbox to suppress spoilage bacteria and to achieve microbial stability. It is not effective against *Acetobacter* or spoilage yeasts, such as *Brettanomyces*, nor does it have antioxidant effect, however, unlike free SO_2, lysozyme is most effective in wine at higher pH when spoilage bacteria growth is favored. It does not replace the use of sulfite but it can be used concurrently to reduce the amount of sulfite needed to achieve microbial stability.

Lysozyme can be used in the following specific applications (each is discussed in the relevant section):

[4]This section has been adapted from http://www.scottlab.com/fordras.htm.

- To reduce the risk of spoilage when grapes have a potentially high level of spoilage bacteria (refer to section 4.1),
- To help restart a stuck or sluggish alcoholic fermentation (refer to section 4.7.1),
- To delay or inhibit malolactic fermentation (refer to section 4.8.7), and
- To stabilize and protect wine against microbial spoilage, particularly after malolactic fermentation (refer to section 6.2.4).

Lysozyme is best added to juice or wine as a 5% solution. Rates of addition are presented in the relevant section for each application.

Prepare a 5% solution by dissolving 5 g of lysozyme in 100 mL of cool or lukewarm water – do **not** use hot water – and stirring very gently for approximately one minute while avoiding any foaming. Allow the mixture to stand for approximately 45 minutes. Stir and let stand again until the lysozyme has completely dissolved and the solution is completely clear. Store any unused solution in a thoroughly sanitized container in the refrigerator for up to one year.

For every 50-mg/L increment of lysozyme required, simply add 1 mL of the 5% solution for every liter of juice. For example, if you need to add 150 mg/L of lysozyme, you will need 3 mL of solution per liter.

Some manufacturers now produce lysozyme in a practical, easy-to-use liquid format for direct addition to must or wine or first mixed with water. For example, Lallemand's LALLZYME LYSO-Easy is available in 250-mL bottles, ideal for home winemaking. The 22% LYSO-Easy solution is added at a rate of approximately 4 mL/hL of wine for every 1 g/hL of lysozyme desired. Be sure to always follow the manufacturer's instructions and recommended rate of addition.

When lysozyme is to be used concurrently with SO_2, **first** add SO_2, mix the juice or wine thoroughly, let it bind, and then add lysozyme.

*Caution: Do **not** use bentonite and lysozyme concurrently; bentonite deactivates lysozyme. Wait for bentonite to completely settle out, follow with a careful racking, and then add lysozyme. If wine has already been treated with lysozyme, wait a minimum of one week before adding bentonite to allow the lysozyme to inhibit the bacteria. Before bottling, you should perform a protein stability test to ensure that the lysozyme will not cause any stability problems. If the stability test is positive, do another bentonite fining until the wine is protein stable. Refer to section 5.2.1 for more information on* *bentonite fining and section 6.1.2 for more information on protein stability.*

Caution: Do not use metatartaric acid in wine treated with lysozyme; a heavy haze may result. Refer to section 6.1.1 for more information on metatartaric acid.

3.4.3 MEASURING THE AMOUNT OF FREE SO$_2$

It is good practice to monitor the amount of free SO$_2$ in musts and wines regularly throughout winemaking, particularly before and after any operation that affects the free SO$_2$ concentration. At a minimum, measure free SO$_2$ before any sulfite addition to avoid over-sulfiting, which could negatively impact vinification or compromise the quality of the finished wine.

You should test all musts made from grapes or fresh juice immediately following crushing, before adding any sulfite. Shippers most often use sulfur when packing grapes to prevent spoilage in transit, and this will find its way into the must. This is particularly important for vinification where the free SO$_2$ concentration is critical, e.g., in malolactic fermentation (MLF) where "good" bacteria are sensitive to free SO$_2$ and could become inhibited even at very low levels.

Keep good records of all sulfite additions and free SO$_2$ measurements to ensure that musts and wines are well protected but kept within the recommended maximum level without over-sulfiting.

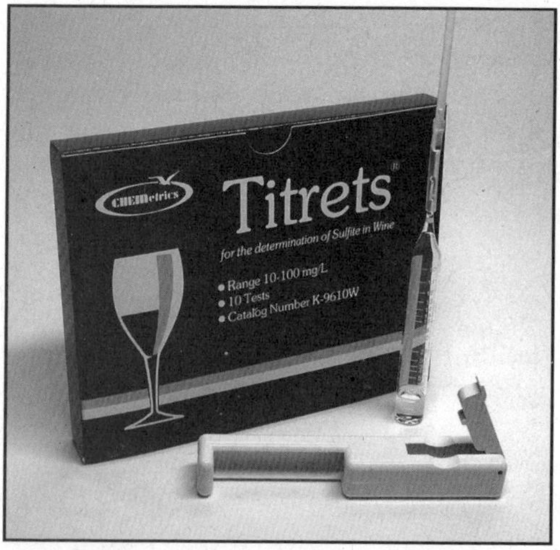

Figure 3-20: Titrets sulfite titration kit

The most effective, practical and inexpensive method in home winemaking for determining the amount of free SO$_2$ is by Ripper-method titration. It gives sufficiently good results for home winemaking applications. The aeration-oxidation (AO) laboratory method provides much more accurate results. Both methods are described here.

Ripper method

Ripper-method titration uses titration cells containing an iodide-iodate titrant and a starch indicator as well as phosphoric acid used to adjust the pH level of the wine sample. Figure

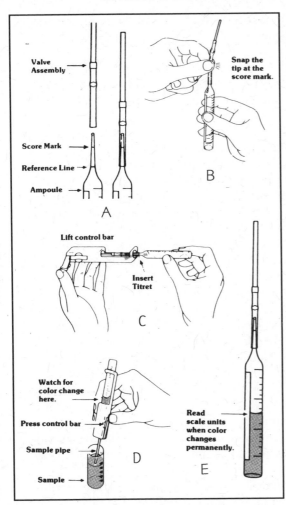

Figure 3-21: How to use a Titrets sulfite titration kit

3-20 shows the components of a CHEMetrics Titrets sulfite titration kit. This kit can measure between 10–100 mg/L of free SO_2, with an error of ±10 mg/L. It includes an ampoule containing the reagent, a valve assembly (shown fitted onto the ampoule) and a Titrettor, a special holder for Titrets cells. The Titrettor has a bar to control the amount of wine allowed to enter the titration cell. Since the reagent is sealed under vacuum, the titration cells have an unlimited shelf life.

Must or wine is allowed to react with the titrant and starch indicator within the titration cell. The amount of free SO_2 is determined by noting the point at which the **deep blue** color changes to **colorless** for **white wines**, or to the color of the **red** wine for **red wines**. The test should be performed on a sample at 20° C (68° F).

Figure 3-21 illustrates how to use a Titrets sulfite titration kit. First fit the valve assembly on the ampoule (Figure 3-21A and B) and snap the tip at the score mark. Lift the control bar of the Titrettor, and then insert and seat the ampoule in the Titrettor (Figure 3-21C). Immerse the tip of the valve assembly in the test sample (Figure 3-21D), and press the control bar firmly but briefly to suck in a small amount of sample. The content will turn to a deep blue color. Shake the ampoule and wait 30 seconds. Once again suck in a small amount of sample, shake the ampoule and wait 30 seconds. Repeat this process until the deep blue color becomes colorless for white wines or changes to the color of the sample for red wines. Remove the ampoule from the Titrettor and

157

turn it right side up to take a reading of the amount of free SO_2 in mg/L, as shown in Figure 3-21E.

*Note: Do **not** press the control bar unless the sample pipe is immersed in the test sample; otherwise, air will enter the ampoule and the vacuum may not be sufficient to complete the test.*

If the ampoule fills completely without a color change, i.e., the color remains blue, the test result is less than 10 mg/L. If the content of the ampoule turns clear immediately – or to the color of the wine sample – the test result is greater than 100 mg/L.

For testing red musts and wines, you should dilute the test sample in water to better detect the color change, and then adjust the result by the dilution factor.

For white musts and wines, the Ripper-method of sulfite content determination is quite accurate and provides fairly reliable results. For reds, phenolic substances – tannins and color pigments – and ascorbic acid (vitamin C) will skew the measurement and yield a false reading. The free SO_2 content will appear higher than the actual amount present. The reading can however be used to confirm the amount of free SO_2 added to musts and wines immediately following sulfiting. For example, if a test measures "15 mg/L" (this is a false reading) of free SO_2 in a red wine and 30 mg/L of sulfite is added, a second test immediately following the addition should read $[15 + (30 \div 2)] = 30$ mg/L (only one-half of the sulfite added will become free SO_2).

Alternatively, the aeration-oxidation (AO) method described below can be used for more accurate determination of free SO_2, particularly for reds.

Fritz Merkel, Vinoferm and ACCUVIN also have titration-method kits or additional equipment and/or chemicals to their basic tests to perform free SO_2 determination, shown in Figure 3-22. All these kits have the same interference problem from ascorbic acid (vitamin C).

Both the Fritz Merkel SULFACOR and Vinoferm ACIDOMETER kits can be used to determine free SO_2 by using a separately-available iodide reagent and similar procedure, and the results interpreted as per the manufacturers' instructions. ACCUVIN's QUICK TESTS AV–Free SO_2 kit can measure free SO_2 up to 130 mg/L with an accuracy of ±6 mg/L in the range 0–40 mg/L and ±15 mg/L in the range 40–130 mg/L. The kit includes two types of vials containing a pre-measured quantity of titrate solution, sampler bulbs for obtaining test samples, and a color chart. One type of vial is for measuring free SO_2 expected to be in the 0–40 mg/L range,

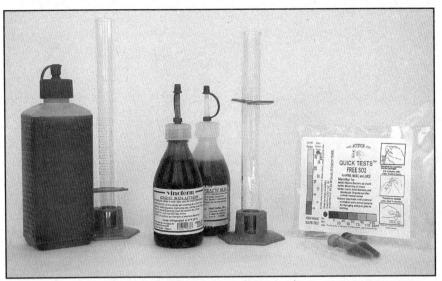

Figure 3-22: Fritz Merkel SULFACOR, Vinoferm ACIDOMETER and ACCU-VIN QUICK TESTS AV-Free SO$_2$ kits

and the second type is for measuring free SO$_2$ expected to be up to 130 mg/L. The method is similar to the TA kit.

Aeration-Oxidation (AO) method

Note: *This is a fairly advanced procedure that requires specialized labware, equipment and chemicals, and laboratory experience; however, it will prove very useful for those wanting to determine SO$_2$ concentrations accurately.*

Aeration-oxidation, or simply AO, is an analytical laboratory procedure used in the determination of both free and bound SO$_2$ (and hence, total SO$_2$) with results accurate to ±2 mg/L or better. The procedure involves removing the free SO$_2$ content from an acidified wine sample by aspiration – hence why it is often referred to as the aspiration method – by passing an air stream through the sample. The released free SO$_2$ is then collected in a peroxide solution to produce sulfuric acid. Standard sodium hydroxide (NaOH) is then used to titrate the sulfuric acid, and, as in acid titration, the amount of NaOH used determines the free SO$_2$ concentration.

Figure 3-23 illustrates the required components and setup for the AO method for determining free SO$_2$. The required apparatus can be purchased as a kit. You will need one of several options to aspirate the test sample: using a Nalgene aspirator pump, sometimes supplied with the kit, using a small vacuum pump, such as a

159

1200 cc fish tank pump, or using a simple aspirator device – the type that aspirates using the flow of water – that can be simply connected to a water faucet using flexible tubing. The latter is the most inexpensive and easiest method to set up.

Note: The following procedure has been adapted from references 8 [Iland et al.] and 22 [Zoecklein et al.].

In this procedure, you will need fresh 0.01N sodium hydroxide (NaOH), 0.3% vol./vol. hydrogen peroxide (H_2O_2) and 25% vol./vol. phosphoric acid (H_3PO_4) solutions. If the solutions are not fresh, the test will yield false results. You will also need an SO_2 indicator solution, such as a methyl red-methylene blue mixed indicator.

Rinse all glassware with **distilled** water and set up the apparatus as per Figure 3-23 or as per your kit's instructions.

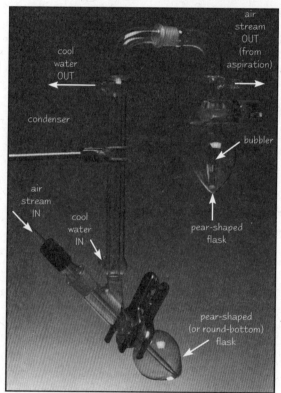

Remove the round-bottom flask from the setup, and add **exactly** 20.0 mL of wine sample followed by 10 mL of 25% phosphoric acid (H_3PO_4) solution. Shake the flask to stir the wine-acid solution thoroughly, and then reconnect the flask to the apparatus.

Remove the pear-shaped flask from the setup, and add 10 mL of 0.3% hydrogen peroxide (H_2O_2) solution and 6 drops of SO_2 indicator solution. Titrate the H_2O_2 solution by adding 0.01N sodium hydroxide (NaOH) solution until the color changes from **violet** to **turquoise** and persists for at least 30 seconds.

Figure 3-23: Aeration-oxidation (AO) setup for determining free SO_2

You will only need a few drops of NaOH solution until the color changes; therefore, be sure to add only one drop at a time while stirring the flask. Take careful note of the turquoise color as you will need to match it to the titration endpoint color in a step below.

Connect the aspiration device to the pear-shaped flask and start aspiration. If you are using a water-flow type aspiration device, you simply need to open the water tap; the flow of water will create a suction force and aspirate.

There should be a steady stream of bubbles in the round-bottom flask, without being vigorous. Ensure that the hydrogen peroxide solution in the pear-shaped flask is not overly agitated. It is important that the flow rate is not too fast; otherwise there will be insufficient time for the released SO_2 to be trapped in the pear-shaped flask. Aspirate for 10–15 minutes – the color will turn to a **light violet** and then a **darker violet** during aspiration – and then stop.

Remove the pear-shaped flask from the setup. Using a 10-mL burette, titrate the solution using 0.01N NaOH solution until the color changes to an identical **turquoise** endpoint color as noted above – this is important. Record the precise amount in mL of NaOH solution used. Multiply the result by 16 to obtain the free SO_2 concentration in mg/L. For example, if 1.75 mL of NaOH were used, free SO_2 concentration would be $1.75 \times 16 = 28$ mg/L.

If you are using chemicals of different concentrations than from above, use the following generalized formula to determine free SO_2 concentration in a 20-mL test sample.

$$\text{Free } SO_2 \text{ (mg/L)} = \frac{\text{mL NaOH} \times N \text{ NaOH} \times 32{,}000}{20 \text{ mL wine sample}}$$

Using the concentrations stated above, we have:

$$\text{Free } SO_2 \text{ (mg/L)} = \frac{1.75 \times 0.01 \times 32{,}000}{20} = 28 \text{ mg/L}$$

To determine the amount of bound SO_2, repeat the same procedure but, before starting aspiration, heat the solution in the round-bottom flask with a simple wick burner (or a Bunsen burner) until it boils. In addition, connect a cold-water supply and return to/from the condenser – a small fish tank pump works well for this purpose – making sure that the water feeds into the condenser from the bottom and the water returns from the top of the condenser. Aspirate for 10–15 minutes while keeping the solution to a gentle boil, and then stop and turn off the heat to the flask.

Remove the pear-shaped flask from the setup. Using a 10-mL burette, titrate the solution using 0.01N NaOH solution. The endpoint color should be identical to the **turquoise** color noted above – again, this is important. Record the precise amount in mL of NaOH solution used. Multiply the result by 16 to obtain the bound

161

SO_2 concentration in mg/L. For example, if 12.50 mL of NaOH was used, bound SO_2 concentration would be 12.50 × 16 = 200 mg/L. The same generalized formula as free SO_2 can be used for bound SO_2.

To determine total SO_2 concentration (mg/L), simply add the results of free SO_2 and bound SO_2, i.e.,

$$\text{Total } SO_2 \text{ (mg/L)} = \text{Free } SO_2 \text{ (mg/L)} + \text{Bound } SO_2 \text{ (mg/L)}$$

3.4.4 CORRECTING THE AMOUNT OF FREE SO_2

If the amount of free SO_2 is slightly beyond the desired level, you can reduce it by successive vigorous aerations of the wine until the desired free SO_2 level is reached. Aeration will cause some free SO_2 to dissipate. This is recommended only if you detect a sulfur smell; otherwise, the procedure may increase the risk of oxidation. Another method is to add 18 mL of a 3% hydrogen peroxide solution for each 10 mg/L of free SO_2 to be reduced in 1 hL (approximately 25 gal) of wine. For example, if the free SO_2 of 20 L (5 gal) of wine needs to be reduced from 50 to 35 mg/L, you would need 18 × (20/100) × (50–35)/10 = 5.4 mL of 3% hydrogen peroxide solution.

Caution: The use of hydrogen peroxide requires chemistry laboratory experience and is therefore only recommended for experienced home winemakers. Excessive addition of hydrogen peroxide can negatively affect the quality of wine. Reference 12 [Margalit] in Appendix E details analytical and laboratory procedures to reduce free SO_2 content.

Table 3-5
SO_2 additions from a 10% sulfite solution

Incremental amount of free SO_2 (mg/L)	Volume of 10% sulfite solution to be added to each liter of must or wine (mL)
5	0.09
10	0.18
20	0.35
30	0.53
40	0.70
50	0.88
60	1.05
70	1.23
80	1.40
90	1.58
100	1.75

To increase the amount of free SO_2, first determine the current amount, and then add sulfite up to the desired free SO_2 level.

Perform sulfite additions by dissolving the required amount of sulfite powder in water or by using a convenient 10% dilute sulfite solution.

Prepare a 10% dilute sulfite solution by dissolving 10 g of sulfite in approximately 50 mL of warm water. When the sulfite has dissolved completely, bring the total volume of the solution to 100 mL by adding cool water, and stirring vigorously.

Table 3-5 lists the volume of a 10% sulfite solution, in mL, to add per liter of must or wine to increase the free SO_2 concentration by the required amount. Each increment of 5 mg/L in the desired free SO_2 concentration will require approximately 0.09 mL/L of must or wine.

Here are some examples of sulfite additions using a 10% solution to increase the amount of free SO_2:

Example #1
Volume of must or wine = 20 L
Initial free SO_2 concentration in must or wine = 0 mg/L
Desired free SO_2 concentration = 50 mg/L
Required volume of 10% sulfite solution to be added = 20 × 0.88 = 17.6 mL, or approximately 18 mL

Example #2
Volume of must or wine = 20 L
Initial free SO_2 concentration in must or wine = 10 mg/L
Desired free SO_2 concentration = 50 mg/L
Required volume of 10% sulfite solution to be added = 20 × 0.70 = 14 mL

Example #3
Volume of must or wine = 20 L
Initial free SO_2 concentration in must or wine = 10 mg/L
Desired free SO_2 concentration = 25 mg/L
Required volume of 10% sulfite solution to be added = 20 × (0.18 + 0.09) = 5.4 mL, or approximately 5 mL

Preferably, you should make any free SO_2 correction by adding sulfite to must or wine for better protection **before** performing the next winemaking operation. For example, if you need to increase the free SO_2 in a wine that will be transferred from a tank to a barrel, add sulfite to the wine before the transfer. If the wine needs to be racked, pour the required amount of sulfite solution in the empty barrel or container where the racked wine will be transferred. Following the racking, transfer or other winemaking operation, re-measure the free SO_2 and make any necessary adjustments.

Be careful not to over-sulfite, and maintain the free SO_2 content at the prescribed level. Frequent and timely monitoring of musts and wines are required to prevent potential vinification problems due to excessively low or high free SO_2 content.

3.4.5 SULFITE CALCULATOR

An easy-to-use calculator to determine how much sulfite to add to wine, available at www.winemakermag.com, shown in Figure 3-24, has been developed based on the theory presented in this chapter.

Based on user-entered values for pH, current and desired levels of free SO_2, and volume to be corrected, the calculator determines how much sulfite to add for the type (white or red) of wine to provide protection at 0.8 mg/L molecular SO_2. The calculator uses the type of wine and pH to recommend the desired free SO_2 level. Volume values can be entered in liters or gallons and results are provided in grams or ounces, respectively, of sulfite powder required for the addition. The calculator also determines number of Campden tablets or volume of a 10% sulfite solution required for sulfite additions.

3.5 PHENOLIC ANALYSIS AND CONTROL

Wines, reds particularly, are described as being light, medium or full-bodied. And great red wines are often poetically described using superlatives as having a velvety texture and a round mouth-feel, or a structure having soft and elegant tannins that make the wine approachable in its youth but which will undoubtedly improve with time. Proud winemakers will talk about gentle phenolic extraction that retains subtle flavors without extracting harsh tannins, and perhaps even be more specific by asserting that punching the cap produces more delicate and more balanced wines than by pumping over because no harsh tannins are extracted. (These winemaking procedures are described in detail in chapter 4.)

Wine is indeed a very complex beverage containing countless complex compounds. One of the most important groups of compounds in wines is phenolics, which are responsible for structure, color and flavor.

Émile Peynaud, forefather of modern enology and a former authoritative research enologist and teacher of modern winemaking, defined "structure" as follows: "Diverse flavors from acids, sugars, salts and phenolic substances ... that blend into a form, a more or less harmonious volume which makes up structure.

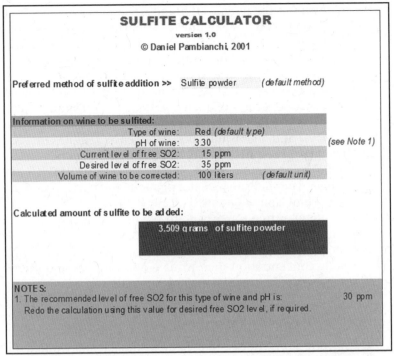

Figure 3-24: Sulfite Calculator available at www.winemakermag.com

[These essential flavors] constitute the bricks and mortar of a wine, its framework, also sometimes described as its bone structure."[5] Hence the reason why structure is often referred to as backbone.

The chemistry of phenolics is quite complex, but their role in winemaking is well understood, and the application of phenolic extraction in home winemaking enables the crafting of many different styles of wine. This is where the art of winemaking intersects with the science of enology. The same batch of grapes can be crafted into many different styles of wine, all under the winemaker's control through a wide variety of process applications.

3.5.1 UNDERSTANDING PHENOLICS

Phenolics, often referred to as polyphenolics, polyphenols, or simply phenols (the chemical name is hydroxybenzene, which is essentially benzene synthesized by the vine), are compounds including many natural color pigments such as the anthocyanins of fruit and dark-skinned grapes, most natural vegetable tannins such as occur in grapes, and many flavor compounds. The amalgam of phenolics constitutes the total phenolic content. There are

[5]Peynaud, Émile. THE TASTE OF WINE: THE ART AND SCIENCE OF WINE APPRECIATION. Schuster, Michael, tr. London: Macdonald & Co. (Publishers) Ltd. 1987. p. 147.

165

many other phenolic compounds in grapes and wine, but we will focus only on the major ones of enological significance and which are under control of the winemaker.

Grapes are very rich in phenolics of which more than half are extracted during winemaking. Phenolic concentration varies greatly between grape varieties as it is determined by such factors as form and structure of grapes, climate and vintage quality (e.g., extent of sun exposure), microclimate (e.g., soil type, drainage efficiency), and harvesting practices. For example, in general, we would expect thin-skinned Pinot Noir grapes to have a lower phenolic concentration than Cabernet Sauvignon, which has a thicker skin and contains more color pigment and tannins, and the reason why Pinot Noir wines are typically lighter colored.

Roughly two-thirds of grape phenolics are found in seeds, up to one-third in the skins, while only a small percentage are found in the juice and pulp. Dark-skinned grapes have a much higher phenolic concentration than white grape varieties and therefore, red wines have a significantly higher phenolic concentration than white wines (refer to Table 1-3 on page 54). That is because juice is allowed to macerate with the skins to extract phenolics in red winemaking, but there is typically no maceration in white winemaking – only juice and pulp are extracted and vinified.

Tannin is the phenolic that impacts wine structure, quality and aging potential the most, and is most often associated with bitterness (as in tonic water) and astringency (as in black tea). For simplicity, tannin can be classified as good or bad. Grape skins, juice and pulp contain good tannins whereas seeds and stems contain what are generally considered by winemakers as bad tannins that impart an overly bitter taste and harsh sensation.

Bitterness and astringency from good tannins must complement the acidity to balance sweetness in wine. Tannins and acidity work in opposite direction: **A low-acidity wine can support a higher tannin concentration and vice versa.** A high-acidity wine coupled with a high tannin concentration would be overly astringent and harsh, possibly making the wine undrinkable. Sweetness comes from any residual sugar as well as perceived sweetness from alcohol content.

Tannins not only affect taste and flavors in wine but also interact with anthocyanins (phenolics responsible for color in red wines) to provide color stability, and protect wine from premature oxidation effects resulting in improved aging potential. During the aging period, tannin concentration decreases because of oxidation and precipitation with protein resulting in increased suppleness, a chemical process known as polymerization. In general, white wines do not age well because of their considerably lower tannin concentration – up to six-fold less than reds.

One important chemical principle to keep in mind is that, whereas **anthocyanins are very soluble in juice, tannins are much more soluble in alcohol; therefore, tannins will be extracted at a faster rate in the presence of alcohol.**

3.5.2 MANAGING PHENOLIC CONCENTRATION

Phenolic concentration can be measured quantitatively, but unfortunately, advanced laboratory procedures, equipment, and skills well beyond the scope of home winemaking are required. Home winemakers will have to rely on a visual inspection to assess color and gustatory senses to assess flavors and structure; basically, much like most commercial wineries.

Phenolic concentration is also not a parameter that winemakers need to constantly monitor to prevent, for example, spoilage, as is the case for parameters like pH and free SO_2. Rather, winemakers know how much phenolic extraction they need based on a desired style and, with experience, learn how to manipulate the various winemaking processes to extract the desired level of phenolics, and how other factors such as environmental and equipment affect extraction.

Following is a list of winemaking processes and equipment as well as environmental factors to consider along with recommendations and guidelines for phenolic extraction. Some will apply only to winemaking from grapes, or specifically red winemaking from grapes, while others will apply to all types of musts. Each is discussed in more details in relevant sections, and specifically, the topics of crushing, maceration, aeration, delestage, pressing and fermentation are presented in depth in chapter 4.

First, choose a fermentation vat with a fairly large opening relative to its volume. When red wine juice starts fermenting, the grape solids raise to the top of the liquid phase to form a cap. For optimal phenolic extraction, the surface-to-volume ratio must be optimized. A very tall but slim vat will not optimize the amount of grape solids in contact with the fermenting wine, and will therefore reduce the rate of phenolic extraction. A fermentation vat with a diameter-to-height ratio between 0.5–1 is recommended. For example, a 1-m (3.3-foot) tall plastic drum with a 75-cm (30-inch) opening would have a ratio of approximately 0.75.

Your crusher should be equipped with two rollers that are set apart sufficiently to allow seeds that contain bad tannins through without crushing them. Crush at a slow and steady pace to minimize extraction of astringent and bitter tannins. Ideally, the crusher should also be equipped with a destemmer to remove stems from grape bunches. Crusher/destemmers for small home winemaking productions usually crush and then destem, and therefore, some harsh (bad) tannins are unavoidably extracted when stems are crushed. Larger-production destemmer/crushers destem grape bunches prior to crushing; however, these bulky machines are geared and priced for commercial wineries that handle larger volumes of grapes.

At crushing, you may also add macerating enzymes to the must prior to fermentation. Macerating enzymes help break down cell walls of red grapes for a more gentle phenolic extraction resulting in improved color stability and smoother mouthfeel. Lallemand's Lallzyme EX or Scott Laboratories' Scottzyme Color Pro are two examples of recommended macerating enzymes.

If you expect the must to be deficient in tannin because of the grape variety used or because of poor grape condition, you can add enological (grape) tannins to the must at a rate of up to 50 g/hL of calculated juice yield. Dissolve the required amount of tannin powder in a little amount of **warm** water and add the tannin solution into the must while stirring thoroughly.

Cold soaking (the pre-fermentation practice of soaking crushed grape solids in the juice at low temperature) is used in commercial winemaking to increase color intensity, improve color stability, and enhance wine complexity although the philosophy behind this method is often debated. Some winemakers argue that post-fermentation maceration (the practice of letting grape solids soak in wine for an extended period of time following end of fermentation) is more beneficial than cold soaking because it softens tannins, making the wine more approachable when young.

Higher fermentation temperature increases the rate of phenolic extraction. Winemakers often opt for a quick fermentation allowing the temperature to rise up to 30° C (86° F) to allow maximum color extraction, followed by a post-fermentation maceration to soften the tannins. This is in contrast to white winemaking where a cool fermentation as low as 13° C (55° F) is desired to preserve the more delicate aromas.

In reds, most of the color is extracted during the first few days of fermentation, and then intensity drops off considerably and levels out after the first week. Tannin extraction is also rapid in the first week of fermentation but continues after the first 7–10 days, albeit at a much slower rate, and then tannins soften after a long post-fermentation maceration that can last up to three weeks. An additional benefit of this extended maceration is increased color stability, an important consideration in wines destined for cellar aging. The rates of color and tannin extraction during maceration and fermentation are illustrated in Figure 3-25.

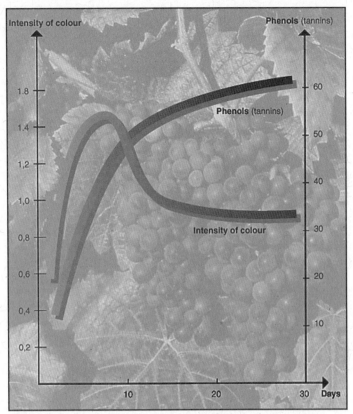

Figure 3-25: Typical rates of color and phenol extractions

Alternatively, you could combine the effects of macerating enzymes and temperature to shorten the maceration period (to reduce phenolic extraction) when a deeper color but less astringency is desired.

Once a cap forms during the alcoholic fermentation phase, it must be broken down to keep the grape solids soaked in the wine, to extract phenolics, and to prevent spoilage. This process is known as cap management and greatly influences the rate and level of phenolic extraction, and quality and aging potential of the wine. There are various cap management techniques; the three most important ones include punching, pump-over, and delestage.

Punching involves breaking the cap using a plunger tool, and is often argued to be a more gentle extraction technique used in making the best wines. Pump-over uses mechanical means, most often a pump, to circulate wine from the bottom of the fermentation vat to the top to soak the grape solids. Advocates of this technique maintain that aeration and heat dissipation, as a result of pumping, optimize phenolic extraction. Others will argue that the pump's rough handling of the wine compromises quality by extracting too much bad tannins and imparting too much astringency and bitterness. Delestage, discussed in depth in section 4.5, is a two-step "rack-and-return" process whereby fermenting red wine juice is separated from the grape solids by racking and then returned to the fermenting vat to re-soak the solids, and then repeated daily. This technique gently extracts phenolics by oxygenating the juice to produce a softer, less astringent wine exhibiting more fruit character. Ultimately, choosing a technique is based on your skills, equipment and desired style of wine.

If you need to add more tannin, you can do so during any of the above processes. Add enological tannin in increments of up to 10 g/hL until the desired results are achieved. Be sure to stir the must or wine thoroughly after each addition.

Aeration, SO$_2$, pH and oak

Aeration during racking, SO$_2$ additions, pH, and oak-barrel aging are other important factors affecting phenolic extraction and wine quality.

Aeration, during racking operations or from delestage, helps soften (polymerize) tannins as phenolics react with oxygen. To avoid premature aging of the wine, handle the wine gently during racking and minimize the number of racking operations after fermentation.

Increased color stability in red wines is a result of tannins binding with color pigments. SO$_2$, through the addition of sulfite, can negatively affect this and destabilize color, and potentially reduce color intensity. Limit sulfite additions to the recommended free SO$_2$ level based on the wine's pH – less at crushing to maximize color extraction during maceration.

Maintain the wine's pH within the recommended ranges provided in Table 3-2 on page 122 keeping in mind that as pH increases, color intensity and stability as well as fruitiness decrease. Higher pH wines will also tend to mature quicker than ones with lower pH, and will be more prone to microbial spoilage.

Oak barrels also play a vital role in tannin management beyond adding oak aromas and flavors; oak wood also imparts good tannins that will soften at a slow rate because of the controlled micro-oxidation of wine through the wood and barrel staves. The additional tannins from oak wood will also bind with the color pigments and improve color stability.

Because of the volume-to-surface ratio, large barrels have less oxygen-exchanging surface per liter of wine, allowing for a slower, more controlled reaction.

3.5.3 ADJUSTING THE AMOUNT OF TANNINS

You should taste your wines regularly and assess the evolution of phenols, particularly tannins to ensure that you maintain a proper balance between acidity, bitterness and astringency.

Once the wines are stabilized and you are getting close to bottling, you can make tannin adjustments depending on your desired style. To the extent possible depending on the types of wines on hand, the best option is always to blend wines to adjust tannins, i.e., blend a highly-tannic wine with a low-tannin wine to reduce or to increase the amount of tannins, respectively, in the former or the latter.

If you need to increase the amount of tannins, add enological tannins in steps of up to 10 g/hL until the desired results are achieved based on bench trials. You will need to wait approximately 4 weeks before racking and bottling the wine. Refer to section 5.2 on how to conduct bench tests.

If you need to reduce the amount of tannins, you can do a simple fining using PVPP. PVPP, short for polyvinylpolypyrolidone, is a synthetic polymer that is effective in absorbing and precipitating polyphenols responsible for browning in wines as well as excessive bitterness in red wines.

Add PVPP powder **directly** to wine at a rate of 25–75 g/hL of wine. Settling occurs very fast, as fast as 1–2 hours depending on the type of PVPP used, which must be racked immediately after settling. Follow the PVPP manufacturer's instructions on specific use. For additional information on PVPP, refer to section 5.2.8.

4
MAKING WINE

The science of winemaking is fairly well understood, and involves a relatively simple, centuries-old sequence of processes that turns raw material, whether grapes, juice or concentrate, into wine.

First, all equipment must be thoroughly cleaned and sanitized to avoid any microbial spoilage. The raw material, or must, is then prepared for alcoholic fermentation. In the case of winemaking from grapes, this will involve crushing, destemming, maceration (for red winemaking), and pressing operations before alcoholic fermentation. Maceration is typically used in red winemaking only although it can be used in white winemaking. Certain types of wines can also be malolactic fermented to soften the acidity. The wine is then clarified and stabilized to protect it from microbial spoilage, oxidation, renewed fermentation, which may occur in the bottle, and cold temperatures, prior to bottling. Optionally, it can be aged in oak barrels and/or blended with wines from different grape varieties for added complexity.

However, the difference between an ordinary wine and a wine that can only be described using superlatives lies in the art of winemaking. This chapter outlines the science of winemaking but also provides insight in the art of winemaking. Use the winemaking flowcharts illustrated in Figure 1-10 to Figure 1-15 on pages 58 to 64 as reference for the science, and experiment, endlessly, to learn what styles of wines you prefer based on the raw material you are able to get.

4.1 HANDLING THE RAW MATERIAL

The condition of the raw material in reconstituted juice and concentrate is not a concern since these are properly processed by producers to ensure that the must is sound and stable. In most cases, pre-packaged fresh juice should also not be a concern since they are stabilized, although you should always ask and confirm this; however, you still cannot ascertain the quality of the grapes used for the juice. You are basically buying juice "as is", trusting your supplier that the juice is sound.

You have to be very vigilant though when making wine from grapes. It is easy to negatively affect the quality of the finished wine if grapes are not sound. In the worst case, the wine may spoil and become undrinkable. Volatile acidity (VA) is a common culprit and a good indicator that the raw material was less than ideal, assuming all other winemaking practices were performed properly. Ideally, you should make wine from sound and undamaged grapes free of any kind of spoilage, such as rot, mold, and spoilage bacteria, such as *Lactobacillus* or *Pediococcus*. If there is any kind of damage or spoilage, it could very well compromise the quality of the wine. Reject the load of grapes, if you can, if there is considerable fruit damage or spoilage.

If you harvest grapes from your own vineyard or if you buy grapes from a local grower, you should transport the grapes to the crusher as quickly as possible while minimizing any handling. Ideally, harvest early in the morning when the temperature is cooler; grapes will break down faster at higher temperature, especially if harvested under a scorching sun.

When you receive and accept your load of grapes, as a first step, remove any foreign and undesirable vineyard matter such as critters (yes, you could come across one kind of insect or another) or other type of vegetation, and remove any leaves still present in your load of grapes. Hand-harvested or house-packed grapes have the least amount of leaves whereas machine-harvested grapes will tend to have a substantial amount of leaves.

Then, try and sort grapes to the extent possible to remove moldy bunches, or rotten or spoiled berries. Discard grapes and bunches that look damaged or unhealthy. This can be time-consuming, however, it minimizes the risk of problems down the road.

A very small amount of rot is acceptable, but, in spite of all the above warnings, if you have decided to proceed with grapes with a high level of spoilage, you should treat the crushed grapes with lysozyme at a rate of 100–200 mg/L of juice. Use the maximum rate for grapes with extensive damage or spoilage. You can add lysozyme by preparing a 5% solution or by adding LYSO-Easy, according to instructions described in section 3.4.2.

And it is worth repeating here that all kinds of musts, whether concentrate or fresh grape juice, are most susceptible to oxidation during handling, and whites considerably more than reds because the latter have a higher concentration of phenolic compounds, which inherently ward off hungry oxygen molecules. Handle the raw material as efficiently and rapidly as possible.

4.2 CRUSHING AND DESTEMMING

Crushing is the process of breaking the grape skins by mechanical means to expose the juice to yeast for alcoholic fermentation. Crushing of grapes is a necessary operation in red winemaking; it does not apply to winemaking from fresh juice, reconstituted juice and concentrates. Although it is optional for white winemaking, crushing is performed in home winemaking simply to ease the pressing operation for extracting juice; it does not serve any other function. Crushing plays a major role in red winemaking where grapes need to be processed adequately in preparation for what is known as phenolic extraction, as outlined in section 3.5.

Crushing is the first operation where tannins are extracted. When whole-bunch clusters of grapes are crushed, tannins are extracted from grape skins, seeds and stems. Of these, stems are the only tannin-imparting component that can be removed prior to crushing. And because stems also cause an increase in pH, which will reduce color intensity, fruitiness and freshness, this is another reason to remove them. These effects will manifest themselves to a larger extent with green stems than with the more mature woody stems (which usually denotes the full physiological maturity of the grape). In any case, it is far more common to see green stems on California grapes, save for in exceptional years.

Although a small amount of stems may be beneficial to add some tannin, generally, the bulk of the stems are removed before the grapes are crushed – a process known as destemming. Some winemakers destem grape clusters before crushing, and then add in a small amount of stems, e.g., 10%, for minimal tannin extraction. Stems add bitter and harsh tannins, therefore only a small quantity should be added back. This practice of adding stems back may be beneficial in red wines. On the other hand, white wines become easily unbalanced with minimal tannin, and therefore, stems are usually removed entirely in white winemaking. Destemming can also be done following crushing although more tannin will be extracted because the tannin-imparting stems are crushed along with the grape berries.

Vinification using 100% of the stems will yield a highly tannic wine that will take several years to mellow down to a drinkable level. This is not recommended for premium-quality wines that will undergo barrel aging or for wines to be aged solely in glass. Highly tannic wines aged in glass containers would display even tighter-wound tannins, for wine aged in glass ages more slowly, not having the benefit of the controlled oxidation of barrel aging. Therefore, the wine will not achieve the desired organoleptic balance.

The decision to destem before or after crushing depends on your equipment at hand, time and patience. Inexpensive crushers (the type without a destemmer) require that stems be removed manually after the grapes have been crushed. This is both tedious and messy. Alternatively, you can use the more expensive but still affordable crusher/destemmers to remove stems efficiently. Their drawback is that they first crush and then destem causing an appreciable amount of harsh tannins to be transferred to the must, and ultimately to the wine. Destemmer/crushers are the ultimate solution, albeit expensive, as they first destem the grape stalks and then crush the grapes.

A manual destemmer can be easily built using a wire mesh made of non-corrosive material in a wooden frame. Holes in the mesh should be just wide enough to allow grape berries to pass through. Stems will not pass through during destemming. Place the destemmer over a large container and slide the grape bunches with a back-and-forth motion over the mesh. Grape berries will fall into the container and the stems will remain behind. You can then crush the grapes with any type of crusher. This process is somewhat tedious but achieves good results for those who are patient.

In red winemaking where the juice and grape solids are to be transferred to a tank, low-capacity home winemaking equipment, such as 1½-in hoses and an economical impeller pump, makes this a painstaking task. If you do not destem grape bunches, hoses will clog and the pump will get damaged. Commercial wineries use a (very expensive) must pump that typically displaces must through 3-in hoses. A simple solution is to crush and destem grapes into 20-L (5-gal) buckets and to transfer the must manually from the top of the tank.

In white winemaking where only juice (without grape solids or stems) is moved through winemaking equipment, you can use a pump with 1-in hoses to transfer the juice to the tank via the top, or via the racking valve, which has the advantage of minimizing oxygenation of the juice. Once the juice has settled and is ready to be racked in preparation for yeast inoculation and fermentation, rack it to another container from the racking valve, empty the tank of solids from the bottom, and re-transfer the juice into the tank for fermentation.

4.3 MACERATION

Maceration is the process of letting the crushed grape berries soak in the juice before, during and/or after fermentation. It is generally used only in red winemaking, partially in rosé production, and seldom in white winemaking. This process does not apply to winemaking from concentrate, reconstituted juice, or fresh juice although purveyors of fresh grape juice now supply grape skins with some juices, and there are even wine kits with grape skins included.

4.3.1 RED WINE MACERATION

Maceration in red winemaking is the process of letting the crushed grape berries soak in the juice before fermentation, in wine during fermentation, or in wine post fermentation for the purpose of extracting phenolics, including color (anthocyanins). Maceration during fermentation is obviously required for making red wine to extract color from grape skins; however, pre- and post-fermentation maceration are optional and only used at the discretion of the winemaker based on the desired style to be crafted. It is during maceration that red wines acquire part of their structure, color and flavors, and that the wine's aging potential can be influenced.

Maceration of crushed grape berries with the juice before fermentation is known as pre-ferment soak or cold soak because the maceration is usually carried out at a cold temperature to inhibit fermentation. As anthocyanins are water-soluble, the objective of cold soak is to increase color extraction before start of fermentation. A benefit is improved color stability as well as flavor complexity.

At the onset of fermentation, phenolic extraction is primarily by heat and then by alcohol as fermentation progresses. Color is mainly extracted by heat within the first few days to one week, and then subsides; there is very little color extraction after the first week. Tannins are more soluble in alcohol than in water and, therefore, as fermentation progresses and alcohol increases, tannins are extracted at a greater extent. Refer to Figure 3-25 on page 169.

Maceration of crushed grape berries with the wine following completion of fermentation is known as post-fermentation maceration, or extended maceration, a process used for additional phenolic extraction to increase mouthfeel and soften tannins.

Table 4-1
Recommended maceration periods

Type of wine	Recommended maceration period	Amount of phenols extracted
Rosé	up to 24 hours	very low
Light-bodied, light-colored	3 – 4 days	low
Medium-bodied, medium-colored	5 – 7 days	medium
Full-bodied, deep-colored	up to 21 days	high

Post-fermentation maceration can last anywhere from one week to one month.

The amount of phenols and aromatics extracted during maceration depends on a number of factors that will need to be carefully managed and controlled. These include cold soaking, if any, the maceration period and temperature, cap management (includes punching down and pumping over operations), and aeration.

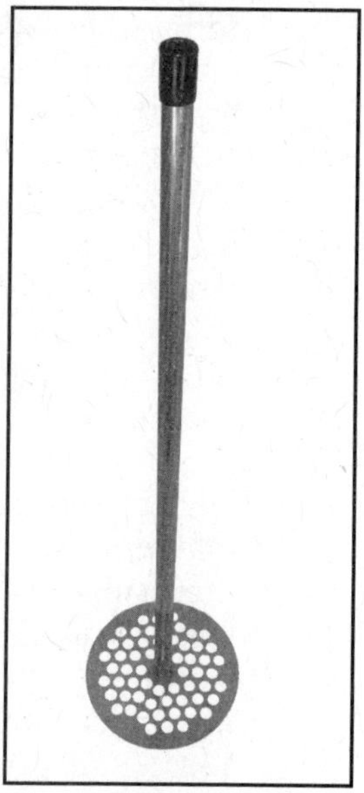

As a general rule of thumb, the longer the maceration/fermentation period, the more tannins, color and flavors that will be extracted, and the more full-bodied and colored a red wine will be. Table 4-1 provides guidelines on maceration periods (which include the fermentation period) for desired wine styles using traditional grape varieties such as Cabernet Sauvignon, Merlot and Syrah. Note that these guidelines depend on the grape varieties as well as their condition.

If you are making wine from very dark-colored, inky-juice grapes such as Alicante Bouschet, you will need to shorten these intervals depending on the desired wine style. You will need to take into account subsequent winemaking operations such as fining, filtering and even aging, which

Figure 4-1: Plunger tool for breaking and punching down the cap

tend to lighten the color of red wine, and therefore, you may want to extract more color.

If you are looking for more depth of color, for example, in varieties, such as Pinot Noir, known to produce a relatively light color even with extended maceration, a clever trick is to run off a small percentage of juice, in the order of 10%, at crushing time. This increases the volume ratio of solids to juice and will therefore increase phenolic concentration in the remaining juice and wine, resulting in increased depth of color as well as tannin and flavor concentration. The run-off juice is vinified separately using white winemaking techniques.

For maximum phenol extraction, prolong the maceration period as much as possible until little or no extraction occurs. The challenge is to retard and slow down fermentation, which would otherwise greatly reduce the maceration period and the level of extraction. The fermentation temperature will rise rapidly up to 32° C (90° F) or more, if not controlled, and will cause a rapid fermentation or may cause a stuck fermentation. The solution is pre-fermentation cold soak maceration.

4.3.2 Cold soak maceration and cap management

By dropping the temperature of the must (juice and grape solids) down to 8° C (46° F) or lower, maceration is effectively prolonged and fermentation is inhibited. For a full-bodied, deep-colored red wine using grapes that have been cold-shipped to your home winery, cold soak the must up to 1 week or 10 days before initiating fermentation by placing sealed freezer bags full of ice or plastic jugs with frozen water into the juice, or if you have a stainless steel tank with a cooling jacket, you can use a refrigerant to cool down the must, as described at the end of this section. You will first need to refrigerate freshly picked grapes in a cooler – not a practical solution for most home winemakers – before cold soak maceration.

Add up to 50 mg/L of sulfite to the must depending on the condition of the grapes to prevent volatile acidity (VA) from forming, and stir the must during cold soaking to distribute the temperature evenly. "Punch down" the grape solids at least twice a day, using a plunger tool, preferably a stainless steel model such as the one in Figure 4-1 or one built using white oak wood, as shown in Figure 4-2. Clean and sanitize the plunger tool before each use and thoroughly rinse after each use. Reload the freezer bags with new ice or use more jugs of frozen water when the old ice has thawed.

When ready to start fermentation, let the must warm up to room temperature and then inoculate with yeast to initiate fermentation. The yeast's rate of fermentation is an important factor

179

Figure 4-2 (from top): Punching the cap, and pumping over or *remontage*

to be considered when choosing a strain. Too quick a fermentation may considerably shorten the maceration period. Refer to section 4.7 for more information on fermentation, and yeast characteristics and selection.

During cold soak maceration, keep the fermentor covered and properly sealed with a tarpaulin or tank lid to prevent flies from invading the sweet juice. Ensure that there is enough room at the top of the fermentor for grape solids that will form a fairly solid mass, known as the cap, and rise to top and float on the wine during fermentation. Carbon dioxide (CO_2) gas produced during fermentation will get trapped between the cap and the cover/lid thereby protecting the juice from oxidation and microbial spoilage.

During cold soaking when no gas is produced, inject an inert gas such as carbon dioxide (CO_2), nitrogen (N), argon (Ar), or a combination of these under the cover/lid to purge air and protect juice or wine from oxidation and spoilage organisms. A small tank of compressed CO_2 is fairly inexpensive and lasts a long time, and is easy to use. CO_2 is heavier than air; therefore, when injected at the top of the fermentor above the grape solids, air is displaced and purged out of the fermentor to make room for the expanding CO_2 gas.

To inject gas and purge the air out when using stainless steel tanks not equipped with a sampling valve, you can install a simple gas-injection valve with a relief valve and bung, and seat the assembly in the hole where the fermentation lock is usually installed. Connect the gas tank outlet tube (from the regulator) to the gas-injection valve. First open the relief valve, then open the gas-injection valve. Slowly open the gas tank valve and let gas flow into the tank for up to 10 seconds or more, depending on tank size and headspace volume. You should feel air being pushed out through the relief valve. When done, shut the gas tank flow and quickly close the relief valve. Once daily, open the lid, thoroughly stir the juice or wine, and re-inject gas.

Alternatively, you can forego the gas-injection valve assembly and simply inject gas via the hole for the fermentation lock.

Remove the bung and fermentation lock, inject gas for a few seconds through the opening using a tube from the gas tank, and quickly re-seat the bung and fermentation lock into place.

If the tank is equipped with a sampling valve, you can inject gas into the wine tank by connecting the gas tank tube to the sampling valve. Ensure that you have a properly installed fermentation lock or relief valve at the top of the tank. Open the gas tank valve and let the gas bubble up through the wine for 10 seconds or more, depending on the tank size and headspace volume, and then close the gas tank valve.

Caution: NEVER inject gas into a tank with a closed lid having no fermentation lock or relief valve; this could cause the tank to explode and cause serious injury.

During fermentation, the grape skins will form a cap and rise to the top of the wine. To prevent spoilage and to maximize phenolic extraction, punch down the cap thoroughly two or three times a day using a plunger tool until the solids are well immersed in the wine. This has the added advantage of evenly distributing the fermentation temperature in the wine, as well as encouraging the multiplication of the yeast population in the early stages of fermentation. Separately or in addition to punching the cap, the wine can be pumped over the cap – a process termed *remontage*. Punching of the cap and *remontage* operations are part of what is known as cap management.

Pumping over involves using an electric pump to recirculate wine from the bottom of the fermentor to the top over the grape solids, as shown in Figure 4-2. This has the added benefit of also dissipating some heat from the fermenting wine and encouraging yeast multiplication. Douse the entire cap being careful not to overdo it to avoid oxidizing the wine. If using stainless steel tanks, pump over the juice with an electric pump from the racking valve through the sprinkler mechanism, if the tank is so equipped. Activate the pump for only a short period; only one or two minutes are required to thoroughly soak the cap. Again, ensure that the fermentation lock or relief valve is working properly – considerable fermentation gas will be expelled from the tank.

Refer to section 5.3.2 or consult a retailer about choosing an appropriate pump for this procedure. Not any pump will do since it has to be able to displace grape solids. A 1-hp positive-displacement impeller pump with at least 1½-inch hoses is the recommended minimum. If no pump is available, you can collect some wine from the bottom of the fermentor with a bucket and then pour it over the cap. This is where a vat or fermentor equipped with a spout, as shown in Figures 2-9 and 2-18 on pages 76 and 92, respectively, will prove very practical for cap management procedures.

As the tarpaulin or tank lid will be removed frequently during punching of the cap and pumping over, the protective CO_2 gas will escape. During the vigorous phase of fermentation, sufficient gas is produced to provide adequate protection. When fermentation subsides, you will need to inject some CO_2 gas under the cover/lid.

When fermentation is complete and the Brix level is $-1.5°$ (SG is 0.995) or lower, for a dry red wine, an additional week to 10 days of post-ferment maceration will be beneficial in softening the tannins. Post-ferment maceration, or extended maceration, is carried out in the same fashion, and with the same precautions, as cold soak maceration. Monitor the wine closely during this phase to avoid unpleasant surprises, such as microbial spoilage. Extended maceration is not recommended for high pH wines since these do not benefit as much from long extraction and are more prone to microbial spoilage.

To maximize the benefits of phenolic extraction, use an inert fermentor that provides an adequate ratio of juice surface to volume. A greater surface allows more juice to be in contact with the grape solids, thereby increasing extraction. Refer to section 2.3 on selecting a fermentor. As a reminder, be sure to account for volume from the rising cap when choosing the size of a fermentor.

When high color and tannin extractions are desired without cold soak or extended maceration, fermentation can be carried out at the high end of the recommended temperature range of $22°$–$28°$ C ($72°$–$82°$ F). This method can also be used with low-tannin grapes where extended maceration provides no benefit. It also has the advantage of minimizing the risk of oxidation and microbial spoilage since the duration of must exposure to air is reduced. Many great wines are made using "high" temperature fermentation!

Additionally, or optionally, you can add enological tannins for increased color extraction, particularly for varietals with little color intensity (low anthocyanins) and/or lower tannin concentration. The added tannins will help reduce precipitation of anthocyanins and hence reduce color loss. Add enological tannins at a rate of 30–50 g/hL by dissolving the powder in a little warm water, pouring the solution in the must, and then stirring or pumping over the must thoroughly.

Macerating enzymes can also be added to the must at crush time to increase juice yield and to prevent possible pectin-related problems, such as haze, at bottling time. Macerating enzymes help break down cell walls of red grapes for a more gentle phenolic extraction

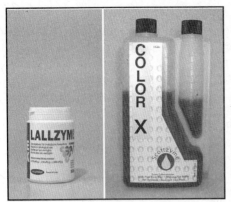

Figure 4-3: Lallzyme EX and Scottzyme COLOR X macerating enzymes

resulting in improved color stability and smoother, rounder mouthfeel. Lallemand's Lallzyme EX or Scott Laboratories' Scottzyme COLOR PRO, for early-drinking reds, or Scottzyme COLOR X, for heavier, more extracted reds, are some examples of recommended macerating enzymes (see Figure 4-3). Follow the manufacturer's instructions and recommended rates of addition for best results.

Since these products are mainly used in commercial winemaking, they are mainly available in formats larger than most home winemaker's needs. Lallemand's Lallzyme EX is now available in small format good for 20-L (5-gal) batches. Alternatively, you can buy larger formats and share with fellow home winemakers. A package can be used for two vintages if it is stored in a well-sealed container in a refrigerator.

To avoid extraction of overly harsh tannins, do not use macerating enzymes if macerating with stems. For the same reason, wait approximately 8 hours after crushing and adding macerating enzymes before (if) adding enological tannins.

The effects of macerating enzymes and temperature can be combined to shorten the maceration period (to reduce phenolic extraction) when a deeper color but less astringency are desired.

To transfer the pomace (the leftover grape solids after the wine has been racked) from the vat to the press, use a large, food-grade scoop or container. Remember to clean and sanitize all your equipment. If transferring from a tank equipped with a bottom manway, open the lid on the bottom manway, place a food-grade plastic bin under the tank opening, transfer the pomace into the bin with your hands or a small, food-grade plastic shovel, and then transfer the pomace to the press. Repeat this until the tank is emptied. Depending on the size of your press, you may need more than one press run.

Cold maceration in tanks equipped with a cooling jacket

In home winemaking, you can certainly chill wine for cold maceration in stainless steel tanks equipped with a cooling jacket, but be prepared for some serious work, ingenuity, and handyman skills. Commercial wineries have very expensive refrigeration plants for this purpose. Following are several poor man's refrigeration system alternatives that will work well in home winemaking applications.

The easiest method to emulate a refrigeration system is to cool a food-grade refrigerant down as low as possible in a camping cooler using frozen jugs of water immersed in the refrigerant. Food-grade glycol in an aqueous solution is the recommended refrigerant for this method because it can be cooled to –29° C (–20° F) without freezing. Prepare a 40% solution using propylene glycol – the type used in potable water plumbing systems, available from home renovation centers. You will need at least as much glycol solution as the cooling jacket will hold, plus the volume of all hoses and pump used in the set-up.

Bring the temperature of the glycol solution down as much as you possibly can using a system of rotating frozen jugs. Freeze several 4-L (1-gal) jugs of glycol solution in a deep freezer. Leave some headspace to allow for expansion in the jugs. You will need to rotate jugs approximately three times daily to get the glycol temperature down. This method can get the temperature of 500 L (130 gal) of wine down to the 10°–13° C (50°–55° F) range.

Use a low-speed pump to circulate the glycol solution from the cooler through the cooling jacket and back to the cooler. Glycol should always enter the cooling jacket from the bottom valve of the cooling jacket and back out from the top valve to ensure that the jacket fills up completely.

If you have an old chest freezer, you can put it to good use and turn it into your home winemaking refrigeration system. Drill two holes in the freezer door, just large enough to pass the hoses that will be moving glycol in and out of the freezer. Place a keg (the type used in beer making) inside the chest freezer and fill the keg with glycol solution. Attach a hose to the OUT port of the keg and run it through the hole in the freezer door to the pump's inlet. Attach a hose from the pump's outlet to the bottom valve of the cooling jacket. Attach a hose from the top valve of the cooling jacket through the freezer door and connect it to the IN port of the keg. Be sure that glycol is drawn from the bottom of the keg, i.e., from the OUT plug. When you are all set and with the freezer running, allow the glycol to cool down, and then start the pump.

In both methods, you can hook up the pump to a timer to turn it on/off at pre-determined time intervals to allow proper cooling of the refrigerant. You can also let the pump run continuously at very low speed to allow the glycol to cool down in the keg and to properly cool the must or wine in the tank.

If you are a handy person with good knowledge of refrigeration systems, you can build a compressor-evaporator easily from used parts. This would be the most effective solution as it saves consid-

Figure 4-4: A 20-L (5-gal) glycol chiller

erable space and has a built-in thermostat to control the temperature of the refrigerant. Alternatively, you can purchase a glycol system, such as the one shown in Figure 4-4, suitable for home winemaking applications. This system is fully integrated with a compressor and glycol holding tank.

If you work with open-top, variable-capacity tanks not equipped with a cooling jacket, you can use an immersion (cooling) plate, shown in Figure 2-14 on page 83, inserted in the must or wine, and hooked up to a glycol source similar to the above methods. Immersion plates work quite efficiently to cool small volumes of must and wine if the recirculating water can be kept sufficient cold.

The above methods can all be used also to reduce fermentation temperature, to maintain a low temperature during aging, or for cold stabilization if/when you have an adequate cooling system capable of delivering glycol at very low temperature. Refer to section 6.1.1 for more information on cold stabilization.

4.3.3 WHITE WINE MACERATION

White wines do not benefit from maceration since no color extraction is required and, in general, tannins are not desirable. Some winemakers still allow their crushed white grapes to macerate in the juice for up to 24 hours to give their wines a little more structure and color, particularly for fuller-bodied whites, such as oak-aged Chardonnay. This practice is seldom used in California in modern winemaking although still used in Europe.

For home winemakers, a short maceration period of up to 4 hours is acceptable. A longer maceration period is not recommended in home winemaking because the wine becomes highly susceptible to oxidation, from exposure to air, and to phenol over-extraction. Sulfite the must after crushing, and then cool down to a temperature between 10°–14° C (50°–57° F) to conduct maceration and to prevent fermentation from starting prematurely.

4.4 MACRO- AND MICRO-AERATION

Two common winemaking practices that can be beneficial in the production of premium wines are macro-aeration and micro-aeration; the latter is more commonly referred to as micro-oxygenation.

185

Macro-aeration refers to the practice of aerating, or oxygenating, fermenting wine by vigorous racking to produce a softer, less astringent wine exhibiting more fruit character and improved color stability.

Micro-oxygenation refers to the controlled process of oak-barrel aging where wine is allowed to interact very slowly with a miniscule amount of air penetrating through the barrel. Apart from flavors and tannins imparted by the wood, oak-barrel aged wines will exhibit more complexity than wines aged in stainless tanks or glass containers because of micro-oxygenation.

4.4.1 MACRO-AERATION

Macro-aeration is only used in red winemaking as it involves vigorous splashing of wine during pump-over or racking operations. The effect is to soften the astringent tannins and produce a softer wine that is approachable much younger, and to stabilize color. The high phenolic content protects the wine from negative oxidation effects. In contrast, white wines have a very low tannin content making them much more prone to the negative effects of oxidation. Therefore, macro-aeration is never practiced and not recommended in white winemaking.

Macro-aeration is also beneficial in red winemaking by providing yeast cells with oxygen and ensuring a healthy fermentation. Yeasts require oxygen in order to thrive and to convert sugar into alcohol. Such yeasts are said to be aerobic, i.e., they are active in the presence of oxygen. If oxygen is not sufficiently available, yeasts can become inhibited and cause a stuck fermentation.

Another benefit of macro-aeration is reduced hydrogen sulfide (H_2S) production. A common cause of H_2S in wines, detected as a rotten-egg smell, is vinification from grapes that have been over-treated with sulfur-based vineyard mildew and fungus inhibitors. Red wines made from grapes are more prone to H_2S problems as the juice is allowed to macerate with the grape skins therefore diluting sulfur compounds into the juice. In white wines from grapes, it is not a problem because the juice is not macerated with the skins, at least not for an appreciable amount of time. By aerating the wine abundantly by racking it against the wall of the container will reduce the amount of potentially harmful H_2S. If not treated early, H_2S will react in the wine to form first into mercaptans followed by disulfides (oxidized mercaptans) – all of which are foul-smelling compounds that cause wine to spoil. The presence of either compound is practically irreversible in home winemaking.

There are several ways to macro-aerate wine, each having varying degrees of effectiveness, which fall into two main categories: 1) by splashing wine and 2) by injecting oxygen into wine.

The most common method of splashing wine used by home winemakers is to let the wine splash against the wall of a carboy when racking. Commercial wineries often use delestage fermentation, also known as the rack-and-return method, described below in section 4.5, where fermenting wine is racked by gravity flow into a vat and then returned to the tank with a pump.

Although these techniques are proven, some industry experts argue that the wine is still too protected by the layer of carbon dioxide gas forming over the wine volume during racking, and therefore the wine does not absorb sufficient air to benefit from macro-aeration. Their solution? Inject oxygen into the wine.

Commercial wineries use a venturi attachment to their hose when returning wine to the top of the tank during the pump-over operation. The venturi attachment is a simple inverted-T connector that allows air to be drawn into the wine stream when the wine is being pumped over. A check valve may be used to prevent back-flow.

In home winemaking, the T-connector can be easily made using polyethylene tubing and plastic barb adapters. Insert the T-connector into the racking line by cutting the tube midway and connecting each end to the barb adapter. You will need to test with various lengths of tube on the leg side of the T until 'burping' stops when racking. Alternatively, if you use a pump for pump-over and it is equipped with a valve on the suction side, open the valve when working the pump.

4.4.2 MICRO-AERATION (MICRO-OXYGENATION)

A miniscule, controlled amount of oxygen during wine aging can be beneficial for wine to develop and show its full potential. It allows wine to develop and age gracefully while softening tannins, stabilizing phenols, and increasing flavor complexity – a phenomenon known as micro-aeration, micro-oxygenation or sometimes as micro-oxidation – which does not happen in air-tight, inert containers such as stainless steel tanks or glass carboys.

Until recently, micro-oxygenation mainly occurred in barrels and bottles where wine would "breathe" through the wood and head and stave joints (the tight space between the pieces of wood forming the heads and walls of a barrel), and through the cork, respectively, during the aging process. However, new advances in winemaking technology now make it possible to micro-oxygenate wine in controlled fashion at any stage of the process, such as tank aging, for example, and replicate the benefits of barrel-aged wines, albeit in a much shorter time period.

Note: Results are not conclusive as to whether wine should be micro-oxygenated before or after MLF, and therefore that decision remains in the hands of the winemaker.

In commercial wineries, micro-oxygenation is achieved by injecting a continuous, miniscule supply of compressed, industrial-grade oxygen gas using a stainless steel, micro-size diffuser installed inside at the bottom of the tank. The amount of oxygen injected is controlled via an automated control box. StaVin, a provider of barrel alternative solutions, has developed such an apparatus, the OxBox, based on Dr. Jeff McCord's research, Director of Research at StaVin.

No such micro-oxygenation equipment is yet available to home winemakers, but if you are a resourceful and handy person, you could find a gas diffuser and assemble it to an oxygen tank using polyethylene tubing. Be sure to use a regulator on the oxygen tank. Then, you can run some tests by injecting gas in varying amounts and rates into wine samples to determine what results work best for you, since there is no control box.

When barrel-aging wine, no special micro-oxygenation equipment or process is required; the barrel does all the work. Your only tasks are to check the wine level every 3–4 weeks and top up the barrel to avoid "bad" oxidation, and smell and taste the wine to ensure that everything is developing as planned according to your desired taste.

For bottle-aging wine, natural or agglomerated corks are recommended. There is much debate about screw caps and synthetic corks because they do not have the long track record of natural corks. Some winemakers maintain that screw caps and synthetic corks provide too much of an airtight seal depriving wine of micro-oxygen that is necessary for wine to evolve gracefully. They argue that airtight seals inhibit micro-oxygenation and completely stifle graceful evolution; more on this in section 9.4.1.

4.5 DELESTAGE

Often, rich, full-bodied wines can be overly astringent in their youth, particularly those that have spent some time in oak barrels, and may not be approachable before a few years of aging to tame the tannins. A technique called delestage fermentation can be used to make full-bodied wines more approachable when young and that exhibit a fruitier nose with a rounder, less astringent mouthfeel.

Delestage (from the French *délestage* meaning "lightening" in reference to the separation of juice and grape solids, and pronounced *day-leh-staj*) is a fermentation/maceration technique used in red winemaking from grapes, which gently extracts phenolic compounds by oxygenating the juice to produce a softer, less astringent wine exhibiting more fruit character. In fact, Dr. Bruce Zoecklein's research at Virginia Tech has demonstrated that delestage-fermented wines have a lower concentration of tannins and a higher concentration of esters – key compounds that contribute fruitiness.[1] Given the lower concentration of tannins, delestage-fermented wines will generally not age as long as traditionally fermented, tannin-rich, oak-aged wines, but this is strictly a matter of style and preference.

Although many wineries use this technique, particularly in making Pinot Noir, delestage is practically unknown to home winemakers because its practice and benefits are not covered in home winemaking literature. And, being labor intensive, delestage is a process best suited for commercial wineries fitted with the appropriate equipment. A simple process adaptation to home winemaking can significantly reduce the effort and still provide the benefits.

4.5.1 HOW DELESTAGE WORKS

Delestage is a two-step "rack-and-return" process whereby fermenting red wine juice is separated from the grape solids by racking and then returned to the fermenting vat or tank to re-soak the solids, and then repeated daily.

Racking the fermenting juice oxygenates, or aerates, the wine and softens the astringent tannins through oxidation, and also stabilizes its color. Racking during maceration and fermentation is the underlying difference from traditional maceration-fermentation where the juice ferments under a layer of carbon dioxide (CO_2) gas and is seldom aerated until racked at the end of fermentation. Pump-over (the recirculation of wine from the bottom of the fermentation vat to the top to soak the grape solids) is sometimes used to aerate the wine but does not provide the same effects as delestage because the wine is never separated entirely from the grape solids.

During delestage racking, the cap slowly falls to the bottom of the vat while the wine is allowed to drain completely under the weight of the grape solids. Once the wine is completely racked, as much grape seeds as possible are removed to avoid imparting harsh tannins from seeds to the wine. Seeds are removed while racking via a faucet or valve from the bottom of the fermentation vat or tank, respectively.

Following racking, the grape solids are allowed to settle separately from the fermenting wine for 1–2 hours or more depending on the size of the fermenting vat. The fermenting wine is returned to the vat over the cap using a gentle, high-volume pump to com-

[1]Leahy, Richard. "Délestage Fermentation: From Bitter to Better Reds." Vineyard & Winery Management. Sept./Oct. 2000, Vol. 26, No. 5.

pletely soak the grape solids for maximum color and flavor extraction while minimizing extraction of harsh phenols.

This process is repeated daily until the end of fermentation. As fermentation progresses, more seeds are released from the grapes, and again, as much seeds as possible are removed during each racking operation.

An advantage of delestage is that the rack-and-return operation favors juice extraction from grape solids and increases free-run yield, and therefore requires less pressing of the solids at the end of fermentation. Macerating enzymes can also be used to help break down cell walls of red grapes for a more gentle extraction of phenolic compounds thereby increasing the effects of delestage. Macerating enzymes are added to the must at crushing, i.e., before the start of fermentation, otherwise they will be inhibited by the presence of alcohol.

4.5.2 DELESTAGE FOR HOME WINEMAKERS

Delestage can be made to be a relatively easy process for home winemakers while achieving the same benefits as commercial wineries. Figure 4-5 illustrates delestage for home winemakers; the top of Figure 4-5 illustrates the "racking" operation, and the bottom illustrates the "return" operation.

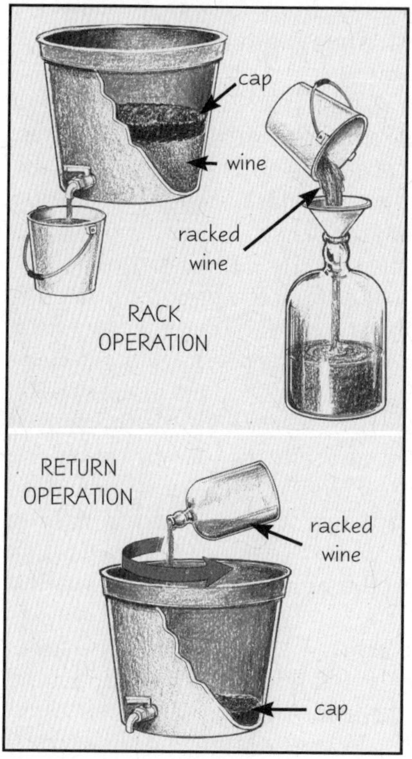

Figure 4-5: Rack and return operations in delestage

The fermentation vat should be equipped with a faucet at the bottom. Position the vat in a slanted position to allow fermenting juice to drain freely from the faucet during the racking operation while allowing the removal of as much seeds as possible. You will not be able to remove all the seeds; expect to remove one-third or more by the end of fermentation. Use a standard 20-L (5-gal) pail for receiving the wine being racked along with a sieve to separate seeds and other grape solids from the wine.

Have sufficient small demijohns or carboys for fermenting wine during the racking and settling period. Use small 20- or 23-L glass containers – or better yet, PET carboys – as you will need to lift these up above waist level during the "return" operation. Hire an

190

extra pair of hands to help you and avoid injuring your back. Commercial wineries use gentle, high-volume pumps to displace large volumes of wine during delestage. The much smaller volume in home winemaking does not warrant the cost of a pump. In addition, special paraphernalia or fermentation tanks with special screens are required to separate the seeds from the juice. Home winemaking pumps are not designed for this type of juice handling.

When planning capacity and carboys required, figure roughly, on average, 70 L of juice or wine (free and press runs) for every 100 kg of grapes, or 8 gal per 100 lbs of grapes. The yield will initially be lower but will progressively increase following each daily racking operation. The maximum total yield depends mainly on the grape variety and fruit quality, as well as on the use of enzymes.

To perform delestage, let fermentation start and allow it to proceed until the cap forms on top of the fermenting juice. This may take up to two or three days depending on temperature of the fermentation area. Adjust the temperature to avoid having the fermenting wine exceed 30° C (86° F), which could otherwise cause fermentation problems. And be sure to protect the must with a heavy tarpaulin to keep fruit flies out and to protect it from spoilage bacteria during fermentation.

Once the cap has formed, place the sieve and pail under the faucet, open it slowly and completely until the pail is filled. Close the faucet, transfer the wine to a carboy, and remove whatever seeds have been collected in the sieve. Repeat this until all the wine is completely drained.

During racking, the cap will slowly and gradually fall to the bottom of the vat. While the cap rests at the bottom, more wine will drain under the weight of the grape solids. Leave the faucet open with the pail under it until no more wine drains. Depending on your grape volume, this may take up to one hour or two, possibly more. Transfer this wine to a carboy, and then ensure that all containers are properly topped up and protected with fermentation locks.

At the end of the racking period, i.e., when no more wine drains, wine in carboys must be returned to the fermenting vat. This is the part of delestage where an extra pair of hands will be required. Alternatively, you can use a high-volume, home winemaking pump in this operation because the wine is free of large solids and does not require any special handling. The idea is to douse the grape solids quickly and thoroughly so that the wine rises faster than the solids while pouring or pumping. This maximizes interaction between the cap and the wine, and optimizes the effects of delestage. If pouring from a carboy, have someone help you to lift and hold the heavy container. If you make more than 200 liters (50 gallons) per year, consider investing in a good pump if you intend to ferment using delestage.

Repeat the rack-and-return procedure each day or every other day. Perform delestage in conjunction with cap punching, i.e., continue breaking and submerging the cap as usual, two or three times daily, to maximize color extraction and protect the wine from spoilage bacteria.

Delestage from a stainless steel tank is even easier. First, connect a hose to the discharge valve. Open or remove the top lid slightly (to prevent the tank from imploding during racking), open the discharge valve and let the wine flow to another tank or into an open vat. Filter out the seeds using a basket sieve. Close the valve and discard the seeds. Repeat this process until there is no more wine flowing out. Then, transfer the racked wine back to the tank using an electric pump. A strong flow rate is required to douse the grape solids for maximum phenolic extraction. Repeat this process each day during the active fermentation phase. Delestage is not recommended in tanks without a sloped or conical bottom and discharge valve as the only valve – the racking valve – sits above the seeds.

4.5.3 MAXIMIZING THE BENEFITS OF DELESTAGE

The benefits of delestage – higher concentration of fruity flavors, softer tannins, and more stable color – can be optimized through the use of selected fermentation yeasts and macerating enzymes.

Use a low-foam yeast strain specifically recommended for reds where supple mouthfeel and concentrated fruit aromas are desired. Foamy yeasts tend to inhibit the benefits of delestage. Refer to section 4.7.1 for more information on selecting wine yeasts.

Macerating enzymes, described in section 4.3.2, can also improve color stability and enhance mouthfeel for smoother reds through a more gentle extraction of phenolic compounds. Macerating enzymes are added to the must before the start of fermentation, when there is no alcohol present; they do their work during the maceration phase in red winemaking.

4.6 PRESSING

Pressing is the process of extracting grape juice or wine by pressure, and only applies to winemaking from grapes.

In red winemaking, grapes are first crushed to allow the grape solids to macerate with the juice, and then fermentation kicks in. Just before or at the end of fermentation, grape solids are transferred to the winepress for pressing.

In white winemaking, either crushed or whole (uncrushed) grape bunches can be pressed; pressing of crushed grapes is always performed before fermentation. In home winemaking, pressing is only recommended on crushed grapes, not whole grape bunches. Although whole white grape bunches can be pressed for extracting clearer juice, it is not recommended on standard home winepresses because they are not designed to withstand the high pressure necessary to extract juice from whole bunches. Only pneumatic or tank presses capable of withstanding the high pressure should be used. Pressed, crushed white grapes will yield a cloudy juice that will settle and then clarify during vinification, i.e., racking, fining and/or filtering, and therefore, crushing is usually not an issue. However, in some cases, such as in sparkling wine production where phenolic extraction should ideally be kept to the strictest minimum, whole grape bunch pressing is most desirable, so be sure to use a strong winepress for this purpose.

Juice extracted from pressing will not be of consistent quality. The free-run juice extracted by the weight of the must and, optionally, from a light pressing will be of higher quality. Press-run juice will generally be of inferior quality depending on the extent of pressing. As pressing pressure is increased, more phenolic compounds, namely tannins, are extracted from grape skins, seeds and stems. Press-run juice will have a lower total acidity with an increased amount of volatile acidity and a higher pH, resulting in a wine having reduced color intensity, fruitiness and freshness, and that may lack the required balance to produce a premium wine. Generally, it is recommended to conduct fermentation of free-run and press-run juices in separate vessels, and to blend the finished wines according to the desired quality.

You can improve yield and pressing efficiency by using pressing aids, such as cellulose or rice hulls, shown in Figure 4-6, which facilitate pressing and juice or wine drainage, particularly with grape varieties with slippery skins, such as Muscat. Sprinkle rice hulls over crushed grapes, as you are loading the press, at a rate of approximately 1:100, for example, 1 kg per 100 kg of grapes. Cellulose pressing aid is easier to use and not as messy as rice hulls. Use a cellulose pressing aid at a rate of approximately 1:133, for example, 0.75 kg per 100 kg of grapes. Alternatively, you could add back a small por-

Figure 4-6: Rice hulls

tion of stems, e.g., 10%, if you destemmed grape bunches at crushing, which will also ease the pressing operation.

Sieve pressed juice or wine using double-cheesecloth to remove as much solids as possible and transfer it immediately to a glass container by pouring the juice or wine against the wall of the vessel – as opposed to straight down – to minimize the effects of aeration and oxidation.

For white winemaking, let the juice settle for 12 hours before racking to a glass fermentor leaving behind all sediment. Some winemakers believe in a light bentonite fining at this stage (refer to section 5.2.1) to ensure a clean must and a firm deposit for ease of racking. Keep the must temperature below 15° C (59° F) during this period to prevent fermentation from starting; otherwise, if fermentation starts, it will be impossible to rack the clear juice up because carbon dioxide gas produced during fermentation will stir sediment back into suspension.

You can coarse filter some of the dense juice at the bottom, just above the heavy sediment, once it has settled (refer to section 5.3) to recover some clear juice that you can ferment. This is generally not recommended because the procedure is extremely difficult to perform and requires considerable time and effort as the dense juice contains a very high concentration of solids. Commercial wineries use centrifugal clarifiers for this operation.

For each juice, free- and press-run, fill the fermentor three-quarters only to allow for expansion during fermentation. The amount of volume required depends on the amount of foam expected during fermentation, which depends on a number of fermentation factors such as temperature and type of yeast.

4.7 ALCOHOLIC FERMENTATION

Alcoholic fermentation, the conversion of must into wine, is the single most vital and critical vinification procedure. In addition to grape variety and quality of the raw material, a wine's organoleptic qualities and structure are influenced by the winemaker's ability to control the various vinification factors such as temperature, sugar concentration, acidity and pH, SO_2 level, rate of fermentation, tannin level and color, to name a few. The various transformations and rapid evolution of ingredients require many quick decisions. Constant care and supervision during fermentation is a mandatory practice. Fermentation can progress free of problems if all instructions are followed as outlined.

Perhaps one of the most critical factors, however, is yeast selection. Yeast is more than merely a fermentation agent; yeast shapes the style of wine, influences organoleptic qualities, and reduces the risk of fermentation problems. Therefore, you should understand yeast properties and select an appropriate yeast strain to achieve predictable results.

4.7.1 YEASTS AND YEAST NUTRIENTS

Yeast plays a very important part in the fermentation process by converting sugar in the must into alcohol. Once fermentation has begun, yeast cells will multiply and will stimulate a faster rate of sugar conversion. Yeast activity will cease if the fermentation environment does not favor cell multiplication – e.g., lack of nutrients, not enough oxygen, too low or high a temperature, or too much SO_2 – or if the cell count is low.

Fermentation can start on its own from wild (indigenous) yeasts, which have formed on grape skins and in the winery, or can be enabled using dry- or liquid-format cultured yeast. Traditionalists still use wild yeast in the production of some wines. Such winemakers must inevitably invest considerable time and energy to monitor and control the wild-yeast fermentation to prevent any problems. Wild-yeast fermentation is prone to microbial spoilage if not managed properly. Cultured wine yeast, on the other hand, allows for a controlled fermentation with relatively minimal monitoring. For home winemaking using grapes or fresh juice, it is recommended to inhibit wild yeast and to use selected cultured yeast specific for a desired wine style. Concentrates and reconstituted grape juices have been stripped of all yeast, therefore, they always require the addition of cultured yeast. Always use yeast supplied by the manufacturer of the kit, concentrate or reconstituted grape juice to ensure problem-free fermentation. Manufacturers go to great length to test and determine the best yeast to use with their raw material.

A plethora of cultured yeast strains is available for various wine styles, although the selection for home winemaking is very limited because most are packaged in volumes for commercial wineries. Cultured yeast strains are taxonomically identified by their

---

What's in a name?

The current (new) yeast taxonomy classifies the previous *S. bayanus* selected wine yeast strains as *S. cerevisiae*. Former *S. uvarum* yeast strains are now called *S. bayanus*, e.g., Lallemand's Lalvin S6U. This is now the only Lallemand *S. bayanus* yeast commercially available. Some manufacturers have chosen to use the terminology *S. cerevisiae bayanus* to avoid confusion with winemakers used to the old terminology. Other manufacturers may use *S. cerevisiae galactose* or "subspecies *bayanus*" while some no longer even mention the scientific classification, but some still use the *bayanus* name. Tables 4-2 to 4-5 list the data as supplied by each manufacturer.

195

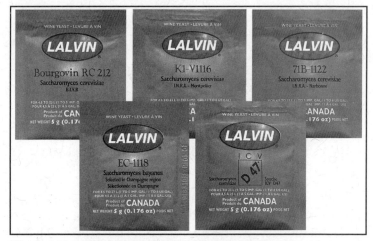

Figure 4-7: Lalvin cultured wine yeast strains

© Courtesy of Fermentis - Division of S.I.Lesaffre

Figure 4-8: Red Star cultured wine yeast strains

genus and species names, such as *Saccharomyces cerevisiae* or *S. cerevisiae*, as is the common practice to abbreviate the genus, and their commercial name. The commercial name is a manufacturer's brand name that represents a specific strain with specific properties often reflecting the area where the yeast was isolated or cultured. For example, Lalvin's Bourgovin RC 212 is a *S. cerevisiae* yeast for strain number 1105-02, which was selected from fermentations in Burgundy by the *Bureau Interprofessionnel des Vins de Bourgogne (BIVB)*, recommended for Pinot Noir.

Cultured wine yeast strains used in home winemaking are mainly from the *Saccharomyces cerevisiae* species. There are many

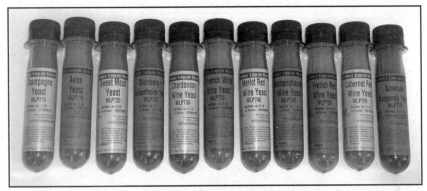

Figure 4-9: White Labs cultured wine yeast strains

strains within each species, each having different microbiological and biochemical properties that not only affect vinification results, but more important, that influence wine's organoleptic qualities.

Lallemand (Lalvin) and Lesaffre (Red Star) are major producers of dry, cultured wine yeasts for home winemaking, while White Labs and Wyeast Laboratories (Wyeast) are major producers of liquid, cultured wine yeasts. Their respective list of cultured wine yeast types and strains available to home winemakers, and strain characteristics along with recommended usage, type of wine and examples of varietals are depicted in Figures 4-7 to 4-10 and Tables 4-2 to 4-5.

Many other yeast strains are available although they are packaged in volumes suitable for commercial winery applications. Some home winemaking supply shops now repackage some of the more popular yeast strains in smaller volumes to ferment 20 L (5 gal) of juice. It is worthwhile then to search out these suppliers for special yeast strains. The most common of these are Lallemand strains. Table 4-6 (see pages 206 to 209) provides a list of other Lallemand yeast strains – those mainly used in commercial winemaking – along with recommendations and usage notes that you can use as a guide and reference to determine and research a desired style of wine. Full details of these Lallemand yeast strains are available at www.lallemandwine.us.

When choosing a yeast type and strain, you will need to consider the following yeast properties and fermentation factors based on desired results:

• Type of wine
• Fermentation temperatures
• Alcohol tolerance
• Rate of fermentation
• Foam production

Text continued on page 201

197

Figure 4-10: Wyeasts cultured wine yeast strains

List of abbreviations used in Tables 4-2 to 4-5 and 4-7

B	Barolo	C	Chardonnay	CB	Chenin Blanc	CF	Cabernet Franc	CS	Cabernet Sauvignon	Gr	Grenache
Gw	Gewürztraminer	Gy	Gamay	M	Merlot	MS	Medium-Sweet	Mu	Muscat	N	Nebbiolo
PB	Pinot Blanc	PG	Pinot Grigio	PN	Pinot Noir	PS	Petite Syrah	R	Riesling	RS	Residual Sugar
S	Syrah	SB	Sauvignon Blanc	Sé	Sémillon	SF	Stuck Fermentation	Sv	Sangiovese	Va	Valdepeñas
VI	Vidal Icewine	Z	Zinfandel						

Table 4-2: Properties of Lallemand's Lalvin home winemaking yeast strains

Yeast strain (Strain #)	Bourgovin RC 212 (1105-02)	ICV/D-47 (1080-02)	71B-1122 (1022-02)	K1V-1116 (1016-02)	EC-1118 (1018-02)
S. species	cerevisiae	cerevisiae	cerevisiae	cerevisiae	cerevisiae
Recommended for	Red varieties where full tannin and color stabilization are desired	Premium-quality white wines, esp. full-bodied, barrel fermented	Fruity wines from concentrates	Fruit wines and low-nutrient musts; restart stuck fermentation	White and sparkling wines; ideal for quick fermentations
Type of wine	Tannic red; light young red	Dry white; MS / Rosé	MS / Rosé; light young red	Dry white; MS / Rosé; light young red; Icewine	Dry white; Sweet; Sparkling; Icewine
Example of varietals	CS, CF, M, N, PN	C, Gw, PG, R	Gy, Gw, R, Z	CB, PG, SB	Sparkling C, VI
Fermentation temperature range	15–30°C 59–86°F	10–35°C 50–95°F	15–30°C 59–86°F	10–42°C 50–107°F	7–35°C 45–95°F
Alcohol tolerance	14%	15%	18%	18%	18%
Rate of fermentation	moderate	moderate	moderate	fast	very fast
Foam production	low	low	low	very low	very low
Flocculation	low	medium	medium	low	low
VA production	low	low	low	low	low
SO_2 production	low	low	very low	low	moderate
ML compatibility	more	more	more	less	less
H_2S production	low	low	low	very low	very low
Nutrient requirements	high	normal	normal	very low	normal

Table 4-3: Properties of Lesaffre's RED STAR home winemaking yeast strains

Yeast strain (Strain #)	Pasteur Red (Davis #904)	Montrachet (Davis #522)	Côte des Blancs (Davis #750)	Pasteur Champagne (Davis #595)	Premier Cuvée (Davis #796)
S. species	cerevisiae	cerevisiae	cerevisiae	bayanus	bayanus
Recommended for	Full-bodied reds where varietal fruit flavors & complex aromas are desired	Full-bodied intense-color reds & whites	Reds, whites & sparkling as well as wines with RS	Whites & some reds; not for sparkling; restarts SF	Reds, whites & esp. sparkling; restarts SF
Type of wine	Tannic red; light young red	Dry white; tannic red	MS / Rosé; sweet; light young red; sparkling	Dry white; light young red	Dry white; sweet; sparkling; Icewine
Example of varietals	CS, CF, M, Z	CS, CF, C	C, Gw, R	CS, CF, C	Sparkling C, VI
Fermentation temperature range	18–30° C 64–86° F	15–30° C 59–86° F	18–30° C 64–86° F	15–30° C 59–86° F	7–35° C 45–95° F
Alcohol tolerance	16%	13%	12–14%	13–15%	18%
Rate of fermentation	fast	fast	slow, moderate	fast	fast
Foam production	low	moderate	low	moderate	very low
Flocculation	low	low	low	medium-low	low
VA production	low	low	low	low	low
SO$_2$ production	low	low/moderate	very low	low	moderate
ML compatibility	more	more	not recommended	more	less
H$_2$S production	low	high	low	low	very low
Nutrient requirements	normal	normal	high	normal	normal

- Flocculation
- Volatile acid (VA) production
- Sulfur dioxide (SO$_2$) production
- Malolactic (ML) compatibility
- Hydrogen sulfide (H$_2$S) production
- Nutrient requirements

Based on the grape variety or varieties at hand, first determine your desired type and style of wine to help you make a better decision on selecting a yeast strain. Will you be making a dry white? Will it be made in a light style or will it be barrel-fermented for a more full-bodied style? Will it be used as a base for sparkling wine? Or will it have residual sugar for an off-dry or medium-sweet wine, or perhaps even an Icewine? Will you be making a dry red for early drinking or do you prefer a big, bold, tannic red meant for aging? Will you be blending different batches or different varietals? Are you expecting a difficult fermentation because, for example, of high sugar? Will you want to put your wine through malolactic fermentation (MLF)?

Each cultured yeast strain has been isolated and developed to allow specific grape varieties to express their full, individual organoleptic characteristics for a desired style of wine. For example, a white wine strain may be recommended for a specific varietal to allow it to exhibit its characteristic fruitiness while a red wine strain may be recommended for greater phenolic stabilization for increased mouthfeel and improved color stability. Beyond contributing to the sensory profile, strains may be specifically recommended to address specific fermentation requirements, such as restarting a stuck fermentation or favoring MLF.

Fermentation temperature should always be within the recommended range. Yeast activity can cease if the temperature deviates outside this range and cause a stuck fermentation. The lower temperature-tolerant yeast strains are recommended for white wine vinification where fermentation is often conducted at low temperatures, or where a cooler fermentation is desired in red wine vinification. When a cool temperature cannot be achieved during red wine vinification, a higher temperature-tolerant yeast strain is recommended because fermentation temperature will rise significantly.

Some strains can tolerate alcohol levels up to 14% or 15% alc./vol. while other strains can tolerate up to 18% alc./vol. Lower alcohol-tolerant yeasts can cause fermentation to cease and become stuck when high alcohol levels are required – for example, in the production of Sauternes- or Port-style wines. For these high-

Text continued on page 210

Table 4-4: Properties of White Labs' home winemaking yeast strains

Yeast strain (Strain #)	Champagne (WLP715)	Avize (WLP718)	Sweet Wine (WLP720)	Steinberg-Geisenheim (WLP727)	Chardonnay (WLP730)
S. species	bayanus	cerevisiae	cerevisiae	cerevisiae	cerevisiae
Recommended for	Dry, crisp & esp. sparkling wine	Complex white varietals, esp. barrel fermented	Wines with residual sweetness	White varietals where high fruit & esters are desired	Whites where enhanced varietal character is desired
Type of wine	Dry white; Sparkling	Dry white	MS / Rosé; Sweet	Dry white; MS / Rosé	Dry white; MS / Rosé
Example of varietals	Sparkling C; Vl	C	Gw, R, White Z	Gw, R	C, CB, PG, SB
Fermentation temperature range	21–24° C 70–75° F	16–32° C 60–90° F	21–24° C 70–75° F	10–32° C 50–90° F	10–32° C 50–90° F
Alcohol tolerance	17%	15%	15%	14%	14%
Rate of fermentation	moderate–high	slow	moderate	moderate	moderate
Foam production	moderate	low	low	low	low–moderate
Flocculation	low	low	low	low	low–medium
VA production	low	medium	low	low	low
SO_2 production	low	low	low	low	low
ML compatibility	less	less	more	more	more
H_2S production	low	low	low	low	low
Nutrient requirements	normal	normal	normal	normal	normal

Table 4-4, *continued*

Yeast strain (Strain #)	French White (WLP735)	Merlot Red (WLP740)	Assmanshausen (WLP749)	French Red (WLP750)	Cabernet Red (WLP760)	Suremain Burgundy (WLP770)
S. species	cerevisiae	cerevisiae	cerevisiae	cerevisiae	cerevisiae	cerevisiae
Recommended for	Whites where a creamy, rich texture is desired	Reds that must ferment to dryness	Whites for spicy, fruity aromas; reds for enhanced velvety texture	Classic Bordeaux-type blends	Full-bodied whites & reds	Barrel-fermented whites & reds that emphasize fruit aromas
Type of wine	Dry white	Light young red; tannic red	Dry white; light young red; tannic red	Light young red; tannic red	Dry white; tannic red	Dry white; light young red; tannic red
Example of varietals	SB, Sé	CS, CF, M, PN, S	PN, Z	CS, CF, M	C, CB, M, Sv	C, PB, PN
Fermentation temperature range	16–32° C 60–90° F	16–32° C 60–90° F	10–32° C 50–90° F	16–32° C 60–90° F	16–32° C 60–90° F	16–32° C 60–90° F
Alcohol tolerance	16%	18%	16%	17%	16%	16%
Rate of fermentation	moderate	moderate	slow	slow/moderate	moderate	moderate
Foam production	low	low	low	low	low	low
Flocculation	low	low	low	low	low	low
VA production	low	low	low	low	low	high
SO_2 production	low	low	low	low	low	low
ML compatibility	more	more	less	less	more	more
H_2S production	low	low	low	low	low	low
Nutrient requirements	normal	high	normal	normal	normal	high (to avoid VA)

Table 4-5: Properties of Wyeast's home winemaking yeast strains

Yeast strain (Strain #)	Pasteur Champagne (4021)	Chateau Red (4028)	Chablis (4242)	Chianti (4244)
S. species	bayanus	cerevisiae	cerevisiae	cerevisiae
Recommended for	Dry, crisp, & esp. barrel fermented whites, & sparkling	Early-drinking reds & as well as reds for aging	White varietals with extremely fruity profile, high esters, & "bready," vanilla notes	Rich, very big, bold, well-rounded reds
Type of wine	Dry white; sparkling	Light young red; tannic red	Dry white; MS / Rosé	Tannic red
Example of varietals	Gw, Mu, PB, SB	CS, CF, Gy, PN, S	C, CB, Gw, PG	N, Sv
Fermentation temperature range	13–24° C 55–75° F	13–32° C 55–90° F	13–24° C 55–75° F	13–24° C 55–75° F
Alcohol tolerance	17%	14%	12–13%	14%
Rate of fermentation	fast	slow/moderate	fast	fast
Foam production	very low	low	moderate	very low
Flocculation	medium	medium	medium	medium
VA production	medium	medium	low	low
SO_2 production	low	low	low	low/moderate
ML compatibility	less	more	more	more
H_2S production	low	low	low/moderate	low/moderate
Nutrient requirements	normal	normal	normal	normal

Table 4-5, *continued*

Yeast strain (Strain #)	Bordeaux (4267)	Portwine (4767)	Rüdesheimer (4783)	Zinfandel (4946)
S. species	*bayanus*	*cerevisiae*	*cerevisiae*	*cerevisiae*
Recommended for	High-sugar musts & rich, intense berry, Bordeaux-style reds	Dry whites & big reds with mild fruit profile, & high-sugar musts	German-style whites with rich flavors & fruity profile	High-sugar musts; restarts SF
Type of wine	Tannic red	Dry white; tannic red	Dry white; MS / Rosé; Icewine	Dry white; tannic red; Sparkling
Example of varietals	CS, CF, M, PN, PS	CS, CF, S, Z, C, CB, Mu	R, R Icewine, V Icewine	PN, S, Z
Fermentation temperature range	13–32° C 55–90° F	16–32° C 60–90° F	13–24° C 55–75° F	16–29° C 60–85° F
Alcohol tolerance	14%	14%	12–13%	18%
Rate of fermentation	moderate	very fast	slow/moderate	fast
Foam production	moderate	low	moderate	moderate
Flocculation	medium	medium	medium	medium
VA production	high	medium	low	high
SO$_2$ production	very low	low	low/moderate	moderate
ML compatibility	more	more	more	more
H$_2$S production	low	low	low	low
Nutrient requirements	normal	normal	normal	normal

Table 4-6: Quick reference guide[2] to other Lallemand yeast strains

Yeast strain	Recommendations[3]					Characteristics & usage notes
	R	W	B	LH	SF	
Uvaferm 43	✓			✓	✓	Highly recommended for restarting stuck fermentations
Rhône 4600		✓	✓			Well suited for fermenting fruit forward, elegant Rhône-style whites, Chardonnay & rosés; enhances apricot and tropical fruit aromas
58W3		✓				Enhances spicy, floral & fruit descriptors in Alsatian-style aromatic whites, e.g., Gewürztraminer & Pinot Grigio
AMH (Assmanshausen)	✓					Enhances spicy & fruity aromas & flavors, esp. in Pinot Noir & Zinfandel
BA11		✓	✓			Intensifies mouthfeel and fresh fruit aromas in whites
Enoferm BDX	✓					Minimizes color loss; enhances flavors & aromas, esp. in Merlot & Cabernet Sauvignon/Franc
BGY (Burgundy)	✓					Used mainly with Pinot Noir; not easy to use
Lalvin BM45 (Brunello di Montalcino)	✓					Slow fermentor & therefore well suited for long maceration programs; enhances mouthfeel & color stability; reduces vegetal characteristics
BM4X4	✓	✓				A blend of Lalvin BM45 and another yeast known for its fermentation reliability; similar to Lalvin BM45 but with a timelier and more secure fermentation; brings roundness to the mouthfeel & facilitates MLF
BRL97 (Barolo)	✓					Highly recommended for full-bodied, age-worthy reds, esp. Barbera, Merlot, Nebbiolo & Zinfandel

[2]Adapted from Lallemand's yeast product information. Details available at www.lallemandwine.us.
[3]R=Red; W=White; B=Rosé (blush); LH=Late Harvest; SF=Stuck Fermentation

Table 4-6, *continued*

Yeast strain	Recommendations[3]					Characteristics & usage notes
	R	W	B	LH	SF	
Cross Evolution		✓	✓			Ideal for aromatic whites & rosés with high alcohol potential, low fermentation temperatures & low nitrogen levels; recommended for Chardonnay, Chenin Blanc, Gewürztraminer, Pinot Blanc, Pinot Grigio, Riesling, Sauvignon Blanc & Viognier
CHP (Champagne)		✓		✓	✓	Has strong fermentation characteristics & ability to produce enhanced floral & direct fruit whites under low temperature & highly clarified juice
CSM (Cabernets, Merlot)	✓					Reduces herbaceous character in underripe fruit; promotes MLF
Lalvin Bourgoblanc CY3079		✓				Highly recommended for rich, full-bodied, barrel-fermented Chardonnay & *sur-lie* aging
DV10	✓	✓		✓	✓	Can ferment under stressful conditions of low pH, high total SO_2 & low temperature
Lalvin ICV-D21	✓	✓	✓			Inhibits development of cooked-jam & burning-alcohol sensations in highly mature & concentrated Cabernet Sauvignon, Merlot & Syrah; blend with ICV-D254 & ICV-D80 fermented wines for fresh, deep fruit & continuous intense sensations carrying through the aftertaste
Lalvin ICV-D254	✓	✓				Enhances mouthfeel; blend with ICV-D80 fermented reds for fuller body
Lalvin ICV-D80	✓	✓				Contributes big tannin volume with ripe fruit, smoke & a licorice finish; blend with ICV-254 or Syrah fermented wines for more tannin intensity

[3]R=Red; W=White; B=Rosé (blush); LH=Late Harvest; SF=Stuck Fermentation

Table 4-6, *continued*

Yeast strain	Recommendations[3]					Characteristics & usage notes
	R	W	B	LH	SF	
Lalvin ICV-GRE	✓	✓				Use with short skin contact regimens to reduce vegetal & undesirable sulfur components; try with Cabernet, Grenache, Merlot & Syrah in reds, & Chenin Blanc, Riesling & Viognier in whites
Rhône L2056	✓	✓	✓			Maintains good color stability & is excellent for forward-fruit reds
Enoferm L2226	✓			✓	✓	Tolerant to high alcohol; recommended for high-sugar reds & LH wines
M05		✓				Gives roundness and lower acidity in *sur-lie* aged wines; recommended for low-maturity whites from cool regions
M69		✓				Increases aromatic complexity & acidity balance of neutral white varieties; very resistant to high concentrations of sugar; recommended especially for warm region neutral whites
M83	✓		✓			Produces round & balanced rosés with enhanced fruit aromas & more stable color
MT	✓	✓				Recommended for long-aging Bordeaux varieties for increased color intensity, tannic structure, & strawberry jam & caramel aromatics
Enoferm QA23		✓		✓		Ideal for fresh, fruity, clean wines, esp. Chenin Blanc, Colombard, Sauvignon Blanc & Sémillon
R2		✓	✓	✓	✓	Helps produce intense fruit in whites, such as Gewürztraminer, Riesling & Sauvignon Blanc
RA17	✓					Liberates cherry & fruit aromas in varieties such as Gamay & Pinot Noir

[3]R=Red; W=White; B=Rosé (blush); LH=Late Harvest; SF=Stuck Fermentation

Table 4-6, *continued*

Yeast strain	Recommendations[3]					Characteristics & usage notes
	R	W	B	LH	SF	
R-HST		✓				Retains fresh varietal character (e.g., floral & mineral characteristics) while contributing body & mouthfeel in aromatic whites, such as Riesling; produces crisp, premium whites & Pinot Noir intended for aging
SIMI WHITE		✓				Contributes aromas, flavors & creamy fruit to Chardonnay
SVG (Sauvignon Blanc)		✓				Enhances typical Sauvignon Blanc varietal character (e.g., mineral, citrus & spicy notes); diminishes acidity by metabolizing malic acid; also recommended for aromatic white varieties such as Riesling & Pinot Grigio
SYRAH	✓					Offers good mouthfeel & stable color extraction, esp. in Carignane, Merlot & Syrah
T306		✓				Use in fruit-focused whites, e.g., Chardonnay, Chenin Blanc, Pinot Grigio & Sémillon, for imparting aroma characters of exotic fruit & pineapple
T73	✓					Enhances natural aromas & flavors of reds produced in hot climates
VQ15	✓					Used in concentrated reds, particularly Cabernet Sauvignon, Merlot, Syrah & Zinfandel, where a moderate fermentation rate is desired for rich, lush, balanced mouthfeel and full-bodied wines
VRB	✓					Enhances varietal characteristics & ester perception, esp. in Barbera, Sangiovese & Tempranillo; provides good color intensity & stability with increased phenolic structure
W15	✓	✓	✓			Recommended for dry whites with bright fruit & heavy mouthfeel, or light reds
W27	✓	✓				Recommended for slow & steady fermentation of whites & reds, particularly for reds where temperature control is not available; a popular choice of organic wine-makers due to low production of SO_2

[3] R=Red; W=White; B=Rosé (blush); LH=Late Harvest; SF=Stuck Fermentation

Continued from page 201

alcohol types of wines, a higher alcohol-tolerant yeast strain is recommended.

A fermentation that is either too slow or too fast can cause hydrogen sulfide (H_2S), a sulfide compound that imparts an unpleasant rotten-egg or sewer smell, and which can develop into mercaptans, sulfide compounds that impart an unpleasant rotten-cabbage or burnt-rubber smell. A moderate and steady rate of fermentation is recommended for vinification of premium-quality wines to favor maximum retention of volatile fruit aromas and extraction of other phenolic compounds although, in general, a slow fermentation is desired in whites and a quick fermentation in reds. Rate of fermentation also depends on temperature, i.e., the higher the temperature, the higher the rate of fermentation. Therefore, when selecting a yeast strain, consider the desired rate of fermentation taking into account the temperature of the surrounding winemaking area. For example, too high of a fermentation temperature will cause a yeast with a slow rate to still ferment rapidly.

Foam production is an important consideration in the selection of fermentation vessel capacity, which is also greatly affected by the amount of solids and proteins in the must. Ferment musts inoculated with higher-foam production yeast in higher-capacity vessels to avoid overflowing. And remember to choose a low-foam yeast when making wine by delestage to maximize its benefits.

Flocculation refers to the yeast's ability to become flocculent, i.e., to settle out after fermentation and sediment to the bottom of the fermentor. This is an important consideration because 1) for early-drinking wines, particularly those made from concentrates or kits, sedimentation must happen quickly to allow early racking of the wine from the spent yeast and to bottle the wine early, and 2) an appreciable amount of wine is lost depending on the volume and compactness of the spent yeast that forms at the bottom of the fermentor.

Volatile acids and acidity (VA) are vital components of a wine's bouquet, but only in very small concentrations. At higher concentrations, volatile acids will negatively affect the quality of wines and can potentially cause spoilage; therefore, choose a yeast strain that avoids the production of volatile acidity.

Although sulfur dioxide (SO_2) is naturally produced during fermentation, bacteria used in MLF can become inhibited if the amount of SO_2 exceeds the bacterium's SO_2 tolerance. Alcoholic fermentation alone may produce SO_2 beyond the bacterium's tolerance and inhibit MLF. And if you added sulfite at the start of fermentation, e.g., to inhibit wild yeast or when dealing with rot, that will further inhibit the bacteria's ability to start MLF; you will need to wait until the SO_2 reduces. If you intend to process wine through MLF, choose a yeast strain with very low SO_2 production. In addition, some yeast strains are more compatible than others with malolactic bacteria necessary for MLF, and so, select a malolactic-compatible yeast strain if you intend to process your wine through MLF. Where MLF is not desired, select a less compatible strain. Refer to section 4.8 for more information on malolactic fermentation (MLF).

Hydrogen sulfide (H_2S) in excessive amounts can be detected as an unpleasant rotten-egg or sewer smell. *S. cerevisiae* yeast, even when properly fed, may produce minuscule quantities of H_2S that cannot be detected by smell and may or may not be harmful to wine. Another source of H_2S is the condition or quality of the juice or raw material, which may contain residual elemental sulfur from late applications of vineyard sprays.

Nutrient requirements is an important consideration when producing wines where the yeast will be subjected to adverse fermentation conditions, such as in high-sugar musts, when the grapes are deficient in yeast nutrients, when using a yeast strain that produces high VA, or as a preventative measure when the source or quality of fruit or juice cannot be ascertained. Grapes from a poor, rainy, or gray rot-affected vintage will typically be deficient in yeast nutrients. Some yeast strains may also have naturally higher nutrient needs to ferment successfully. Nutrients, including nitrogen essential for healthy yeast cell growth, are recommended in all such cases to favor yeast survival, multiplication and fermentation, and to avoid potential off-flavors in the wine.

The above fermentation factors are subjective as they are interrelated, e.g., the rate of fermentation is a function of temperature and nutrient requirements. The chemical behavior of these factors also depends on the composition and quality of the must. As such, use these factors as guidelines in choosing cultured wine yeast strains for desired wine types.

In general, it is good practice to add yeast nutrients when making wine from grapes or fresh juice to ensure a problem-free fermentation. When making wine from concentrate or reconstituted juice, follow the manufacturer's instructions and add the nutrients if supplied. These types of musts may have been adjusted during the production process, and therefore do not require additional nutrients.

Yeast nutrients can be added to yeast at the rehydration stage, or directly into the must/wine before or during an active fermentation. Yeast nutrients are available in powder form and may be premixed with all the necessary ingredients, and may include

Figure 4-11: Lallemand's GO-FERM yeast nutrients

either diammonium phosphate (DAP) or a mix of sodium phosphate and ammonium sulfate, thiamin (vitamin B_1) and other vitamins such as biotin and pantothenic acid, and other ingredients. Thiamin is the most important vitamin in yeast nutrients for these to feed yeast in a successful fermentation. Generic yeast nutrient formulations or specific wine yeast nutrients are available, such as Lallemand's GO-FERM, shown in Figure 4-11, and Fermaid K, and Lesaffre's Superfood.

If using DAP or generic yeast nutrients, dissolve the powder in water and add at a rate of 10–20 g/hL of must and add to the must before the start of alcoholic fermentation, e.g., at yeast inoculation, if all fermentation pre-conditions are normal.

GO-FERM is a natural yeast rehydration nutrient enabling a stronger fermentation. Use at a rate of 30 g/hL by first rehydrating the required amount in water and then adding the selected yeast culture. Follow the manufacturer's rehydration instructions making sure not to add any other nutrients concurrently, which could otherwise inhibit the yeast.

Fermaid K is a blend of nutrients including DAP, nitrogen, minerals, thiamin and other vitamins, which achieves best results when used with yeast rehydration nutrients, such as GO-FERM. Use at a rate of 25 g/hL by first rehydrating the required amount in water and then adding it directly to an active fermentation when sugar has depleted by one-third. For example, if the starting Brix (SG) was 24.0 B° (1.101), add Fermaid K when the Brix (SG) reaches 16.0 B° (1.065).

Superfood is a complete yeast nutrient that contains yeast hulls, yeast extracts, vitamins and minerals, and is particularly recommended for sluggish fermentations or fermentations expected to produce higher levels of H_2S. Add Superfood at a rate of 50–100 g/hL.

Two other recommended natural yeast derivative nutrients are Lallemand's OptiWHITE and OptiRED shown in Figure 4-12. The following has been adapted from Lallemand's product descriptions.

OptiWHITE is a specific inactivated yeast with high antioxidant properties that protect against oxidation of phenols and aromas. It provides rounder mouthfeel, greater aromatic complexity and freshness, and better color preservation in white wines. For a round mouthfeel contribution, antioxidative color protection

Figure 4-12: Lallemand's OptiRED natural yeast derivative nutrients

and aromatic freshness, add OptiWHITE to juice at the beginning of fermentation at a rate of 30–50 g/hL. For mouthfeel contribution and better integration of wood and alcohol, add OptiWHITE post fermentation at a rate of 20–30 g/hL.

OptiRED is a natural yeast preparation used to obtain fuller bodied, more color stable, smooth palate red wines. OptiRED can be used alone or in conjunction with enological macerating enzymes such as Lallzyme EX. Add OptiRED to the must, i.e., at the beginning of red wine fermentation, at a rate of 20–25 g per 100 kg (220 lbs) of grapes. To rebalance herbaceous characters or harsh polyphenols into smoother more approachable tannins, add OptiRED post fermentation at a rate of 30 g/hL.

Use a single yeast strain only for one batch of wine, i.e., do not use different strains concurrently unless they are known to be compatible, otherwise, yeast cells from the different yeasts may start competing for valuable resources and may yield unexpected results. To take advantage of the organoleptic features of different yeast strains and create a wine with greater complexity, ferment each batch with a different strain and then blend batches as desired.

Many other specialized yeast strains are available to make Sauternes-style, Champagne-style and Port-style wines, for example. Although these strains are marketed under the wine-style name, such strains may contribute to the wine's flavors and aromas as per the intended style; however, they do not necessarily affect the sugar and alcohol contents, acidity, pH, or tannin level of the intended style. Flavors and aromas are determined by both the selected yeast strain and the vinification and winemaking techniques used. Therefore, when selecting strains with generic names, you should inquire and establish the yeast type (genus and species) and specific strain. For example, a Sauternes-style wine – a late-harvest sweet white wine produced from shriveled sugar-rich grapes affected by "noble rot" (*Botrytis cinerea* fungus) – will contain approximately 14% alc./vol. and residual sugar content greater than 100 g/L. A yeast strain labeled "Sauternes" may impart typical flavors and aromas found in Sauternes wines; however, you must ensure that the yeast strain can survive in a sugar-rich must and be able to convert the sugar into alcohol. You must also be able to cease fermentation when the desired alcohol and residual sugar contents are achieved. The yeast strain alone cannot produce the labeled style of wine on its own.

Cultured wine yeast is available in both dry and liquid formats. Dry yeast cultures come in small packets of vermicelli-shaped granules that must be rehydrated prior to inoculation – the process of adding yeast to the must – while liquid cultures can be added directly to the must. The advantages of dry cultures are that they have a longer shelf life, approximately 2 years, if kept away from moisture and if refrigerated between 4°–10° C (40°–50° F), and they are also more stable than their equivalent liquid cultures.

For home winemaking, dry yeast cultures are available in 5-g packets, good for up to 23 L (6 gal) of must, providing a rate of addition of approximately 20 g/hL. To use (refer to Figure 4-13), rehydrate one packet in 50 mL of water at a temperature between 35°–40° C (95°–105° F) for 15 minutes, or as recommended by the manufacturer. Follow these temperature recommendations strictly to avoid killing the yeast, and do **not** rehydrate the yeast longer than the manufacturer's recommended time. Use a container with a capacity of at least double the water volume, as rehydrating yeast may bubble up. Use multiple packets for larger volumes and rehydrate in the appropriate amount of water. For example, for a 100-L (25-gal) batch, use five 5-g packets and rehydrate in 5×50 mL, or 250 mL, of water.

You can rehydrate the dry yeast by adding it to water and stirring lightly. Manufacturers mention that there is no need to stir; however, a very gentle stir ensures that all the yeast will be properly rehydrated. After the rehydration period, stir the yeast culture, now referred to as the inoculum, and add directly to the must while stirring gently.

Increase the yeast rate of addition to 30 g/hL to avoid stuck fermentation in high-sugar musts, i.e., use one and a half packets for a 23-L batch. It is also recommended to supplement the yeast with nutrients, such as GO-FERM. Be sure to maintain a ratio of 1 part yeast to 1¼ parts GO-FERM. For example, add 7 g of GO-FERM with one 5-g packet of dry culture to a 23-L batch, or 10 g in high-sugar musts.

Liquid yeast cultures are packaged for inoculating up to 23 L of must. A key advantage is their ease of use; they can be simply added directly to the must, although some

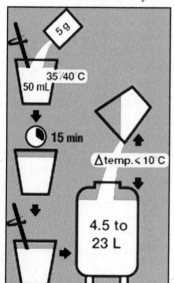

Figure 4-13: Dry yeast culture rehydration procedure

manufacturers may recommend conditioning the yeast in a small volume of must and providing a good supply of oxygen before adding the inoculum to the batch.

The use of a yeast starter is also often recommended as an inoculum to favor a successful fermentation when using grapes or when fermenting under difficult conditions, e.g., where the cellar temperature is rather cool.

A yeast starter is prepared by using a small volume of must from concentrate, fresh juice, or grape juice and adding yeast to start fermentation. This is done several days before inoculation of the entire must to be fermented. A starter volume of 2% of the must to be inoculated is recommended; for example, to inoculate a 54-L (14-gal) batch, prepare 1 L of yeast starter. Optionally, add yeast nutrients if a difficult fermentation is anticipated. With the yeast starter at room temperature, let fermentation start and once it becomes vigorous, add the starter to the bulk of the must.

If you expect a sluggish fermentation, possibly because of a high spoilage bacteria population or high pH (where SO_2 would not be as effective), treat the juice with lysozyme to inhibit the growth of bacteria. Lactic acid bacteria (LAB) can start feeding on sugar and form excessive VA, and, at high concentrations, they can inhibit yeast.

Add lysozyme at a rate of 250–300 mg/L (25–30 g/hL) of red or white must using a 5% solution or LYSO-Easy, according to instructions described in section 3.4.2.

4.7.2 CONDUCTING ALCOHOLIC FERMENTATION

Conducting alcoholic fermentation is a simple and trouble-free operation when basic precautions are followed. The chemistry of fermentation is a well-understood science, and various enological products and techniques are now available to ensure successful fermentations in home winemaking.

And this is the part of winemaking where there are significant differences in fermenting reds and whites. Namely, reds are macerated and fermented in open vats at relatively higher temperatures, and pressed near or at the end of alcoholic fermentation. Whites are almost never macerated, and the pressed juice is immediately transferred to a closed container and inoculated with a yeast culture to start fermentation, which is carried out at a much cooler temperature. The following details the specific differences.

Red wine fermentation

In red winemaking, following any cold soak maceration, the vigorous phase of fermentation is carried out in an open fermentor – a vat or other open container. To minimize the effects of oxidation,

215

to reduce the risk of spoilage and to keep dust and fruit flies away from the fermenting must, cover the open fermentor with a heavy plastic sheet or tarpaulin. This will help maintain a protective layer of carbon dioxide over the fermenting must therefore minimizing the risk of oxidation or spoilage. Account for must/wine volume expansion during fermentation to prevent overflowing by allowing approximately 25% headspace volume in fermentors.

As a first step prior to yeast inoculation, allow the must to reach a suitable temperature by adjusting the temperature in the surrounding area. The temperature should be well above the yeast's minimum fermentation temperature, and ideally, it should be at least at 20° C (68° F), but not much higher considering that heat from fermentation will quickly and easily rise to 30° C (86° F) or more on its own. Place a large floating thermometer in the must for the duration of fermentation to monitor the temperature continuously, and adjust the surrounding temperature as required to maintain a proper fermentation environment. Fermenting red must can easily exceed the prescribed maximum temperature very quickly if not controlled and, therefore, can inhibit yeast activity, which can cause fermentation to become stuck.

Take an initial sugar content reading to determine the starting Brix (SG) and potential alcohol level. Record all must measurements and quantities of chemicals and ingredients added so "recipes" can be adjusted in the future. If something should go wrong, the evolution of the wine can be traced from these records. A handy winemaking log chart is provided in Appendix C and is also available for download at www.vehiculepress.com.

When ready, inoculate the must with the hydrated or liquid yeast culture or starter and nutrients, if any. Fermentation should start within 48 hours following inoculation, or earlier if the temperature is higher than the recommended range.

Once fermentation begins, monitor progress on a daily basis by taking two Brix (SG) and temperature measurements, one in the morning and one late afternoon, and mapping the measurements on a fermentation curve. Fermentation should progress according to the curve shown in Figure 3-3 on page 112.

*Caution: Fermentation of large volumes of must will release asphyxiating quantities of carbon dioxide gas. To eliminate any potential health hazards, properly ventilate the fermentation area to the outside. And **never** conduct fermentation in a closed container without the use of a properly functioning fermentation lock; otherwise, consequences of an exploding fermentor can be disastrous.*

When fermentation has subdued and the Brix (SG) is below −1.3 B° (0.995), rack the wine and transfer it to another fermentor, and press the pomace to extract the press-run wine. If you prefer less phenolic extraction, optionally, you can rack and press when the Brix (SG) reaches 7.6 B° (1.030), and then ferment the wine in a closed container. Fermentation can be safely assumed to be complete when the Brix (SG) is steady at −1.3 B° (0.995) or lower for a few days. Red wine fermentation will typically last about 7 days, depending on fermentation temperature and other environmental factors. If you can adequately protect the wine against oxidation and microbial spoilage, carry out an extended post-ferment maceration, as outlined in section 4.3, to extract more tannins. Additionally, if you want to enhance varietal aromas, you can add pectolytic enzymes to the wine at the end of fermentation to help release aromatic compounds. One such enzyme is RAPIDASE AR2000, shown in Figure 4-14. Add at a rate of 2–3 g/hL of wine by first dissolving the powder in ten (10) times its weight in wine. For example, if you need to add 2 g into your 100-L (25 gal) batch, dissolve the powder in 20 mL of wine, introduce the mixture into the wine **after fermentation**, stir thoroughly, and let stand for at least 2 months. Lastly, to prevent further enzymatic reactions and stability problems, inactivate the pectolytic enzymes with a bentonite treatment following the waiting period. Refer to section 5.2.1 for more information on the use of bentonite.

For fermentation from concentrate or reconstituted juice, where there is no maceration, follow the same racking regimen as above, ensuring that the Brix (SG) is steady at −1.3 B° (0.995) or lower for a few days before the final racking.

In all cases, do not leave the wine for too long on its gross lees

Figure 4-14: RAPIDASE AR2000 pectolytic enzymes

(the heavy sediment formed during fermentation) to avoid potential spoilage from a reaction known as autolysis. This reaction is a result of decaying dead yeast cells. The gross lees consist mainly of dead yeast cells and grape solids when vinifying from grapes (although fresh juices do include some grape solids in suspension). The length of time a wine spends on the gross lees is also dependent on the health of the grapes at crush or harvest. For instance, you should separate the wine from the gross lees as soon as possible if grapes are from a vintage with a high percentage of rot. Sediment formed after the removal of the gross lees are referred to as fine lees. Refer to section 4.7.3 for a detailed description of gross lees and how to use fine lees for crafting different styles of wine, and section 5.1.1 more information on the timing of racking operations.

Throughout the fermentation period up until completion, test the wine for the presence of H_2S, which can be detected as a rotten-egg or sewer smell. If detected early, you can easily correct this potential problem by racking with aeration without adversely affecting the quality of the finished wine. Otherwise, prolonged presence of H_2S can ultimately spoil the wine. Refer to section 14.7 for a description of how to treat H_2S.

When fermentation is complete, measure key parameters to determine the level and timing of any adjustment that may be required; at a minimum, measure TA, pH and free SO_2 content. TA and pH will have decreased and increased, respectively, while the SO_2 content may have increased slightly due to SO_2 generated by fermentation, or perhaps even decreased depending on your winemaking. For example, if the must or wine has been subjected to racking operations, the free SO_2 content may have decreased. Make necessary SO_2 additions at this time to achieve your desired free SO_2 level.

At this point, you can clarify and stabilize the wine; however, it will improve greatly if first allowed to age for up to 6 months in a cool place. During the aging period, change the sulfite solution in fermentation locks monthly. Monitor the wine level in all containers and top up as required. If cellar temperature rises, remove some wine, as it will expand when it gets warmer. When this happens, there is a danger the wine will come into contact with the sulfite solution in the fermentation lock as it overflows and spills. The wine can spoil if the sulfite solution has not been changed as it may have developed spoilage organisms. Rack the wine again before clarification if it has been aged.

White wine fermentation

In white winemaking, musts should always be fermented in a properly air-locked fermentor, for example, a glass carboy or a stainless steel tank, to minimize the risk of oxidation, and with 25% headspace to allow for expansion during fermentation. As white winemaking from kits is more tolerant to the effects of oxidation, manufacturers often instruct that the vigorous fermentation should be conducted in an open container. Undoubtedly, closed-container fermentation reduces any risk of oxidation, and so, this is the recommended practice.

In white winemaking, in contrast to red winemaking, there is no requirement for color or tannin extraction, except in full-bodied whites, such as Chardonnay, where some very short maceration and oak-barrel aging are beneficial. Therefore, in general, there is no pre- or post-fermentation maceration of juice/wine and skins, and there is no need for a hot fermentation. In fact, a cooler fermentation in conjunction with an appropriate yeast strain is most beneficial for optimal flavor and aroma development. Cool fermentation in white winemaking has a number of benefits essential in making fruit-forward wines.

Most important, the cooler fermentation, usually carried out in the 13°–18° C (55°–65° F) range, significantly slows down fermentation and allows slow aromatic development enabled by a yeast strain specifically chosen to enhance aromas. The temperature must be maintained above the yeast's minimum fermentation to avoid a stuck fermentation. Depending on environmental factors such as temperature and Brix (SG), fermentation can potentially take several weeks.

As great effort goes into aromatic development, the cooler fermentation preserves the subtle flavors and aromas by minimizing the loss of precious flavor and aromatic compounds that could easily be volatized with an otherwise vigorous fermentation. Additionally, you can add pectolytic enzymes at the end of fermentation to enhance varietal aromas. Important side benefits of a cool fermentation include reduced risk of microbial spoilage and oxidation owing to the lower temperature.

Most white varietals, including those that will be used as a base for making white (*blanc de blancs*) sparkling wine, will benefit from cool fermentation. Examples of wines and styles include unoaked Chardonnay, Sauvignon Blanc, Pinot Grigio (Gris), Gewürztraminer, and Riesling. Red varietals that will be used as a base for making white (*blanc de noirs*) or rosé sparkling wine or to make a rosé still wine using white winemaking techniques will also benefit. Examples of wines and styles include Gamay, Grenache, Pinot Noir, and Zinfandel for making rosé wine, and Pinot Noir for making *blanc de noirs* sparkling wine.

In the case of winemaking from fresh juice or grapes, allow the juice to settle for up to 24 hours in a closed container and then rack to another carboy or tank in preparation for fermentation. Be sure to maintain a cool environment, e.g., below 13° C (55° F) if possible, during the settling period to avoid a spontaneous fermentation from wild yeast. This is not required for winemaking from concentrate or reconstituted juice.

Take an initial sugar content reading to determine the starting Brix (SG) and potential alcohol level. Record all must measurements and quantities of chemicals and ingredients added so "recipes" can be adjusted in the future. Use the handy winemaking log chart provided in Appendix C to record your analytical data.

Assuming you do not have the luxury of temperature-controlled, stainless steel tanks and are instead working with carboys or similar glass containers, you will need one or more large containers that can accommodate carboys in width and height. You will be immersing containers in a chilled-water bath. A 350-L (92-gal) plastic vat, such as the one shown in Figure 2-9 on page 76, works well for this purpose.

Choose an appropriate yeast strain for 1) cool fermentation and determine its temperature range from the manufacturer's specifications, and 2) optimum aroma and/or mouthfeel development. Your desired cool fermentation temperature will need to be slightly higher than the yeast's minimum temperature.

Rack the juice from the sediment and transfer to a clean and sanitized carboy. To reduce the risk of a stuck fermentation, use yeast nutrients, such as GO-FERM, at a rate of up to 30 g/hL by first adding the nutrients to water and then rehydrating the yeast in the nutrient solution as per the manufacturer's instructions. Have the juice at a slightly warmer temperature than the desired cool fermentation and add the yeast/nutrient solution. Secure the carboy with a fermentation lock and let stand. Fermentation should start within 24 hours.

In the meantime, as close as possible to the onset of fermentation, prepare the setup for cool fermentation by pouring sufficient cold water in the vat so that the carboy will be completely immersed to right above the shoulder. The water temperature should be at your desired cool fermentation temperature. Use a large floating thermometer and leave it in the water. Add ice to the water if you need to lower the temperature. Make sure you have a good supply of ice throughout the cool fermentation period to keep the temperature steady. Keep the ambient temperature as cool as possible to reduce the need to chill the water.

As soon as fermentation starts (confirmed by visual inspection), transfer the carboy to the chilled-water vat making sure that the carboy is immersed to the shoulder. Maintain the water at the desired temperature by adding ice as required. As fermentation progresses, temperature will rise and you may need to replenish ice at shorter intervals.

Monitor fermentation progress twice daily by taking hydrometer and temperature readings, and stir the sediment. Do not let temperature fall lower than the desired temperature. Map the measurements on a fermentation curve. Fermentation should progress according to the curve shown in Figure 3-3 on page 112, albeit over a much longer period of time.

Caution: Fermentation of large volumes of must will release asphyxiating quantities of carbon dioxide gas. To eliminate any potential health hazards, properly ventilate the fermentation area to the outside. And **never** *conduct fermentation in a closed container without the use of a properly functioning fermentation lock; otherwise, consequences of an exploding fermentor can be disastrous.*

Fermentation will not be vigorous but will be slow and steady, and can last several weeks, and is complete when the Brix (SG) is steady at −1.3 B° (0.995) or less for several days. For a light-bodied white wine, rack the wine from its fine lees as soon as fermentation is complete. For a fuller-bodied style wine, you can leave the wine on its fine lees for another couple of weeks while stirring the lees once or twice daily. Be sure to keep the container topped up during this time. Add pectolytic enzymes at this point if you want to enhance varietal aromas. Refer to section 4.7.3 for a detailed description of lees and how to use fine lees for crafting different styles of wine, and section 5.1.1 more information on timing of racking operations.

As in red winemaking, test the wine for the presence of H_2S, and measure TA, pH and free SO_2 content. Make necessary SO_2 additions at this time to achieve your desired free SO_2 level.

At this point, you can clarify and stabilize the wine; however, it will improve greatly if first allowed to age for up to 6 months in a cool place. During the aging period, change the sulfite solution in fermentation locks monthly. Monitor the wine level in all containers and top up as required. If cellar temperature rises, remove some wine, as it will expand when it gets warmer. When this happens, there is a danger the wine will come into contact with the sulfite solution in the fermentation lock as it overflows and spills. The wine can spoil if the sulfite solution has not been changed as it may have developed spoilage organisms. Rack the wine again before clarification if it has been aged.

4.7.3 LEES AND THE PRACTICE OF *BÂTONNAGE*

Understanding lees

Lees are the result of an enzymatic reaction called yeast autolysis, responsible for the breakdown of dead yeast cells from alcoholic fermentation. They fall to the bottom of the fermentation vessel to form a dense, creamy sludge. Contact with the lees can add complexity to wine and can give rise to desirable flavor compounds, most often described as yeasty or nutty, but also giving wine a creamy mouthfeel.

The large volume of coarse lees from the vigorous phase of alcoholic fermentation is referred to as gross lees, while the smaller volume of lees resulting from fermentation and aging following racking from the gross lees are referred to as fine lees.

Only fine lees are beneficial though, adding aroma and flavor complexities; gross lees are rich in spoilage organism nutrients and can therefore have a negative impact on wine quality. Gross lees are coarser and include not only dead or living yeast cells but also a myriad of other heavy solids such as pulp and grape skin fragments that may contain sulfur from vineyard spraying, or sulfur dioxide (SO_2) from sulfite additions. Extended contact with gross lees can cause such sulfur-containing compounds to form, which can lead to highly undesirable smells – caused by hydrogen sulfide, or H_2S – or other foul-smelling mercaptans. This can be avoided by racking wine early off its voluminous gross lees. Expect fairly significant volume loss, in the order of 10% or more, when racking gross lees.

Only fine lees – those that continue to sediment during fermentation – will be beneficial for autolysis. Fine lees **must** be stirred to obtain increased aroma and flavor complexities; simply leaving the wine in contact with the lees without stirring can actually cause H_2S to form. By stirring the lees, the yeast is re-suspended thus helping to avoid H_2S to form. Lees should be stirred for several weeks starting at the end of alcoholic fermentation and up to one year.

This technique of lees stirring, known as *bâtonnage* in French, but also referred to as *sur lie* (French for "on the lees") as is common in the Muscadet region, is a traditional white winemaking technique commonly practiced in Burgundy and the Loire Valley, for example. *Bâtonnage* is encouraged and used extensively to make for a more complex white wine in the production of Burgundian-style or rich, full-bodied California Chardonnays, and "Sur-Lie" wines of Muscadet de Sèvre et Maine from France's Loire Valley. It is also often used in red winemaking to help build the wine's structure and stabilize phenolic compounds.

Extended lees contact without stirring is also notably used in the production of crisp, brut, taste-bud-teasing bubbly crafted in the traditional method, such as Champagne, to impart its typical, unmistakable yeasty aromas. There are no gross lees in the production of sparkling wines, and the fine lees need not be stirred as the wine is protected in a sealed bottle under the high pressure of carbon dioxide gas resulting from bottle fermentation. Autolysis of the fine lees can last several years in some of the most expensive Champagnes and other fine sparkling wines of the world. Champagne houses are increasingly marketing their non-vintage sparkling wines with some indication of aging on the lees on labels.

For example, the label might state that the wine was *Mise en Cave en 1997*, or laid down in the cellar in 1997 for its second (bottle) fermentation, and *Dégorgement – 2ème Semestre 2000*, or disgorged in late 2000, for a total of approximately three years of aging on the lees.

Bâtonnage – Stirring the lees
In Burgundy, a *bâtonnage* cane, such as the one shown Figure 4-15, is used for stirring lees in barrels. The practice of *bâtonnage* in barrels and the *bâtonnage* cane are described in more details in section 8.4.1.

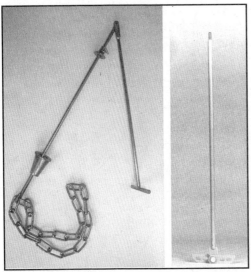

Figure 4-15: Bâtonnage cane and stirring rod

A stirring rod, such as the one shown Figure 4-15, is as an efficient tool as the *bâtonnage* cane and is better adapted to all types of containers including tanks and glass containers. It consists of a rod, which can be attached to a cordless drill, with two plastic paddles that pop up horizontally when the rod is spun. The advantage of this apparatus is that it will come in handy when stirring in fining agents in preparation for clarification.

Be sure to sanitize the cane or rod thoroughly with a caustic solution followed with a sulfite solution prior to use, and rinse completely after use.

Start the lees stirring regimen at the end of fermentation, once a day initially, and then progressively reduced to once a week for a maximum total duration of 12 months depending on the extent of *sur-lie* aging desired. Don't over-stir and don't stir too fast, which would hasten oxidation; however, stir sufficiently to get all lees back into suspension uniformly in the wine. You will need to get close to the lees and all along the bottom surface of the container to ensure that all lees are stirred back into suspension. Also, be careful to avoid over-foaming the wine and making a mess in your cellar or fermentation area; fermentation might be complete but the wine has a lot of dissolved carbon dioxide gas still that can cause vigorous foaming. A variable-speed drill will prove most useful for this purpose.

During the *sur-lie* aging period, maintain the temperature between 18°–20° C (64°–68° F), and a free SO_2 level of approximately 35 mg/L, adjusted up or down based on the wine's pH.

Note: Refer to section 4.8 on free SO₂ restrictions when the wine is to undergo malolactic fermentation (MLF). MLF will also benefit from much-needed nutrients present in fine lees.

Following the lees contact period, rack, fine and/or filter as you would any other wine. Although still done in the Muscadet region, the practice of bottling wine unracked and unfiltered straight from the fermentation vessel is not recommended. It is difficult to rack without getting some lees in the bottle, which would otherwise affect clarity and, more important, it would make the wine unstable and prone to renewed fermentation.

4.7.4 CARBONIC MACERATION

A vinification technique known as carbonic maceration can be used to initiate alcoholic fermentation for styling young, fruity wines that can (should) be drunk within a few months of their production. Carbonic maceration is used to make nouveau-style wines, such as the popular Beaujolais Nouveau, and only applies to winemaking from grapes.

Carbonic maceration triggers fermentation within whole (uncrushed) berries to extract the maximum amount of fruit from grapes. As opposed to full-bodied red wines where the juice is allowed to macerate with the grape skins to extract maximum phenols, including color and tannins, in addition to the fruit, nouveau-style wines macerate for only a short period of time resulting in much reduced phenolic extraction. The result is a light-bodied wine with oodles of fruit and very little tannin that must be drunk within a few months. It is not meant to age; it will actually deteriorate fairly rapidly, usually well within a year, because tannin is what gives wine its structure and contributes to its aging potential. Additionally, carbonic macerated wines have a lower total acidity because malic acid content is reduced, therefore further reducing aging potential.

Carbonic maceration uses carbon dioxide (CO_2) gas to trigger fermentation inside the berries, usually without the addition of cultured yeast, instead relying on indigenous yeast. Grapes are placed in a pressure-resistant, stainless steel tank under a layer of CO_2 gas. The berries essentially consume CO_2 to start fermentation and then the yeast starts to feed on the sugar inside the berries. During this fermentation, referred to as intracellular fermentation, flavor compounds are extracted to give these wines their characteristic fresh fruit aromas, and only a small amount of sugar is converted to alcohol – up to approximately 2% alcohol.

Intracellular fermentation in itself would therefore not be sufficient in making the final wine. Alcoholic fermentation is also required to run in parallel by allowing some juice from crushed grapes to interact with wild or cultured yeast to convert sugar into alcohol to obtain a wine with 11%–12.5% alcohol. The juice is obtained by either crushing a small portion of the grape volume, or by letting the weight of the grapes crush and split grapes at the bottom of the fermenting vat. As the juice at the bottom of the vat starts fermenting, it gives off CO_2 gas and provokes intracellular fermentation of whole berries sitting on top.

As alcoholic fermentation progresses, whole berries undergoing intracellular fermentation become softer and start bursting to release wine. To minimize phenolic extraction, free-run wine is separated only three or four days after the start of fermentation. Free-run wine is essentially wine obtained without any pressing. The must, which will still contain whole but soft berries, is then pressed to extract wine. This press-run wine is still rich in sugar content and is therefore added to the free-run wine, and alcoholic fermentation is then allowed to complete to dryness (the point at which, for all practical purposes, there is no more sugar to ferment).

Wines vinified by carbonic maceration will have a lower total acidity than wines vinified by traditional winemaking. Less acidity is extracted during carbonic maceration, and this in the presence of indigenous lactic acid bacteria. The reduced acidity creates a favorable environment for the lactic acid bacteria to convert the naturally occurring, sharper malic acid into the softer lactic acid by malolactic fermentation (MLF). Refer to section 4.8 for more information on malolactic fermentation.

Since carbonic macerated wines are to be drunk less than a few months after harvest, they need to be fined and filtered to ensure they remain stable once bottled.

Although the exuberantly fruity Gamay grape is used in making red Beaujolais Nouveau, other grape varieties with low tannin content such as Pinot Noir, Carignan or even Concord can be used. Grape varieties such as Cabernet Sauvignon are too tannic and would not be compatible with the light, fruity nouveau-style wines. White nouveau-style wines are also possible using fruity grape varieties having a high acid content, such as Sauvignon Blanc, for example. Low-acid varieties would result in a flat wine with no life or freshness.

Simplified carbonic maceration

Carbonic maceration as practiced by commercial wineries requires special equipment such as pressure-resistant tanks and CO_2 injection apparatus. A simplified variation of carbonic maceration, known as partial carbonic maceration, is the easiest and most practical method for home winemakers for producing red or white nouveau wines. This simplified technique described here does not require any carbon dioxide addition, and unlike true carbonic maceration, it makes use of cultured yeast to start fermentation.

For partial carbonic maceration, crush a portion of the grapes into an open plastic fermentor (vat), for example a minimum of 25% of the total weight, and inoculate with a wine yeast specifically recommended for fruity, light, young red wine, such as Lalvin 71B-1122 strain, Red Star Pasteur Red or Côte des Blancs strains, White Labs Assmanshausen, or Wyeast Chateau Red. Add sufficient yeast for the estimated amount of must, assuming a rough yield of 70 L (18 gal) for every 100 kg (220 lbs) of grapes. There is no need to sulfite at this point since the primary fermentation will be very quick, and you do not want to risk inhibiting the MLF with a high free SO_2 level.

Add the remaining grapes as whole clusters in the same vat, on top of the crushed grapes. Cover the vat tightly and secure with a thick plastic or tarpaulin. This is particularly important if you will not be submersing the cap by punching down. Carbon dioxide gas produced from fermentation will protect the grapes from microbial spoilage if the plastic is tightly secured. If you cannot contain the gas to protect the fermenting juice, break and punch down the cap very gently to avoid damaging the whole berries, which would otherwise affect the fruit flavor extraction during intracellular fermentation. Intracellular fermentation is what gives the wine its desired softness, fruitiness, and low tannic content. If not all the berries burst, it should not be a cause of concern, as they will burst during the pressing operation. If possible use a variable-capacity, floating-lid tank or fill your vat as much as possible to minimize the amount of air over the grapes. This should not be of concern if the fermentation starts rapidly, say within 24 hours. It is more important in the case of white wines because they are more prone to oxidation effects.

During the maceration/fermentation phase, keep the temperature at around 30° C (86° F). Fermentation will occur within the berries and therefore not all the fermenting juice (wine) will burst out of the berries. Let fermentation run its course to dryness – the hydrometer should read –1.3 B° (0.995) or lower – which can take between 4–10 days. For a lighter, less tannic wine style, rack the wine after 3–4 days of fermentation.

Rack or drain the free-run wine into a glass container. The remaining "fermenting" grapes may still very much look like whole berries. Carefully transfer these to the winepress and extract the press-run wine. Transfer the press-run wine to the same glass container with the free-run juice, or alternatively, in a separate container if you wish to vinify free- and press-run wines separately. Beaujolais Nouveau wine is usually blended at this stage. Seal all containers with a fermentation lock, and ferment all wines to dryness.

Let the MLF run its course either naturally, or preferably by inoculating the wine with lactic acid bacteria to avoid a stuck MLF. Be sure to follow the manufacturer's instructions on using lactic acid bacteria culture and guidelines on free SO_2, pH and temperature, which if not observed, may inhibit MLF. For example, the free SO_2 level may need to be below 10 mg/L with a pH above 3.2 at a temperature above 18° C (64° F) for many malolactic bacteria to carry out a successful MLF.

Once the MLF has completed, rack the wine, sulfite between 10–20 mg/L, or the equivalent of 1–2 Campden tablets per 20-L batch, and add a fining agent, such as Kieselsol to clarify the wine, which is particularly effective in low tannin wines. Follow the manufacturer's instructions on adding Kieselsol and let the wine clarify for a minimum of two weeks, and then filter to obtain a brilliant, clear wine. Let the wine rest for a minimum of two weeks before bottling.

You can drink the wine immediately or shortly after bottling, but don't wait too long. You can chill bottles for approximately 15 minutes in the refrigerator before serving to fully appreciate the fruity aromas and freshness.

4.7.5 STOPPING FERMENTATION

There will be instances when you will need to stop an active fermentation, for example, when producing wines that require naturally occurring residual sugar, such as a sweet dessert wine or a fortified sweet Port-style wine. There are various techniques for stopping an active fermentation, but only two are practical for home winemaking: 1) deep cooling of the wine and 2) alcohol fortification. A new product, ProDessert, is now gaining popularity with commercial wineries wishing to simplify the production of sweet wines and to reduce labor and risks associated with the heavy-handed process of stopping fermentation. Refer to section 4.10 for more information on ProDessert.

Note: Potassium sorbate, used to prevent re-fermentation in a finished wine, cannot be used to stop an active fermentation. Refer to section 6.2.4 for more information on the use of potassium sorbate.

Stopping fermentation by deep cooling
Stopping alcoholic fermentation by deep cooling is a tedious and cumbersome task for home winemakers as this method requires the wine to be placed in a cold refrigerator or a freezer at a tem-

perature between –5° and –2° C (23° and 28° F). This is the ideal temperature range to quickly stop fermentation although a temperature of up to 4° C (40° F) will work. This method can only be done practically in small quantities.

To stop an active fermentation, you must first create and condition the environment to favor yeast inhibition. At the start of alcoholic fermentation, use only half the inoculum amount and do not add yeast nutrients, which would otherwise encourage fermentation and making it more difficult to stop. Conduct fermentation at the low end of the recommended temperature range. When fermentation is to be stopped, sulfite the wine to achieve a free SO_2 level of 50 mg/L and immediately place the wine in cold storage. Since fermentation will not cease spontaneously, plan to chill the wine at a slightly higher Brix (SG) than the desired final Brix (SG) to account for some residual fermentation during chilling. The time required for fermentation to completely stop depends on the temperature, the amount of sulfite present and the alcohol content. Stopping fermentation by deep cooling will require some testing and experience to determine when the cooling operation should be performed.

After two weeks, rack, clarify and stabilize the wine. Stabilization should include stabilizing filtration, also known as membrane filtration, to remove any active yeast still present, which could otherwise restart fermentation in bottled wine. Refer to section 6.2.5 for more information on stabilizing filtration. As a last step, store the wine in a cold environment, such as a refrigerator, at a temperature between 5°–8° C (41°–46° F) for up to 6 months before bottling. The wine can be further chill-proofed by adding metatartaric acid (refer to section 6.1.1).

Chapter 13 describes the use of this method of stopping fermentation to produce homemade Icewine-style wine from grape juice.

Stopping fermentation by alcohol fortification
Stopping fermentation by alcohol fortification is an effective method although the resulting wine is of a very different style because a distilled spirit, such as brandy, is added to the fermenting wine to stop fermentation. The addition of a high-alcohol spirit will invariably result in a wine with alcohol content greater than 16% alc./vol. Most yeast strains cannot survive at such a high alcohol level therefore halting fermentation. The finished wine will consequently have higher residual sugar content. Alcohol fortification is the key and most critical step in the production of Port wines.

Before stopping an active fermentation by alcohol fortification, determine the desired style of wine by establishing the desired residual sugar and alcohol levels. Alcohol fortification is very effective and, as such, fermentation will cease very quickly; therefore, time the addition of your distilled spirit of choice to coincide with your desired residual sugar level, which can be increased by adding sugar just before bottling, and alcohol level. The final alcohol content will be a function of alcohol content and volume of both the wine and the distilled spirit, and is easily calculated using the Pearson Square, outlined in section 7.4. The alcohol content in the wine before fortification is calculated as the difference in potential alcohol measured (using the hydrometer) just before fortification and before the start of fermentation. Taking a hydrometer reading after fortification will skew results because of the higher alcohol concentration, but it also assumes that fermentation will stop almost immediately. Additionally, the resulting wine will also be lighter in color since the high-alcohol spirit acts as a clarifying agent and also dilutes the wine color.

To stop an active fermentation by alcohol fortification, first determine the volume of distilled spirit required to achieve your numbers and then add that volume to the fermenting wine. How quickly fermentation stops depends on the amount of active yeast and fermentable sugar left over, the must temperature and the alcohol concentration of the distilled spirit. Here is an example to illustrate the calculations.

Example using a 20-L (5-gal) batch of wine
Initial Brix (SG) and potential alcohol level: 24.0 B° (1.101) and 12.6% alc./vol.
Desired Brix (SG) at fortification: 6.0 B° (1.023), which corresponds to 2.6% potential alc./vol.
Alcohol level of distilled spirit: 40.0% alc./vol.
Desired final alcohol level: 20.0% alc./vol.

To stop fermentation in the 20-L batch of wine and to achieve the desired final alcohol level, you will need to add 10 L of the distilled spirit, based on the Pearson Square calculation, when the desired Brix (SG) is reached. At that point, the alcohol level in the wine is 12.6 – 2.6 = 10.0% alc./vol.; after the addition of the distilled spirit, it rises to 20.0%.

4.8 MALOLACTIC FERMENTATION (MLF)

Malolactic fermentation, or simply MLF, is the partial or complete transformation of naturally-occurring, sharper tasting malic acid (think green apples) into the softer lactic acid (think sour milk products, such as yogurt) induced by indigenous or cultured lactic acid bacteria (LAB). It is not a new winemaking practice though not well understood, at least not in home winemaking; however, there has been extensive research done that has not only shed some light on this practice but has also turned MLF into a hotly-debated topic in academia and the industry.

Until recently, the practice was fairly straightforward: 1) malo (winemaking jargon used to describe the action of letting a wine go through MLF) medium- to full-bodied reds since they would benefit from it, 2) in whites, only malo full-bodied varieties such as Chardonnays, and high-acid whites that require deacidification, and 3) do not malo white varieties, such as Rieslings, where refreshing acidity is a prerequisite.

Although recent research supports these guidelines, the decision to malo or not must also be based on your desired style in terms of flavors and mouthfeel, which are primarily determined by the variety as well as the LAB. Therefore, the key to successful MLF is knowing what varieties will benefit from it, how to select a LAB culture, and how to conduct and monitor the MLF, and where MLF is not desired, how to inhibit it during winemaking and how to prevent it once wine is bottled.

4.8.1 How MLF works

MLF is a secondary fermentation occurring when lactic acid bacteria (LAB) become active in the presence of malic acid converting it into lactic acid and giving off carbon dioxide (CO_2) gas, and resulting in a decrease in total acidity (TA) in the wine. Malic acid will be converted in roughly equal proportions of lactic acid and carbon dioxide (CO_2) gas, resulting in a TA decrease equal to roughly half the malic acid concentration.

Another important MLF by-product is diacetyl, responsible for the common buttery/nutty flavor found in malolactic-fermented Chardonnays, although not desirable in reds.

As for the bacteria, there is "good" LAB and there is "bad" LAB. The latter can cause off-flavors in wine or spoil the wine altogether. Examples of bad LAB include bacteria from the *Lactobacillus* genus, which can give a spoiled-milk taste to wine, and bacteria from the *Pediococcus* genus, which give wine an oily texture and which produce a high level of diacetyl, giving wine an objectionable buttery or cheesy smell. The main good LAB for MLF are from the *Oenococcus* genus, and are often referred to as malolactic bacteria, or MLB, to differentiate them from bad LAB.

MLB may be indigenously present in fresh grape juice or wines to cause what is known as a spontaneous MLF, or can be inoculated with a selected MLB culture, liquid or dry, or may be acquired from oak barrels previously used for MLF.

In the spontaneous method, the wine is allowed to ferment (alcoholic) to completion and stored in a cold room or cellar during the winter months. As the cellar temperature rises in the spring months, the wine temperature rises to a level favoring MLF. This explains why carbon dioxide bubbles re-appear in the spring. This method poses a potential microbial infection risk, as the wine is stored for several months at a low sulfite concentration, and results can be unpredictable because the type of bacteria cannot be ascertained. Undesirable bacteria, or even bad LAB, may spontaneously set off MLF and impart off-flavors and aromas to the wine. Spontaneous MLF also produces significantly higher levels of biogenic amines, such as histamine, which are believed to be responsible for red wine headache. Unless you have experience in relying on and controlling spontaneous MLF using indigenous bacteria, the many unknowns can make this very risky and potentially result in spoilage.

In the inoculation method, selected LAB capable of converting the malic acid are used as the MLB culture. This method allows winemakers more control, and the MLF period is usually much shorter, therefore, reducing the risks of unsuccessful MLF or microbial infection.

Relying on bacteria from a previous MLF in oak barrels or, better yet, adding a selected culture will yield reliable and predictable results, and also provides more control on the process and therefore reduces the risks of a stuck MLF.

Generally, MLF adds complexity to wine and is most beneficial in red wines. Highly tannic, malolactic-fermented red wines can be drunk earlier because the acidity is much reduced, and the astringent sensation imparted by tannins is softened appreciably.

However, not all grape varieties or styles of wine will benefit from MLF; in fact, some wines, particularly aromatic whites, will be negatively affected possibly to the point of being undrinkable. The flavor transformations and/or acid reduction may simply not be compatible with the varietal at hand, or may contribute unpleasant off-flavors that include acetic acid, wet leather, mousiness, or rancid yogurt. Therefore, MLF is generally not recommended for white wines, except for Chardonnay and highly acidic grape varieties.

MLF lowers a wine's TA and raises its pH level, and is therefore recommended for wines with high TA – due to malic acid – and low pH but it is not recommended in wines with a low acid concentration because the wine would have little acidity and be too thin or flat. As explained in section 3.2, you should first establish which acids are present in a wine as well as their relative concentrations before proceeding with MLF, or any acidification or deacidification procedures for that matter, to ensure that a proper balance

231

between TA and pH is maintained. The reason is that different acids, contributing to the wine's TA, have different strengths, i.e., pH.

For highly acidic white wines, use a deacidification solution followed by MLF to reduce TA. Conversely, if TA following MLF is below the desired level, you can add tartaric acid to raise TA for a more balanced wine. Do **not** use acid blends containing fermentable malic acid to avoid the possibility of restarting a second MLF.

Do **not** attempt MLF in kit wines because these types of juices have been tartrate-stabilized during their production and thus contain a very high proportion of malic acid, which would be converted to lactic acid. The wine would have very little acid, and a high pH making it very susceptible to bacterial infections.

Table 4-8 on pages 248 and 249 lists styles of wines with examples of varietals along with recommendations on whether to malo or not.

MLF does however have drawbacks and dangers for home winemakers.

Citric acid is partly transformed to acetic acid during MLF, which will increase the level of volatile acidity (VA) – an undesirable effect. The level of citric acid in grapes and wines is usually low and should not be of concern. For the same reason, do not use acid blends that contain citric acid when you need to raise the TA; instead, add tartaric acid.

Progression of MLF also requires careful monitoring and control. If allowed to progress to an unusually high pH level, the wine will oxidize prematurely and will become prone to bacterial infection. Paper chromatography techniques are used to monitor progression. Kits that include all the necessary chemicals and apparatus for paper chromatography analysis can be purchased from home winemaking supply shops. Section 4.8.6 describes the paper chromatography procedure for the determination of malic acid presence in malolactic-fermented wines. Rudimentary guidelines to monitor and control MLF are also provided below.

4.8.2 SELECTING AN MLB CULTURE

Oenococcus oenos (*O. oenos*), formally known as *Leuconostoc oenos* (*L. oenos*), is one of the most common MLB in home winemaking and is available in either liquid or freeze-dried format. Liquid cultures are easy to use as they can be added directly to wine (direct inoculation); however, they are less stable than freeze-dried cultures and therefore have a shorter shelf life. Although some freeze-dried cultures are available for direct inoculation, the majority needs to be rehydrated before inoculation, and this is the recommended practice.

Two popular, direct-inoculation liquid cultures are Wyeast Laboratories' Vintner's Choice and White Labs' WLP675 Malolactic Cultures, shown in Figure 4-16.

Figure 4-16: Wyeast's VINTNER'S CHOICE and White Labs' WLP675 liquid MLB cultures

Wyeast Laboratories' Vintner's Choice liquid culture is a blend of OSU (Oregon State University) Er1a and Ey2d *L. oenos* strains, and is available in 114 mL (4 fl oz) packages for inoculating 20 L of wine; it is particularly effective at lower pH and temperature levels.

White Labs' WLP675 Malolactic Cultures is available in pitchable vials for inoculating 20 L (5 gal) of wine. It has high tolerance to low pH (3.0), low temperature (13° C or 55° F), and high alcohol (up to 15% alc./vol.).

Lallemand offers two types of freeze-dried MLB cultures: MBR (Microbe Be Ready) for direct inoculation and STANDARD for preparing a build-up culture. Most packets are available in 2.5-g format for inoculating up to 2.5 hL (65 gal) of wine, as the smallest format. As such, these are used for inoculating large volumes in commercial winemaking but are also highly recommended for home winemaking. If you make considerable wine every year, or if you can share with fellow winemakers, these cultures are worth seeking out. They can be stored up to 18 months in a refrigerator or 30 months in a deep freezer.

Recommended freeze-dried MBR cultures include Lalvin 31 and ENOFERM ALPHA shown in Figure 4-17.

A recommended STANDARD culture is Vinquiry's MCW, shown in Figure 4-18. This strain is known for its high diacetyl contribution, and has superior tolerance to low temperatures, to pH below 3.0, and to alcohol levels up to 15%. These characteristics make this strain suitable for the most difficult MLFs. For home winemaking, this culture is available in a 2-g format for preparing 19 L (5 gal) of starter. It is also available in liquid format.

Lallemand's Lalvin Bacchus *O. oenos* MLB culture, shown in Figure 4-19, is a relatively new MLB product specifically developed for home winemaking needs. It is available in 1-g format for direct inoculation of 4.5 to 23 L (1 to 6 gal) of wine immediately following

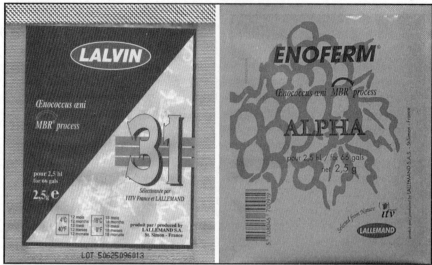

Figure 4-17: Lalvin 31 and ENOFERM ALPHA dry MBR MLB cultures

completion of alcoholic fermentation. It is effective in wine with a pH as low as 3.1, alcohol up to 13.5% and free SO_2 up to 20 mg/L.

Manufacturers may provide valuable information on culture characteristics and environmental needs such as temperature, tolerance to free or total SO_2, pH and alcohol. Table 4-7 provides typical environmental specifications for a favorable MLF vs difficult and very difficult MLFs as well as the recommended MLB

Figure 4-18: Vinquiry's MCW dry STANDARD MLB culture

inoculum and method, and is depicted graphically in Figure 4-20. Tolerance to alcohol is seldom a problem unless the selected culture has an unusually low tolerance, in which case it would be inhibited by the high alcohol content. Make sure you select a culture that is appropriate for your wine's alcohol level. The other factors are more critical for successful MLF, and are described below.

4.8.3 PREPARING FOR MLF

Your first decision on whether to process the wine through MLF should first be based on the desired style; however, you also need to consider the impact on TA as MLF will reduce TA, possibly appreciably depending on the concentration of malic acid. Therefore, if you do not want to reduce TA in a low-acid wine (e.g.,

234

Figure 4-19: Lalvin Bacchus *O. oenos* MLB culture

below 6.0 g/L), you should forego and inhibit MLF. A wine with very low TA will be flabby and unbalanced. Refer to section 4.8.7 for more information on inhibiting MLF.

If you need to increase the TA in anticipation of conducting MLF, do so before the start of alcoholic fermentation using tartaric acid. Do not use acid blends because they contain a different type of malic acid that does not get converted by the MLB. Some blends also contain citric acid, which may cause acetic acid formation, increase volatile acidity (VA), and impart a vinegar taste and smell.

Conducting an MLF is not difficult but can be tricky if the wine is not "MLF ready" as wine can be a hostile environment for MLB, which can easily become inhibited. Here are some guidelines on creating a favorable environment for a successful MLF.

First, for the alcoholic fermentation, select a *S. cerevisiae* yeast strain from Tables 4-2 to 4-5 that is compatible with MLF. Choosing a yeast strain that is malolactic-compatible will greatly increase the chances of a healthy MLF.

Table 4-7
MLF environmental specifications

		Favorable MLF environment	Difficult MLF environment	Very difficult MLF environment
Temperature	(°C)	>18	14–18	<14
	(°F)	>64	57–64	<57
Free SO₂ (mg/L)		<5	5–10	>12
pH		>3.2	<3.2	<3.1
Alcohol (%alc./vol.)		<13	13–15	>15
Type of inoculum		MBR or STANDARD	MBR or, preferably, STANDARD	STANDARD
Method		Distilled water	Distilled water with, optionally, apple juice	Distilled water with apple juice

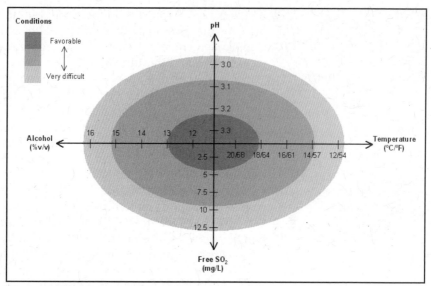

Figure 4-20: ML Growth conditions

Second, ensure that the wine's free SO_2 content is less than the maximum (typically less than 5 or 10 mg/L) prescribed by the culture manufacturer because MLB are very sensitive to SO_2. Therefore, be sure to only sulfite the must or wine very lightly for any batch that you plan to take through MLF.

Third, ensure that the pH is higher than the prescribed minimum (typically 3.2) because MLB are also sensitive to low pH. Add potassium bicarbonate at the rate of 1 g/L of wine for each 0.1 unit increase in pH required. For example, for a 20-L (5-gal) batch of wine with a pH of 3.2, 40 g of potassium bicarbonate is required to increase the pH to 3.4.

Fourth, have the wine above 18° C (64° F) throughout MLF for the bacteria to become and remain active. Warm up a cool cellar, or move the wine to a warmer room without exceeding 25° C (77° F). Alternatively, use a heating belt wrapped around the carboy or container to increase the temperature of the wine. Another option is to wait until spring warms up the cellar if it is not temperature-controlled.

Fifth, feed the MLB with plenty of nutrients, which can be found abundantly in the fine lees – the deposits formed during alcoholic fermentation. Rack the wine off its gross lees from the vigorous alcoholic fermentation, let the alcoholic fermentation complete, which will produce fine lees, but do not rack the wine. During MLF, once daily for the first week and then once a week, stir the lees into suspension **very gently** being careful not to aerate the wine excessively. Stirring vigorously will accelerate oxidation of

MLB and can potentially render these ineffective; racking would have the same effect.

Also verify the oxygen requirements of the MLB strains from the manufacturer's specifications or description as different strains have different needs. Most MLB cultures grow and survive much better with very little or no oxygen. Protect anaerobic MLB species from exposure to air by avoiding such practices as racking during MLF. And follow the manufacturer's recommendations to the letter as different MLB cultures have different environmental requirements, such as maximum alcohol tolerance.

If you expect to conduct the MLF under adverse conditions, prepare an inoculum using a STANDARD (i.e., not direct inoculation) MLB culture, and acclimatize it by diluting the inoculum into an equal volume of commercial apple juice – the kind containing no preservatives. Apple juice has a high malic acid concentration, which will "jump-start" the bacteria. For example, if the manufacturer's instructions require rehydrating the culture in 50 mL of distilled water, add the inoculum to 50 mL of apple juice. Loosely cover the container ensuring that there is little air space and let the inoculum stand for two to four days before adding it to the wine.

A word of caution! Many of the above environmental conditions favor growth of spoilage organisms. Use extra sanitary precautions to avoid potential problems. Ask your supplier for the full set of manufacturer's instructions when buying MLB culture, and strictly follow these.

Optionally, for conducting MLF under adverse conditions, you can add malolactic nutrients, such as Lallemand's OPTI'MALO PLUS, shown in Figure 4-21, to wine before inoculating with MLB culture to help absorb potential MLB inhibitors. Add OPTI'MALO PLUS at rate of 20 g/hL by first dissolving it in a small amount of wine and then adding the solution up to 48 hours before MLB inoculation.

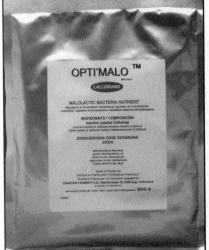

Figure 4-21: OPTI'MALO PLUS

4.8.4 TIMING OF THE MLF

MLF can be initiated at one of several different stages of vinification. Each method has its share of proponents and benefits as well as opponents and drawbacks. Pros and cons are often a matter of preferred style and not necessarily based on scientific data. The best advice is to experiment to deter-

237

mine what results work best for your style of wine. Here are the three MLF timing options.

First, MLF can be initiated at the same time as yeast inoculation or during active alcoholic fermentation, a technique known as co-inoculation, the intent being that both fermentations are concurrent; however, this is precisely what many claim as a drawback – that the two fermentations interfere with each other and compete for important nutrients. More important, the MLB can metabolize unfermented sugar and increase the possibility of off-flavors and VA, i.e., acetic acid. MLB cultures for co-inoculation that circumvent potential nutrient competition are now available.

Second, MLF can be initiated as soon as alcoholic fermentation completes, i.e., when the wine has reached total dryness, a technique known as a post MLF. This seems to be the most widely practiced method as the two fermentations are kept separate with no competition for nutrients, and the MLB has no unfermented sugar to metabolize, therefore reducing the risk of VA. In fact, in reds, MLF is best initiated on the yeast lees at this stage since the lees curtail the production of diacetyl and therefore limit the buttery/nutty flavors, which are undesirable in reds.

Third, MLF can be initiated some time after alcoholic fermentation has completed to allow the wine to age for a short period and develop more flavors, and to stabilize prior to MLF. The wine would have to sojourn in an MLF-friendly environment until MLF is initiated. Of the MLF environmental requirements, SO_2 would be the most critical since it would need to be kept low, therefore increasing the risk of spoilage. If you add sulfite during this time, you will need to reduce the free SO_2 level before initiating MLF; this could prove difficult to do and may result in a stuck MLF. For these reasons, this MLF timing method is generally not recommended, especially at higher pH since the risks are too great for the rewards.

And remember! **Never** conduct MLF in a wine to which potassium sorbate has been added (to prevent refermentation in wine with residual sugar); the result would prove disastrous – a strong, off-putting smell of geranium. Refer to section 6.2.4 for more information on the use of potassium sorbate.

4.8.5 CONDUCTING MLF

When ready to initiate the MLF, inoculate the wine with the selected MLB culture, making sure all environmental conditions are maintained favorably throughout this phase.

If using a STANDARD culture, rehydrate the content of the packet in 25 mL of **distilled** water at 25°–30° C (77°–86° F) and wait 15 minutes. Stir the inoculum lightly and then add it directly to the wine according to the chosen timing, making sure that the Brix

(SG) is at the required level. Make sure the wine's parameters, i.e., temperature, free SO2, pH and alcohol, are all within the prescribed ranges of the MLB culture. Under a more difficult MLF environment, condition and acclimatize the inoculum using commercial apple juice, as outlined above. Remember! The apple juice must not contain any preservatives.

To inoculate several batches, withdraw a 5–10% volume of wine actively undergoing MLF and inoculate another batch with this second-generation sample. For example, withdraw approximately 1 L to inoculate a 20-L batch. Be sure to minimize the sample's exposure to air. This method of cross-inoculation reduces the cost of MLB cultures to be used but does not always work as reliably as straight inoculation and is risky as you may end up cross-inoculating more than good MLB.

Conduct MLF in glass or PET carboys, stainless steel tanks or in oak barrels. Oak-barrel, malolactic-fermented wines are considered to be more complex than their glass/PET or stainless steel counterparts.

Oak barrels used for MLF will become heavily populated with MLB. Successive vintages can be malolactic-fermented in the same barrels without adding any bacteria. Simply transfer the wine to barrels, and MLF will start on its own. The challenge is in preventing formation of other spoilage bacteria. To minimize such risk, you can re-inoculate the wine each year when it is to be aged in the barrel for an extended period of time. Although the need for oak-aged, non-malolactic-fermented wines is rare, you should not use oak barrels that have previously been used for malolactic-fermented wines if MLF is not desired.

Monitor MLF progress throughout this phase, and stir the lees to re-suspend nutrients for the MLB, without over-stirring, which could otherwise inhibit MLB. During active MLF, you should notice tiny and rapid-forming carbon dioxide bubbles rising from the bottom. MLF should normally complete within approximately one to three months if temperature is held above 18° C (64° F). You can use ACCUVIN's QUICK TESTS AV–Malic Acid and AV–L-Lactic Acid strips or ML paper chromatography to determine the MLF endpoint. Alternatively, as a quick test (which should be confirmed analytically shortly thereafter), the absence of any carbon dioxide activity can be used to confirm the endpoint. You should confirm this technique of observing bubbles during MLF with the manufacturer's instructions as newer cultures on the market may behave differently.

When MLF has completed, confirmed through analytical tests, stabilize the wine by adding sulfite to obtain a free SO_2 level in the range 35–50 mg/L, optionally add lysozyme at a rate of 15–25 g/hL for microbial stabilization, top up containers and return the wine to the cellar for aging at a cooler temperature. Refer to section 6.2 for more information on microbial stabilization.

Measure TA and pH levels once the MLF has completed to determine the extent of acid reduction and pH increase, and to ensure that the wine is chemically stable. You can adjust TA and pH levels, if desired, following cold stabilization of the wine. When a wine's TA is abnormally low (high pH), increase acidity before MLF, and ideally before alcoholic fermentation, to avoid any potential spoilage problems.

4.8.6 ML DETERMINATION BY PAPER CHROMATOGRAPHY

The ability to monitor and control MLF progression is critical in achieving the desired quality and style of wine. MLF is complete when malic acid is totally converted into lactic acid, or when it is purposely stopped for a partial MLF. ML determination by paper chromatography is a qualitative, industry-accepted analytical procedure to detect the presence or absence of malic and lactic acids. When used carefully, quantitative determinations of acid concentrations can be made. The procedure is based on the ability of separating the acid components in wine, namely tartaric, citric, malic, and lactic acids. Separation is accomplished regardless of the number of components and their respective concentrations, and is based on the relative adsorption of each acid component.

The procedure, often referred to as vertical-style chromatography, uses cellulose chromatography paper, specifically manufactured for this purpose, which is immersed in a solvent (also referred to as reagent) containing a color indicator. The chromatography paper is "spotted" with reference acid solutions and samples of wines to be analyzed. As the solvent is adsorbed and travels up the paper, acid components in the reference solutions and wine samples are adsorbed at different rates and cause spots to form, which become visible as the paper dries out. Based on the relative adsorption rate of each component, a qualitative identification of components is possible as well as fairly good quantitative results, or at least relative concentrations of each acid. The different adsorption rate of each component will cause spots to travel different distances up the paper.

Paper chromatography procedure
You will need the following laboratory apparatus and chemicals to perform vertical-style paper chromatography tests:
- 20 cm × 30 cm Whatman #1 chromatography paper,
- 4-L (1-gal) wide-opening jar with a tight-closing lid,
- Disposable micropipets (capillary tubes are very expensive),

- Chromatography solvent (a solution of n-butanol, formic acid and bromocresol-green indicator) – color of solvent is orange,
- 3.0 g/L (0.3%) malic-acid solution,
- 3.0 g/L lactic-acid solution,
- 3.0 g/L tartaric-acid solution (optional),
- 3.0 g/L citric-acid solution (optional), and
- A small sample of each wine to be tested and analyzed

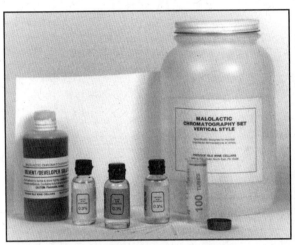

Figure 4-22: Paper chromatography kit

Inexpensive paper chromatography kits, such as the one produced and assembled by Presque Isle Wine Cellars shown in Figure 4-22, comprising of all necessary material and chemicals are available from specialized laboratories or winemaking supply shops providing wine analysis products. Assembling all required material and chemicals individually can be very costly and a challenging task. Another advantage of kits specifically designed for wine analysis is that the chromatography solvent is ready to use. References 4 [Boulton et al.], 12 [Margalit], and 15 [Ough and Amerine] in Appendix E provide detailed instructions on how to prepare the chromatography solvent.

Caution: Chromatography involves the use of dangerous chemicals and requires knowledge and experience in laboratory procedures. You should not attempt to prepare the solvent unless you are very familiar with the handling of these chemicals. Always conduct chromatography tests in a well-ventilated area as the solvent has a very powerful and irritating smell.

Using a **lead pencil** (ink will run when absorbed by the solvent), label a sheet of Whatman #1 paper as shown in Figure 4-23 with a reference dot or "x" marked on the line for each sample to be used. Label the reference dots as "T" for tartaric acid, "C" for citric acid, "M" for malic acid, "L" for lactic acid, and WS for each wine sample to be tested. Tartaric and citric acid reference dots are optional. Space the dots at a minimum of 2.5 cm (1 in) from paper

241

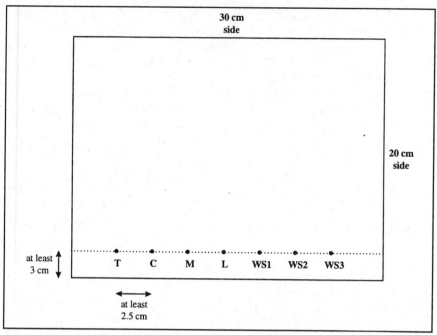

Figure 4-23: Labeling Whatman #1 paper for spotting

edges and from adjacent dots. The line with reference dots should be at least 3 cm from the bottom edge of the paper.

Using a different micropipet for each solution and wine sample, immerse the micropipet in the acid reference solution or wine sample to withdraw a small amount, making sure to spot each reference dot with the correct reference solution or wine sample. Spot each dot four (4) times being careful not to let the paper absorb too much liquid; spot lightly and quickly for best results. If you use too much liquid when spotting, these will become large and will make the analysis of results more difficult.

Once the paper has been spotted, let dry for approximately 15–30 minutes, or better yet, use a blow dryer to speed up the drying. If the spots are not allowed to dry adequately, results will be more difficult to analyze and determining relative concentrations might prove impossible.

Curl the paper into a cylindrical shape with the axis along the 20-cm side of the paper. Hold the two 20-cm ends together, without overlapping, and then staple the ends. The paper must form a perfect cylinder without the ends overlapping. This is important.

Pour approximately 100 mL of the solvent in the jar and insert the paper inside and in the solvent. The line drawn on the chromatography paper should be above the solvent level for the test to work properly. Lastly, close the jar tightly with a lid and let stand.

The solvent will start traveling up the chromatography paper and will cause separation of acid components. Spot formation will not be visible yet. Let the solvent reach the top of the paper, which can take up to 6 hours. You can leave the paper in the jar safely overnight. When completed, remove the paper from the jar and then remove the staples to uncurl it. Hang the paper to dry in a warm, well-ventilated area to volatilize the solvent and to allow spot colors to form. Return the leftover solvent to its original container; it can be reused for other chromatography tests.

After approximately 3 hours, yellowish spots will appear on the paper. Although results will be visible, spots will become much clearer after several hours or as much as one day when the paper becomes completely dry. At that point, the paper will become blue-green while the spots will have a yellowish color. Use a blow dryer to accelerate the drying time.

Interpreting chromatography results
The chromatography result is referred to as a chromatogram. Figure 4-24 illustrates a typical chromatogram showing how the spots have traveled and formed. To interpret the results, the following relationship applies relative to distance traveled:

tartaric < citric < malic < lactic

This relationship indicates that tartaric acid spots will travel the least distance while lactic acid spots will travel the most distance. You can also compare the size of each wine sample acid spot to the reference acid solution. A spot smaller in size and of lower intensity than the reference spot indicates that the acid concentration in the wine sample is less than 3.0 g/L. Similarly, a more intense and larger spot indicates an acid concentration greater than the reference 3.0 g/L-solution. This quantitative analysis is only valid if the same precise volume of each sample is used in the spotting process. The acid concentration of samples will be different when different volumes are dispensed, even if by a single drop.

In Figure 4-24, the chromatogram confirms that wine sample WS1 has not started MLF, as a malic acid spot is present and there is no lactic acid spot visible. WS1 also contains tartaric acid as well as citric acid. Wine sample WS2 has completed MLF due to the absence of a malic acid spot and the presence of a lactic acid spot. There is no citric acid present in sample WS2. In wine sample WS3, MLF has begun but is not complete. The malic acid spot has started disappearing while the lactic acid spot has started appearing. Citric acid concentration is also less than 3.0 g/L. As wine contains many other different acids, other spots may become visible

243

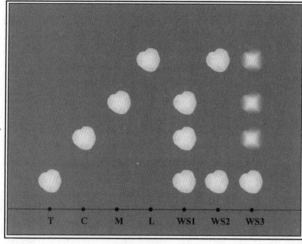

Figure 4-24: A chromatogram

depending on the acid concentrations. The spots will typically be very small or not visible as concentrations of secondary acids are very small.

Note that, due to the different chemical structure of malic acid additives, any must and/or wine acid correction using malic acid will yield invalid chromatography results. Therefore, you should perform acid correction using malic acid additives post MLF, if desired. Tartaric acid is, however, the preferred and recommended choice for acid correction.

Note: Although a malic acid spot may be absent, a small amount may still be present in the wine. Therefore, it is recommended to let MLF carry on for another week or two before stabilizing the wine.

4.8.7 INHIBITING MLF

MLF is often not desirable for certain varietals, or you may simply prefer wines that are not malolactic fermented, in which case MLF must be actively inhibited.

There are several methods, used independently or in combination, to inhibit MLF. The most effective methods include sulfiting the must beyond the prescribed maximum before alcoholic fermentation, followed by a racking, using a special enzyme known as lysozyme, or by stabilizing filtration to strip the wine of any yeasts or bacteria that might otherwise favor MLF. Refer to section 6.2.5 for a description of stabilizing filtration.

Note: Stabilizing filtration is more commonly referred to as sterile filtration; however, the latter terminology is not accurate and is misleading in a winemaking context. Stabilizing filtration is also known as membrane filtration in reference to the filter medium used.

An alternative method for white winemaking is to conduct alcoholic fermentation at a temperature between 10°–14° C

(50°–57° F), i.e., which is below the normal range for MLF. Both white and red wines must be stored within this temperature range during the maturation and aging processes to prevent MLF. You can also carry out the alcoholic fermentation with a yeast strain that is less favorable to MLF. Such strains are more competitive for nutrients, produce higher amounts of SO_2, and may produce compounds that help inhibit MLF.

Although the pH level is another parameter that can be controlled, it is not recommended to alter a wine's pH to inhibit MLF unless absolutely necessary.

Lysozyme[4]

One of the most common applications of lysozyme is suppressing LAB, both good (e.g., *Oenococcus*) and bad (e.g., *Pediococcus* and *Lactobacillus*), that could compete for fermentable sugars with some yeast strains during alcoholic fermentation. In such a case, lysozyme can be used to delay the onset of MLF until alcoholic fermentation has completed. It is also used to prevent MLF by inhibiting LAB, and is particularly effective at higher pH when LAB growth is favored and free SO_2 is less effective.

To delay MLF in red or white wines, add lysozyme at a rate of 100 mg/L (10 g/hL) of must using a 5% solution or by adding LYSO-Easy, according to instructions described in section 3.4.2.

To prevent MLF completely, increase the rate of addition of lysozyme to 200–500 mg/L (20–50 g/hL). Since lysozyme cannot absolutely guarantee complete blocking of MLF – some LAB strains may be resistant to lysozyme – it is recommended to add SO_2 concurrently with lysozyme in this application.

In red wine, use the lowest dosage whenever possible as lysozyme binds with tannins and other phenolic compounds, resulting in a decrease in mouthfeel and color. The effects, if perceptible, should be noticeable within the first few days of treatment. Always run bench tests on every wine to be treated with lysozyme to ensure results will be as expected. Test results are usually conclusive overnight, i.e., treat samples, let stand overnight, and assess mouthfeel and color in all samples the next day.

Lysozyme will cause further lees precipitation that will need to be racked. Rack approximately one week after the treatment.

4.9 STYLES OF WINE

Table 4-8 on pages 248 and 249 summarizes this chapter's techniques that are required to make specific styles of wine.

---

[4]This section has been adapted from http://www.scottlab.com/fordras.htm.

4.10 HOW THE PROS DO IT

Over the last decade or two, the average alcohol level in commercial red wines has increased steadily, very often exceeding the 14% or 15% mark. The trend is definitely to make richer, bolder, and higher alcohol wines.

Vineyards are constantly "pushing the envelope" to try and harvest higher Brix grapes without compromising flavors or quality. This may not always be possible, particularly in cooler climate winemaking regions or when high sugar development is unachievable under poor vintage conditions.

So how do the pros manage to churn out high alcohol wines even when grapes are harvested at, say, 23 B° (1.096), or approximately 12.0% potential alcohol? The answer: Reverse osmosis and vacuum distillation technologies – very expensive technologies that only big wineries can afford but few, if any, will admit to using.

Reverse osmosis (RO) – the flow of water through a semi-permeable membrane when pressure is applied to juice/wine on one side of it, also known as nanofiltration – and vacuum distillation, where must is heated under vacuum, are technologies used in concentrating the must (grape juice) by removing water content, thereby increasing the sugar concentration and potential alcohol.

Vacuum distillation is primarily used for must concentration as RO tends to be problematic with unclarified juices. RO is mainly used for removing alcohol as well as removing volatile acidity (VA) from a finished wine.

To complete the picture on modern technology and alcohol manipulation, some wineries also use a spinning-cone column that uses centrifugal force and vacuum to reduce alcohol in wines when looking for better balance in the event that grapes have not ripened to their optimum level.

Although the above technologies may seem foreign, these are all employed by wine-kit manufacturers to produce their products used by home winemakers.

Another new "technology" gaining popularity with commercial wineries is encapsulated yeast. ProDessert, one such new product from Proenol of Portugal using encapsulated technology, is used in the production of dessert or sweet wines. Specifically, ProDessert is an encapsulated *S. cerevisiae bayanus* yeast added to the must and then removed from fermentation when the desired residual sugar level is obtained. Since the yeast remains encapsulated and does not escape into the wine, there is less handling, and fermentation is easier to stop, resulting in superior wine quality. Encapsulation technology involves embedding the yeast in a calcium alginate shell that prevents the yeast from getting into the fermenting wine. The ProDessert beads are placed in a nylon bag that is then inserted and suspended in the fermenting vessel. The bag is simply removed to stop fermentation at the point that the desired residual sugar is achieved. Clever!

Table 4-8: Summary of techniques and recommended yeast strains for specific styles of wine

Style of wine	Characteristics	Ex. of varietals[5]	Crushing	Pressing	Maceration	Yeast for Alcoholic Fermentation	MLF	Oak Aging
Base for sparkling wines	High TA	C, PN, R	No	Whole-cluster	No	EC-1118, Premier Cuvée, Champagne, Pasteur Champagne**	No	No
Low-acid or aromatic whites	Low TA High aromatics	Gw, Mu, PG, V	Yes	Light	No	ICV/D-47, 71B-1122, Côte des Blancs, Sweet Wine, Steinberg-Geisenheim, Pasteur Champagne**	No	No
Light-bodied whites where refreshing acidity & fruitiness are to be preserved	Med to high TA Fruitiness Light bodied	R	Yes	Light	No	ICV/D-47, 71B-1122, Côte des Blancs, Sweet Wine, Steinberg-Geisenheim, Rüdesheimer	No	No
Light-bodied, aromatic whites where refreshing acidity & fruitiness are to be preserved but where more body is desired	Med to high TA Fruitiness Medium bodied	SB	Yes	Light	No	K1V-1116, Pasteur Champagne*, French White, Pasteur Champagne**	Partial only	No

"*"=RED STAR Pasteur Champagne; "**"=Wyeast Pasteur Champagne; [5]Refer to page 198 for a list of abbreviations

Table 4-8, continued.

Style of wine	Characteristics	Ex. of varietals[5]	Crushing	Pressing	Maceration	Yeast for Alcoholic Fermentation	MLF	Oak Aging
Full-bodied whites	Med TA, Full bodied, Higher %alc, Age-worthy	C	Yes	Moderate	No	ICV/D-47, Montrachet, Chardonnay, Chablis	Yes	Yes
Rosé	Med to high TA, Off-dry, Fruitiness, Light bodied	Gr, Z	Yes	Light	Very short	71B-1122, Côte des Blancs, Sweet Wine, Rüdesheimer	No	No
Light-bodied reds fermented by carbonic maceration (e.g., Beaujolais Nouveau)	Med TA, Fruitiness, Light bodied, Little/no tannins	Gy	Partial	Light	Carbonic	K1V-1116, Pasteur Champagne*, Assmanshausen, Chateau Red	No	No
Light-bodied reds	Medium TA, Fruitiness, Light bodied, Little/no tannins	Gy, Va	Yes	Light	During fermentation only	71B-1122, Pasteur Champagne*, Suremain Burgundy, Chateau Red	Yes	Short, if any
Medium- to full-bodied reds	Med TA, Full bodied, Higher %alc, Age-worthy, High tannins	CS, CF, M, PN, S, Z	Yes	Full	Cold soak and/orPost-fermentation	Bourgovin RC 212, Pasteur Red, French Red, Bordeaux	Yes	Yes

"*"=RED STAR Pasteur Champagne; "**"=Wyeast Pasteur Champagne; 5Refer to page 198 for a list of abbreviations

5
CLARIFICATION

Wine can only be fully appreciated if it is clear and free of suspended particles and/or sediment. Although sediment in premium wines is acceptable, if not expected, and often considered a sign of quality by wine connoisseurs, winemakers need to control the type of sediment that will form and that is considered acceptable. That being said, sediment in young wine is generally not acceptable, just as cloudiness and haze are unacceptable in any wine, and are considered faults because these point to physical or chemical instabilities (and poor winemaking) that affect physical appearance and organoleptic qualities. Wine must be adequately processed to prevent such instabilities and faults.

Stabilization is the winemaking practice of safeguarding juice and wine from the time the must is handled in preparation for vinification, through vinification and aging, to bottling and until consumed, and "includes two sorts of operations: one to counter physical and chemical changes and another to counter microbiological changes."[1]

[1]Robinson, Jancis, ed. THE OXFORD COMPANION TO WINE – THIRD EDITION. Oxford: Oxford University Press. 2006. pp 661-662.

In this chapter, we are specifically concerned with clarification – the general class of physical and chemical stabilization processes used to achieve and maintain clarity throughout the wine's life, and includes racking, fining and filtration. Other classes of physical and chemical stabilization processes, such as cold stabilization and protein stabilization, are discussed in section 6.1. Stabilization processes to counter microbiological changes are discussed in section 6.2.

Traditional clarification of wines is achieved strictly through sedimentation and racking only because it is considered a natural process. Suspended particles are allowed to naturally precipitate to the bottom before the wine is separated, or racked, from the sediment. Wine can also be clarified using fining agents that coagulate and precipitate particles in suspension, or by mechanical filtration.

Whereas racking is always used in clarification, fining and filtration are optional and are used according to the winemaker's practice and intended style, most often dictated by when the wine is to be drunk; for example, early-drinking wines are always filtered. Clarification by fining or filtration is a much-debated topic in winemaking circles. Traditionalists believe in natural, non-interventionist winemaking methods that do not make use of "chemicals" or even mechanical processing in the belief that such processing alters the wine's structure, taste and color, and hence quality. Modern winemakers, on the other hand, advocate the use of fining agents and filtration although many do not filter their premium wines; in general, filtration is a shunned practice for ultra-premium wines. Many commercial premium wines are now labeled "unfiltered" – a marketing tactic to promote unfiltered wines as being of higher quality. However, Émile Peynaud, one of the greatest enologists of the twentieth century, commented on "the sensory consequences of filtering" in his book KNOWING AND MAKING WINE [reference 16], "that the mechanical action of filtering has never had a negative influence on quality."[2]

In general, wine is clarified throughout vinification by several rackings, and if desired, by fining after alcoholic and malolactic fermentations, and optionally by filtration prior to bottling. In red winemaking from grapes, you should always expect some amount of sediment in the bottle, depending on the extent of clarification, particularly when the wine is aged for an extended period of time, because red musts have a high concentration of total dissolve solids (TDS). On the other hand, red wines from concentrate, which are fined, filtered and bottled quickly, will not throw any

[2]Peynaud, Émile. KNOWING AND MAKING WINE. Spencer, Alan F., tr. New York: John Wiley & Sons, Inc. 1984. p. 307.

sediment because concentrates have the lowest concentration of TDS.

5.1 CLARIFICATION BY RACKING

Fermentation, fining and stabilization winemaking processes produce sediment that needs to be separated, or racked, from the wine. Racking wine from its sediment is key to producing clear and stable wines free of substances that might otherwise interact with the wine when bottled. Racking is performed either by gravity by siphoning wine from one container to another or by using a pump. Figure 5-1 illustrates the setup to rack wine from its sediment by gravity. Section 2.5.2 describes the siphoning procedure. Figure 5-2 illustrates how to rack using PET carboys and accessories; racking of wine is done completely under the protection of an inert gas.

If you are working with tanks, racking wine could not be easier. Simply connect an appropriate hose to the racking valve, open it, and let the wine flow into another container, such as an oak barrel; no pump is required as long as you are racking to a

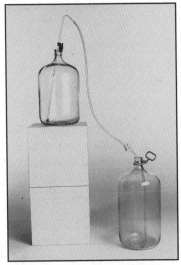

Figure 5-1: Setup for racking wine by gravity

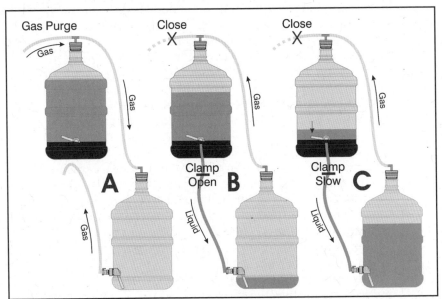

Figure 5-2: Racking made easy with Better Bottle containers and accessories

container below the wine level in the tank. The screen behind the racking valve inside the tank, if so equipped, prevents large solids from flowing out. If the tank is not equipped with a screen, filter the wine through a basket sieve while racking.

Although you can rack wine as little or as often as you deem necessary, notwithstanding the negative effects of over-processing and extended exposure of wine to air, a clear wine requires a minimum recommended racking schedule. Racking according to the recommended schedule will help prevent development of bad flavors from autolysis if wine is left in contact with the gross lees for an extended time, or at least reduce any such risk. White and red wines require slightly different racking schedules.

5.1.1 RACKING SCHEDULE

For white wines, the first racking is performed on the pressed juice approximately 24 hours following pressing to allow the mud-like sediment to settle to the bottom of the container. This first racking is done before yeast inoculation and the start of alcoholic fermentation, and is only required for winemaking from grapes or fresh juice if previously unracked by the producer.

For red wines, the first racking is performed from the primary fermentor to closed containers near or at the end of the alcoholic fermentation phase or following any post-ferment maceration. The timing of this first racking depends on the desired level of phenolic extraction. For the first racking, either let the free-run wine flow from the fermentation vat or container through the faucet, if so equipped, before transferring the leftover pomace to the wine-press for pressing, or transfer the pomace and then rack the wine.

A second racking is recommended at the end of the alcoholic fermentation phase, which produces heavy sediment, or gross lees. Wine to be malolactic-fermented can either be racked once, following both fermentations, or twice, i.e., just before MLF and right after completion of MLF. The latter is recommended as the finer lees provide nutrients beneficial for malolactic fermentation (MLF). Racking can be performed when the Brix (SG) has stabilized at -1.3 B° (0.995) or lower for at least 2 weeks for a dry wine.

The third racking follows fining and stabilization procedures, and prepares the wine for bulk aging. The amount of sediment depends on the extent of the fining procedure, the fining agent used, and if the wine is cold stabilized. The timing of the third racking depends on the fining agent and any stabilization. Guidelines are provided in relevant sections.

A fourth and final racking is required after the wine has aged and is ready for filtration or bottling. The amount of sediment is relatively smaller than in previous rackings although it may still be significant depending on vinification and winemaking methods used. This fourth racking is not required for red wine vinified by carbonic maceration, as it will not undergo any aging and is intended to be bottled immediately after fining, stabilization and filtration.

If the wine is to be oak-aged, rack every 3–6 months. Extracted oak tannin will act as a clarifying agent causing suspended particles to sediment. Heavily fined oak-aged wines will throw a heavy deposit and will require very careful racking. You can achieve excellent clarity without the need for filtration if the wine is aged for an extended period of time, e.g., more than 18 months, although some sediment in the bottle is to be expected, which many consider a sign of high quality.

5.1.2 TOPPING UP

Racking always results in a smaller volume of clear wine as the sediment volume is separated and discarded. The lost volume should always and immediately be replaced with more wine using a procedure referred to as topping up. The practice of topping up wine in containers and oak barrels is required to minimize exposure of the wine to air that could cause spoilage. By maintaining minimum air space – known as ullage – between the bung and the wine surface, the risk of spoilage is greatly reduced.

Through careful planning and management of your total wine production and capacity, using different size containers, you can easily ensure that these are always topped up. You can transfer any small volume of wine left over following racking to smaller containers, which minimizes the volume of topping wine required. You should preferably use the same wine from the same vintage for topping. If this is not possible, use wine of the same variety and quality from a previous vintage. Unless done in very small proportions, do not use water to top up as this will dilute the wine, which can result in a thin wine with diluted flavors and aromas, particularly if the wine is already light.

Alternatively, when you cannot fully top up a container, store the wine under a layer of non-toxic inert gases – a technique used by commercial wineries – to protect the wine from oxidation. Use beer gas (CO_2+N_2) for larger operations or a can of Private Reserve, shown in Figure 5-3, which contains a blend of nitrogen, carbon dioxide and argon gases, available

Figure 5-3: Private Reserve for protecting wines from oxidation

255

from wine shops or liquor stores. This blend is tasteless and inert, and therefore does not alter the composition or organoleptic qualities of the wine.

If you do not top up containers regularly and allow the ullage to increase, you risk causing excessive oxidation that could result in volatile acidity (VA), acetic spoilage and/or mycoderma. Acetic spoilage, or acetification, is caused by *Acetobacter*, the aerobic vinegar bacterium responsible for acetic acid and ethanol oxidation. Mycoderma is the more advanced and irreversible condition of excessive oxidation resulting from the presence of film-forming yeast from the *Mycoderma* genus. This condition will manifest itself by a white film forming on the wine's surface, as shown in Figure 3-16 on page 148, and is impossible to completely eradicate to produce a good wine.

Using a keg for topping barrels

Barrels will need regular topping to replace wine absorbed by the wood and that evaporates through barrel joints. On average, barrels need topping once a month; however, frequency depends on factors such as cellar temperature and humidity, size, age and condition of barrels, and type of wine. If your winemaking involves many barrels, it can become a tricky chore, as you will need to carefully manage bottled or bulk wine for topping. The solution is a topping device that greatly eases topping many barrels and that makes wine readily available whenever you need it. No need to uncork bottled wine or leave other containers partially empty.

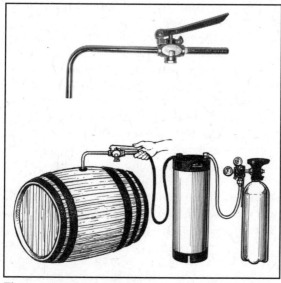

Figure 5-4: (top) A topping gun, (bottom) Topping a barrel with a topping gun

You can easily build such a topping device using a stainless steel pressure-resistant container or keg, such as a Cornelius soda keg and a topping gun, shown in Figure 5-4. Specifically, you will need:

- 9.5- or 18.9-L (2.5- or 5.0-gal) Cornelius keg, depending on our topping volume needs

- One keg disconnect (black) for wine and one keg disconnect (gray) for gas
- Gas tank fitted with a nitrogen regulator, filled with nitrogen gas
- Stainless steel topping gun or food-grade faucet
- ¼-in and ½-in tubing for gas line applications
- ¼-in adapters

Assemble the equipment as per Figure 5-4 and use the following instructions for topping up.

1. Sanitize all equipment that will come into contact with wine.
2. Transfer bulk wine to be used for topping into the keg. Fill to just under the inlet port (the tube protruding just below the top portion of the keg, on the inside; the outlet port has a tube protruding from the top to the bottom of the keg on the inside), and replace the keg lid making sure it is airtight.
3. Fit the nitrogen regulator on the nitrogen tank and attach a ¼-in tube on the regulator using a ¼-in adapter.
4. Connect the ¼-in tube from the regulator to the **gray** keg disconnect. Snap the keg disconnect to the IN port of the keg.
5. Purge the headspace in the keg by opening the relief valve on the keg lid and by opening the gas tank and regulator valves. Let the gas run for approximately 10–15 seconds to displace air out of the keg. Close the relief valve and then the regulator valve. Listen for any sound emanating from the keg lid seal. If you detect any sound, then the seal is not airtight, in which case you will need to reposition the lid or change the seal if the problem persists.
6. Connect a ¼-in tube from the **black** keg disconnect to the topping gun. You may need a ¼–½-in adapter depending on your gun assembly. Make sure that the topping gun valve is in the CLOSED position and snap the keg disconnect to the OUT port of the keg.
7. To top barrels or other containers, open the regulator valve slightly and then open the valve on the topping gun. Wine should start flowing from the keg through the gun. Increase the pressure if wine does not flow, but stop as soon as it does as very little pressure is required. Try and keep pressure well under 1 bar to avoid excessive pressure in your system and to avoid dissolving gas into the wine.
8. When finished topping, close all valves, remove both keg disconnects, and clean the wine line and gun. The remaining wine in the keg is protected by nitrogen gas; however, it is recom-

mended purging the headspace once a week to ensure against any gas that may have leaked out.

5.2 CLARIFICATION BY FINING

In home winemaking, fining, the process of clarifying wine using products known as fining agents that coagulate and precipitate particles in suspension, is required for early-drinking wines produced from fresh juice or grapes. These have higher concentrations of total dissolved solids (TDS) and proteins that will cause sediment in the bottle and clarity instability that could result in cloudiness in wine. Wines from concentrate or reconstituted juice are designed for quick production and bottling and therefore should also be clarified by fining to achieve clarity quickly.

The choice of a fining agent depends on the type of wine (white or red) to clarify, tannin concentration, desired results relative to color, and lees compactness.

Fining agents have varying levels of effectiveness in white and red wines because the latter have a much higher concentration of phenolic compounds, namely, anthocyanins (color pigments) and tannins. Tannin concentration is the most significant difference in the context of clarification and may cause improper clarification with some fining agents resulting in a cloudy wine or bottle sedimentation.

Table 5-1
Recommended fining agents and their compactness rating

Fining agent	White wine	Red wine	Lees compactness
Bentonite	Yes	Yes	Poor
Casein	Yes	No	Good
Egg whites	No	Yes	Good
Gelatin	Yes*	Yes	Good
Isinglass	Yes	No	Poor
Kieselsol	Yes	Yes	Good
Pectic enzymes	Yes	Yes	Good
PVPP	Yes	Yes	Good
Sparkolloid	Yes	Yes	Poor
Tannin	Yes§	Yes	Good

*Requires the addition of tannin. Refer to section 5.2.4.
§Only if used in conjunction with gelatin.

Wines, white and red, will always become lighter in color as suspended particles naturally precipitate; fining agents hasten this process but should not negatively impact color. Over-fining (when too much of a fining agent is used) can strip wine of color; therefore, you need to be careful to use only the recommended dosage rate and to properly time the addition of the fining agent and racking of the wine.

Different fining agents will create varying amount and compactness of lees, which will impact the volume of wine and make the racking operation easier or more difficult. Some agents are known to create a voluminous or non-compact deposit. Compactness is rated in terms of lees density as either poor or good. For example, a fining agent with a poor lees compactness rating will cause a greater volume of sediment to form and/or may require a second racking as sedimentation is less effective. Fining agents with a poor lees compactness rating will result in an appreciable reduction of wine volume.

Table 5-1 lists commonly available fining agents, shown in Figure 5-5, for clarifying white and red wines, including lees compactness rating for each. Although grape tannin is not classified as a fining agent, proper clarification often depends on the presence of tannins, and so it will be treated as a fining agent in this section. Activated carbon is considered a fining agent but it is not discussed here as such because its use is not recommended in healthy wines; rather, it is used to treat flawed wines. Specifically, activated carbon is used to reduce or remove brown color or "bad" odors or flavors. Refer to section 14.4 for more information.

Always dissolve fining agents in **water**, unless specified otherwise, before adding to the wine to be clarified. Fining agents lose their effectiveness if dissolved or introduced directly into the wine.

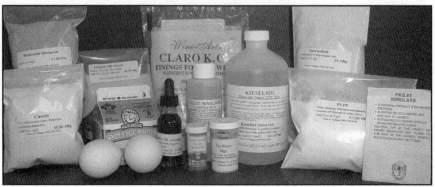

Figure 5-5: Fining agents

Conducting bench tests

Fining is part science, and part art and experience. Fining agent effectiveness can vary based on the rate of addition, pH and composition of the wine (e.g., acids, proteins, phenols), temperature, and other factors that can influence results. As with any wine additive or winemaking operation, you should be able to predict results to understand the impact on wine quality before any fining agent addition or fining operation is performed on the whole batch. If you are unsure about the expected results of a fining agent, for example, because you have never clarified that specific varietal before with that fining agent, or if you are using a fining agent for the first time, you should conduct bench tests, or laboratory tests, as they are commonly known in the industry, before using the fining agent in a batch of wine.

Because no two wines are ever the same from a chemical composition standpoint, experienced winemakers, particularly in commercial winemaking, most often conduct bench tests to avoid any surprises prior to bottling. This year's Cab may require a different rate of addition of your favorite fining agent or perhaps a different agent altogether from last year's vintage.

To conduct a bench test, start with a small volume of wine sample, for example, 1 L (¼ gal). Measure and record as much data about the wine as possible including TA, pH, as well as a qualitative assessment of color, aromas, flavors, body, and tannin concentration. Proceed with the fining operation of the test sample according to the instructions, rate of addition and fining (settling) period for the selected fining agent. Start with the lowest rate of addition in the recommended range and increase the rate as desired based on results. Rack the wine sample at the end of the fining operation.

Once again, perform quantitative and qualitative assessments, and compare these results to the initial assessments. Are the results as you expected? Have there been any significant changes in any of the data points? If you are satisfied with the results, proceed with fining the entire batch of wine; otherwise, try increasing or decreasing the rate of addition if the clarity of the wine does not seem to have changed or if the color has become too light, respectively. Temperature of the wine may also affect the results, and you may need to shorten or extend the fining period accordingly. If the results are simply not satisfactory, perform a bench test using a different agent.

Bench tests are critical in achieving desired results. Choose the right fining agent for your wine, and understand its effect to predict the results. Avoid any surprises!

5.2.1 BENTONITE

Bentonite is a natural absorptive type of clay that binds to and precipitates oppositely charged suspended particles. It is used in clarifying both red and white wines although highly recommended for white wine applications because it inhibits haze caused by naturally occurring proteins in juice (refer to section 6.1.2). Bentonite's clarifying effectiveness makes it a popular choice as a fining agent amongst winemakers although the heavy deposit translates into more wine loss. One of its advantages over other fining agents is that it minimizes color reduction and therefore provides a safeguard against over-fining.

Bentonite is added as a solution to wine after the first or second racking, or before cold stabilization, but it can also be added to must **before** the start of alcoholic fermentation, a technique known as counterfining, to improve fining in high-protein musts.

Add bentonite at a rate of 25–100 g/hL of must or 25–50 g/hL of wine if the addition is to be done at the end of fermentation. Prepare a bentonite solution by adding the granules to a volume of warm water equal to 10–15 times its weight, e.g., 50 g in 500 mL, in a closed container. Shake the solution vigorously for a few minutes, and then let it stand for 24 hours while shaking the container occasionally during this period. The granules do not absorb water easily; you may need to stir the content a couple of times until all the granules absorb water and form a thick, heavy sludge. Bentonite's effectiveness is much reduced if not dissolved properly.

Add the solution at a rate of 10 mL/L to must or 5 mL/L of wine, and stir well. Using the above example, this rate provides 1.0 g (50 g × 10 mL ÷ 500 mL) of bentonite per liter of must, or 100 g/hL, or 0.5 g (50 g × 5 mL ÷ 500 mL) of bentonite per liter of wine, or 50 g/hL. Store wine treated with bentonite at a temperature between 15°–25° C (59°–77° F) during the fining period. Rack the wine as per your kit's instructions or when the wine is crystal clear.

When making wine as a base for sparkling wine, reduce the rate by approximately one half to ensure a good effervescence and a good refermentation in the bottle.

Note: Bentonite inactivates enzymes, and specifically, it should not be used concurrently with lysozyme. Refer to section 6.2.4 for more details on using bentonite and lysozyme.

5.2.2 CASEIN

Casein, a phosphoprotein of milk that flocculates to absorb and precipitate suspended particles, is primarily recommended for clarifying white wines, especially for reducing tannin content in

261

Figure 5-6: Fining with egg whites

over-oaked white wines, and for reducing browning resulting from oxidation. Drawbacks include color stripping if excessive casein is used, and requires a second fining with bentonite to avoid clogging filter pads when wine is to be filtered.

Add casein at a rate of 50–100 g/hL of wine by dissolving the powder in a small volume of water – use 100 mL of water for each gram of casein powder – and then quickly add the solution to the wine while stirring vigorously. To avoid over-fining, use the lowest rate of addition and increase if the wine was aged in oak barrels. Rack the wine after a couple of days or within one week at the most. For white wines affected by browning due to oxidation, increase the rate of addition to the maximum depending on the severity of the problem. Follow the casein fining with a bentonite treatment.

Warning: *You should rack casein-fined wines very carefully because some people may experience allergic reactions to casein. Do not disturb the sediment during racking and rack until the wine is just above the sediment level to avoid getting sediment into the wine.*

5.2.3 EGG WHITES

Fining with egg whites, shown in Figure 5-6, a traditional method of clarifying red wines, is still widely used in modern winemaking as it proves to be an excellent fining agent. An important advantage of egg white as a fining agent is that the loss of color is minimized. Being rich in albumen, egg white has the added advantage of softening a wine's astringency and is therefore most appropriate for highly tannic wines or wines undergoing barrel aging. Egg white fining is mainly used for wines produced from grapes.

Add egg whites at a rate of 5–10 g/hL of wine, or 1–2 egg whites per 100 L. First separate the egg white from the yolk, discard the yolk, and then add to slightly salted water. Salt prevents the solution from getting cloudy. Alternatively, use pure, refrigerated egg whites, the type sold in small cartons in your grocer's dairy section. Typically, approximately 30 mL (2 tbsp) of pure egg white is equivalent to 1 large egg white. For each egg white, dissolve a pinch of table salt in 100 mL of water and then combine with the egg white. Add the saline egg white solution to the wine directly into the barrel and stir gently but thoroughly. Rack the wine in 1–2 weeks, no later.

5.2.4 GELATIN

Gelatin, derived from animal tissues, is a good fining agent for red wines because of its affinity to bind with phenols in precipitating suspended particles and for reducing tannin content. For this reason, it is usually not recommended for fining white wines as it will reduce the amount of tannins, and in fact, may not fine adequately if the tannin content is too low. To avoid over-fining with gelatin in white wines, add grape tannin powder before the gelatin fining. For excessively tannic red wines, gelatin is an excellent fining agent. Red wines vinified by carbonic maceration will benefit from a gelatin fining if the tannin content is too high. It is also effective in fining wine with high pectin content, which could otherwise cause haze in bottled wine.

Add gelatin at a rate of 1–5 g/hL of wine, or up to 25 g/hL for wines having a higher-than-normal concentration of suspended particles or having high pectin content. Prepare a gelatin solution by soaking (unflavored) gelatin powder in approximately 25 times its weight of warm water. For example, if you want to add 10 g/hL of gelatin in 20 L (5 gal) of wine, then dissolve 2 g of gelatin in 50 mL of warm water. Stir the gelatin thoroughly until completely dissolved. Some gelatin manufacturers may recommend soaking the gelatin in cold water and then heating it to parboil.

Mix the warm gelatin solution with a little wine – about twice the amount of water used – and then add to the rest of the wine, and stir the wine thoroughly. Rack the wine in 2–3 weeks time.

5.2.5 ISINGLASS

Isinglass, a pure gelatin prepared from the swim bladders of cichlids (tropical spiny-finned freshwater fishes), is a popular fining agent amongst home winemakers because it acts quickly and it strips color to a lesser extent than other protein-based fining agents such as gelatin or casein. It is most effective in clarifying white wines, particularly oak-aged whites. A drawback is that it throws a heavier deposit that tends to cling to the carboy glass wall making racking a little tricky. A second fining with bentonite alleviates this problem and avoids clogging filter pads when wine is to be filtered.

Isinglass is available either in liquid format used at a rate of up to 1 mL/L of wine, or in powder format, used at a rate of between

1–3 g/hL of wine. The powder format has proven to be more effective.

Dilute liquid isinglass in a small quantity of **wine** and then stir the solution into the wine after fermentation is complete.

When using the powder format, completely dissolve the isinglass powder in water at a temperature between 16°–18° C (61°– 64° F) and stir thoroughly. Let the solution stand for 15 minutes and then stir again for 2 minutes. Add the solution to the wine and stir vigorously for 2–3 minutes. Rack the wine in 2–3 weeks time.

5.2.6 KIESELSOL

Kieselsol, a silicate suspension that electrostatically binds to and precipitates proteins, is an excellent fining agent for both white and red wines and is specifically effective in wines with low tannin content. Kieselsol is therefore recommended for wines produced from concentrate, reconstituted or fresh juice, or wines that have not been oak-aged in barrels.

Kieselsol is most often used in conjunction with gelatin, such as Wine-Art's Claro K.C., to increase its effectiveness. Separate packages are required for white and red wines as the necessary gelatin quantities are different.

Add the kieselsol suspension at a rate of 25–50 mL/hL of wine, **directly into the wine** and stir gently. After 24 hours, add gelatin to the wine as per the instructions above or as per the package's instructions. Rack the wine in 2–3 weeks time.

5.2.7 PECTIC ENZYMES

Pectic enzymes are not classified as fining agents but they greatly improve fining and filtering operations of high-pectin white and red wines by breaking down pectin, which occur naturally in wine but are often the cause of cloudiness. Pectic enzymes are especially beneficial for press-run wines (from grapes) as well as fruit and country wines because these tend to have much higher pectin content. Pectic enzymes can also be used at crushing to increase the yield of free-run juice or as a preventive additive to minimize the potential of pectin haze formation.

Add pectic enzymes at a rate of 1–2 g/hL or 2–4 g/hL of must or wine, for whites and reds, respectively, or as per the manufacturer's instructions. First dissolve the powder in cool water and add the solution to the must following the crushing operation, as a preventive additive, or following fermentation for fining. The must or wine should be at a minimum temperature of 27° C (80° F) for pectic enzymes to be effective.

If cloudiness persists after fining, it is an indication that the wine may contain excessive pectin. To test for the presence of pectin, add 50 mL of wine to 200 mL of methanol. If heavy whitish sediment forms, the wine contains excessive pectin and you should treat it again with pectic enzymes until it becomes clear. It is highly recommended that you filter wine treated with pectic enzymes to further clarify the wine.

Caution: Methanol is poisonous. Be sure to discard the methanol-treated sample immediately following the test to avoid mistaking it for a wine sample and ingesting it.

5.2.8 PVPP

PVPP, short for polyvinylpolypyrolidone, is a synthetic polymer that is effective in absorbing and precipitating polyphenols responsible for browning in wines as well as excessive bitterness in red wines. PVPP can also be used as a preventive fining agent to avoid such problems.

Add PVPP powder **directly to wine** at a rate of 25–75 g/hL of wine. Settling occurs very fast, as fast as 1–2 hours depending on the type of PVPP used, which must be racked immediately after settling. For example, two popular PVPP products are Polyclar V and Polyclar VT. Polyclar V acts in as little as 1–2 hours and is used at a rate of 10–35 g/hL and must be filtered following the racking operation. Polyclar VT is used at a rate of 25–75 g/hL and does not require filtering although it is strongly recommended.

Note: There are different PVPP formulations requiring different rates of addition and shorter or longer settling periods. The above instructions are provided as guidelines; be sure to follow the manufacturer's instructions for the PVPP product you purchase.

5.2.9 SPARKOLLOID

Sparkolloid, a proprietary fining agent derived from alginic acid salt found in brown algae, is very effective in settling finely suspended particles and is therefore recommended for red wines although suitable for white wines also. A benefit of Sparkolloid's effectiveness is increased filter throughput, when the wine is to be filtered, due to the greater extent of lees compactness.

Although Sparkolloid is a very effective fining agent, it has disadvantages. It will tend to throw very heavy sediment causing an appreciable loss in wine. More important, the fining operation requires a much longer period of time – up to 6 months – to allow proper sedimentation of particles in suspension. To accelerate the fining operation for earlier bottling, you can use a second fining agent recommended for red wines. Perform the second fining at least one month following the Sparkolloid fining.

Add Sparkolloid add at a rate of 10–40 g/hL of wine. First prepare a Sparkolloid solution by boiling water in an enamel, stainless steel or other heat-resistant saucepan. Add the Sparkolloid powder to the boiling water and stir well. Let the solution boil for 20 minutes while stirring continuously to dissolve all the powder. Add the hot Sparkolloid solution to the wine and stir well. Let the wine clarify for approximately 6 months before racking.

Scott Laboratories has developed a new formulation, Cold Mix Sparkolloid NF, which can be dissolved into water without the need for boiling; you simply need to add the Sparkolloid solution to wine and stir thoroughly. The rate of addition is 12.5–25 g/hL.

When using Sparkolloid to clarify white wines, you will need to add grape tannin to the wine, several days before fining, if the tannin content is too low.

5.2.10 TANNINS

Tannins play a determining role in a wine's structure, mouthfeel and aging potential. A secondary but very useful role in winemaking is their ability to precipitate proteins that are often the cause of haze in cloudy wines, a condition known as protein haze, which can be difficult to clear. As such, it is an effective fining agent in both red and white wine applications.

During red wine aging, tannins and proteins bind to precipitate, which clarify the wine naturally and also results in a corresponding reduction in tannin concentration. In white wines, which inherently have a low-tannin concentration, tannins are used to avoid over-fining when using protein fining agents, such as gelatin or casein, which have an affinity in binding to tannins.

Add enological or grape tannin powder at a rate of 10–30 g/hL, or up to 50 g/hL when fining high-pectin wines with gelatin. Prepare a tannin solution by dissolving the powder in warm wine and then add it directly to the wine batch, 3–5 days before adding the fining agent. Stir the solution in thoroughly and then rack the wine in 2–3 weeks. Follow the manufacturer's instructions on preparing protein-fining agents.

5.3 CLARIFICATION BY FILTRATION

The effects of wine filtering on quality are a much-debated topic amongst winemakers. Many seldom filter their premium-quality wines and deem that fining is sufficient and believe that filtering strips wine of key organoleptic ingredients and alters its color, while many traditional winemakers still opt for natural winemaking and forego both fining and filtering operations. The decision to filter, then, is up to the winemaker and the style of wine to be crafted, namely, is the wine to be consumed early or is it intended for aging?

Young wines produced for early consumption should always be filtered, with or without fining; otherwise, unfiltered young wines will still throw a deposit, even when fined. Sediment in a young wine is generally not acceptable and is a sign of poor winemaking.

Sediment in older vintage or age-worthy premium wines is very acceptable, if not expected, and many will equate that to higher quality. In these premium wines, you may opt for fining and/or filtration, or neither.

When making wine from a kit, always follow the manufacturer's instructions on fining and filtering, as the kit was designed to provide expected results according to the instructions.

Although the effects of filtering on wine quality can be debated, it is proven that filtering will yield a lighter-colored wine depending on the tightness of the filtering. The major drawback of filtration involves the additional processing time that may expose the wine to air and therefore accelerating oxidation. For this reason, you should always measure and adjust the free SO_2 content before and after filtration.

5.3.1 UNDERSTANDING FILTRATION

Filtration, the process of filtering or passing wine through a filter for the purpose of mechanically separating particles out from suspension, is used in winemaking to obtain a polished, crystal clear wine. The process involves passing wine through a filter medium – the physical, porous interface that entraps particles during filtration – or successively through a series of filter media, which mechanically separate intended particulates.

Filtration is always discussed in terms of the size of intended particulates to be filtered out, referred to as retention rating. The basic unit for specifying retention rating is the micrometer, more commonly referred to as micron (μm), where one micron, 1 μm, is defined as 10^{-6} meter. As a reference, the average size of a human hair is 70 μm.

Filter media retention ratings are often stated as either nominal or absolute. A nominal retention rating is an arbitrary retention rating value assigned to filter media to denote that particles greater than this value will be filtered out. The actual retention can vary greatly from the stated nominal retention rating. An absolute retention rating is a much more precise retention rating value assigned to filter media to denote that the majority of particles greater than this value will be filtered out. The actual retention can also vary from the stated absolute retention rating, but the variance is much smaller.

Evidently, retention ratings can be confusing because there can be a wide divergence between the stated retention and actual retention because actual retention, commonly referred to as filtering efficiency, is impacted by such factors as precision of medium manufacturing, concentration of particles, filtration capacity, and operating pressure, to name a few. We will keep it simple here and refer to filtration in terms of expected particle size to be filtered out; however, you should never expect that 100% of particles greater than the stated rating would be filtered out. In fact, even particles smaller than the rating may be filtered out.

In winemaking, clarification by filtration is specifically concerned with the removal of particulates larger than 5–10 μm for coarse or rough polishing, particulates larger than 1–4 μm for clarifying or polishing, and particulates larger than 0.5–0.8 μm for fine or pre-sterile (pre-membrane) filtration, and makes use of depth filtration technology and equipment. Membrane filtration is discussed in details in section 6.2.5.

Depending on the type and clarity of the wine, you may need multiple filtration passes of the same type; for example, a young red wine with heavy particles still in suspension might need one coarse filtration at 10 μm and a second at 5 μm before polishing filtration. Unfined, unfiltered wine will have much larger particles, particularly reds with their high color pigment concentration, which will clog up the filter medium very quickly.

In depth filtration, wine is filtered throughout the thickness of a filter medium, such as disposable, single-use depth filter sheets or pads, manufactured from layers of cellulose fibers, and non-pleated cartridge filters, which look like tall rolls of bathroom tissues, manufactured from polypropylene spun microfibers. Wine is forced through the filter medium by mechanical action, e.g., using a pump, and particulates larger than the filter medium's rating become trapped throughout the thickness. As a result, depth filtration has high particle retention or filtering capacity. Filtering efficiency can however vary significantly from the specified retention rating, and therefore, the filtering tends to be imprecise although it is sufficient for the intended application.

5.3.2 FILTRATION EQUIPMENT AND SYSTEMS

There are various types of depth filtration systems available for winemaking applications depending on your budget and annual production. A pressurized-wine filtration system that forces wine through filter pads using air pressure is sometimes used for kit wines but has the major drawback of accelerating wine oxidation, and is for this reason not recommended for premium wines. Suction or vacuum-type depth filtration systems are costlier but provide better results. These are the most popular systems in home winemaking, and equipment is available for any budget. Avoid gravity-flow and venturi filtration systems as these unnecessarily prolong the filtering operation and hasten oxidation. Such systems make use of gravity and water pressure, respectively, and are not efficient for filtering wine.

In a suction-type filtration system, wine is forced through the filter pads by a suction force and transferred into an open container, such as a carboy or tank. This system works well for small and larger productions.

In a vacuum-type filtration system, a suction force creates a vacuum and displaces the wine through filter pads and into a closed container. The complete filtering operation is performed under vacuum, therefore minimizing exposure of wine to air. The type of equipment used in this system is best suited for small productions, limited to carboys and demijohns.

The main components of a depth filtration system are the pump, the assembly that houses the filter pads, and the filter pads. The two most popular and effective filtration systems used in home winemaking are the round-plate system, mainly used in small applications, and the plate-and-frame system for larger applications. Both types use cellulose fiber pads as the filter medium.

Pumps

The choice of a good pump is essential for efficient filtration. There are several considerations when purchasing a filtration system equipped with a pump. The most important factors are the type of pump, priming requirements, the rate of fluid displacement, its maximum height above the pump, and whether the pump can or will be used for other wine processing applications, such as racking or wine transfers.

Pumps are classified according to the fluid displacement method, either positive displacement or centrifugal, and the priming method, either unprimed or self-priming. Priming refers to the process of filling a pump's cavity with the fluid to be displaced prior to the pumping operation.

Positive displacement pumps, commonly used for small-scale operations, consist of a mechanical device, such as pistons, diaphragms or impellers, which is capable of displacing a liquid by suction without the need for priming. Such pumps are termed self-priming. Although priming is not required, some positive displacement pump types cannot run dry. These pumps are often referred to as wet pumps or water system pumps as they require a liquid to be displaced for proper operation.

A water system pump, such as the one shown in Figure 5-7, works very well in filtering operations and will also prove indis-

Figure 5-7: A water system pump

pensable in racking and transfer operations. This pump model is equipped with a ¼-horsepower, variable-speed motor capable of displacing 10–15 L (2.5–4 gal) of wine per minute; the variable speed feature will come in very handy. It is also equipped with inlet and outlet adapters of varying diameters for connecting to various devices such as filtration plates and racking tubes.

An in-line strainer with stainless steel mesh, shown in Figure 5-8, is a useful add-on specifically designed to protect and lengthen the life of the check valve in the pump shown in Figure 5-7. It is placed at the input side of the pump to restrict large particles such as oak chips, grape skins and tartrate crystals from entering and damaging the pump.

Pumps, such as the diaphragm pump from Barnant Company depicted in Figure 5-9, which are capable of running dry, are termed vacuum-type pumps owing to their ability to create a vacuum in a container. This is another important consideration in the purchase of a pump. Very often, the pump will inadvertently be left to run dry and can damage if it was not specifically designed to run dry. This type of pump will also be very useful in degassing wine, i.e., wine that contains an appreciable amount of residual carbon dioxide gas from alcoholic and/or malolactic fermentation that needs to be removed in preparation for bottling.

Figure 5-8: A pump pre-filter or in-line strainer

Note: Wine to be degassed using a vacuum-type pump must be racked from its sediment; otherwise, the pump action will cause the sediment to go back into suspension.

For larger productions, a high-throughput positive displacement or centrifugal pump is recommended, although the latter can be quite expensive. Positive displacement pumps are quite affordable; the one shown in

Figure 5-9: Barnant diaphragm pump

Figure 5-10: A positive displacement pump with rubber impellers

Figure 5-10 is equipped with a 1½-hp motor and rubber impellers, and is capable of displacing up to 100 L (25 gal) of wine per minute.

Centrifugal pumps generate their pumping action by imparting a centrifugal force to the liquid to be displaced as opposed to a suction force in positive displacement pumps. The pump's cavity must be filled with juice or wine to be displaced before the pump can reach its normal operating pressure and start displacing the liquid. A centrifugal pump requiring manual priming is termed unprimed, whereas a self-priming pump will automatically fill its cavity prior to displacing the liquid. Centrifugal pumps will generally displace liquids at a higher rate than positive displacement pumps. As such, medium- and large-scale filtration systems will generally be equipped with centrifugal pumps.

If your cellar operations include displacing wine to a container placed above the pump, the pump must have the ability of delivering juice or wine against gravitational pull. Above a certain height, the pump may no longer be able to displace liquid. The maximum height above the pump that liquid can be displaced is called the head, and is usually specified on pumps by manufacturers. Determine your juice/wine displacement needs and choose a pump with an adequate head, keeping in mind that a higher head decreases the rate of fluid displacement.

If you intend to use a pump for displacing grape solids in addition to your filtration needs, choose a type that can accommodate 50-mm (2-in) hose adapters on the inlet and outlet, and that it has adequate horsepower. If you intend to move stems along with grape solids, e.g., from the crusher to a tank, you need 75-mm (3-in) hose adapters; anything less is asking for trouble. Grape solids and stems will stress the pump, which can become easily clogged and damaged if small hoses are used.

And when choosing a pump, always ensure that it is rated as food-grade, i.e., it is specifically designed with materials that are food-safe and that will not contaminate food, or juice or wine in a winemaking application. Similarly, all fittings and any other materials such as hoses that will come into contact with juice or wine should be food-grade. Particularly, stainless steel fittings are always recommended in winemaking applications; never use brass fittings as they can contribute to some lead contamination. .

Plate and plate-and-frame filtration systems

For home winemaking applications, plate and plate-and-frame systems are the most popular and most efficient models. The choice of a filtration system depends on your capacity needs, namely, the type – white or red – and amount of wine to be filtered in one operation. These will determine the required filtration surface area, and therefore, will also determine the number of filter pads for any specific system.

Two popular and practical filtration systems for small-scale home winemaking are the round-and-grooved plate model, shown in Figure 5-11, and the Buon Vino Mini Jet plate-and-frame model, shown in Figure 5-12. These are ideal for filtering small batches of up to 23 L (6 gal) of wine.

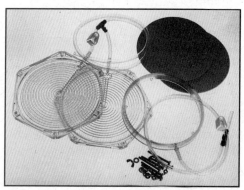

Figure 5-11: Filtration plates and filter pads

The round-and-grooved plate model consists of a short cylindrical ring with a single 8-mm (5/16-in) inlet and tubing, two grooved plates with 6-mm (1/4-in) outlets and tubing connected to a T-connector and a single tube, two disposable filter pads, and bolts, washers and wing nuts to assemble the unit.

To assemble the unit, place one filter pad in each plate with the smooth side facing the grooves in the filtration plate. Place the cylindrical ring over one pad-plate pair and then place the second pad-plate pair on top, and secure the whole assembly with bolts, washers and wing nuts. Gradually tighten opposite wing nuts to ensure even pressure around the plates' cir-

Figure 5-12: Buon Vino Mini Jet filtration system

cumferences and a tight

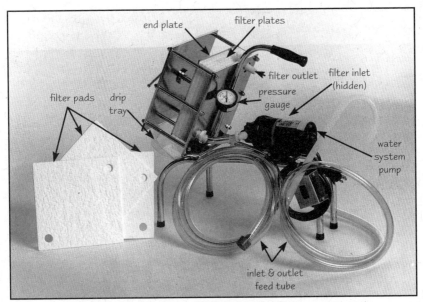

Figure 5-13: Buon Vino Superjet filtration system

seal. If the seal between the pads, cylindrical ring and plates is not proper, air will leak in and diminish filtering efficiency, and possibly not filter at all. And double-check that the smooth sides of the pads face out, i.e., the rough sides of the pads should be facing each other.

During filtration, unfiltered wine from a carboy will flow into the plates from the inlet in the cylindrical ring and into the rough sides of the pads, under the action of a pump, and filtered wine will flow out from the smooth side, through the grooves and out to the outlet tubes. The filtered wine is then collected in a second container. The water system pump shown in Figure 5-7 can be used with this filtration system in a suction-type configuration. The vacuum-type pump shown in Figure 5-9 can be used with this filtration system in a vacuum-type configuration using a special bung assembly. These configurations and the use of the special bung assembly are outlined in more details in section 5.3.3.

The Buon Vino Mini Jet filtration system consists of a plate-and-frame assembly with an integrated water system pump, three filter pads, and the necessary tubing. This type of system operates in a suction configuration.

To assemble the unit, insert a plate and pad pair in the frame assembly making sure that the rough side of the pad faces the side of the assembly with the two tightening knobs. Repeat for the second and third plate-pad pair, and then secure by tightening the two knobs. Connect the racking tube to the pump's inlet and the

Figure 5-14: Pillan F.6 filtration system

outlet tube to the outlet at the top of the assembly, and secure both tubes with fastening clips. The inlet and outlet are equipped for 10 mm (⅜-in) plastic tubing.

For medium-scale filtration, e.g., 50–100 L (13–25 gal), a plate-and-frame filtration system is recommended. Popular models include the Buon Vino Superjet, shown in Figure 5-13 and the Pillan F.6 system shown in Figure 5-14.

The Buon Vino Superjet system uses an integrated water system pump with three filter pads and plates anchored in a frame assembly, and is equipped with a gauge to monitor pressure during filtration that indicates when pads are becoming clogged. When pressure exceeds the prescribed maximum, the filter pads must be replaced. The inlet and outlet are equipped for 10-mm (⅜-in) plastic tubing. Assembly is the same as the Mini Jet filtration system.

The Pillan F.6 system is equipped with an unprimed impeller pump, a plate-and-frame assembly for six filter pads, and a pressure gauge. The inlet and outlet are equipped for 13-mm (½-in) plastic tubing.

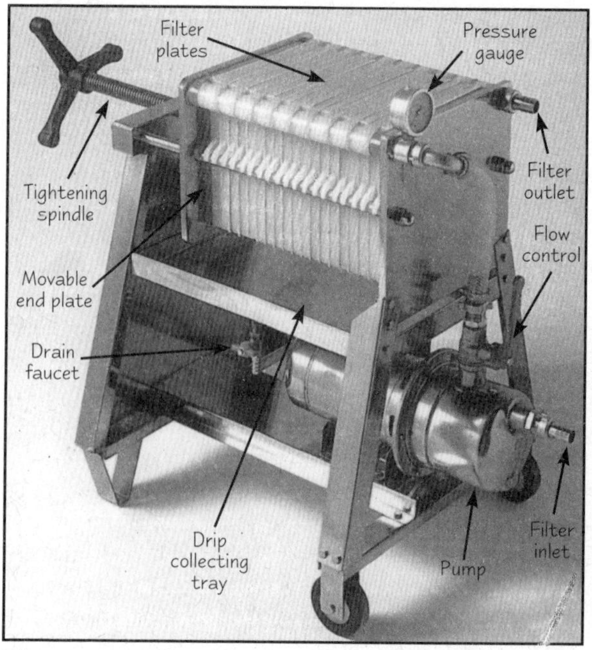

Higher-capacity plate-and-frame filtration systems using 10, 20, 30 or more filter pads, with or without an integrated pump, are also available for large-scale filtration, albeit very expensive. A typical model is the Pillan F.20 system shown in Figure 5-15, set on casters for ease of mobility, which can filter on average in

Filter plates

Pressure gauge

Filter outlet

Flow control

Tightening spindle

Movable end plate

Drain faucet

Drip collecting tray

Filter inlet

Pump

Figure 5-15: Pillan F.20 filtration system

excess of 300 L (80 gal) of wine. The filtration system's inlet and outlet are equipped for 20-mm (¾-in) plastic tubing.

Manufacturers will often state their system's filtering rate or throughput – defined in liters per hour – in their product specifications or marketing literature. Although a useful indicator, filtering rate can vary widely depending on pump characteristics, filtration type (a function of filter pad rating), clarity of the wine, and type of wine, i.e., white or red wine. Therefore, when evaluating a filtration system against your needs, use the advertised filtering rate only as a guideline.

Depth filter pads

Depth filter pads manufactured from layers of cellulose fibers come in a variety of grades, i.e., retention ratings, and sizes for various applications and volumes of wine to be filtered.

Manufacturers may assign an easy-to-remember number, code or intended type of filtration instead of a retention rating; for

Table 5-2

Depth filter pad ratings and equivalents for various manufacturers

Filtration type	MANUFACTURER							
	Buon Vino		Flomaster		Pall Seitz Schenk		Gruppo Cordenons	
	Filter grade code	µm	Filter grade code	µm	Filter grade code	µm	Filter grade code	µm
Coarse					K900	9–10		
			AF1	8	K800	7–8	CKP V4	8
	1	5	AF2	4.5	K700	5–8		
Clarifying (Polishing)					K300	3–4	CKP V8	3
			AF3	2.5	K250	2–3		
	2	1.8			K200	2.0		
					K150	1.5	CKP V12	
					K100	1.0	CKP V16	0.95
Fine (Pre-sterile)			AF4	0.8	KS80	0.8	CKP V18	
	3	0.5			KS50	0.5		
Sterile					EK	0.45	CKP V20	0.45
			AF5		EK1	0.35		
					EKS	0.25	CKP V24	0.2

example, #1 or K800 for rough polishing, and #3 or K100 for higher polishing clarity. Table 5-2 lists depth filter pad ratings from various manufacturers for selecting filter pads or for determining equivalent replacements across manufacturers for a specific filtration type.

Coarse-rated pads are mainly used for coarse or rough filtration of wines with a high concentration of suspended particles. They are used to collect and/or break down large particles but will not show a significant change in the wine. Clarifying or polishing pads are finer and are used for brightening and polishing wine. These will show a significant change in the wine's clarity and brightness. Fine and pre-sterile pads will further enhance the clarity and brightness of wine, and are typically used just before bottling to minimize sediment forming in the bottle. Sterile-grade filters are used for sterile filtration to remove any latent active yeast and/or bacteria and prevent re-fermentation, or to remove other spoilage organisms in suspension. The use of sterile-grade filters is discussed in section 6.2.5.

Pad size is also important when assessing filtering efficiency and capacity. Since pads filter throughout the thickness, the filtering volume of each pad must be considered, and given that the standard pad thickness is 4 mm (5⁄32-in), the surface area is most often used. Pads with a greater surface area will filter more effec-

Table 5-3

Key characteristics of popular filtration systems

Model	No. of pads	Type of pads	Size of pads (cm × cm)	Approximate total pad surface area (cm²)
Buon Vino Mini Jet	3	rectangular	14.5 × 13.0	525
Round plate system	2	round	22	760
Buon Vino Superjet	3	square	20 × 20	1,200
Pillan F.6	6	square	20 × 20	2,400
Pillan F.10	10	square	20 × 20	4,000
Pillan F.20	20	square	20 × 20	8,000
Pillan F.30	30	square	20 × 20	12,000

tively and more volume than pads with a smaller surface area. The total surface area is the aggregate of surface areas of all pads combined in a system. Table 5-3 lists key characteristics of various filtration systems presented in this section, including approximate total pad surface area. For example, the total pad surface area in the three 20×20-pad Buon Vino Superjet filter is 3×20×20=1,200 cm^2.

*Note: Black carbon-type filter pads are also available and are used to increase the effectiveness of the filtering operation, particularly in wines contaminated with unwanted particles. Do **not** use carbon-type filter pads for filtering healthy wines as they will be excessively stripped of color and flavor compounds.*

Reminder: Filter pads have a smooth side and a rough side. For proper filtration, always filter wine into the rough side of the filter pad and out from the smooth side. Discard filter pads after use; they are not reusable.

5.3.3 FILTRATION

The type of filter pads to use and timing of filtration depend on the type and clarity of wine, and how soon it will be bottled. The shorter the period between fermentation and bottling, the higher the need to filter, particularly if the wine has not previously been fined.

In general, it is recommended that successive finer filtering be preceded by one or more lower-grade filtrations depending on the wine's clarity and/or amount of suspended matter, or total dissolved solids (TDS), particularly for wines made from grapes or fresh juice, which have a higher TDS concentration; otherwise, the filtering operation will take a very long time or may not be possible at all if the pads clog. Specifically, first do a coarse filtering followed by a clarifying filtering and then a fine filtering. You may skip the coarse filtering in clear whites – and possibly skip clarifying filtering in well-fined whites – or reds that have been adequately fined. Kit wines also need one single, fine filtering because of the relatively low TDS concentration when properly fined.

If you are using a filtration system that accommodates different grades of pads for the same filtration type, you can do successive filtrations to prepare the wine for improved filtration efficiency in the next stage. For example, you can first filter using K300 pads followed by K200 for clarifying filtration, and then fine filter using KS80 pads.

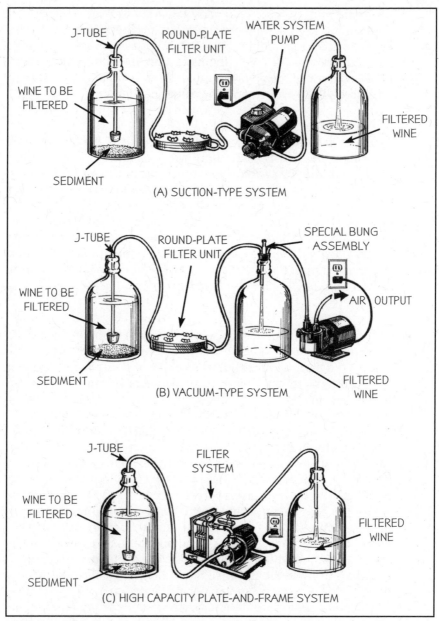

Figure 5-16: Filtration setups - (A) suction-type system, (B) vacuum-type system, (C) high capacity plate-and-frame system

Note: *Never combine filter pads of different ratings in the same filtration run on the same filter unit to reduce the number of operations; this will not work and may compromise filtration efficiency and quality.*

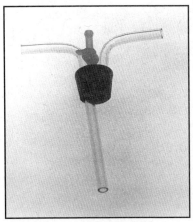

Figure 5-17: Special bung assembly

Figure 5-16 illustrates set-ups for the most common wine filtration systems used in home winemaking. Figure 5-16A and B illustrate the use of a round-plate system in a suction-type and a vacuum-type configuration, respectively. Figure 5-16C illustrates the set-up for plate-and-frame systems.

To create a complete vacuum, the system shown in Figure 5-16B requires a special bung assembly, shown in Figure 5-17, on the container receiving the filtered wine. The special bung assembly allows the pump to withdraw all the air and create a vacuum in the container to receive the filtered wine. The filtration system then forces the wine through the filter pads under vacuum. The wine is totally filtered under vacuum and is therefore better protected from oxidation effects.

Set up your filtration system according to one of the configurations in Figure 5-16. First, saturate the pads with clean water and let any excess drip before inserting the pads in the filtration unit. Assemble the system as per instructions in section 5.3.2 or as per the manufacturer's. Be sure to position, align and secure pads properly, particularly if the pads have holes that channel wine in and out of the system, so that the rough side faces the inlet.

Next, sanitize the entire filtration system, including the pads, before filtering wine. Fill a carboy with approximately 20 L (5 gal) of water, turn on the pump, and collect the water in the receiving carboy and discard. This operation ensures that all components are rinsed properly and removes any carton flavor from the pads, which could otherwise be imparted to the wine. Repeat this step with approximately 10 L (2.5 gal) of 1% effective SO_2 sulfite solution (see section 2.6.3) to sanitize the entire system. You can add a small amount of citric acid (just discernible to the taste buds) to the sulfite solution to increase its effectiveness. The resulting drop in pH of the solution increases the SO_2 effectiveness, but the addition of citric acid also "sweetens up" the pads and avoids any cardboard taste. Additionally, the drop in pH increases the filtering efficiency of the pads by increasing the absorption efficiency, which would otherwise only increase when wine passes through the filter pads. As a final step, flush the system using approximately 10 L of clean or distilled water, preferably, to rinse out any sulfite solution remaining in the filtration system. The system is now ready for wine filtering.

It is recommended to filter wine when cold, e.g., at cellar temperature, for a more effective filtration operation. Before filtering, add a small amount of sulfite to the wine to protect it from oxidation, particularly when using suction-type systems. Bring the free SO_2 level to 25–30 mg/L, and then, at bottling, add more sulfite to reach your desired free SO_2 level.

Once you have double-checked that everything is set up properly and you are ready to filter, start the pump. For a round-plate filtration system, when starting the filtering operation, lock the control clip on the outlet tube on the upper plate to restrict flow of wine into it so that the filter unit fills bottom-up. When the filter unit is full, open the clip. When filtering is completed, lock the clip again to drain any remaining wine out of the filter unit.

While filtering wine, do not disturb the sediment at the bottom of the carboy; otherwise, sediment can go back into suspension, into the filter line and filter pads, and clog the pads and slow down the filtration process, possibly requiring a change of pads. Also, the first half to one liter of liquid to pass through the system may contain water. The volume of diluted wine depends on the amount of water left in the unit during the flushing operation. Discard the diluted wine by filtering it out to a waste container and then returning the outlet tube to the receiving carboy when the wine seems wholesome.

If the filtration system is equipped with a pressure gauge, monitor the filtering pressure, and stop the pump and replace the clogged pads if/when the manufacturer's recommended maximum pressure is reached. Typically, a pressure increase indicates that the pads are becoming clogged, which will cause the filtering to leak and spray wine.

When filtration has completed, discard the filter pads, rinse and sanitize the entire system again with water and a sulfite solution as outlined above for the filter set-up phase.

*Note: Once the pump is turned on and filtering has started, do **not** turn the pump off/on or interrupt the operation by any other means; this will greatly decrease filtering efficiency and may affect the wine's clarity.*

6
STABILIZATION

Wine is an amazingly complex beverage, one that has life, and that therefore evolves and transforms over its lifetime. This evolution and transformation can be good or bad, depending on the intended style.

The best wines with long aging potential are expected to age gracefully over time. Flavors should develop and contribute to the wine's complexity; tannins should soften and become better integrated and balanced with other elements, and so on. They will also tend to throw a deposit, light to heavy depending on the type and age of wine. Wine connoisseurs perfectly accept, if not expect, this natural phenomenon, often regarded as a sign of quality.

But a wine's evolution and transformation can suddenly become altered because of a latent oversight during winemaking, because of some spoilage yeast or bacterium that infiltrated the wine, or because that special bottle of Cabernet Sauvignon you gave to a close relative has traveled across the country in a hot car. There are countless factors that can alter wine during the course of its evolution. The result is a wine that may lack the intended character or no longer reflects the true style, or, in the worst case, the wine has become spoiled and undrinkable.

When you simply make and store wine in your cellar and then drink the wine at home, you only need minimal processing, or stabilization, to ensure a problem-free wine; however, even if you enter a couple of bottles of fine wine in a competition and ship it across the country, your wine is suddenly at risk. Although a wine may be clear with a brilliant color when bottled, it can become cloudy during aging or transportation, in your relative's scenario, if not properly stabilized.

To reduce the risk of the wine "changing" or spoiling, you need to stabilize wine to the extent possible taking into account the wine's chemistry and assuming a reasonable set of environmental conditions that the wine might be subjected to over its lifetime. For example, will the wine have residual (fermentable) sugar? Will it have undergone MLF? Does the wine have a high pH that might cause chemical stability and color problems? Could the wine potentially be stored in a cellar colder than normal? Or would it be able to withstand cellar temperature swings between cold and warm, or even hot? There is nothing worse than fine bottles of wine starting to re-ferment or spoil!

As defined in chapter 5, stabilization is the winemaking practice of safeguarding juice and wine from the time the must is handled in preparation for vinification, through vinification and aging, to bottling and until consumed, and "includes two sorts of operations: one to counter physical and chemical changes and another to counter microbiological changes."[1] In this chapter, we examine stabilization processes that ensure 1) physical and chemical stabilization, in addition to those covered in chapter 5, and 2) microbiological, or microbial, stabilization.

6.1 PHYSICAL AND CHEMICAL STABILIZATION

Physical and chemical stabilization procedures discussed in this section are those specifically used to prevent adverse effects when wine is subjected to very low or very high temperatures, referred to as cold and heat stabilization, respectively. The latter is more commonly referred to as protein stabilization.

6.1.1 COLD STABILIZATION

When wine is subjected to cold temperatures for an extended period of time, a natural chemical process known as tartaric acid crystallization causes tartrate crystals, or tartrates – chemically known as potassium acid tartrate, the potassium salt of tartaric

[1]Robinson, Jancis, ed. THE OXFORD COMPANION TO WINE – THIRD EDITION. Oxford: Oxford University Press. 2006. pp 661-662.

acid – to form. The amount of tartrates that can form is greatest in wines with high tartaric acid concentration, such as in a Riesling from a cool-climate viticultural area, and depends on temperature, pH, and concentration of alcohol, potassium, and other compounds such as tannins and proteins.

Although completely harmless, tartrates affect the appearance of wine because they form at the bottom of the bottle and/or on the face of the cork exposed to wine. In white wine, the colorless crystals look like tiny shards of broken glass, which can be a cause of panic with new wine consumers. In red wines, the crystals absorb some red pigments from the wine and are therefore reddish in color. It is usually considered acceptable to find a small amount of tartrates in premium wines; however, the majority of wines are processed to safeguard against tartrates to alleviate any consumer concerns.

The process of protecting wine against tartrates is known as cold stabilization, or tartrate stabilization; the former is adopted here. If your cellar temperature is higher than 15° C (59° F) and you never expect your wine to be stored for any extended period of time at a lower temperature, then you do not need to cold stabilize it. It is good practice however to always cold stabilize wines as future storage conditions can never be guaranteed.

The first test you should do before undertaking cold stabilization is to determine whether your wine is cold stable; it might already be cold stable and, therefore, may not require any further processing to safeguard it against tartrates. The best and quickest test is the conductivity test, but this requires specialized equipment beyond the needs and scope of home winemakers. The simple alternative is to hold a sample of wine in a bottle or stoppered flask at a temperature of –4° C (25° F) for three days, i.e., 72 hours. This temperature might be difficult to achieve in a home winemaking environment; however, setting the refrigerator at the coldest temperature, for example, at 4° C (39° F), and leaving the wine sample in for one week will work just as well. Alternatively, set the freezer temperature higher than normally used for food storage to –4° C (25° F). At the end of the test period, hold up the bottle or flask against a bright light, simply invert it and look for any tartrate crystals that fall down. If there are no crystals, the wine is considered cold stable and requires no further processing against tartrates.

Wine can be made to be cold stable by chilling or by adding metatartaric acid. Cold stabilization by chilling is a natural process and is permitted in commercial winemaking, whereas, cold stabilization by addition of metatartaric acid is not permitted in all winemaking regions. As a home winemaker, you have a choice depending on your facilities and geographical location.

Cold stabilization by chilling

Cold stabilization by chilling is the process of cooling wine down to a temperature favoring tartaric acid crystallization – a process often referred to as chill proofing – until it is cold stable, i.e., cold temperatures will no longer cause tartrates to precipitate. Inevitably, cold stabilization by chilling will cause total acidity (TA) to decrease, with a small rise in pH, due to the crystallization of tartaric acid. The drop in TA is equivalent to the amount of tartaric acid precipitated as tartrates.

Cold stabilization by chilling is carried out by placing the wine in cold storage at a temperature between –4° C (25° F) and –10° C (14° F) for up to 2 weeks. You do not need to rack the wine before cold stabilization. Where a cold temperature is not possible, a minimum of 4° C (39° F) will work although it will take several weeks to cold stabilize wine. The lower temperature is always more effective and faster.

Try to time cold stabilization with cold weather; it's the easiest and cheapest method. If you live in a hot-climate area with no cold winter season, your only options are to use a home refrigerator if you make small batches, use a large commercial refrigerator if you have a friend in the grocery business that can accommodate large batches, or use the metatartaric acid method described below.

Alternatively, you can use a glycol system, such as the one show in Figure 4-4 on page 185, which can deliver glycol at very low temperature to chill and stabilize wine.

You can also add potassium bitartrate to wine during the chilling period as a seed to promote tartrate crystallization. Add potassium bitartrate powder at a rate of 50–100 g/hL of wine, stir thoroughly, and maintain temperature at the higher end of the recommended range above.

Following cold stabilization, **gently** stir the wine to hasten precipitation of crystals that may have clanged to the wall of the container, and let settle until fully precipitated. **Be careful not to aerate the wine, which could hasten oxidation, as oxygen is more soluble at colder temperatures**. Then rack the wine gently, again being careful not to over-aerate.

Note: Cold stabilization by chilling in oak barrels is not recommended because it would be extremely difficult, if not impossible, to remove tartrate crystals from the inside wall of barrels.

Cold stabilization using metatartaric acid

Cold stabilization by addition of metatartaric acid can be used in home winemaking to safeguard against tartrates when the chill-proofing temperature cannot be achieved. Metatartaric acid is a safe additive when used within the recommended guidelines. It should only be used in early-drinking wines because its effect cannot be guaranteed beyond a few months unless the wine is continuously stored at cold temperatures well below normal cellar temperature – an impractical and unsafe assumption. If the temperature were to rise, metatartaric acid would transform to tartaric acid and increase TA. Gum arabic, described in section 6.2.4, can be used to enhance the action of metatartaric acid by inhibiting tartrate crystal growth.

To prevent precipitation of tartrate crystals in early-drinking wines, add metatartaric acid powder at a rate of up to 10 g/hL of wine. Dissolve 2.5 mL (½ tsp) of metatartaric acid powder in 25 mL of cold water and stir well to completely dissolve the powder. Measure the required amount carefully because metatartaric acid is fairly strong and is therefore easy to over-compensate. Add the solution at a rate of 1 mL/L of wine just before filtration or bottling and then stir thoroughly. This addition will be more effective if done at cellar temperature or cooler.

Store metatartaric acid powder in the refrigerator to prolong its shelf life. It quickly (approximately 2 months) loses effectiveness if stored at room temperature. For this reason, store wines treated with metatartaric acid in a cold cellar and drink them early, before the cellar temperature starts rising.

*Note: Do **not** use metatartaric acid in wine treated with lysozyme; a heavy haze may result. Refer to section 6.2.4 for more information on the use of lysozyme.*

6.1.2 PROTEIN STABILIZATION

Proteins are very complex amino acid (organic acid containing the amino group NH_2) compounds essential to all living cells and synthesized from raw materials by vines. They are generally found in relatively high concentrations in grapes and remain soluble in white wine whereas tannins and color pigments in red wine will cause proteins to precipitate. Protein concentration in white wine is therefore higher than in red wine.

Proteins are very sensitive to heat (think of egg white changing from colorless to white when heated) and, in wine, they can coagulate and cause a haze when temperature starts rising. The extent of haze depends on temperature and on the concentration of proteins, which can change throughout vinification due to changes in such factors as alcohol concentration, temperature, and pH.

285

White wines, particularly varietals such as Sauvignon Blanc and Gewürztraminer that have a higher than normal concentration of proteins, are at a higher risk and much more susceptible to temperature variations, even in crystal clear wine previously fined and/or filtered. Such wines are said to be protein or heat unstable, and must be treated for protein stabilization. Red wines with low phenolic concentration are also at risk, albeit much lower, whereas those aged in oak barrels have almost no risk.

Bentonite is the ideal fining agent to reduce protein concentration and achieve protein stability. Since it interacts with proteins, bentonite can be added to grape juice before fermentation, to an active fermentation, or to wine at the end of fermentation; this process is known as counterfining. Refer to section 5.2.1 for specific usage instructions and rate of addition.

Prevention is the best cure for protein haze as the condition is practically impossible to correct. The best advice then is to test must or wine for protein stability and counterfine accordingly, or simply counterfine as a standard practice, in whites or low phenolic reds. Protein stability is determined using a heat stability test, which should be performed at various stages of winemaking in high-risk wines, or at minimum, before bottling.

A heat stability test consists of subjecting wine samples to various temperatures for various durations. There are no industry standards for this test; however, a simple procedure recommended in reference 22 [Zoecklein et al.] in Appendix E, developed by Ribéreau-Gayon and Peynaud, is most practical in home winemaking applications.

Start with a small, fine-filtered sample (e.g., 200 mL) of juice or wine and pour it in a non-reactive container, such as a small, narrow cooking pot, and insert a thermometer with a range of up to at least 100° C (212° F) in the juice or wine. If the sample is not adequately clarified, other forms of precipitation may cause confusion with protein precipitation. Heat the sample to 80° C (176° F) and maintain at that temperature for 10 minutes. Turn the heat off, remove the pot from the heat source, and let cool for 15 minutes. Transfer the sample to a laboratory flask and place it in a freezer for several hours. Retrieve the flask and allow the sample to warm up to room temperature. If the sample shows any sign of haze or precipitation, then the juice or wine is not protein/heat stable and requires a bentonite treatment.

6.2 MICROBIAL STABILIZATION

Microbial stabilization is the process of safeguarding wine against microbiological changes or spoilage due to unwanted or undesirable yeasts and bacteria that may start feeding on residual sugar, malic acid or other nutrients and cause unexpected results. Here, "unwanted or undesirable yeasts and bacteria" refers to latent cultured yeasts and bacteria that were specifically introduced during the winemaking process as well as wild or spoilage yeasts and bacteria that have not been kept in check or that were introduced by contamination, for example, from unclean equipment, fruit flies, or airborne organisms.

Microbial stabilization, then, deals with the removal – or at least reduction to an acceptable level – and inhibition of such yeasts and bacteria, either chemically, using preservatives or stabilizing agents, or mechanically by filtration.

In many wines, or specifically those considered dry and having undergone MLF, the risk of oxidation or microbial spoilage can be effectively prevented using preservatives and stabilizing agents, many of which are found in every day food and beverages, and include sulfite, ascorbic acid, potassium sorbate, and lysozyme, or products which combine one or more of these agents with possibly other enological products. Lysozyme is a relatively new stabilizing agent, or more precisely, an enzyme that safeguards against lactic acid bacteria (LAB) microbial spoilage.

In high risk wines, such as those having high residual sugar content or not having been malolactic fermented, mechanical filtration is used to remove undesirable yeasts and bacteria that could otherwise adversely affect wine.

Although not absolutely necessary, you can also perform tests using readily available kits to screen for unwanted or undesirable yeasts and bacteria to help you determine an appropriate course of action, if required, before proceeding with any stabilization treatment. Table 6-1 lists available kits, or screening tools, and the type of screening each performs.

Note: There are countless wild and spoilage yeasts and bacteria. Here, for the sake of simplicity, we will focus only those that are most important and most prevalent in a home winemaking context. For a complete study of microbiological organisms relevant to wine, please consult reference 6 [Fugelsang].

6.2.1 SCREENING FOR WILD YEASTS (*Saccharomyces*)

Wild or indigenous yeasts are ubiquitous organisms, meaning that they are found everywhere – in the vineyard on grape berries, in the winery on equipment, in must and wine – and easily become airborne or transmitted by insects to contaminate just about anything. Fortunately, most strains of concern in winemaking are sensitive to free SO_2 and can therefore be inhibited quite easily with a small dose of sulfite; most are only capable of fermenting to

Table 6-1
Yeast and bacteria detection kits

Kit (section)	Type of screening	Target yeast or bacterium
Wild Yeast Test Kit (6.2.1)	Wild yeasts	*Saccharomyces*
MicroQit DETECT (6.2.2)	Spoilage yeasts	*Brettanomyces*
Wallerstein (WL[2,3]) Test Kit (6.2.3)	Wild and spoilage yeasts	*Brettanomyces*
	Bacterial contamination	• *Acetobacter* • *Lactobacillus* • *Pediococcus*
ACCUVIN QUICK TESTS AV–D-Lactic Acid kit (6.2.3)	Bacterial contamination	D-Lactic acid

approximately 5% alc./vol., obviously not adequate for making wine. There are some wild yeast strains that can make wine – even great wines in some cases – used by many traditional or minimal-ist winemakers, such as Burgundians whose wineries have been in existence for a century or more, during which time they have suc-cessfully isolated desirable strains that ferment under rigorous sanitary conditions – not your typical home winemaking scenario. Home winemakers would not be able to isolate wild yeast strains and ensure successful fermentation. In fact, results can be very unpredictable and may negatively affect the quality of the wine or even cause spoilage.

Wild yeast strains can belong to many different yeast genera; however, here we will focus on those from the *Saccharomyces* genus.

White Labs Wild Yeast Test Kit, shown in Figure 6-1, can be used to screen for *Saccharomyces*-type wild yeast strains. The kit includes Lin's wild yeast media (LWYM) plates and all the necessary paraphernalia. The test involves inhibiting, or markedly restricting, growth of cultured yeast while permitting growth of a variety of wild yeast, and can be per-formed on juice, wine, equipment or air samples.

[2]"WL" is an acronym for the no longer extant Wallerstein Laboratories, which orig-inally marketed the media. WLD refers to WL-Differential plate media that uses cycloheximide while WLN refers to WL-Nutritional plate media without cyclohex-imide. Cycloheximide (actidione) is essentially an antibiotic that inhibits the growth of cultured yeast to isolate bacteria.
[3]Fugelsang, Kenneth C. WINE MICROBIOLOGY. New York: Chapman & Hall (International Thomson Publishing). 1997. p. 107.

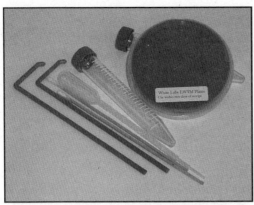

Figure 6-1: White Labs Wild Yeast Test Kit

The media plates must be stored in a refrigerator at 4° C (39° F); they have a shelf life of less than 2 weeks and should ideally be used within 2 days of reception from the supplier, and so you must plan your tests accordingly.

To prepare a sample from equipment, such as tanks or carboys, simply swab the surface of the equipment with a sterile swab dampened with sterile water, or alternatively, run sterile water over the surface of the equipment and collect the water in a sanitized container.

To prepare an air sample, simply leave an LWYM plate open in the area of concern for approximately one hour.

To perform a test, take one LWYM plate out from the refrigerator one hour before start of test. If you are performing multiple tests on various samples, be sure to label each plate with appropriate sample identification. Choose an area where there will be no draft, either from air current or foot traffic.

Turn the LWYM plate over so that the media is now on the bottom. Using a sterile transfer pipet with graduations supplied with the kit, add 0.25 mL of sample to a small, peripheral area of the plate and then replace the cover. Although not absolutely necessary, it is preferred that this last step be performed underneath the protection of a flame, such as from a small alcohol lamp.

Carefully remove one cell spreader from the sterile package, being careful not to touch the "L" portion of the spreader as contamination can result. Place the "L" portion on the media (opposite your sample). Introduce the spreader into the sample and spread evenly over the plate, and then replace the cover. The consistency of the media is that of "Jell-O" so be sure to use a light touch when spreading to avoid gashing the media. If you are using a swab, i.e., when testing equipment, swab the area to be tested and streak over the entire surface of the LWYM plate. Set aside the plate for approximately 15 minutes or until the sample dries completely, and then turn the plate media side up. Repeat this procedure for all samples to be screened.

To help you compare results, you may want to prepare a control plate, or "negative" plate, by adding 0.25 mL of sterile water to a plate and performing the same test.

Place the plates next to a heat source capable of keeping the samples at approximately 30° C (85° F) for up to 3–4 days, or use an incubator if you have access to such equipment. Preliminary results are visible after 48 hours.

Examine the plates, specifically the color and number of colonies that have developed. Positive colonies are pink or white in color and usually range 3–5 mm in size. "Tiny" or micro-colonies are considered negative results.

A clean sample should have 0 (zero) colonies. One (1) to 5 colonies signifies a problem that needs attention while over 5 colonies signals a serious wild yeast problem.

If wild yeast is detected in juice or wine, treat with sulfite at a rate of 20–35 mg/L, less if the juice is still to be fermented AND which will then be malolactic fermented. Follow the MLB manufacturer's instructions on the maximum free SO_2.

If wild yeast is detected on equipment, clean, rinse, sanitize and rinse again all equipment as per instructions in section 2.6.

6.2.2 SCREENING FOR SPOILAGE YEASTS (BRETTANOMYCES)

Wines are often described as having a barnyard smell. Personal taste and preferences notwithstanding, if a barnyard aroma is subtle, it is considered acceptable and is often desired by many winemakers who assert that it adds complexity to certain styles of wines. But when the aromas are dominated by a strong barnyard smell, then it is considered a fault. And such is the nature of the indigenous *Brettanomyces* yeast, more affectionately known as Brett; it can have both a positive influence on wine, for those who like it, or it can spoil wine outright. It is responsible for barnyard, medicinal, sweaty, "Band-Aid" and rancid aromas resulting from three main compounds, 4-ethylphenol, 4-ethylguiacol and 3-methylbutyric acid, also known as isovaleric acid, which can be detected at very low concentrations.

Note: Brettanomyces and Dekkera species are different but equivalent and are therefore quite often used interchangeably in wine analysis.

The challenge with *Brettanomyces* yeast is that it easily thrives throughout the winery and is difficult to eradicate, particularly that it seems to adapt to changing environments. It is an anaerobic microorganism, meaning that it thrives in the absence of oxygen. Specifically, it thrives in oak barrels feeding on cellulose, or in wines with residual sugar (RS), high pH or high polyphenol concentration. Red wines are inherently more susceptible to Brett owing to their higher pH and high polyphenol concentration. RS is usually not a problem in whites because (if) they are well protected with SO_2; in reds, however, where the style is meant to be a dry wine, RS can be a source of food for Brett.

Eradicating *Brettanomyces* is nearly impossible except by stabilizing filtration, discussed below in section 6.2.5. Brett is sensitive to free SO_2, and so it is easily preventable using sulfite. Here is a list of additional tips in preventing Brett:

- Ferment red wines to dryness as much as possible for dry-style red wines.
- Maintain a low pH in the recommended range for your style of wine.
- Use SO_2 judiciously, taking into account the wine's pH, being extra vigilant with high-phenol wines.
- Do not age wine on the lees for too long as they are a source of nutrients for Brett.
- Store wine in a cool cellar, ideally at 13° C (55° F).
- Keep carboys, tanks, barrels and all other containers well topped up.
- Stabilize filter wines prior to bottling.

Prahl Biolab A/S of Denmark has developed the MicroQit DETECT test kit, shown in Figure 6-2, now available through White Labs, which provides a qualitative assessment of *Brettanomyces* detection in must and wine, as well as a crude quantitative approximation of cell count down to 1,000 Brett cells/mL. The kit can also be used for checking the sterility of previously infected barrels. Refer to section 8.7 for more information on barrel spoilage problems. The detection plates in the kit have a shelf life of approximately 12 months when stored at 4° C (39° F).

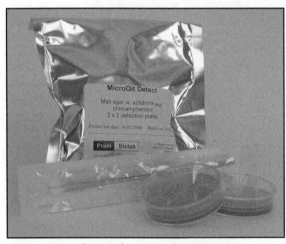

Figure 6-2: White Labs MicroQit DETECT

To perform a test with the MicroQit DETECT test kit, first draw a small sample of wine from a carboy, tank, barrel or other container into a beaker. Make sure that any laboratory apparatus that will come into contact with the wine sample is clean and sanitized,

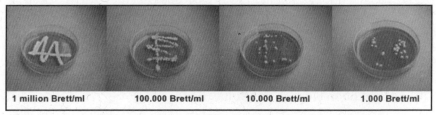

Figure 6-3: MicroQit Brett cultures at various cell count concentrations

and handle the test kit apparatus with great care to avoid contaminating it with foreign organisms.

Take one sterile cotton-tipped applicator and dip the cotton tip end into the wine sample. Take a detection plate out from its sterile packaging and remove the lid. Wipe the cotton tip of the applicator over the gel surface in a Z-movement, and place the lid back on the plate immediately. If you are testing more than one sample, be sure to mark each plate with an appropriate identification. Put the detection plate back in the plastic bag and incubate it at 25–30 °C (77–86° F) for 6–7 days, preferably in a dark place.

Following incubation, visually inspect the detection plate. *Brettanomyces* infections will appear as white or cream-colored colonies in the plate. To obtain an approximate estimate of the infection level, compare your results with the pictures in Figure 6-3. Heavy infections appear as smeared lines in the plate, representing a cell count of approximately 1 million Brett cells/mL. Loosely scattered colonies represent a cell count of approximately 1,000 Brett cells/mL.

Alternatively, you can use a Wallerstein Test Kit, used to screen for spoilage bacteria and described below in section 6.2.3, to screen for *Brettanomyces*.

If the wine has acquired a barnyard smell that you deem acceptable and the screening test confirms a low-to-moderate population of *Brettanomyces*, perform a stabilization filtration, as outlined in section 6.2.5, to reduce the amount of Brett yeast, or simply blend the wine with one that has no Brett.

If the wine has acquired a strong barnyard smell and the screening test confirms a heavy population of *Brettanomyces*, the wine is beyond salvage. If the wine was aged in oak barrels, the barrels too may be spoiled and may need to be discarded.

6.2.3 SCREENING FOR SPOILAGE BACTERIA (*ACETOBACTER, LACTOBACILLUS* AND *PEDIOCOCCUS*)

In sections 3.2.1, UNDERSTANDING ACIDITY, and 4.8, MALOLACTIC FERMENTATION (MLF), the role and significance of "good" and "bad" bacteria in enology were presented. Specifically, good lactic acid bacteria (LAB), or malolactic bacteria (MLB), convert malic acid into lactic acid, or more precisely, MLB convert L-malic acid into L-lactic acid during malolactic fermentation (MLF). On the other hand, bad LAB can wreak havoc in wine and cause spoilage.

Acetobacter feeds on alcohol to produce acetic acid and imparts the familiar sour taste and smell of vinegar. A very small concentration of ethyl acetate can also develop, which is detectable as an off-putting aroma of nail polish remover at higher concentrations. The usual culprit of the bacterium is the dreaded fruit fly, commonly pervasive around winemaking season.

Acetobacter is always present in wine but, being aerobic, it only thrives in the presence of oxygen to cause spoilage. It is usually the result of poor or defective winemaking equipment, excessive manipulation of wine during transfers or other cellar operations, or simply, careless winemaking, such as a poor topping regimen.

Lactobacillus and *Pediococcus* are the two most important LAB genera and of greatest concern in winemaking because they can produce D-lactic acid and cause spoilage if not controlled. Specifically, they give rise to a problem known as lactic taint, or *piqûre lactique* in French, which gives wine an unpleasant sour-milk taste. *Acetobacter* is also a by-product of this spoilage reaction.

Spoilage LAB can originate from a number of sources including previously contaminated equipment, possibly from contact with spoiled and contaminated wine, or damaged grapes. These anaerobic bacteria can multiply easily in wine under favorable environmental conditions, and if the D-lactic acid they produce rises above 300 mg/L, it will compromise the quality of the wine. Bacteria can also nestle in nooks and crannies of equipment that can be difficult to clean, such as pumps, hoses and barrels, as well as in poorly sanitized equipment, such as carboys and tanks.

White Labs WL (Wallerstein Laboratories) Test Kit, shown in Figure 6-4, can be used to screen for *Acetobacter*, *Lactobacillus* and *Pediococcus* bacteria, as well as *Brettanomyces*,

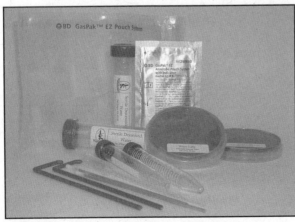

Figure 6-4: White Labs Wallerstein Test Kit

293

while ACCUVIN's QUICK TESTS AV–D-Lactic Acid kit, shown in Figure 6-5, can be used to screen for D-lactic acid.

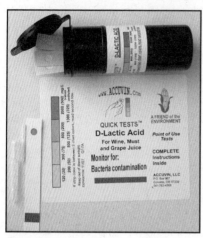

Figure 6-5: ACCUVIN QUICK TEST AV-D-Lactic Acid Kit

The WL Test Kit includes what is known as Wallerstein Differential (WLD) blue-green media plates with cycloheximide and Wallerstein Nutrient (WLN) blue-green media plates without cycloheximide, and all the necessary paraphernalia. Cycloheximide (actidione) is essentially an antibiotic that inhibits the growth of cultured yeast to isolate bacteria and wild yeast. In addition, WL media allow for easy detection of acid-secreting bacteria via its bromcresol green pH indicator component. By plating a sample on both the WLD and WLN media plates, you can perform a direct comparison of bacteria or wild yeast growth (seen on WLD) versus cultured yeast growth (seen on WLN).

Note that the kit includes everything to perform aerobic incubation to screen for *Acetobacter*. To screen for *Lactobacillus* and *Pediococcus* bacteria and *Brettanomyces* yeast, you will need optional anaerobic pouches to perform anaerobic incubation.

The media plates must be stored in a refrigerator at 4° C (39° F); they have a shelf life of approximately 30 days.

To perform a test, take the required number of WL plates out from the refrigerator and prepare test samples as per the Wild Yeast Test Kit instructions in section 6.2.1. Remove the parafilm and place the plates with the media side up. Allow the plates to reach room temperature before plating. If you are performing multiple tests on various samples, be sure to label each plate with appropriate sample identification. Choose an area where there will be no draft, either from air current or foot traffic.

Turn the WL plate over so that the media is now on the bottom. Using a sterile transfer pipet with graduations supplied with the kit, add 0.25 mL of sample to a small, peripheral area of the plate and then replace the cover. Although not absolutely necessary, it is preferred that this last step be performed underneath the protection of a flame, such as from a small alcohol lamp.

Carefully remove a cell spreader from the sterile package, being careful not to touch the "L" portion of the spreader as contamination can result. Place the "L" portion on the media (opposite your sample). Introduce the spreader into the sample and spread evenly over the plate, and then replace the cover. The consistency of the media is that of "Jell-O" so be sure to use a light touch when spreading to avoid gashing the media. Spread your sample over the entire media surface. If you are using a swab, i.e., when testing equipment, swab the area to be tested and streak over the entire surface of the WL plate. Set aside the plate for approximately 20 minutes or until the sample dries completely, and then turn the plate media side up. Repeat this procedure for all samples to be screened.

To help you compare results, you may want to prepare a control plate, or "negative" plate, by adding 0.25 mL of sterile water to a plate and perform the same test.

Place the plates next to a heat source capable of keeping the samples at approximately 30° C (85° F) for up to 3–4 days. Preliminary results are visible after 48 hours.

If testing for anaerobic yeast or bacteria, place the plates into the optional anaerobic (Gas Pak) pouch, media side up. Each pouch can hold up to 4 plates. Remove the outer foil packaging of sachet and place the plates inside the pouch, between the plates and pouch. Seal the pouch by pressing the zipper together and incubate as described above.

Examine the plates, specifically the number of colonies, plate and colony color, and colony texture that have developed. You may have more than one type of bacteria or wild yeast colonies on a single plate. The WL media will lighten in color significantly in the presence of acid-secreting bacteria turning the blue-green media to yellow or light green.

A clean sample should have 0 (zero) colonies. One (1) to 5 colonies signifies a problem that needs attention while over 5 colonies signals a serious wild yeast problem.

If undesirable bacteria are detected in juice or wine, treat with sulfite at a rate of 20–35 mg/L, less if the juice is still to be fermented AND which will then be malolactic fermented. Follow the MLB manufacturer's instructions on the maximum free SO_2.

If undesirable bacteria are detected on equipment, clean, rinse, sanitize and rinse again all equipment as per instructions in section 2.6.

ACCUVIN's QUICK TESTS AV–D-Lactic Acid kit is another simple bacterial contamination screening test that can measure D-lactic acid concentration in musts and wines up to 500 mg/L. The kit includes test strips, vials containing a dilution mixture to dilute must or wine samples, which also reduces the concentration of interfering substances, sampler bulbs for obtaining test samples, and a color chart.

To determine D-lactic acid concentration, simply transfer the test sample to a vial using a sampler bulb, close the vial and shake **once** only. Aspirate a sample from the vial using a new sample bulb, transfer the test sample on the absorbent layer on the test strip using a sampler bulb, wait 4 minutes for the color to develop, and then compare the color of the dot on the reverse side of the strip against the color chart provided. The chart shows both diluted and undiluted concentrations, so no correction is required. Be sure to compare colors under incandescent or natural lighting, not fluorescent lighting. If the test result indicates a contamination above 300 mg/L, the wine may be salvageable depending on the extent of spoilage or, in the worst-case scenario, the wine is completely spoiled and is best poured down the drain.

Chapter 14 outlines common root causes of defects in wine and procedures to address the problems. The following sections will help you avoid the potential of such problems.

6.2.4 PRESERVATIVES AND STABILIZING AGENTS

Sulfite
Potassium metabisulfite, or sulfite, is the industry-accepted chemical additive for preserving wines. It is a common preservative in the food and beverage industry. Sulfite is very effective in inhibiting spoilage yeasts and bacteria that can restart fermentation, and in warding off oxidation.

Add sulfite powder to achieve a nominal free SO_2 level between 35 mg/L and 50 mg/L based on the pH and type of the wine. Refer to sections 3.3 and 3.4 for situations where the pH exceeds 3.5.

To add sulfite, first completely dissolve the powder in a small quantity of warm water and then stir the sulfite solution gently into the wine. Never add sulfite powder directly to wine because it will not dissolve properly and, as such, it will not provide expected protection. Alternatively, you can use Efferbaktol or Oenosteryl tablets, which make sulfite additions easy, as outlined in section 3.4.

Note: Sodium metabisulfite is another source of sulfite as Campden tablets or as a powder. If for health reasons you are concerned about sodium intake in your diet, opt for the potassium form of sulfite.

Ascorbic acid (vitamin C)
Ascorbic acid (vitamin C) is an ingredient often used in home winemaking for its antioxidant properties; however, its use is not well understood.

Ascorbic acid only has an extremely transitory antioxidant effect on wines. It fixes to dissolved oxygen in wine and quickly converts to dehydroascorbic acid – a weak organic acid – within 3–4 days. Following this oxidation, ascorbic acid is exhausted and serves no further function. It is mainly used to scavenge oxygen in wine before bottling or other operations where the wine will be subjected to little and temporary aeration.

Another function of ascorbic acid is in preventing a condition known as ferric (iron) casse, which is caused by oxidation of iron supplied from the soil and present in wine. Ferric casse will cause wine to become cloudy and hazy when there is a high concentration of oxygen (typically from excessive exposure to air) in high-iron content wines. High-iron content wines that are handled with minimal exposure to air do not need to be treated with ascorbic acid. This is difficult for home winemakers to assess because there is no simple tool to measure iron content; however, ferric casse is a very rare occurrence nowadays because iron-rich equipment is no longer used for handling wine. Most equipment is now manufactured from food-grade plastic or stainless steel. As a reminder, avoid brass fittings on pumps and hose attachments.

Add ascorbic acid crystals at a rate of 2–3 g/hL of wine just before bottling by first dissolving the crystals in water. Only add ascorbic acid if/when the wine is adequately protected with the recommended minimum level of free SO_2; otherwise, it may actually favor oxidation of the wine. And **never** exceed 10 g/hL to avoid imparting an off-taste to the wine.

Potassium sorbate

Potassium sorbate – a salt derived from sorbic acid and often simply referred to as sorbate – is a widely accepted food and beverage additive used to inhibit growth of yeast and mold. In winemaking, its main application is in stabilizing wines with residual sugar, specifically to prevent renewed yeast activity and fermentation once the wine is bottled. Any fermentable residual sugar can potentially restart fermentation if there is any yeast. If wine starts re-fermenting, it can cause bottles to explode. It is therefore good practice to use potassium sorbate in making sweet wines. It is not required for properly sulfited dry wines where the residual sugar content is almost nil.

When making wine from kits or when the wine is to be bottled soon after fermentation and stabilization, it is highly recommended to add potassium sorbate. Wine kits very often include potassium sorbate as novice winemakers often unintentionally do not ferment the wine to dryness and then bottle prematurely. As a preventive measure, add potassium sorbate if the amount of residual sugar cannot be determined. It will not have any adverse effect on the wine and the wine will be protected.

Potassium sorbate is commonly available as vermicelli-shaped crystals. Add potassium sorbate at a rate of 10–20 g/hL of wine, following clarification or before bottling, by first dissolving the crystals in water. Use the higher rate within the recommended range if the wine's pH approaches or exceeds 3.5, or when the alcohol level is relatively low; potassium sorbate becomes less effective at lower alcohol levels. Before adding the potassium sorbate solution to the wine, ensure that the free SO_2 level is at least at the minimum recommended level. Stir the sorbate solution vigorously into the wine.

An alternative method to prevent re-fermentation is stabilizing filtration, outlined in section 6.2.5.

*Note: Potassium sorbate **cannot** be used to stop an active fermentation; it can only inhibit a renewed fermentation.*

*Caution: Do **not** use potassium sorbate to stabilize a wine having undergone MLF. Sorbic acid in potassium sorbate reacts negatively with lactic acid bacteria, which will result in an unpleasant geranium-like odor – a serious wine fault.*

Tannisol

Tannisol, shown in Figure 6-6, is a product that packages potassium metabisulfite, ascorbic acid and tannin into a convenient format for home winemaking. It is available in a package of 10 tablets each weighing 10 g and consisting of 95% potassium metabisulfite, 3% ascorbic acid and 2% tannin. The recommended dosage is 1 tablet per hL (25 gal) of wine to be preserved. You can increase the dosage to 2 tablets for wine with faults and needing a higher concentration of free SO_2. For sweet wines, increase the dosage to 3 tablets per hL of wine. You can easily split tablets in half or quarter pieces for demijohn (54-L) and carboy (23-L) batches, respectively.

To add Tannisol to wine, first crush a tablet to a powder and then dissolve it in a small quantity of warm water. Stir the Tannisol solution into the wine and mix thoroughly.

Figure 6-6: Tannisol tablets

Lysozyme[4]

Lysozyme, a purified and freeze-dried enzyme isolated from egg whites, and now also available in liquid format, is a relatively new tool in the winemaker's toolbox used to suppress spoilage bacteria

[4]This section has been adapted from http://www.scottlab.com/fordras.htm.

after MLF and to achieve microbial stability. It is not effective against *Acetobacter* or spoilage yeast (e.g., *Brettanomyces*), nor does it have antioxidant properties, however, unlike free SO_2, lysozyme is most effective in wine at higher pH when spoilage bacteria thrive the most. As such, it cannot replace the use of sulfite but can be used concurrently to reduce the amount of sulfite needed to achieve microbial stability.

The recommended rate of addition for microbial stability is 200–300 mg/L (20–30 g/hL) immediately following completion of MLF. Supplement the lysozyme treatment with a sulfite treatment to ensure that any residual LAB that might potentially start feeding on non-fermentable sugars does not produce VA.

In white wine, reduce the rate to 100 mg/L if added just before bottling. In red wine, use the lowest dosage whenever possible as lysozyme binds with tannins and other phenolic compounds, resulting in a decrease in mouthfeel and color. The effects, if perceptible, should be noticeable within the first few days of treatment. You should always run bench tests on every wine to be treated with lysozyme to better predict results. Test results are usually conclusive overnight, i.e., treat samples, let stand overnight, and assess mouthfeel and color in all samples the next day.

To treat wine, use a dilute 5% solution prepared as per instructions in section 3.4.2 or a commercially-prepared solution, such as LYSO-Easy. Lysozyme will cause further lees precipitation; wait approximately one week and then rack the wine off the lees.

Caution: Do not use bentonite and lysozyme concurrently; bentonite deactivates lysozyme. Wait for bentonite to completely settle out, follow with a careful racking, and then add lysozyme. If wine has already been treated with lysozyme, wait a minimum of one week before adding bentonite to allow the lysozyme to inhibit the bacteria. Before bottling, you should perform a protein stability test to ensure that the lysozyme will not cause any stability problems. If the stability test is positive, do another bentonite fining until the wine is protein stable.

Caution: Do not use metatartaric acid in wine treated with lysozyme; a heavy haze may result. Refer to section 6.1.1 for more information on metatartaric acid.

Gum arabic

The use of gum arabic is unknown in home winemaking but commercial wineries use it in a number of applications, one being to improve stabilization in wine. At Maleta Winery, Head Winemaker Arthur Harder recommends its use for rounding out tannins in reds, for increasing mouthfeel in both whites and reds, and for increasing persistence of bubbles in sparkling wines.

Gum arabic is a natural gum extracted from specific species of African Acacia trees. As a colloid dispersion[5] of saccharides and glycoproteins, it is used in food and beverage processing not only as a stabilizer but also as syrup for making soft drinks or for making gummy candies and chewing gum.

In wine processing, gum arabic from *A. Seyal* and *Senegal* species is available in a dilute solution, for example, 20%, such as Arabinol, shown in Figure 6-7, which is used for a number of applications.

It can be used to enhance the action of metatartaric acid by encasing tartar crystals thereby keeping them completely separated and inhibiting tartrate crystal growth.

It can improve aromatic intensity and complexity as well as "palate" balance.

It can be used in the stabilization of red wine color pigments in young wines, by acting as a protective colloid. This aids in preventing pigment precipitation. Gums can reduce tannin astringency. As such, they can increase the perception of body or volume, reduce the perceptions of acidity and tannin harshness, while adding body.

Figure 6-7: Arabinol (gum arabic)

In bottled red wine, it stabilizes color and hinders their precipitation. It is also used in preventing ferric casse in high-iron content wines, and to enhance perlage or bubbling in sparkling wine (see section 11.4).

Older literature states that gum arabic could plug final filters; however, modern products are sterile filtered in order to ensure that the gum is completely sterile and easy to filter after its addition to wine.

As a 20% dilute solution, add gum arabic at a rate of 0.5–5 mL for every liter of **filtered** wine, or as directed by the manufacturer, **after the final fining or before final filtration prior to bottling**. Do not treat wine with fining agents after a gum arabic treatment.

[5]A colloidal dispersion, or simply, colloid, is a homogeneous mixture consisting of minute particles suspended in a medium, both of which can be gas, liquid or solid. The particles are dispersed in a manner that prevents them from being filtered easily or settled rapidly.

Perform bench tests on a small sample before treating the whole batch of wine to determine the desired rate of addition. Be sure to read and follow manufacturers' directions as product use can vary.

6.2.5 STABILIZING FILTRATION

Dry wines with no appreciable amount of residual fermentable sugar that have been malolactic fermented and processed in a clean, sanitized environment and adequately protected and stabilized with preservatives are generally sufficiently stable to be bottled without the need for further microbial stabilization. Most red wines are dry and malolactic fermented, and therefore at much lower risk of post-bottling problems.

Wines with residual fermentable sugar or which have not been malolactic fermented, or as added insurance against microbial spoilage, must undergo sterile filtration prior to bottling to prevent renewed fermentation or even spoilage due to residual yeast and/or bacteria. White wines are often crafted in a non-dry style ranging from off-dry to sweet and often also without being malolactic fermented, putting them at much higher risk of post-bottling problems.

Specifically, microbial stabilization by sterile filtration is concerned with the removal of residual or latent yeast cells and lactic acid and spoilage bacteria that could start feeding on residual sugar or that could cause other unexpected microbiological problems, such as that distinctive barnyard smell in some red wines, which is caused by *Brettanomyces* spoilage yeast. Yeast cells are larger than 1.2 µm while lactic acid and spoilage bacteria are larger than 0.65 µm, and therefore require a minimum filtration of less than 0.65 µm. This is typically done using 0.6-µm filtration although 0.4-µm is the standard and recommended winemaking practice. Because the filter medium's filtering efficiency is not always guaranteed 100%, some winemakers choose to filter down to 0.2 µm for added protection and insurance.

Sterile filtration is somewhat misleading terminology because we cannot achieve an absolute sterile environment and filtration in the strict sense of the word, at least not in winemaking. To do so would require specialized tools and expertise, akin to pharmaceutical manufacturers. In winemaking, wine is considered sterile if it is microbiologically stable. This means that yeast cells and spoilage bacteria have been sufficiently removed to ensure that the wine, once bottled, is stable and is protected from renewed fermentation or other activity arising from unwanted yeast or bacteria. A more accurate term then for sterile filtration in a winemaking context, which we adopt here, is stabilizing filtration, and refers to a minimum filtration of 0.6 µm.

Figure 6-8: A capsule filter

Stabilizing filtration makes use of membrane filtration technology and equipment. In membrane filtration, wine is filtered at or near the surface (much like the action of a sieve) of a disposable or reusable membrane filter medium, manufactured from specialized material, such as cellulose esters or other polymers, with miniscule holes or pores. Wine is forced through the tiny pores in the membrane by mechanical action, e.g., using a pump, and particulates larger than the membrane's rating are filtered out. The filtering action is similar to water filters, such as the ones found in water-dispensing fridges.

Being a surface filtration technology, membrane filtration has low particle retention or filtering capacity. However, due to the membrane's manufacturing technology, membrane filtration provides much more precise and efficient filtering that meets the stricter requirements in preventing microbial spoilage, unlike depth pad filtration. It is also used in a microbiologically affected wine to remove spoilage microorganisms in an attempt to correct the problem, though the extent or severity of the problem may not always make it possible to correct.

Membrane filtration equipment
The first decision in getting started with membrane filtration is determining your needs, budget and filtering requirements. Membrane filtration equipment can range from the simple and inexpensive for small batches to the sophisticated and expensive for any size batch. There are various types of equipment available, two of which are capsule filters and filter housings.

Capsule filters, such as the one shown in Figure 6-8, are disposable filters self-contained in a polypropylene housing assembly providing various filtration areas, for example, 300 cm^2 (0.3 ft^2), 500 cm^2 (0.5 ft^2), 1000 cm^2 (1.1 ft^2), or 2000 cm^2 (2.1 ft^2), and retention ratings down to 0.4 µm suitable for winemaking applications. As a guideline, a 300-cm^2 capsule filter would be adequate for occasional small batches of up to 23 L (6 gal). A 2000-cm^2 capsule filter could support even the largest of home winemaking needs of 1,000 L (263 gal).

Filter housings are made of either polypropylene or 316L stainless steel – a highly corrosion resistant type of stainless steel – typically specified by the length of cartridges that it can house, for example, 2.5, 5, 10, 20, or 30 inches, providing effective filtration

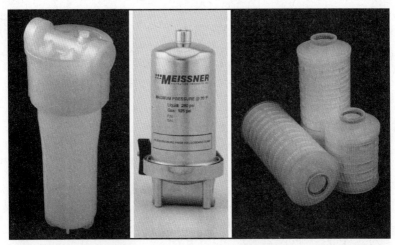

Figure 6-9 (left to right): A 10-inch polypropylene housing, a 5-inch 316L stainless steel housing, and cartridges for either housing type

areas of up to 1.95 m² (21 ft²). For winemaking applications, they can house cartridges rated down to 0.2 μm. Figure 6-9 illustrates a 10-inch polypropylene housing, a 5-inch 316L stainless steel housing, and cartridges for either housing type.

Both capsule filters and filter housings are equipped with standard inlet and outlet interfaces, or ports, that can also be fitted with various valves and connector types including NPT[6] connectors, hose barbs, and sanitary flanges, such as Tri-Clover fittings.

The inlet and outlet sides of the filter equipment, where the wine flows into and out from, are commonly referred to as the upstream and downstream sides, respectively.

Capsule filters and filter housings can be used either in an upright or upside-down position. The upright position refers to the setup where wine flows from the upstream side to downstream side by filling the capsule or housing bottom-up; the upside-down position refers to the setup where wine flows from upstream side to downstream side by filling the capsule or housing from the top.

A vent valve on the capsule or housing is used to let air out when the capsule or housing is first filled with wine. The vent valve is also used to drain wine when the capsule or housing needs to be emptied, by flipping over the capsule or housing, or to sample wine during filtration. Some models may be equipped with both a vent valve at the top and a drain/sampling valve at the bottom. But remember ... vent from the top, drain from the bottom.

Filter housings can be further configured with more "bells and whistles" for increased filtration process control and more operat-

[6]NPT, short for National Pipe Thread, is a U.S. standard for tapered threads used to join pipes and fittings.

ing flexibility by installing pressure gauges and ball valves at any or all ports.

Specifically, you can install a pressure gauge on the vent port at the top of the housing unit to monitor pressure inside and ensure that the housing's maximum operating pressure is not exceeded. You can also use a T-connector to install a vent valve to ease housing filling during startup.

More important, although not a necessity, you can equip both the upstream and downstream ports with pressure gauges to monitor differential pressure, which gives an indication when to clean or change the cartridge. A filter medium that no longer filters as per filtering efficiency specifications is said to fail integrity, which should be confirmed by what is known as a bubble point test, and needs to be replaced.

Pressure gauges at the upstream and downstream ports can be equipped with ball valves to control the flow of wine in and out of the housing. Always match the size of the upstream and downstream port interfaces so as to minimize differential pressure and achieve maximum filtering efficiency; for example, do not use a ½-inch hose barb at the inlet and ¼-inch hose barb at the outlet, or vice versa, but rather, use ½-inch hose barbs on both ports. Ball valves at the ports are useful when you need to adjust the rate of flow inside the housing, and particularly when you need to let air out of the housing when first starting to pump wine.

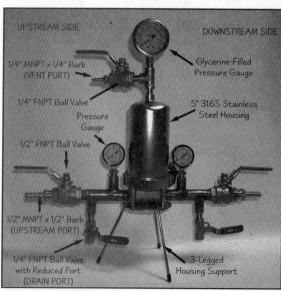

And if your filter housing model is not equipped with drain/sampling ports, again, you can easily install small sampling valves at the upstream and downstream ports.

Figure 6-10 illustrates a fully configured, 5-inch, 316L stainless steel filter housing.

Evidently, a filter housing equipped with the various ports can be flexibly configured to your needs and skills. And if you don't need some of the ports, simply leave the supplied port plugs in place.

Figure 6-10: Fully configured 5-inch, 316L stainless steel housing

The last but equally important piece of equipment required is a good pump. A centrifugal pump is best because it is most efficient and allows for recirculation or bypass when the maximum operating pressure is reached; however, they tend to be pricey and are mainly the domain of commercial wineries.

Positive displacement pumps are the norm in home winemaking applications. They are quite inexpensive and are available for small batch runs to large batches at high operating pressures. The only disadvantage of inexpensive positive displacement pumps in filtration applications is that they are not equipped for recirculation/bypass, or pressure control in general; therefore, choose a pump that provides a safe maximum operating pressure, ideally equipped with variable-speed control and with reversible flow switches to create flow in either direction, which is great for draining the filter line at the end of filtration.

Wine will be moved through various processing equipment all rated at different operating pressures. A pump's rated maximum pressure should never exceed the maximum of any component along the process line. Manufacturers usually specify the maximum operating pressure on filtration equipment and media. In all cases, always choose a pump that can deliver a constant and steady flow of wine to the filter. Do not use pulse-type pumps; they tend to reduce filtering efficiency and capacity.

Preparing the wine
Stabilizing filtration is normally the penultimate step in winemaking, performed immediately preceding bottling, so that wine is bottled with the greatest assurance that it is microbiologically stable. To reduce the probability of microbial contamination as much as possible, you will need to have the minimum amount of equipment between membrane filtration equipment and bottling equipment, all of which have to be exceptionally well sanitized, and a meticulously clean working environment.

Then, the wine to be filtered must be "stabilizing filtration ready", at least one day prior to membrane filtration and bottling. This cannot be over-stated. A wine should not be filtered for microbial stability until it is physically and chemically stable. This means that the wine must have completed its alcoholic fermentation as well as malolactic fermentation (MLF), the latter if expressly desired, be adequately sulfited for the type of wine, be cold and protein stabilized, and be adequately (pre) filtered. Wine with residual sugar does not need to be stabilized with potassium sorbate to prevent renewed fermentation; stabilizing filtration will accomplish this by filtering out yeast that could otherwise start feeding on any residual sugar.

It is important that the wine be fine filtered at 0.5–0.8 µm before membrane filtration. This pre-membrane filtration is required to avoid clogging up the membrane, which would otherwise reduce filtering efficiency as well as the life of the membrane. You should always pre-filter wine first with depth filter pads rated at least at 2.4 µm or 1.2 µm if you will be stabilize filtering with a membrane rated at 0.6 µm or 0.4 µm, respectively. To save on processing time, pre-membrane filtration can be performed in line (before) with membrane filtration, i.e., wine is filtered first via depth pads followed by a membrane on the same line.

Stabilizing filtration

Note: *The following instructions are based on a fully configured membrane filtration set-up that includes a filter housing, upstream and downstream control valves, vent and drain valves, and pressure gauges. For capsule filters or basic set-ups that are minimally configured, follow the same instructions while skipping any reference to control equipment not available on your set-up.*

The day you plan to stabilize filter and bottle, you will need to get a head start to set up and sanitize all the equipment. Do not be tempted to skip any sanitization step; you will otherwise greatly reduce filtering efficiency and increase the risk of microbial contamination.

Whether you are using a new or used cartridge filter, you should first assess its integrity, i.e., its ability to filter as per specifications, by conducting a bubble point test, outlined further down below, to ensure that it performs at the specified filtering efficiency.

Then, you will need to clean and sanitize the entire membrane filtration line and bottling equipment according to winemaking specifications. This means that all equipment from the carboy or holding tank through to the depth (if any) and membrane filters, hoses, valves, bottle filler and bottles must be sanitized thoroughly prior to bottling. Some commercial wineries use steam to sanitize the filtration/bottling line, however, this is costly and not practical for home winemaking, and should not be used in any case on any material other than stainless steel, unless recommended otherwise by the manufacturer. A simple and effective alternative procedure is to clean using a caustic solution and **filtered** water, and sanitize with a sulfite solution; however, you should first refer to your filter manufacturer's instructions to confirm what procedure and chemicals are compatible with the filter medium. Filtered water used in rinsing the membrane filtration line during cleaning and sanitizing should be filtered to a minimum of 5 µm, i.e., larger than 5 µm absolute, or, ideally, it should be filtered through the prefilter in use at either 0.8 µm or 1.2 µm.

Set up the complete membrane filtration line and bottling equipment from the carboy or holding tank that will be used for holding the caustic solution and filtered water as per Figure 6-11.

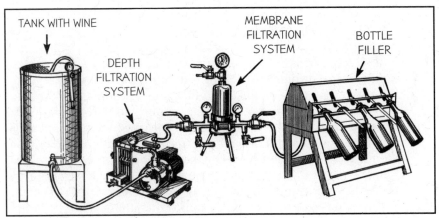

Figure 6-11: Setup for membrane filtration

*Note: If your set-up involves depth filtration in line with membrane filtration, do **not** hook up your depth filter equipment at this point. The caustic solution treatment for the membrane filtration equipment can damage filter pads, unless specifically endorsed by the pad manufacturer. Use a sulfite solution to sanitize depth filter pads.*

Your set-up should ideally feed filtered wine from the membrane filter directly to your bottling equipment for immediate bottling to reduce the possibility of microbial contamination from airborne microorganisms or from contaminated downstream processing equipment. You want to bottle filtered wine as quickly as possible using the shortest distance in terms of amount of equipment between the membrane filter and the bottling equipment. This is very important.

Fill the holding tank with **filtered cold water**; you will need sufficient water to run through the line for approximately 15 minutes. When ready to start sanitizing, open the vent valve on the filter housing, if so equipped, and close the downstream valve. With the filter housing in either the upright or upside-down configuration, the vent valve is always at the top, the idea being that liquid should always fill the housing bottom-up for proper filtering. Start the pump on the filter and, as soon as water spews out from the vent valve, open the downstream valve and quickly close the vent valve.

Wash the entire line by running water for 15 minutes followed by **filtered hot water** at 60° C (140° F) for 15 minutes at a slow flow rate. The objective here is to perform a thorough wash, not fast throughput. Completely drain the water from the entire line. Re-open the vent valve and close the downstream valve.

Prepare a 3% caustic solution by dissolving soda ash or sodium percarbonate at a rate of 30 g/L of filtered, ambient-temperature water into the carboy or tank. Ensure that the caustic powder is thoroughly dissolved to avoid clogging the cartridge, or ideally, try to source liquid caustic to alleviate any concern. You will need as much solution as the entire line can hold – you will need to guesstimate the total volume including filter housing, hoses, etc.

Start the pump on the filter and again, as soon as caustic solution spews out from the vent valve, open the downstream valve and quickly close the vent valve. Run the caustic solution through the line until it starts discharging from the membrane filter, then immediately stop the flow. Let the membrane soak for approximately 10 minutes. Then pump the solution through the entire line for at least 15 minutes by recirculating the solution from the membrane filter back to the holding tank. When done, drain the entire line of the caustic solution by opening all vent and drain valves, and rinse the whole line again thoroughly with **filtered ambient temperature water** followed by a **cold-water** rinse. Drain the line of all water. As a precaution, you can measure and compare the pH of the water both upstream and downstream to ensure that the caustic solution has been thoroughly drained (the pH values should be identical).

Some literature recommends back-flushing the line by running hot water in the opposite direction. Unless specifically recommended by the manufacturer, back flushing is not recommended; otherwise, it could in fact add contaminants in the filter and water pressure in the opposite direction can damage the membrane.

You are now ready for stabilizing filtration. Hook up the upstream side of the depth filtration equipment to the carboy or holding tank with the wine to be filtered and the downstream side to the membrane filter as per Figure 6-11. Start the pump of the depth filter and the one on the membrane filter. Follow the same procedure as above to filter the wine. Feed the filtered wine directly into your bottling equipment and hire some well-rested family members or friends to bottle and cork at the end of the line.

During filtration, the differential pressure (psid), the difference in pressure between the upstream and downstream sides, should ideally be below 15 psid, but at least below the membrane manufacturer's specified maximum differential pressure. Once it starts exceeding that maximum (usually 80 psid at ambient temperature), the integrity of the cartridge is compromised and filtering efficiency diminishes, and the cartridge needs to be replaced. Check the manufacturer's specifications for operating parameters specific to your equipment. The ability to monitor psid is the advantage of having a pressure gauge at each of the upstream and downstream ports in the membrane filtration configuration.

When done, open all vent and discharge valves to empty the line of any wine remaining. Remove the depth filtration equipment from the line and rinse it separately, and rinse, flush, sanitize, and flush again the entire line as per instructions above.

Filter integrity and the bubble point test

An important advantage of membrane filtration is that a cartridge filter can be re-used over and over until it no longer filters to the stated specifications. A cartridge's ability to filter to specifications is referred to as integrity. You should always establish the integrity of a cartridge prior to **and** following filtration. Why following filtration if it was checked apriori? To ensure that the wine just filtered has indeed been stabilize filtered with an integral cartridge that might otherwise have been altered during filtration, therefore compromising microbial stability.

The bubble point test is a relatively simple, non-destructive test used to determine the integrity of a cartridge. Compressed gas, such as air or nitrogen, is introduced in the upstream direction through the cartridge at increasing pressure until the downstream flow of gas in a water vessel becomes a steady and vigorous stream of bubbles.

To perform the test, set up the filtration system as per Figure 6-12, making sure that the downstream valve is beyond the valve to the water vessel, and close all valves. Open the filtered water source, and open the upstream valve followed by the vent valve to wet the cartridge and to allow trapped air to escape from the housing. When water spews out of the vent valve, open the downstream valve, and let water flow through the filter for a few minutes to ensure the filter is properly wetted. **It is very important that the filter be fully wet with water for this test to be done correctly.** Then, stop the water source and close both the upstream and vent valves.

Slowly open the compressed gas feed from the tank to the upstream port. This will empty the total volume of water from the housing, and so be sure to perform this test in an area that can get wet and not on a tabletop.

Open the compressed gas tank valve to start feeding pressurized gas into the water in the vessel, and then close the downstream valve. Slowly increase the gas pressure until the flow

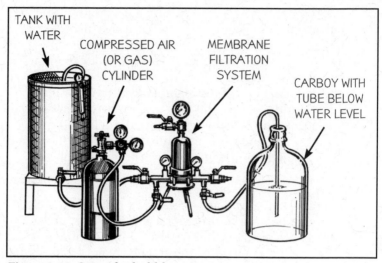

Figure 6-12: Setup for bubble point test

of gas in the water vessel becomes a steady and vigorous stream of bubbles, record the pressure, and close the gas feed.

If the final observed pressure is lower than the cartridge's **minimum** bubble point, then integrity has failed and the cartridge needs to be replaced. Check the cartridge manufacturer's specifications for exact minimum bubble points. If integrity fails, you can repeat the test to confirm results; be sure to rewet the cartridge before retesting.

Storing cartridge filters

Cartridge filters must be properly stored in between uses to optimize their filtration efficiency, particularly if stored for long periods of time.

At the end of the filtration procedure, following rinsing, sanitizing and flushing operations, drain all the water out of the filter housing by opening upstream and downstream valves or drain valves if so equipped on the housing.

If you intend to reuse the cartridge filter within a day or so, you can leave it in the housing and fill the housing with a sanitizing agent or preservative compatible with the cartridge filter, as recommended by the manufacturer, and housing material. For example, you can use a 70% ethanol solution, or inexpensive 100-proof vodka, in a stainless steel housing, or a 1% effective SO_2 sulfite solution in a polypropylene housing. When ready to reuse the cartridge filter, drain the housing completely and flush abundantly with fresh, clean water by running the filtration line.

If you need to store the cartridge filter for a longer period of time, it is best to store it in a separate closed container or a sealed plastic bag.

Choose a suitable container with a lid that will accommodate the cartridge filter. Retrieve the cartridge filter from the housing unit and place it in the container. Pour a sufficient amount of fresh 1% effective SO_2 sulfite solution (or another manufacturer-recommended storage solution if sulfite is contraindicated) in the container to completely immerse the cartridge filter, and replace the lid and ensure a tight seal. Store the container in a cool, dry place.

Alternatively, you can let the cartridge filter dry outside its housing in an area where humidity is not too high or over a source of warm – not hot – dry air. Once the cartridge filter is completely dry, place it in a plastic bag and seal properly.

When ready to reuse the cartridge filter, place it in the housing and flush abundantly with fresh, clean water by running the filtration line, then sanitize and rinse again.

Refer to section 2.6.3 on page 102 for instructions on preparing a 1% effective SO_2 sulfite solution.

The above procedure was adapted from Meissner's Product Notes on cartridge filter storage.

7
BLENDING

Traditionally, in Old World winemaking regions, wines were commonly a blend of two or more varietals – a varietal is a wine produced from a single grape variety. The final blend was subject to regional winemaking laws and/or local traditions. Winemaking laws in Europe date back more than a century and were created to mandate and control the types of blends and percentage of each varietal used in the final wine.

More recently, consumers' increased appreciation of wines and awareness of associated varietals coupled with new marketing tactics from wineries have led to varietal wines, e.g., Chardonnay, Sauvignon Blanc, Cabernet Sauvignon, Merlot and Pinot Noir; however, blending, known as *assemblage* in French, is still widely practiced in modern winemaking to produce different styles of wines, or to craft wine whose sum is greater than the sum of the parts, if not because of laws or traditions. Premium Bordeaux red wines – blends of up to five varietals – still command very high prices on the open market and at auctions.

The underlying art and science of blending is that each varietal contributes its specific characteristics. In vintage wines, only wines from the same vintage can be used for blending. In non-vintage wines, different vintage wines can be blended. Non-vintage blending is a practice mainly used to maintain a consistent level of quality and style from year to year, such as in non-vintage Champagne. But the practice of blending is not limited to blending different varietals. It can include blends of one or more varietals that have been vinified using different techniques, or blends of batches each fermented with a different yeast strain to achieve higher complexity.

A blending practice used by many commercial winemakers that gives rise to interesting wines is to blend a small percentage of malolactic fermented wines back into their non-malolactic fermented base wines to add flavor complexity while retaining flavors of the base wines. Other winemakers choose instead to only partially malolactic ferment their wines without blending to add flavor complexity but retain the flavors of the base wine. Another example is an oak-aged wine having an affinity for oak may be blended with a wine that has benefited from MLF. The resulting wine has an oak aroma with reduced acidity and greater complexity.

Once combined, the blending wines will marry into one and enhance the complexity of the final wine; however, style and complexity are shaped by the many elements in wine that must all be present in balance, and include color, aromas and flavors, alcohol, sweetness, acidity, and bitterness. And that's what great winemaking is all about: Achieving balance in wine.

7.1 BALANCE IN WINE

When we drink wine, we expect all elements to be in balance and to complement each other for a desired style. If any one element dominates, the effects of the other elements are diminished, causing the flavor profile and wine to be unbalanced. For example, excessive, hard tannins would be unsuitable for an early-drinking, fruity red wine. Unlike a cup of coffee where one adds milk and/or sugar to taste, wine is produced in bulk and cannot be adjusted in every serving. The wine must be produced in balance according to its intended style. Beyond that, it comes down to a matter of taste. For example, some people may be partial to red wine only and may not like sweet, dessert wine, while others may not enjoy sparkling wine.

Achieving balance in wine can therefore be a formidable challenge for winemakers. Consider all the vineyard management, winemaking, and cellaring factors such as weather, pruning techniques and timing, fertilizer selection, maceration techniques, yeast selection, malolactic fermentation, oak-aging regimen, maturation period, and the myriads of other factors can become quite overwhelming. And winemakers who purchase grapes or juice have no control over the quality of the raw material in producing a well-balanced wine.

There is no exact science or tools to guide home winemakers in making well-balanced wines, but there are some simple guidelines to follow. Émile Peynaud in his authoritative book THE TASTE OF WINE: THE ART AND SCIENCE OF WINE APPRECIATION [reference 17] affirms the following guiding principles in achieving balance:

"A wine tolerates acidity better when its alcoholic degree is higher; acid, bitter and astringent tastes reinforce each other; the hardest wines are those which are at the same time acid and also rich in tannins; a considerable amount of tannin is more acceptable if acidity is low and alcohol is high.

The less tannic a red wine is, the more acidity it can support (necessary for its freshness); the richer a red wine is in tannins (necessary for its development and for its longevity) the lower should be its acidity; a high tannin content allied to a pronounced acidity produces the hardest and most astringent wines."[1]

Let's examine specific wine styles along with Émile Peynaud's guiding principles to help us better understand balance.

Note: In the following sections, ranges for acidity (TA), and sugar and alcohol concentrations are provided only as typical or as representative values for the type of wine discussed. Some wines can have concentrations outside these ranges.

Fresh, dry white wines
Fresh, dry, unoaked white wines, such as Riesling and Sauvignon Blanc, have a delicate flavor profile but are relatively easy to balance. These wines are characterized by a relatively high acidity and low tannin concentration as there is no extraction of phenolic compounds, i.e., there is no maceration in white winemaking. Tannin is not agreeable in these wines because the high acidity would reinforce bitterness excessively.

If alcohol is high, in varietals such as in Chenin Blanc and Chardonnay, the wine can tolerate and benefit from a higher acid-

[1]Peynaud, Émile. THE TASTE OF WINE: THE ART AND SCIENCE OF WINE APPRECIATION. Schuster, Michael, tr. London: Macdonald & Co. (Publishers) Ltd. 1987. p. 157-158.

ity and will be better balanced. Likewise, low acid, high alcohol varietals such as Gewürztraminer, Pinot Blanc and Viognier, will definitely show better by increasing their acidity. Conversely, low alcohol varietals such as Colombard and Trebbiano (Ugni Blanc), will benefit from increased alcohol, either through blending with a higher-alcohol wine or by chaptalizing (the practice of adding sugar prior/during fermentation to increase alcohol).

Full-bodied, dry white wines

Chardonnay is one of the rare white varietals that has an affinity for oak aging. Acidity in oak aged Chardonnays must however be reduced, through MLF, to offset bitter tannins imparted from oak barrels, particularly for extended barrel aging. Acidity and tannins must be carefully balanced with the typically higher alcohol content found in full-bodied Chardonnays.

Sweet white wines

Rich, sweet white wines pose an additional challenge trying to balance the high sugar content with alcohol and acidity. Two examples are Icewine, a sweet wine made from syrupy juice extracted from naturally frozen grapes that have been harvested during the cold months of December or January, and Sauternes wine, a sweet wine from the Bordeaux region made from late-harvest grapes affected by noble rot.

Both types of wines are similar in that the juice to be fermented has much-reduced water content with a high sugar content; however, each wine has different balancing requirements.

The high sugar in Icewine is balanced with a higher acidity while Sauternes wine has a lower acidity but higher alcohol. A typical profile for an Icewine would be 11% alcohol, TA between 9–10 g/L with an RS of 200 g/L. A typical profile for a Sauternes wine would be 14% alcohol, TA of 7 g/L with an RS of 125 g/L. Note that Sauternes wine could well benefit from higher acidity owing to its higher alcohol.

At the other end of the sweet wine spectrum are lightly sweet, low alcohol wines such as Moscato d'Asti, a deliciously sweet and refreshing wine from the Piedmont region in northern Italy made from Muscat grapes. The low alcohol, typically in the 5–9% range in Moscato d'Asti, requires a lower acidity for proper balance and to still provide freshness, usually in the 6–8 g/L range.

Sparkling white wines

Sparkling wine is probably the style of wine that is the least understood and for which consumers are polarized towards either a bone-dry (brut) style or a sweeter style, with a plethora of styles in between.

Alcohol in sparkling wines generally ranges from approximately 11% to as high as 13%. In certain styles, such as Brut Champagne, acidity can be quite high, compounded by acidity from carbon dioxide gas. TA can be as high as 10 g/L, and therefore, sugar (known as dosage in sparkling wine production parlance) is added to balance acidity.

Table 7-1 maps residual sugar (RS) ranges for common sparkling wine styles.

Table 7-1
Residual sugar (RS) ranges for
common sparkling wine styles

Style	RS (g/L)
Extra Brut	0–6
Brut	0–5
Extra Dry	12–20
Dry	17–35
Semi-Dry	35–50
Sweet	50+

Dry red wines

Red winemaking always poses a greater challenge, not only because of grape or juice quality and vinification techniques, but also because it is more difficult to achieve balance, and an improperly balanced red wine can be unappealing or downright undrinkable.

There are four elements to consider in red winemaking: acidity, sweetness, alcohol, and tannin.

Of these, tannin is the element that is the most difficult to manage because it develops and transforms during maturation and aging. Home winemakers also have no tools to measure tannin concentration and must therefore rely on taste evaluation. It is also the one most often cited as the culprit in wines lacking balance. Descriptors such as harsh or hard tannins, bitter, astringent, green or rough are often used for improperly balanced red wines. It is the winemaker's challenge then to extract the "right" amount of tannins during maceration (and avoid crushing stems by destemming first, and avoiding pressing seeds), to mature the wine in oak barrels for the "right" duration, and to age it for the "right" amount of time in bottles before releasing the wine for consumption. The right amount of tannin depends on the other three elements and the desired style of wine.

Most red wines are dry and have an RS less than 2 g/L. Acidity can lie in the 5–7 g/L range with alcohol ranging between 11–14%. A wine meant to be dry and that exceeds 2 g/L of RS will be unbalanced. Although acidity and alcohol can counterbalance the sweetness, the high perceived sweetness would still be considered inappropriate for the style of wine.

The most important point to remember when dealing with balance in red wines is that acid and tannin (bitterness) will reinforce each other, and therefore, only acidity or tannin should be high with the other low. If both are high or low, try and keep the alcohol midrange to avoid an imbalance. High alcohol with both low acidity and tannin will increase perception of sweetness and will make the wine overly hot, in terms of sensation in the mouth. Similarly, low alcohol with both high acidity and high tannin will make the wine taste very light, and very bitter and acidic with no perception of sweetness for balance.

Table 7-2 provides guidelines for obtaining balance and for avoiding imbalance in red wines. Use the ranges discussed above for determining LOW, MED, HIGH contents. For fruity, light-bodied, young, early-drinking reds, aim for low tannin with higher acidity and keep the alcohol mid-range. For making age worthy, full-bodied reds, aim for higher tannin and lower acidity with alcohol in the mid- to high-range.

Table 7-2
Guidelines for obtaining balance and for
avoiding imbalance in red wines

Acidity	Tannin	Alcohol
Balanced		
LOW	HIGH	LOW-MED-HIGH
HIGH	LOW	MED-HIGH
MED	MED	LOW-MED-HIGH
Unbalanced		
LOW	LOW	HIGH
HIGH	HIGH	LOW

Port

Port is the famous fortified, sweet red wine from Portugal. In Port wine production, a distilled spirit is added to halt alcoholic fermentation (to inhibit yeast) to fortify the wine and to retain residual sugar, which can be as high as 100 g/L or more. The wine then spends a sojourn in oak barrels for two years or more depending on the type of Port being produced.

A typical profile for Port wine is 20% alcohol, 6 g/L acidity, and 80 g/L RS. Referring back to the table for dry red wine balance, it can be seen why Port is such a great wine with harmonious balance; high alcohol and high tannin coupled with low acidity with a good dose of sugar.

7.2 ACHIEVING BALANCE

Achieving balance is a mix of both art and science, and can be quite a challenge when working with fruit or juice that is not balanced, and is most often achieved through blending of different varietals or different batches (*cuvées*) of the same wine. As a winemaker, you must become versed in selecting appropriate varietals or *cuvées*, and be able to control the many parameters of each varietal and *cuvée* in producing a specific style. A specific style will be achieved through extensive tasting of the endless combinations and permutations of blends. The challenge is also not to disturb the balance of each wine when blending. Often when trying to balance one element, another element may become unbalanced, and the blended wine may not meet expectations. For example, if an oak-aged wine is blended with a very fruity wine, the final blend may have the desired oak aroma but it may also hide the much-desired fruitiness. For these reasons, blending has become an art requiring skillful craftsmanship and experience. Blending will require extensive experimentation until the final desired result is achieved.

You should continually perform both taste tests, i.e., visual, olfactory and gustatory, and analytical tests throughout the winemaking process, from growing or selecting grapes or juice, through vinification to cellaring. Keep tab of test data, particularly quantifiable data such as acidity, sweetness, and alcohol to assess the wine's development and to make necessary adjustments to achieve a well-balanced wine.

Blending is also used to correct or mask wine faults. The objective is still to produce a wine of higher quality than the individual wines. If a fault can be corrected or masked, blending is recommended. It is not recommended if a wine has faults that cannot be corrected, or is spoiled. A spoiled wine blended with a sound wine will spoil the final blend. Chapter 14 describes procedures to prevent and to correct wine faults without the use of blending.

Refer back to Table 1-1 and Table 1-2 on pages 50 to 53 describing the characteristics of various grape varieties, to help you select wines for blending to produce a desired style.

Blend wines according to well-established classical blends at first to become acquainted with the art. This will reduce the probability of producing undesired results as many varietals are not well suited to blending, and others should only be blended.

Following is a sample of classical blends for white and red wines:

- Chardonnay and Pinot Blanc
- Sauvignon Blanc and Sémillon
- Cabernet Sauvignon, Cabernet Franc, and Merlot
- Barbera and Nebbiolo

You can blend these varietals in any proportion. For example, Château Pétrus (Pomerol) typically uses 95% Merlot and 5% Cabernet Franc, while Château Mouton-Rothschild (Pauillac) typically uses approximately 80% Cabernet Sauvignon, 10% Cabernet Franc, 8% Merlot and 2% Petit Verdot (a *V. vinifera* variety), and Château d'Yquem (Sauternes) most often uses 80% Sémillon and 20% Sauvignon Blanc. Pomerol, Pauillac and Sauternes are Bordeaux appellations.

You can blend at any stage of the winemaking process, including the blending of must from crushing or pressing; however, it is best to blend wines as a last step before bulk or bottling aging or bottling when the wines to be blended have been clarified, stabilized and oak-aged. This will ensure that no further changes in the wine's structure will occur after blending, and also provides more control over the final blend.

7.3 BLENDING PROCESS

Blending requires careful planning and preparation. First, establish a desired wine style and assess the component characteristics of each blending wine. Quantitatively assess residual sugar content, alcohol content, TA and pH, and qualitatively assess fruitiness, color intensity, tannin level and oak character. Have plenty of tasting glasses available to taste the various test blends. Conduct the tasting experiments at room temperature, if possible, with even, natural lighting to verify color intensity in the wines.

Then, blend required wines in small and increasing proportions until you get the desired style. Taste as many blends with different combinations and permutations of varietals and proportions. Some will work, some won't.

If you are blending to "achieve the numbers", you can measure residual sugar content, TA and pH repeatedly until you obtain the desired level of a specific element. You can easily calculate alcohol content and TA for each blend whereas you will need to rely on your olfactory and/or gustatory senses for the desired level of fruitiness, oak flavor and tannins. Color intensity can be determined by visual inspection.

When blending wines of different alcohol contents, the final alcohol content of a blended wine can be determined as follows:

$$\% \text{ alc./vol. of blended wine} = \frac{(A \times D) + (B \times E)}{(D + E)}$$

where:

    A = % alc./vol. of first wine
    B = % alc./vol. of second wine
    D = volume of first wine
    E = volume of second wine

For example, if 5 L (1¼ gal) of a 13.5% alc./vol. wine is blended with 10 L (2½ gal) of a 12% alc./vol. wine, the resulting blended wine will have an alcohol level of:

$$\frac{(13.5 \times 5) + (12 \times 10)}{(5 + 10)} = 12.5\% \text{ alc./vol.}$$

You can perform a similar calculation for TA.

When you have achieved the desired style, set aside a sample of the blend in the cellar for up to four weeks. This is important as the blend may evolve and taste different from when first assembled. Following the storage period, re-taste the blended wine and make any blending adjustments as required. Age or bottle the final blend as desired.

Blend all wines selected in creating the final wine in a large container capable of holding the total volume to ensure that each bottle of wine is of consistent quality. Large variable-capacity stainless steel tanks are very practical for blending.

7.4 THE PEARSON SQUARE

The Pearson Square is an easy-to-use tool to calculate the number of parts of wine of a given concentration, i.e., alcohol content or TA, required to bring the concentration of another wine to a desired level. You can use this tool in lieu of the mathematical relationship presented above.

There are five parameters involved:

A = concentration of the wine to be used
B = concentration of the wine to be "corrected"
C = calculated or desired concentration
D = number of parts of wine to be used and is equal to C–B
E = number of parts of wine to be "corrected" and is equal to A–C

By placing these parameters in the following Pearson Square, you can easily determine any parameter if the other four are known quantities.

A	D
C	
B	E

Using the example in section 7.3, where a final alcohol level of 12.5% is desired by blending two wines having 13.5% and 12% alcohol, respectively, you can use the Pearson Square as follows to determine the required volumes:

13.5	0.5
12.5	
12	1.0

The value of D and E are 0.5 and 1.0, respectively, meaning that for every liter of the 13.5% alc./vol. wine, 2 L of the 12% alc./vol. wine are required.

You can perform similar calculations for TA determination in blended wines. Using the example in section 3.2.3 on page 132, to increase the TA of 20 L (5 gal) of wine from 5.0 to 6.0 g/L using a 7.5-g/L blend wine, use the Pearson Square to determine the number of parts required of each wine.

7.5	1.0
6.0	
5.0	1.5

   Therefore, for every 1.5 L of the 5.0-g/L wine, 1.0 L of the 7.5-g/L wine would be required. Then, for 20 L (5 gal) of 5.0-g/L wine to be increased to 6.0 g/L, 20÷1.5=13.3 L of the 7.5-g/L wine would be required.

8
OAK BARRELS

Oak barrels are seldom used in home winemaking. Their high price, and perceived high maintenance and high risk of wine spoilage have made oak barrels unattractive to amateur winemakers. Yet, barrels have been used since the early days of winemaking. It is well known that oak-aging benefits far surpass the perceived disadvantages. Some knowledge and experience of barrel maintenance coupled with the wine's new organoleptic dimensions should make their use very attractive and the investment worthwhile.

A wine's quality, complexity and aging potential are greatly enhanced by aging in oak barrels such as the one depicted in Figure 8-1. Oak imparts a distinctive aroma to wine and increases the tannin level improving the wine's aging potential. Barrel-aged wines also benefit from the minute, gradual, controlled oxidation, or micro-oxygenation, that occurs in barrels – and not in glass containers or stainless steel vats. Because wood is a porous material, both oxidation and evaporation occur between and through the wood staves. Even old (but well-kept) barrels concentrate the wine through this minute oxidation/evaporation, lending the finished wine a perfume, a bouquet never possible in inert, totally hermet-

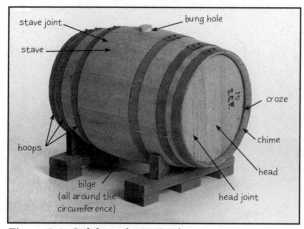

Figure 8-1: Oak barrel terminology

ically sealed aging containers. Oak barrels also improve a wine's limpidity and, in the case of red wines, they provide a deeper color.

If your winemaking preference is young, early drinking wines and you are simply looking to impart oak aromas, oaking alternatives may be best for you. If you are looking to craft full-bodied, complex wines like a bold California Cab, a First-Growth Bordeaux, an opulent Chardonnay, or a delicate yet intense Pinot Noir, barrel aging is the solution.

This guide will demystify the centuries-old tradition of oak aging and will help you understand how barrels can transform a great wine into a superior, full-bodied wine with layers of complex aromas and flavors, exquisite balance and long cellaring potential. Specifically, it will help you understand the physics and chemistry of barrels to not only give you an appreciation of why barrels are different from oaking alternatives, but also to guide you in your purchasing and oaking regimen decisions.

This chapter also provides detailed practical instructions on storing, maintaining, preparing and reconditioning barrels, and avoiding spoilage problems. With some experience and routine checks, winemaking using barrels will prove to be relatively simple and will reward you with great wine.

8.1 HOW BARRELS WORK

Oak, specifically white oak as it relates to wine, is a type of wood that is rich in "good" tannins – as opposed to harsh, undesirable tannins found in grape seeds and stems – essential in shaping the structure and body of wine, defining its aging potential, as well as acting as a natural clarifying agent. Tannins contribute to mouthfeel, which can create a "puckery" feeling, akin to drinking cold tea. They are imparted through the simple contact of wine with wood, and the extent of extraction depends on contact time. Over-extraction would cause wine to become overly astringent.

The underlying barrel physics and chemistry responsible for the evolution and development of wine can be distilled down to an easy-to-understand explanation – the basic phenomenon is called micro-oxygenation. Wood, being a porous material, allows the barrel to "breathe" by allowing alcohol (ethanol) and water to evaporate to the outside and air to penetrate to the interior and oxygenate the wine. The tight but porous joints between stave and head segments hasten evaporation and oxygenation. Evaporation and wine absorption into the wood cause wine volume inside the barrel to decrease; the resulting headspace is known as ullage. Barrels must be regularly filled, or topped up, to replenish evaporated wine and avoid over-oxygenation, which would otherwise oxidize and spoil the wine. By keeping the barrel full, the infinitesimally small oxygenation, or micro-oxygenation, is controlled and essential to the wine's development.

During the aging (maturation) period, micro-oxygenation softens tannins and increases bouquet complexity by allowing a very small amount of oxygen to interact with the wine's compounds and transform them into more complex aromas and flavors. In addition, oak aging – specifically, toasted oak – stabilizes pigments thereby intensifying and stabilizing color.

8.2 BARREL TYPES

There is a plethora of barrel types now available to home winemakers with a choice of provenance of the wood, drying and seasoning methods, toast level, and size; the most common sizes range from 19 to 225 L (5 to 60 gal).

Nowadays, white oak is the wood of choice for winemaking; however, not all white oak is the same, nor are all barrels manufactured the same way. First, there are various species of white oak within the *Quercus* (oak) genus, each having somewhat different characteristics. *Q. robur* is the most widespread species in Europe while its subspecies *Q. sessilis* and *Q. pendunculata* are most often used for French barrels, and *Q. alba* is predominantly used for American and Canadian barrels, which tend to impart more oakiness. Second, wood and barrels are processed and built differently in different countries. Methods used in drying and sawing wood, for example, can impart significantly different characteristics, and consequently, oak species and manufacturing methods directly influence cost.

Such are the reasons why winemakers request barrels from specific countries, the most popular being French, American and, to a large extent, Hungarian oak barrels, although Eastern European and Canadian barrels are also available. It is also not uncommon to find French barrels manufactured using a mix of French and/or Eastern European wood, and, in some cases, winemakers can specify provenance down to a region or forest, the most common being Allier, Limousin (*Q. pendunculata*), Nevers (*Q. sessilis*), and Tronçais. Each wood type has its own special characteristics or is preferred for specific wines. For example, Chardonnay has an affinity for Limousin oak while Cabernets, Merlot, Bordeaux-style blends, and Pinot Noir have an affinity for Nevers and Tronçais. Provenance can also be specified for American oak and includes areas or states such as Minnesota, Appalachians, Kentucky, and Indiana.

Drying and seasoning methods used in preparing oak wood destined for barrels also play a significant role in the style and quality of wine. To make barrels more affordable, they may be manufactured from wood that has been kiln-dried – a quicker and cheaper production process. In contrast, premium barrels are manufactured from wood that has been air-dried for two or three years, for example. The advantage of air-dried wood compared to kiln-dried is that the former imparts more subtle aromas and softer tannins to wine. Likewise, the longer the air-drying period, the better; for example, very young air-dried wood would impart undesirable green oak aromas and harsh tannins. Manufacturers of premium barrels usually provide a choice of two- or three-year air-dried wood, albeit at different prices.

The type of toasting is as important as the type of wood or drying and seasoning methods. It complements the wine by imparting another level of complexity to the bouquet and flavor profile not otherwise possible with oaking alternatives. Before barrel heads are seated onto the ends, open-ended barrels are placed over an open fire for toasting. The high toasting temperature acts on the wood components, namely, cellulose, hemicellulose and lignins, to soften tannins and release desirable aromas such as vanilla, caramel, coffee, chocolate, and aromatic sweetness.

Three levels of toasting are available based on the desired wine style: Light, medium and heavy. Some manufacturers also provide a medium-plus toast for added toastiness without it being too heavy. Usually, only the barrel staves are toasted; however, barrels can be ordered with toasted heads if extra "toastiness" is desired. Toast level is most often identified on a barrel head; for example, MT-TH stands for "Medium Toast – Toasted Heads". If you are new to oak aging, choose Medium Toast barrels as they provide a good compromise between aging period and risk of over-oaking.

8.3 BARREL-BUYING CONSIDERATIONS

Before deciding to invest in oak barrels, establish a budget and whether it is worth investing time and patience to care for the barrels. Oak barrels are expensive and require proper preparation and maintenance that can prove to be a tedious task, especially when encountering barrel spoilage problems, if you do not care for them properly. When shopping for barrels, inquire about barrel origin, the type of oak used and the extent of toasting, if any. These factors will affect price.

Before purchasing barrels and filling them with wine, ensure that your cellar provides an adequate environment to store full barrels, and then map out your desired wine style.

First, lay out a reserved area in your cellar to receive the barrels. Choose a suitable and practical location as chances are that you will not be moving the barrels around much. Cellar temperature should ideally be around 13° C (55° F) with a relative humidity (RH) around 65%. These are ideal conditions for barrel aging; otherwise, barrels may shrink and expand, causing excessive wine loss through evaporation, or possibly causing mold buildup in an excessively humid cellar.

Second, establish the desired level of oakiness and toastiness, flavor profile, and maturation period. These will help you determine the required type and size of barrels. Experimenting with different barrel types and maturation periods will help you establish a preference, which you can then replicate year after year. There is no single method or regimen for maturing wine; it all comes down to preferred style. For example, you can try blending half a batch of wine aged in American oak and the other half in French oak, and then blending the two at bottling time. Compare that wine with one aged in American oak for half the maturation time and then moved to French oak for the other half of the maturation period. The results will undoubtedly surprise you.

The maturation period depends on the desired style, barrel size and age. New oak imparts more oak flavor and tannins than older wood, and therefore, a shorter maturation period may be in order. Likewise, smaller barrels have a greater surface-to-volume (S/V) ratio than larger barrels, and therefore, they impart oak flavors at a proportionately higher rate. For example, a 55-L barrel has more than 1.5 times the S/V ratio of a 225-L barrel.

In home winemaking, 15-gal or 57-L barrels are recommended because they are most convenient to handle in the cellar, even when full. The more common 60-gal or 225-L barrels used by commercial wineries are cumbersome and not easy to handle, even when empty. Keep in mind that smaller, lower-capacity barrels are costlier, in terms of cost per unit volume, than larger, higher-capacity barrels although the latter are very bulky for home winemaking. The 57-L (15-gal) barrel provides a good compromise between cost and size.

Oak barrels are now almost exclusively available with galvanized hoops. Avoid barrels with steel hoops as these will rust and spoil the wine if it comes in contact with the hoops. Wine can seep through the stave joints and become contaminated from hoop rust on the exterior surface of the barrel.

The useful life of a barrel is approximately 5 years, after which time it is said to be neutral as it no longer imparts any appreciable amount of oak flavor or tannins, unless you have the time and patience for extended barrel aging. At that point, you can use the barrel as a storage vessel, possibly in conjunction with other oaking alternatives such as oak chips or staves, or it can be reconditioned to expose new oak and extend its life. Keep good records of barrel uses to establish the residual lifetime before they become neutral.

8.4 BARREL USES

Barrels are used for alcoholic fermentation, malolactic fermentation (MLF) and aging, commonly referred to as maturation, to impart oak flavors and tannins to wine, and to add another level of complexity to the flavor profile.

8.4.1 BARREL FERMENTATION

Without a doubt, barrel-fermented wines are more complex and of superior quality over wines fermented in glass, stainless steel, or other types of fermentation vessels. Wines that have been barrel-fermented also absorb the oak qualities in a softer way, as opposed to picking up the harsher principles when merely oak-aged.

Barrel fermentation is used extensively in white wine production, especially for Chardonnay. The fermentation of white grape juice in oak barrels is a traditional Burgundian technique that can yield high-quality wine. However, as it is quite easy to oxidize white wine if it is not constantly topped up, only the most meticulous and experienced home winemakers should attempt this technique. Topping of white-wine oak barrels requires constant care and supervision. You can use the topping device in Figure 5-4 on page 256 to help you better manage your barrel topping regimen.

When initiating fermentation in oak barrels, keep the temperature above 15° C (59° F). It can then be lowered, if desired, to 10°–14° C (50°–57° F) for white wines and 22°–28° C (72°–82° F) for red wines to carry out a cooler fermentation. If fermenting wine is transferred to oak barrels, fermentation can be carried out to completion at the lower temperature.

For varieties that have an affinity for oak wood, you can take full advantage of the benefits of *bâtonnage*, discussed in details in section 4.7.3, by stirring the fine lees during barrel fermentation. By stirring the lees, "they act as an even more effective buffer between the wine and the wood, limiting the extent to which wood tannins and pigments are extracted into the wine. Wines subjected to lees stirring therefore tend to be much paler and less tannic than those whose lees are not stirred."[1] In fact, Zoecklein et al. [reference 22] cite research that determined that "barreled wines aged and stirred *sur-lie* had a phenolic content [namely, tannins and color pigments] quite similar to wines aged in stainless steel"[2] but also with greater aging potential.

You can use a stirring rod, or a *bâtonnage* cane, shown in Figure 8-2, to stir the lees. The cane consists of a folding T-shaped rod with a double chain at one end to stir the lees, and a bung hole adapter that can be adjusted for various barrel sizes. To stir the lees, insert the chain end of the cane into the barrel, seat the adapter firmly in the bunghole, and twist the cane using the T-handle.

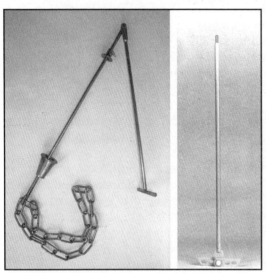

Figure 8-2: A *bâtonnage* cane and stirring rod

Stir the fine lees weekly for the first couple of months and then monthly to increase a wine's complexity and richness. During the *sur-lie* aging period, maintain the temperature in the 18°–20° C (64°–68° F) range. Alternatively, ferment the wine as low as 10° C (50° F) in a glass container or stainless steel tank, and then rack the wine into barrels when the Brix (SG) level has dropped to 10 B° (1.040). The cooler temperature slows down fermentation and helps preserve fruity aromas, particularly in delicate, aromatic white varietals. Throughout the lees contact period, maintain a free SO_2 level between 35–40 mg/L, adjusted up or down based on the wine's pH.

To further increase the complexity of barrel-fermented wines, you can carry out MLF in barrels, but without *bâtonnage* during MLF as the additional aeration could inhibit malolactic bacteria (MLB). It has also been observed that red wines that have been malolactic fermented in barrels retain more of their color than their glass or stainless steel counterparts. And remember to

[1]Robinson, Jancis, ed. THE OXFORD COMPANION TO WINE – THIRD EDITION. Oxford: Oxford University Press. 2006. p. 399.
[2]Zoecklein, Bruce W., Fugelsang, K.C., Gump B.H., and F.S. Nury. WINE ANALYSIS AND PRODUCTION. Gaithersburg: Aspen Publishers, Inc. 1999. p. 160.

respect temperature and free SO_2 requirements during MLF, as outlined in section 4.8.

8.4.2 Oak-barrel aging

Red wine varietals are most suitable for oak aging although white wine varietals such as Chardonnay and Sauvignon Blanc can be aged in oak barrels, albeit for a much shorter period. Don't leave white wines to age in oak barrels for too long, otherwise, the wine will acquire excessive tannins and will become unbalanced, very harsh and, potentially, undrinkable.

Red wine maturation

In red wine production from grapes, wine is usually transferred to oak barrels after pressing to finish fermentation, as it would be impractical to conduct maceration in oak barrels – transferring grapes and pomace in and out would be quite a task – unless you have barrels with one head removed. Instead, transfer wine to oak barrels when the desired level of color and tannin extraction is achieved from maceration and alcoholic fermentation, and then let the wine finish fermenting to dryness, if not completed, with lees contact.

The amount of oak imparted to a wine during maturation depends on the barrel size and age (new vs. old oak), and the barrel maturation period. A small-volume barrel will impart oak flavor quicker than a larger barrel owing to the higher surface-to-volume ratio in a smaller barrel. Different grape varieties will also have different barrel maturation requirements as some may have more of an affinity for oak than other varieties. For example, varieties high in tannin content will require less barrel aging. Therefore, you should monitor and taste regularly wines undergoing barrel maturation to avoid imparting too much of oak taste.

For the first several months – this depends on the size and age of the barrel – smell and taste the wine on a weekly basis to determine when the desired level of oak character has been achieved. This may occur very early as new oak imparts its flavor very quickly. The first and second batches in a new barrel will tend to be high in tannin content. The third and fourth batches will produce the higher-quality wine, and wine can be stored for a much longer period as tannins are transferred from the oak to the wine at a lesser extent.

As guidelines for 57-L (15-gal) American and French barrels, age wine for 2–3 weeks and 1–2 months, respectively, when the wood is new. The next batch of wine can sojourn for twice the amount of time, or 4–6 weeks and 2–4 months, respectively. Double the maturation time until the fourth batch, which will be the best wine out of those barrels. Subsequent batches can spend 1–2 years in barrels and may get blended back with any of the first three batches to balance the wine and achieve the desired style. With experience, you will come to determine how long wine should age in barrels before transferring it out. Be sure to taste barrel samples regularly to monitor the extent of oaking, and to decide when to transfer wine out.

It is recommended not to oak-age all wine so that you can blend aged and non-aged wines later to achieve the right level of oak flavor.

Wine clarifies during barrel aging as it acquires tannins. You can rack unfiltered wine at 3- to 6-month intervals to other barrels during barrel-aging depending on the clarity of the wine. After each racking, rinse the barrel two or three times thoroughly with cold water to remove all deposits.

Store wine at cellar temperature at approximately 13° C (55° F) and RH in the 55%–75% range during the aging process. A RH below this range will favor evaporation of wine from the barrel, whereas humidity above this range will favor growth of spoilage organisms.

During maturation, check the ullage in all barrels and top up every 3–4 weeks – more often in a dry or warm cellar or with new oak. Always use a similar type and equivalent quality of wine for topping up – never use a "faulty" wine, which could otherwise negatively affect the entire batch and possibly the barrel itself. Use a good quality silicone bung to secure the bung hole, and keep the bung area clean to avoid mold buildup.

And here's a trick to reduce the risk of drying up the bung hole area, which could otherwise cause a hairline crack that would allow wine to seep out and air to penetrate the barrel. Top up and bung the barrel, and then rotate the barrel with the bung to the 2-o'clock position. At the next top up, rotate the barrel in the reverse direction with the bung to the 10-o'clock position.

Following the oak-aging period, an additional period of up to 12–18 months of bottle aging is recommended to let the wine evolve and tannins soften, which will further add complexity. Taste the wine at regular intervals during the maturation period to determine when the wine has reached the right balance for your taste.

8.4.3 OAK-AGING CONSIDERATIONS

Some wines have an affinity for oak while others should never be aged in oak barrels. The most important consideration is to maintain balance of aromas, alcohol, acidity (TA), sweetness and bitterness. Here then are some guidelines:

- Barrel age high alcohol wines, typically reds (where TA is usually reduced further through MLF), such as Syrah or Nebbiolo, particularly where TA is low, such as Pinot Noir, or a "heavy" malo-fermented Chardonnay, to balance them with tannins.

- Avoid oaking delicately aromatic or fruit-forward wines to avoid losing freshness or oak masking the fruit.

- Avoid oaking high-acidity wines, particularly whites known to have high TA, such as Chenin Blanc, dry Riesling, or a lively Chardonnay, because the high acidity will reinforce bitterness and astringency, making the wine unpalatable.

- Barrel age sweet wines only if there is moderate to high alcohol content to balance tannins, e.g., Port or Icewine.

8.5 ALTERNATIVES TO BARREL AGING FOR IMPARTING OAK AROMAS

There are no proven alternatives to barrel aging that benefit wines to the extent that oak barrels do. These benefits are a direct result of the barrel's physical properties, namely, the wood's porosity and staves that provide controlled oxidation. However, several inexpensive techniques are available to home winemakers to impart oak aromas and flavors. The most common techniques are the use of what is commonly known as oak adjuncts – oak mor chips, beans or segments and oak staves – and oak extract.

8.5.1 OAK ADJUNCTS

The use of oak adjuncts such as oak chips, beans or segments and oak staves is a common and inexpensive alternative for imparting oak aromas and flavors to wine. This method is becoming increasingly popular in the winemaking industry as an alternative to expensive oak barrels. Some wineries are also experimenting with the use of solid oak planks immersed directly into the wine. These alternatives are the best way to quickly add oak aromas and flavors, particularly to small batches, and are therefore highly recommended for early-drinking wines. Oaking can be accomplished in less than a week, even as little as a couple of days, but it does nothing for aging. You can also toast chips in a small toaster oven to add some toastiness.

Oak mor, shown in Figure 8-3, is available as fine sawdust, and plain or toasted small and large chips in French or American oak. The recommended rate of addition is 1–2 g/L and 2–4 g/L for 1–2 weeks for white and red wines, respectively. You can add more or less depending on your desired oak flavor intensity.

Figure 8-3 (clockwise, from top left): Regular oak-mor, oak shavings, large French oak chips, small French oak chips, and premium oak-mor

You will need to prepare the oak chips as follows before use. Weigh the required amount of chips and wash in a sieve with cool tap water until no more dust or color is being washed out. Optionally, if you wish to add some toasted oak notes to wine, toast the chips, while still moist, under a broiler at about 200° C (392° F) until most are browned – but not burnt – to a crisp. Drop the chips loosely in the wine during the closed-container alcoholic fermentation; they will settle at the bottom in a day or so. Taste and sniff the wine frequently until the desired aromas and flavors reach a good intensity, and then rack the wine carefully away from the chips.

A popular, albeit more expensive alternative is oak staves that can be immersed in any type of vessel. Staves are an attractive alternative because they impart oak more slowly owing to the fact that less end grain is exposed on the wood.

An alternative to replicate oak barrel aging that is gaining popularity in commercial winemaking is in the use of oaking methods, such as the use of oak staves, in conjunction with micro-oxygenation techniques. The practice involves using a closed vessel, such as a neutral barrel or tank, and injecting a miniscule, controlled amount of oxygen into the wine. The required equipment is well beyond the scope of the home winemaker; however, it can be easily replicated, even for carboy-sized batches, using an oxygen tank and gas diffuser.

8.5.2 Oak extract

Oak extract, an additive produced by macerating oak chips in ethanol, is yet another inexpensive alternative to impart oak aromas and flavors to wine. Figure 8-4 shows Vintner's Sinatin 17 oak extract available at winemaking shops. The rate of addition depends on the concentration of oak flavor extracted from maceration. For example, a 10%-oak extract additive, such as Sinatin 17, can be added at a rate of 1–2 mL/L of wine, or as per the manufacturer's instructions or according to your taste and preference.

Oak extract accelerates wine aging and is, therefore, not a recommended practice for premium wine although okay for early-drinking wines. This method is not accepted and not allowed in commercial winemaking.

8.6 OAK BARREL STORAGE, MAINTENANCE AND PREPARATION

It is always advisable to buy new or reconditioned oak barrels, and to avoid used ones if their origin is unknown. Barrels of unknown origin will require extensive preparation before use and are very risky. And if possible, buy barrels when ready to transfer wine into to avoid maintenance of empty barrels; if not, maintenance of empty barrels can be made relatively easy and problem-free by following recommended treatments.

Figure 8-4: VINTNER'S SINATIN 17 liquid oak extract in 30- and 500-mL formats

Thoroughly inspect the condition of a barrel – interior and exterior – before filling it with wine. Inspect the interior for any obvious defects or mold using a light bulb small enough to pass through the bung hole. And inspect the exterior for any obvious defects that might affect the barrel's storing and aging ability. For example, verify that stave and head joints are not too wide, that the bung hole is properly tapered, and that all hoops are properly fastened.

8.6.1 NEW BARREL STORAGE AND MAINTENANCE

Store empty barrels in a wine cellar at 13° C (55° F) and at 55%–75% RH, away from dampness. Wrap barrels in cellophane to improve humidity retention in a cellar with less-than-desirable conditions. Quite often, barrel manufacturers ship barrels already wrapped in cellophane. Simply wrap cellophane around the bilge (the cross-section area of the barrel with the largest diameter) of the barrel to cover staves only, as shown in Figure 8-5. Do not wrap top and bottom head sections; otherwise, the barrel will not "breathe" properly. Head sections wrapped in cellophane will trap moisture causing mold to form and the barrel to spoil beyond repair. Do **not** wrap a barrel in cellophane if its exterior has freshly spilled wine, which can be a source of nutrients for mold and bacteria, or with the slightest growth of mold; cellophane will cause a greenhouse effect and accelerate growth of mold in a moist environment, fur-

Figure 8-5: Wrapping a barrel in cellophane

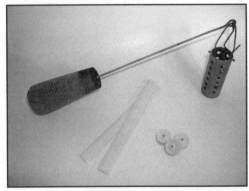

Figure 8-6: Sulfur holder, sticks and discs

ther compounding the problem.

Barrels to be stored empty also require proper sulfiting to prevent growth of spoilage organisms that would otherwise make the barrels unusable. Although a sulfite solution can be used, the best method to sulfite a barrel is by burning a piece of sulfur stick or disc, shown in Figure 8-6, inside the barrel. Sulfur for burning is typically sold in 20-cm sticks or 10-g discs. Burnt sulfur, or sulfur dioxide (SO_2) gas, replaces the air, fills the barrel, and protects it from spoilage organisms. You can store an empty barrel for an indefinite amount of time if properly preserved by sulfur.

To prepare an empty barrel for storage, thoroughly rinse the interior with fresh water, drain well and let dry. Use a sulfur disc or cut a short piece from a sulfur stick and light it with a match or lighter. A 2.5×2.5-cm piece is sufficient for a 57-L (15-gal) barrel. Drop the piece of burning sulfur into a fireproof sulfur holder, such as the one depicted in Figure 8-6, specifically built for this purpose. Discs can be conveniently inserted on the piece of hanging wire to make the whole operation easier. The sulfur holder prevents burning sulfur from dropping inside the barrel, which could otherwise cause hydrogen sulfide (H_2S) to form and wine to spoil later on during wine storage. H_2S imparts a rotten-egg smell and can be very difficult to eradicate. Refer to section 14.7 on how to treat the presence of H_2S.

Quickly introduce the sulfur holder with burning sulfur into the barrel, as shown in Figure 8-7, and make sure the fireproof bung is well seated in the bung hole and that no sulfur gas escapes. Let the sulfur stick or disc burn for several minutes until it is completely burnt and is extinguished. Remove the holder from the barrel and quickly replace with a silicone or wooden bung. To pro-

337

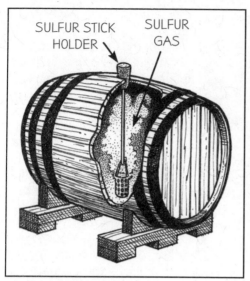

Figure 8-7: Burning sulfur inside a barrel

long the life of the silicone bung, you can cover the bung with a plastic bag, such as a freezer bag, to protect it from the sulfur gas.

On a regular basis, for example, every 3–4 weeks, examine the inside of the barrel for the presence of SO_2 using a small flashlight. If you see or smell the gas, simply put the bung back in place; otherwise, burn more sulfur.

Caution: When burning sulfur sticks or discs, work in a well-ventilated area as sulfur fumes can irritate your nose.

8.6.2 NEW BARREL PREPARATION

Although it is possible to transfer wine directly into a new barrel without any treatment, there is always a risk of leakage between stave joints but most often at the head joints and/or croze – the groove near the end of the staves where each barrel head fits. Not only will this cause wine loss but also it will expose wine to air and cause oxidation, and in the worst case, it may cause spoilage organisms to form on the barrel surface if not properly treated on time.

You can perform a simple procedure to swell a barrel and to test for leakage by partially filling the barrel with water. If the barrel does not leak or stops leaking after the wood has swollen, then the barrel is sound and can be used without worries. When the wood of a barrel swells, staves, head segments and croze will form tighter joints minimizing and/or eliminating wine seepage. If leakage cannot be stopped, the barrel may be unusable and costly to repair. In most cases, a water-tested leaky barrel (which has not been filled with wine) can be returned to the barrel supply shop.

You can swell a new barrel in preparation for aging wine by one of two methods: 1) using a hot-water treatment, a French technique for swelling a barrel, or 2) using an overnight water-soaking treatment. Clean water, if properly used, should be the only treatment necessary for a barrel in good condition. Avoid water that contains any kind of contaminants or that has high iron content. Both methods have the advantage of using no chemicals that would otherwise excessively leach out the oak flavor from the barrel. However, the hot-water treatment method may prove more advantageous; it requires much less water and, because of the much shorter soak period, it does not leach out oak flavor as much as the overnight water-soaking treatment.

As a first step for either method, let out any remaining sulfur gas from the barrel, and thoroughly rinse with fresh, lukewarm water at least twice to ensure that the entire inner surface is cleaned.

To perform a hot-water treatment, pour a small volume of hot water into the barrel. Use a 1:20 volume ratio of hot water to barrel size; for example, use 12 L of hot water for a 57-L barrel. Bung the barrel and then slosh it around to coat the entire interior surface. The vapor pressure created by this action will accelerate any seepage through the stave and head joints and croze. Return the barrel to the upright position, fill the head area with hot water and let the barrel stand for 15 minutes before repeating for the other head area. Initially, the barrel may leak in one or more places but, as the wood swells, all leaks should plug up fairly quickly. When both heads have been properly soaked and swollen and there is no leakage, completely drain the water and allow the barrel to dry and cool down. The barrel is then ready for use. If leakage persists, the barrel may be defective or overly dry; in which case, you should try an overnight water-soaking treatment specifically recommended for very dry barrels that have been in dry storage for a prolonged time.

To perform an overnight water-soaking treatment, place the barrel horizontally and fill it with fresh cool water, making sure that it is properly topped up. Initially, the barrel may leak in one or more places but, as the wood swells, all leaks should plug up within a few hours. Let the barrel soak overnight or to a maximum of 24–36 hours if leakage persists. If there is still leakage after this soaking period, the barrel is defective and should be returned.

Warning: NEVER exceed the maximum soaking period; otherwise, mold can form and spoil the barrel.

At the end of the soaking period, when all leakage has stopped, drain the barrel by placing it in the bung-down position. No puddling of water should remain in the bilge. Allow the barrel to dry and then immediately fill it with wine. If the barrel cannot be filled with wine, you can store the barrel empty by burning sulfur. It is very important that the barrel be drained and dried completely before burning sulfur; otherwise, sulfur gas will hydrate and form into sulfurous acid, and adversely affect the taste of wine and cause spoilage.

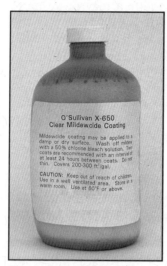

Figure 8-8: Mildewcide

The barrel's exterior surface requires no special preparation although it should be inspected regularly for mold. Section 8.7.2 describes how to prevent and to treat mold that has formed on the barrel's exterior surface. Optionally, it can be treated with Mildewcide (BarrelGuard), shown in Figure 8-8, to inhibit mold. Apply two coats of Mildewcide using a paintbrush and let dry to a clear finish.

Warning: Some manufacturers recommend a soda ash treatment for barrel preparation. Soda ash will leach out oak flavor, and in some cases, impart undesirable flavors to the wood, which will react negatively with wine. For this reason, it is best to avoid using soda ash, although it can be used for treating barrels affected by spoilage organisms. Refer to section 8.7 for more information on treating oak-barrel spoilage problems. And NEVER use chlorine-based chemicals in barrels; they are the primary source of 2,4,6-trichloroanisole, or TCA, the culprit in corked wine. Refer to sections 2.6.2 and 14.17 for more information treating TCA.

8.6.3 USED BARREL STORAGE AND MAINTENANCE

Storage and maintenance of empty used barrels are more tedious, but necessary tasks. If not properly maintained, used barrels can contaminate and spoil wine. When possible, you should transfer new wine into a used barrel after having transferred out aged wine. This has the advantage that the barrel requires no preparation beyond a simple water rinse. For this reason, it is recommended that you have a continuous supply of wine to be aged in oak barrels so that these need not be maintained.

Although not recommended, you can store used barrels empty for a prolonged period of time if treated to prevent them from drying out. This may prove tedious. You will need to soak the barrel using a hot water or overnight water-soaking treatment. Empty the barrel, let it dry and then burn sulfur to prevent mold and bacteria growth. Bung the barrel, and set it aside in a cool area for storage. Repeat this procedure every 6–8 weeks.

If this procedure proves to be inconvenient, and to reduce the risk of spoilage problems, you can use a sulfur-citric holding solution for barrel storage. A holding solution will promote sterility and keep the barrel smelling sweet. This procedure is not recommend-

Figure 8-9: Tartrate buildup in barrels

ed for new barrels or barrels less than one year old; oak flavor will be excessively stripped in the process.

To prepare a holding solution, dissolve 1 g of citric acid and 2 g of potassium metabisulfite in hot water for each liter of barrel volume – or 4 g and 8 g, respectively, for every gallon of barrel volume. Fill the barrel two-thirds with fresh water and then add the holding solution. Top up with fresh water and bung the barrel for storage. Top up the barrel with fresh water or holding solution every 4–6 weeks to keep all wood and bung hole moist. You should also rotate the barrel alternately to the 10- and 2-o'clock positions after each top up to keep the bung hole moist. This procedure allows the barrel to be stored indefinitely without the risk of spoilage, and prevents hairline cracks in the bung hole area.

8.6.4 USED BARREL PREPARATION

Used barrels require no special preparation beyond a simple water rinse, if desired, when transferring wine out and in immediately. If the barrel has been stored with a holding solution, drain and rinse the barrel thoroughly. A neutralizer for the holding solution is not required since sulfur and citric residues are compatible with wine. You can immediately fill the barrel with wine.

If the barrel has tartrate buildup, hot water and a fair amount of athletic barrel swirling will help take out some of the tartrates. You can use soda ash to speed up the process although it will leach out some oak flavor. Swirl the barrel vigorously to splash the hot water solution all over the barrel's inside, and then, rinse the barrel several times with fresh water.

Warning: The sulfur-citric holding solution will etch a concrete floor. Hose the floor with plenty of water if some holding solution is spilled on the floor.

If the barrel has a very heavy tartrate buildup, as shown in Figure 8-9, it will be impossible to remove the tartrate without reconditioning the barrel. Refer to section 8.8 for step-by-step instructions on barrel reconditioning.

341

Figure 8-10: Larvae in the croze of a barrel

Figure 8-11: Typical mold problems in barrels

8.7 OAK-BARREL SPOILAGE

Oak barrels, if properly maintained, should not cause any problems. Spoilage problems can happen, however, since wood is a good breeding medium for bacteria and other spoilage organisms, especially in the presence of water or wine, or other unwanted substances or critters, such as larvae in the croze, shown in Figure 8-10. The risk of spoilage problems is also increased as no chemicals are used in treating barrels. Chemicals leach out much of the oak extract in the wood and are therefore only recommended as a last resort in treating spoilage problems.

8.7.1 TYPES OF OAK-BARREL SPOILAGE PROBLEMS

There are four major types of spoilage problems that can occur in oak barrels: 1) mold, 2) acetic acid, 3) yeast and 4) lactic acid bacteria.

Mold is the most frequent type of spoilage problem encountered and is very difficult to eradicate. Figure 8-11 illustrates three cases of mold formation and growth in barrels. Mold attacks and transforms the wood on the barrel's interior surface, causing mouse-like or mushroom-like flavors in wine. A barrel affected by mold is no longer usable and should be discarded. Tiny amounts of mold growing inside an empty barrel can, however, be treated using sodium percarbonate.

Mold can also form on the exterior surface of a barrel caused from wine seepage, or water residues, or an overly humid cellar. There is little danger of this mold penetrating from the outside of a barrel if removed and cleaned promptly. When barrels are opened for sampling or topping, some mold spores could enter the barrel; however, these molds are aerobic and will not grow in a full barrel.

The most common area of mold formation on the exterior surface is around the bung hole. The bung hole area will absorb wine rapidly due to the increased surface area, and will saturate on the exterior promoting the growth of penicillium mold.

A periodic cleaning of the bung hole area and other parts of a barrel's exterior surface contaminated with wine can prevent this problem. Scrub the affected area using a natural- or plastic-bristle brush. Do not use a wire brush for cleaning a barrel; it will tend to scratch the surface excessively. Prepare a scrubbing solution by dissolving equal parts of potassium metabisulfite and citric acid in water. As the solution is acidic, be careful not to let it come into contact with galvanized hoops. If this happens, rinse the hoops promptly with water. When scrubbing the bung hole area, be careful not to let the solution enter the bung hole or drip in the wine. To avoid this, let the solution dry before pulling the bung.

Mold can also spread to or grow on cork or wood bungs, penetrate the bung hole and contaminate the wine. Silicone rubber bungs are the best choice for storing wine in oak barrels to prevent this risk of spoilage.

A second frequent type of spoilage problem is the formation of *Acetobacter*. These vinegar bacteria, responsible for acetic acid (VA), grow in an aerobic environment and can be prevented by keeping barrels topped up. *Acetobacter* can be easily detected by smelling the interior of the barrel or using a Wallerstein Test Kit, described in section 6.2.3. Volatile acidity in the early stages will smell like clean vinegar, though faint. A wine would require an undrinkable level of VA to produce a pronounced vinegar odor when the barrel is emptied. Therefore, the acetic acid in an empty barrel more likely comes from wine residues having oxidized. This problem is often the result of insufficient sulfuring when the barrel is stored empty. In later stages, the acetic acid combines with alcohol residues to form ethyl acetate, which smells distinctly like nail-polish remover. This problem is very difficult to eradicate in the cleaning process.

The third type of spoilage problem is yeast formation. Many of the spoilage-causing types of yeasts cannot live in an alcohol solution, such as wine, above 10% alc./vol.; these are, therefore, not a cause of concern. However, *Brettanomyces* yeast can cause a serious problem as it can metabolize extremely low levels of sugar, even wood cellulose sugars in new barrels. In wine, it can produce an attractive complexity at low levels, but as it grows, the wine takes on a "medicine cabinet" smell. This type of spoilage problem can be prevented through careful barrel maintenance. *Brettanomyces* can be screened using MicroQit DETECT or Wallerstein (WL) Test Kits, described in section 6.2. Simply pour a small amount of fresh water into the barrel, slosh the barrel around and then pour the water out of the barrel and into a container. Use a small sample of this water (instead of wine) and follow the kit's instructions in section 6.2.2 for the MicroQit DETECT test kit or section 6.2.3 for the Wallerstein (WL) test kit.

The last type of spoilage problem is the formation of lactic acid bacteria (LAB), specifically, *Lactobacillus* and *Pediococcus* bacteria, giving wine a sour-milk taste. These bacteria form in wines with a very high pH (above 3.7), in wines with very low levels of SO₂, or in wines that have had a problem fermenting to dryness. This spoilage problem is best avoided by prevention through careful vinification. *Lactobacillus* and *Pediococcus* bacteria too can be screened using a WL Test Kit.

8.7.2 TREATING OAK-BARREL SPOILAGE PROBLEMS

Depending on severity, oak-barrel spoilage problems most often can be treated if acted upon promptly.

Treating oak-barrel spoilage problems is a multi-step process. First, fill the barrel two-thirds with fresh water. Prepare an alkaline solution by dissolving either sodium carbonate or sodium percarbonate in water, add the solution to the barrel and then top up. The amount of chemical to use depends on the severity of the problem and the barrel size. For mild spoilage problems, dissolve sodium carbonate or sodium percarbonate at a rate of approximately 1 g/L of water. For more serious problems, increase the concentration to 3 g/L of water, but never exceed this concentration as these chemicals could attack the wood and dissolve the oak lignins.

Leave the barrel to soak overnight without exceeding 24 hours as it may develop other spoilage problems. Empty the barrel and rinse thoroughly. Follow with a citric acid solution rinse to neutralize any possible alkaline residues. Trace residues of sodium carbonate or sodium percarbonate in a barrel are not poisonous, but they will affect the taste of wine if allowed to come into contact with it. To rinse with a citric acid solution, first fill the barrel two-thirds with fresh water. Then prepare the citric acid solution by dissolving the required amount of citric acid powder in approximately 4 liters (1 gallon) of water in a separate container. Measure sufficient citric acid powder to achieve a rate of 50–100 g/hL of water in the barrel. Pour the solution into the barrel, top up, and let soak overnight. Lastly, empty the barrel, rinse thoroughly at least twice, drain completely and let dry. Smell the barrel for any off odors to ensure the treatment worked. If the barrel does not smell completely clean, repeat the treatment.

This treatment for correcting oak-barrel spoilage problems is a very tedious process without shortcuts. In addition, the oak extracts from a newer barrel will be stripped in the process. Therefore, the best policy will always be prevention.

In some cases where spoilage is fairly advanced, such as high VA or strong Brett smell, this treatment will likely not solve the problem and your only option is to discard the barrel.

8.8 BARREL RECONDITIONING

Barrels are expensive and home winemakers would like to maximize their investment as much as possible by extending the useful life of barrels. The solution is barrel reconditioning; however, this is not for anyone.

Reconditioning a barrel involves shaving the inside of the barrel to expose new wood, which can extend its life another 3–5 years and reduce oak-aging costs by as much as 50%. Barrels can be shaved two or three times or more depending on the type and thickness of wood, extent of previous shaving, and extent of use for aging wine.

Note: "Shaving" is the term commonly used as wood has historically been removed, as is still practiced today, with a curved hand scraper. The more common practice nowadays is to plane or sand the wood but it is still referred to as shaving.

Figure 8-12: Blisters in a barrel

Barrel reconditioning may also be necessary – and the only solution – if a barrel is afflicted with mold, heavy tartrate buildup, blisters or other serious interior damage that could not be removed otherwise. Blisters in wood can form during the toasting process and then become pockets of wine. A substantial amount of wine remains in pockets even after the barrel has been rinsed and sanitized. The pockets then become perfect hideouts and breeding ground for bacteria and other organisms that can cause spoilage, even while the barrel is stored empty. Bacteria-laden pockets can then cross-contaminate new wine introduced into the barrel. Figure 8-12 illustrates the interior of a barrel affected by blisters.

8.8.1 COOPER'S TOOLS

Reconditioning a barrel requires disassembling and reassembling parts of the barrel. This can be tricky if you have never worked with barrels; however, with the right tools, a little woodworking know-how and some experience, it will become relatively easy to recondition a barrel.

The cooper's essential tools, shown in Figure 8-13, include a hammer, a hoop driver, an awl, and a bumper.

Choose a broad- and smooth-faced, heavy-duty hammer. A true cooper's hammer, such as the one in the Figure 8-13, is specifically designed for cooperage applications. This is an excellent investment if you intend to perform more advanced barrel repairs.

Figure 8-13: The cooper's tools

The hoop driver is a specialized tool for removing and installing hoops on barrels. It looks like a chisel and it can be straight or slightly curved to match the face of a barrel. The latter is recommended as it is more efficient and greatly reduces the risk of slippage while driving hoops. Flat-head screwdrivers do **not** provide a safe or efficient alternative and will damage hoops.

The bumper is a simple tool used to set the barrel heads back into place, which can be easily built using ¾- or 1-inch steel pipe. The pipe should be at least the length of the barrel and should be bent at a right angle at a point slightly shorter than the barrel's half-length. The extra length is to allow the pipe to be inserted fully to one side of the barrel and have extra length to handle the pipe. For example, the bumper pictured in Figure 8-13 was built for use in a 57-L (15-gal) barrel using a 120-cm (48-inch) pipe bent at approximately 45 cm (18 in). Insert a rubber stopper, such as the type used on chair legs, on the end of the short section to minimize damaging the head surface during replacement. Be sure that the stopper can pass through the bung hole. The long section of the pipe is used as a handle to prop up the head during reassembly.

Along with these tools, you will also need an awl, also known as a bradawl – available from any good hardware store – or a long, timber-frame construction nail for handling the barrel head during disassembly and reassembly, a drum sander or a stainless steel wire wheel, and protective clothing including a dust mask, safety goggles or face shield, and steel-toe boots.

8.8.2 HOW TO RECONDITION A BARREL

Reconditioning a barrel involves removing the head, quarter and bilge hoops at one end and then removing the corresponding head section from the croze and chime, which should come out in one piece. The croze is the groove around the circumference of the inside of the barrel towards the end of the staves, and the chime is the part of the staves from the croze to the end of the staves (refer to Figure 8-1 on page 326). The interior of the barrel is then shaven until new wood is exposed. The head is also shaven and then placed back into position. Alternatively, the exterior surface of the head can be sanded to a clean and smooth finish, and then the head is flipped inside out and placed back into position in the croze. Lastly, the hoops are reseated back into their original positions, and the whole procedure can be repeated with the second head unless you want to shave on and around the second head without removing it, and with access from the first removed head section.

Choose a suitable location with adequate ventilation to the exterior, such as a woodworking shop, a garage, or very simply out in the backyard or driveway – if your neighbors won't mind the noise and sawdust.

Before shaving a barrel, it is strongly recommended to soak the interior with water to ease shaving if the barrel is very dry; shaving dry oak will be very tedious. To soak the barrel, pour approximately one quarter of its volume with very hot water, or 15 L for a 57-L (4 gals for a 15-gal) barrel. Seal the bung hole with a silicone bung, slosh the barrel around and roll it to soak the entire surface. Stand the barrel upright on one head for approximately 10 minutes and then repeat for the other head. Then fill the barrel completely with warm water and let stand for about one hour. Drain the water out and let the barrel stand horizontally on its side, bung hole in the down position, for 24 hours to allow it to drain completely.

If you will be removing only one head, choose the one that looks better and free of any defects around the croze or along the joints between head sections; this will make replacing the head that much easier. Using a chalk or a felt pen, draw a line from the chime down onto the head section. This step is important as it will help you properly realign the head section with the staves to its original position, which will minimize any risk of leakage after reassembly.

Remove any hoop nails around all head, quarter and bilge hoops, i.e., on **both** sides of the barrel to avoid hitting nails while

Figure 8-14: Driving a hoop

shaving the inside. Using a cooper's hammer and hoop driver, remove the head and quarter hoops. Hold the hoop driver with the tip of the fingers at a slight angle away from the barrel with the driver tip resting on the hoop edge, whilst standing as shown in Figure 8-14. Do **not** wrap fingers around the hoop driver handle, which could otherwise get caught between the handle and barrel and cause injury. Similarly, loosen the bilge hoop but only slightly and just enough to loosen the head section.

With the hammer, gently tap on the staves around the circumference of the end of the barrel – where the head hoop was – to loosen the head further. Avoid hitting too hard which might otherwise cause the head section to come apart. Once the head is sufficiently loose, remove it from the open barrel; you may need to push the head into the barrel first and then out depending on the type of barrel you have. Lastly, reset all three hoops back into position to keep the staves steady for the shaving operation.

Using a drum sander and coarse wood sandpaper, or your tool of choice, proceed to shave the entire inside surface of the barrel until new wood is exposed, and then some more, trying to keep the surface as even as possible. The amount of wood to be shaved depends on how deep wine has penetrated; however, expect to shave ⅛–¼ inch. Avoid shaving too close to the croze, which could otherwise cause leakage after reassembly – you want to keep that joint with the head as tight as possible.

The trick to reduce the risk of leakage after reassembly is to apply a thick flour-water paste inside the croze, around the entire circumference. You only need to apply a very small amount using a thin and pointy piece of wood.

Figure 8-15: Using a bumper to position a barrel head

Toast the inside of the barrel and heads, if desired, as described below in section 8.8.3.

And now for the most important step in the reassembly.

Drive an awl on the outside face of the head, close to the edge on the opposite side of the chalk mark made during disassembly. The awl is simply used as a handle to set the head into place; therefore, you only need to drive it in sufficiently to be able to handle the head during this procedure.

With the barrel upright, remove the head hoop and loosen the quarter and bilge hoops. Holding the head section using the awl or nail, set the opposite end of the head into the croze **making sure to align the chalk marks**. Gently tap the head into position in the croze using the hammer.

Depending on the type of barrel you have, this might prove difficult, in which case you will need to first insert the head inside the barrel. You may also need to loosen the hoops a little more. Lift the head and raise the end with the chalk mark to set it in the croze and align it with the chalk mark on the stave. Using the awl, raise the opposite end towards the croze. Insert the short section of the bumper through the bung hole and prop it up towards the head section, as shown in Figure 8-15. Apply upward pressure on the end opposite of the chalk mark to push the head into the croze. You will likely need to gently tap around the entire head perimeter to ease it into the croze. Be sure that the chalk marks remain aligned during this procedure.

Reseat the hoops back into position – the order is very important – starting with the bilge hoop followed by the quarter hoop, and lastly, the head hoop while trying to keep hoop rivets aligned on all hoops. To reseat a hoop, tap gently along its circumference using the hoop driver until there is considerable resistance and the hoop is close to its final position. Then, drive the hoops completely and firmly into position by hitting the hoop driver harder. Do **not** drive the hoops excessively, which could otherwise cause hoop or barrel damage.

If the head hoop tends to pop out of place while driving it, use a thick piece of hardwood long enough to span the diameter of the hoop. Rest the wood on the hoop across its diameter and tap on the center of the wood with the hammer. Rotate the wood 90° after

Figure 8-16: A master cooper shaving barrel staves

each couple of taps until the hoop is seated perfectly into position, and then remove any excess paste around the croze. Hoops will be difficult to drive into place if the barrel surface is wet; therefore, be sure to keep the exterior of the barrel dry.

Here's a neat trick from Barrel Builders [reference 2] on how to drive a popping head hoop; it is particularly helpful when the hoop pops due to a damp barrel. "Use a piece of chalk and rub the area where the hoop will sit and then also chalk the inside of the hoop. This will dry the wood and help the hoop stick."

Thoroughly rinse the interior of the barrel several times, making sure to rinse the heads well to remove any excess paste around the interior croze, and soak the barrel to test for leakage using the same procedure as described earlier. If there is any leakage, it should cease fairly quickly, or at least within 24 hours. When all leakage has ceased, drain the water out and let dry for a day with the bung hole in the down position. You should then immediately transfer wine into barrel.

Shaving like a pro

Eddie McMillan is an expert cooper specializing in barrel reconditioning in Ontario's (Canada) Niagara wine region. The following describes his more efficient and quicker method of shaving barrels. Refer to Figure 8-16.

First, remove all hoops, except one head hoop, and both heads. Place the barrel on its end with the remaining head hoop at the top. Try not to disturb the barrel excessively so as not to move the staves out of alignment. Fasten the head hoop and staves with 2 strong spring clamps. Each clamp should hold one stave tight against the head hoop. Leave 2 or 3 staves between each clamp so that you can remove one stave easily from between the clamps. Retrieve one stave between the clamps from under the head hoop. Lay down the stave on a stable surface and, using an electric, portable curved planer, such as Makita's Model 1002BA, shave the stave without getting too close to the end of the stave near the croze. Shave the stave down to new wood. Replace the stave into position under the head hoop, take another stave, and repeat the operation. You simply need to move the 2 clamps along the head hoop to work on the other staves as you progress. Very simple!

When done, replace all hoops and head sections back into position to complete barrel reassembly.

8.8.3 TOASTING BARRELS

Toasting a barrel refers to the practice of "firing" or burning the inside of a barrel, and optionally both heads, over an open fire, as shown in Figure 8-17. A toasted barrel and heads impart more of an oaky aroma to wine as well as toasty notes increasing the wine's complexity.

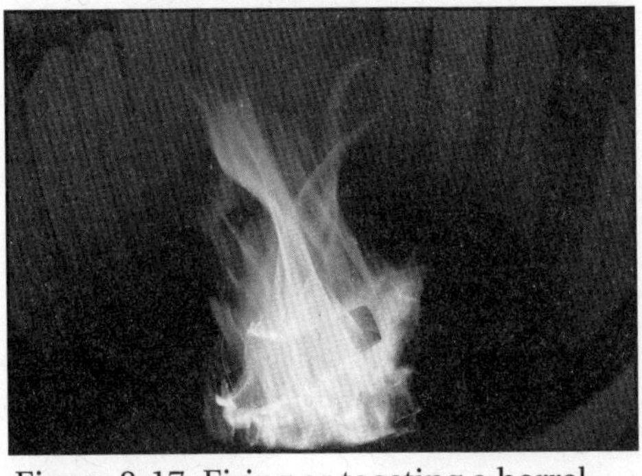

When the barrel is first manufactured, it is toasted without the heads in place. When reconditioning, you can easily retoast, or "refire", with only one head removed.

To retoast a barrel, you will need a fireproof bucket with a metal handle, such as the one

Figure 8-17: Firing or toasting a barrel

351

Figure 8-18: A fire-proof bucket for toasting/refiring barrels

in Figure 8-18; a one-gallon bucket will work well for a 57-L (15-gal) barrel. Punch or drill a few 1-inch holes all around the bucket (not the bottom). Choose a suitable outdoor location away from neighbors. Set the barrel upright with the open head section on top. Lay down two short pieces of two-by-four wood inside the barrel, at the bottom – this will protect the head surface during retoasting. Throw in a pile of small pieces of **oak** kindling wood into the bucket with a small piece of wrapped newspaper. Light the paper and allow the oak wood to catch fire until it burns well and is hot. You may need to replenish the fire with kindling wood to keep it burning well. When ready, place the bucket inside the barrel on top of the two-by-four pieces of wood and allow the staves to toast to your desired toasting level. Be careful not to over-toast; you could otherwise ignite the staves and cause a fire. When the outside of the barrel surface starts feeling warm, it is a good indication that you should stop toasting; this can take 15–30 minutes.

To toast the heads, you can easily build a stationary or hand-held tool to hold the head section over the open fire. Do **not** try toasting a head inside the barrel by placing the head section at the top; this is dangerous as there is no "chimney" to allow the smoke to escape.

Note: Do not try and toast a barrel using a blowtorch; the oak wood will char and will not toast as is necessary for oak-aging wine.

9
BOTTLING

Bottling is the final process in winemaking where aged wine is bottled either for immediate consumption or for further aging. A bottle of homemade wine, garnished with a capsule and personalized label, is the winemaker's ultimate reward. Each bottle is the culmination of several weeks or months, or even years of dedicated work from the high-anxiety labor of (if) growing grapes to meticulous winemaking. Stabilization issues notwithstanding, poor bottling equipment, techniques, or even closures, such as corks, can easily compromise the quality of wine being bottled. As in all winemaking procedures, wine exposure to air should be minimized and only the best closure material available should be used, especially if bottle aging wine for long periods.

Bottling technology and equipment for home winemakers has greatly evolved over the years, and there are now assortments of tools that greatly simplify and accelerate the bottling process although it is still very much a manual process. Whether you are bottling a 20-L batch (approximately 27 bottles) or 1,000 bottles, you can find tools to match your production needs and budget constraints.

Bottling involves assembling bottles and washing, sanitizing, filling, corking, dressing, and labeling each bottle into a finished product.

9.1 BOTTLES

Bottles come in a plethora of shapes and thicknesses, colors or tints, and sizes. Figure 9-1 illustrates the most common bottle shapes. Winemaking aficionados are adamant on bottling wine in their respective traditional bottle shapes.

High-shouldered Bordeaux bottles are commonly used for varietals such as Cabernet Sauvignon, Merlot, Zinfandel and Sauvignon Blanc. Sloping-shouldered Burgundy bottles are used for varietals such as Pinot Noir, Gamay and Chardonnay, while longer sloping-shouldered hock or Alsace-style bottles are used for varietals such as Riesling and Gewürztraminer. For sparkling wines, only use thick-walled, Champagne-style bottles. Never use standard still-wine bottles for sparkling wines because they could potentially explode from the high pressure in the bottle. Heavily tinted or black Port-style bottles should be used to protect long-aging Port wines from light.

Figure 9-1: Bottle shapes (from left) - Bordeaux, Burgundy, Alsace, Champagne, and Port

Bordeaux, Burgundy and sparkling wine bottles often have a punt – an indentation in the bottom of the bottle. Many theories have been offered as to the origin and intended use of the punt in wine bottles. The industry claim is that the punt does not serve any function or purpose except in sparkling wine bottles where, supposedly, it deflects the inside pressure away from the bottom of bottles. By minimizing pressure on this part of the bottle, the risk of bottle explosion is greatly reduced. Another purpose is to allow sparkling wine bottles to be stacked upside down, or *sur pointes*, onto one

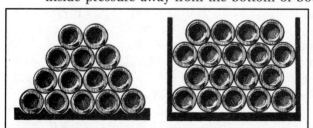

Figure 9-2: Bottle-stacking arrangements (from left) - pyramid and bin

another during the aging phase. In still-wine bottles, the punt is often used to make bottles look bigger.

The Bordeaux bottle shape provides the greatest stability when bottles are to be stacked horizontally on top of one another, particularly in a pyramid-stacking arrangement as illustrated in Figure 9-2. Burgundy, Alsace and sparkling wine bottles provide less stability when stacked on top of one another and are best stacked in a bin, as shown in Figure 9-2. A benefit of the bin-stacking arrangement is that it makes better use of space compared to the pyramid-stacking arrangement.

Dark-colored glass is best because it protects wine from damaging light rays that cause premature aging. Wine exposed to constant light and not protected by colored glass will show signs of fatigue and, in the worst case, will show similar symptoms as an oxidized wine. That explains why vintage Port, which is meant for very long aging – 10, 20, 30 or 50 or more years – is bottled in opaque bottles. The most common colors of glass for wine are green (often referred to as antique green or Champagne green), brown, or yellow (often referred to as dead-leaf green). Clear glass is mainly used for white wines meant to be drunk early, i.e., it is not recommended for wine to be aged.

The choice of bottle size depends on expected drinking needs. A good mix of half-bottles (375 mL), standard 750-mL bottles, and magnums (1.5 L) will allow for the opening of the right-size bottle for the right occasion. The smaller 250-mL and 500-mL bottles are very practical for serving one or two people, respectively. It is also believed that wine ages slower and longer in larger bottles because of the smaller headspace-to-volume ratio.

For home winemaking, the above types of bottles using cork as the closure are still the most popular because they are easily sourced. You can buy bottles from winemaking supply shops or you can simply ask a local bring-your-own-wine (BYOW) restaurant. The restaurant owner will typically be very happy to give away empty bottles. Remove labels and capsules, and be sure to clean and sanitize bottles thoroughly. Label removal can take a little time depending on the glue type used by the wineries where the bottles came from. The best method for removing labels is to fill each bottle with very hot water and then completely immerse each under very hot water in a large sink. Leave the bottles underwater for up to 24 hours. Labels may peel off easily or you may need to scrape them off with a sharp knife.

What about screw cap bottles? They are gaining global popularity, even with many premium wineries. Given the high rate of corked wine (described in more details in sections 2.6.2 and 14.17) from commercial wineries, many are converting from corks to screw caps. In home winemaking, however, this may not be an issue and, given the investment in corking equipment and stock of traditional bottles, amateurs may not be willing or be ready for the change. For more information on the use of screw caps, refer to section 9.4.2.

9.2 BOTTLE WASHING DEVICES

The importance of clean and sanitized bottles cannot be over-emphasized. A number of very effective and easy-to-use tools are available to home winemakers, and include bottle washing devices and the bottle rinser/sterilizer and drainer (more appropriately called a rinser/sanitizer and drainer).

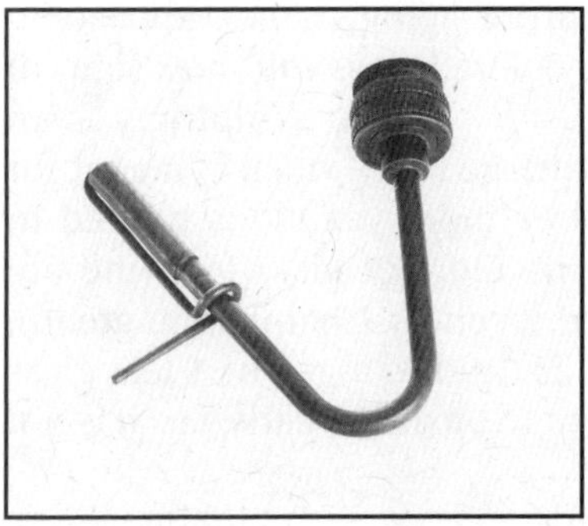

Bottle washing devices connect to a water source to wash and rinse bottles under water pressure. The bottle washer shown in Figure 9-3 has a built-in device to start and stop the flow of water and is most effective when water is sprayed instantaneously several times as opposed to spraying continuously. The latter method will cause water to accumulate inside the bottle and restrict the flow of pressurized water on the inner surface. This bottle washer is very effective for washing and rinsing a small quantity of bottles, and can also be used for washing other glass containers such as carboys and demijohns.

Warning: This bottle washer has been reported to cause pipe problems in some cases due to the spontaneous and very strong on/off action that causes excessive strain on the water pipes. Watch out for strange behaviors in the house water system, for example, if there is no more hot water supply throughout the house after use.

The Fermtech Double Blast Bottle Washer, shown in Figure 9-4, is an alternative device to the bottle washer to improve washing and rinsing efficiency – and to circumvent potential pipe problems. It operates on the same principle as

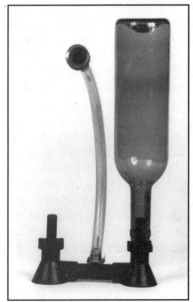

Figure 9-3: Bottle washer for rinsing bottles

Figure 9-4: Fermtech Double Blast Bottle Washer

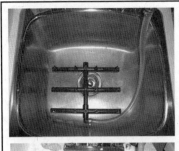

Figure 9-5: 2-in-1 Bottle Washer (from top) - H-shaped array of high-pressure spouts connected to a faucet, tray positioned over spout array without any bottles, and bottles positioned on tray (Note: All 12 bottles must be in place for proper use.)

the bottle washer above, however, it does not cause any pipe problems. And advantages are that it requires much less water and can be used to wash or rinse two bottles at a time as well as carboys, demijohns and siphoning tubes. The spouts are equipped with bottle-activated valves to start and stop the flow of water.

A newer device that handles 12 bottles at a time, the 2-in-1 Bottle Washer from Vintage Shop, shown in Figure 9-5, greatly simplifies washing and rinsing operations, and speeds up the whole bottle sanitization procedure. It consists of a tray that firmly seats 12 standard bottles in the inverted position, and an H-shaped array of high-pressure spouts connected to a faucet. Simply place the tray and bottles over the spout array and open the faucet to rinse the bottles. To further speed up the operation, you can use a second tray; while the first set of bottles is set aside to drip and bottles are removed, the second tray is used to wash/rinse another dozen bottles.

Rinse bottles once with hot water and then set them on a bottle drainer or tree, such as the one shown in Figure 9-6, and allow the bottles to drip. For stubborn stains on the inside wall, fill the bottles with a chlorine-detergent solution and let stand for several minutes to an hour, and then rinse abundantly with water.

The bottle drainer is a device for stacking bottles upside down to completely drain any residual liquid. Its modular design can accommodate up to 90 bottles by stacking ten 9-bottle modules, as shown in Figure 9-6. Although the device can be further expanded, the weight of 90 bottles is the practical limit.

The bottle drainer can also accommodate a pump-action bottle rinser/sanitizer at the top, as shown in Figure 9-6. The bottle rinser/sanitizer is used to rinse and sanitize bottles under pressure using a sulfite solution. Rinse each bottle three or four times with a sulfite solution by exerting pressure on the rinser and then set the

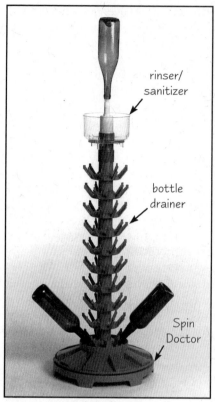

rinser/
sanitizer

bottle
drainer

Spin
Doctor

Figure 9-6: Bottle drainer equipped with a rinser/sanitizer on a Spin Doctor

bottle on the drainer. Optionally, you can rinse bottles one more time under water if there is excess sulfite remaining in the bottle.

To help you place bottles around the drainer, you can mount the bottle drainer on a rotating device, known as the Spin Doctor, shown in Figure 9-6, which allows the drainer and bottles to be rotated full revolutions.

9.3 BOTTLING DEVICES

There are now many types of devices for quick and efficient bottling of still wine.

Bottle fillers are usually classified according to the action used to displace wine from a container and into bottles. There are two types: gravity and electric pump-assisted fillers.

Gravity bottle fillers work on the simple principle of gravity to displace wine, where the wine container must be placed at a higher level than bottles to be filled. These types of fillers therefore require priming by sucking wine through a hose to start the flow, similar to when racking. Pump-assisted fillers use an electric pump and have the advantage that the wine container need not be placed high above floor level.

Bottle fillers are also often referred to as automatic or semiautomatic to highlight that the equipment has some level of automation, such as fill level or making use of a self-activating pump to transfer wine from a carboy to bottles. Whether a particular unit is automatic or semiautomatic is often a question of interpretation. A truly, fully automated bottling system would channel bottles through a bottling line without operator intervention. As such, some of the automatic fillers described below are really semiautomatic; you still need to move bottles around.

Lastly, fillers are also classified as being single- or multi-spout, meaning that either one bottle or many at a time can be filled, respectively. The bottling rate, expressed in number of bottles per hour (bph), depends on the number of spouts and whether the filler is equipped with a pump.

The most popular and widely available bottling devices used in home winemaking include the stem-and-valve filler, the vacuum-stoppered funnel, semiautomatic fillers, and multi-spout fillers.

9.3.1 STEM-AND-VALVE FILLER

The most basic bottling apparatus is the stem-and-valve bottle filler, shown in Figure 9-7, also known as a bottling wand, which is ideal for small batches. It can fill 27 standard 750-mL bottles in less than 20 minutes.

This type of bottle filler consists of a short, clear plastic tube with a stem attachment. The stem has either a simple or spring-activated "foot" valve to control the flow of wine, and uses gravity to displace wine from a carboy to bottles.

To fill a bottle, prime the filler, insert it in an empty bottle and apply pressure by pressing the stem against the bottom of the bottle. Release the pressure when the wine level reaches the top of the bottle to stop the flow of wine. Retrieve the filler to let the wine level fall back down to the desired level for inserting standard 38- or 45-mm (1½- or 1¾-in) corks. For longer corks, fill bottles to the required level below the bottle opening; however, for shorter corks, you will need to manually add a small quantity of wine to each bottle to leave a headspace (ullage) of 1.25 to 2 cm (½ to ¾ in). Use a small, sanitized syringe for this purpose.

Figure 9-7: Stem-and-valve bottle filler or bottling wand

The stem-and-valve bottle filler works well for standard flat-bottom bottles but it is hard to operate when the bottle has a deep punt. The stem will slide down the punt when pressure is applied, and therefore the valve never opens.

9.3.2 VACUUM-STOPPERED FUNNEL

The vacuum-stoppered funnel, shown in Figure 9-8, is a special funnel that fills a bottle to a preset level and stops automatically. Wine is fed into the funnel via a tube by gravity. The funnel has a built-in diverter enabling wine to pour down the bottle wall – as opposed to splashing down, as in a regular funnel – and minimizes aeration and premature oxidation. The vacuum-stoppered funnel with a diverter circumvents this problem.

9.3.3 SEMIAUTOMATIC FILLERS

All semiautomatic or automatic bottle fillers used in home wine-making are really semiautomatic because the entire process is not fully automated. For example, models described below require manual handling of bottles prior to and after fill-up. The use of the word "automatic" refers to manufacturers' descriptions.

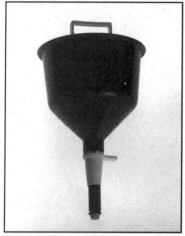

Figure 9-8: Vacuum-stoppered funnel for bottling

Many different types of semiautomatic bottle fillers are available. Buon Vino and Tenco are manufacturers of the most common and popular models used in home winemaking.

Buon Vino's Super Automatic Bottle Filler is the "automatic" version of the vacuum-stoppered bottle filler above. It is completely integrated to minimize aeration and spillage during bottling and can fill 27 bottles from a 20-L (5-gal) batch in less than 15 minutes. The device, depicted in Figure 9-9, withdraws wine from a container and fills a bottle automatically to a preset level. It offers all the features of the vacuum-stoppered funnel in addition to further facilitating the bottling operation. It is well worth the small incremental investment.

To operate the Super Automatic Bottle Filler, insert the siphoning tube (5) equipped with an antidreg tip in the carboy or demijohn and seat the filler in the bottle opening (4). Set the filler in the open position by pulling up on the valve (2), and then suck air from the overflow tube (1) to start the flow of wine from the carboy to the filler (3). Insert the overflow tube in an empty bottle during bottling to collect overflow wine. The filler mechanism will close automatically by pulling down on the valve (2) when the bottle is filled to the preset level. Then, simply transfer the filler to another bottle, and push

Figure 9-9: Buon Vino's Super Automatic Bottle Filler

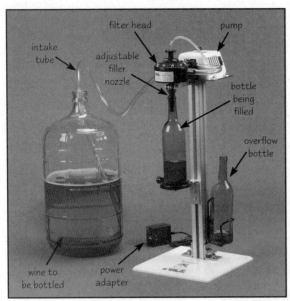

Figure 9-10: Buon Vino's FILLjet (tabletop version)

down on the valve (2) to restart the flow of wine.

Buon Vino has integrated the filler head of its Super Automatic Bottle Filler into the FILLjet, shown in Figure 9-10, a tabletop electric version that uses a small electrical positive displacement pump that can achieve a bottling rate of 200 bph. Its greatest advantage is that heavy demijohns or other containers no longer need to be placed at a height above the bottles to be filled. These can rest right on the floor since the force of gravity is not required to fill bottles.

Operating the FILLjet is very simple. Place the intake hose equipped with an antidreg tip in the carboy or demijohn. Insert the overflow tube into an empty standard bottle to collect overflow wine during bottling. Insert an empty bottle to be filled under the filler head with the bottle opening over the filler nozzle. The bottle holding plate and spring exert an upward pressure on the bottle to create a perfect seal with the filler nozzle to ensure proper operation of the filler head. When ready, power up the pump to start the flow of wine into the bottle. Once the bottle is full, the filler head automatically shuts off the pump. Remove the full bottle and place another empty bottle in position. Press the filling head button to restart the filling operation. The switch on the pump need not be turned ON/OFF; it is left in the ON position for the remainder of the filling operation.

The filler nozzle can be adjusted to accept small and large bottles with different mouth diameters, and to control the fill level depending on the length of corks used.

Follow the manufacturer's instructions for operating, flushing, cleaning and maintaining the FILLjet to ensure many years of problem-free bottle filling.

Tenco's ENOLMATIC filler, shown in Figure 9-11, is a semiautomatic, tabletop bottling system that uses an electric pump to displace wine under vacuum to fill bottles. Although it fills one bottle at a time, it can achieve a bottling rate of over 200 bph, which can be adjusted using a control knob. This is particularly handy for bottling sparkling wine, for example, where the speed must be decreased to the minimum speed setting to minimize foaming during bottling. Displacing sparkling wine at a high rate would cause excessive foaming. The 4-spout ENOLMASTER version, shown in Figure 9-11, can fill up to 500 bph.

The ENOLMATIC filler is convenient because it is compact and light, being manufactured mainly from durable plastic. The pump is self-contained within the unit, and can pull wine up from a container up to 4 meters (13 feet). And because bottling is done under vacuum, the wine is protected from exposure to air, therefore minimizing the effects of oxidation. An inline filter using special cartridges can be installed between the wine container and bottling system to filter and bottle in a single operation.

Operating the ENOLMATIC filler is very simple. First, ensure that the overflow tube is properly connected to the bowl cover. The overflow tube is to allow the small amount of overflow wine to flow into the bowl when the system shuts off once it has reached the fill level in each bottle. Turn the pump to the ON position and place the intake tube into the wine container. Place a bottle under the filler nozzle and let it rest under the unit on the table. Wine will start to flow and fill the bottle. Once the bottle is filled to the (adjustable) preset level, the system automatically stops. Remove the bottle and place another one in position. Filling restarts on its own once the bottle is in place; there is no need to flip the switch. Each bottle is filled to the same level.

Be sure to follow the manufacturer's instructions for proper operation. This is particularly important if you need to switch the unit OFF during bottling; the unit and vacuum will need to be setup again.

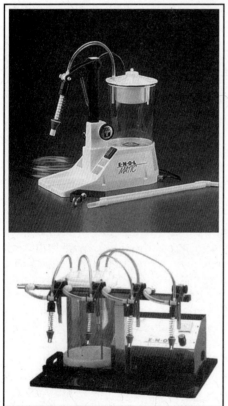

Figure 9-11: ENOLMATIC and ENOLMASTER units

A minor drawback of this system is that the filler nozzle lets the wine drop straight down, causing a splashing action and hastening oxidation. Other fillers described below are designed to let the wine flow down gently along the wall of the bottle.

9.3.4 MULTI-SPOUT FILLERS

For serious home winemakers requiring filling large quantities of bottles, a multi-spout filler (often known as an in-line filler) is recommended to increase bottling efficiency. Unlike the single-bottle devices above, multi-spout fillers allow for continuous bottle filling. The best models are manufactured entirely of AISI 304 stainless steel, which greatly facilitate maintenance and reduce the potential of wine spoilage since they do not rust.

Various models with 3 or up to 8 spouts are available, although the 3-spout filler is a good compromise between cost and speed (250 bph, on average) if you are working alone – a 3-bottle cycle seems to match two hands very well. Figure 9-12 illustrates a 5-spout AISI 304 stainless steel model capable of an hourly production rate of 390 bottles.

This type of filler consists of a small holding tank that is continuously fed by siphon action from a carboy, demijohn or tank, a float valve to control flow of wine into the holding tank, and spouts for filling bottles. Its operation is very simple.

First, siphon wine into the filler's holding tank and then, with wine still in the tubing, attach the tube to the holding tank's inlet. It is important to keep wine in the tubing so as not to lose siphoning action. This first step can be skipped if you are working with a tank and drawing wine by gravity from the bottom valve. Then, prime each spout by siphoning wine from the holding tank, similar to when using a racking hose. Place a bottle under the first spout and lower it to start the flow of wine. Secure the bottle with the clip to allow you to move on to the next bottle. Repeat this procedure for all spouts. As each bottle fills and automatically stops to the adjustable preset fill level, simply remove it

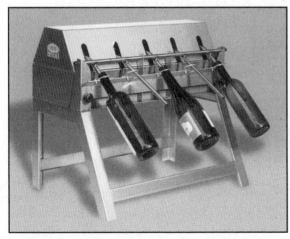

Figure 9-12: High-production bottle filler (5-spout AISI 304 stainless steel floor model shown)

363

and place another empty bottle over the spout. All bottles are filled to the same exact level (ullage).

Choose a model that allows you to adjust the ullage to your desired level. The best models have a front bottle support attachment that can be raised or lowered. The float ball and valve inside the tank can also be raised or lowered to adjust the ullage. Models without these features may cause low fill levels, and will require manual top up of each bottle, which can be quite a chore.

You can easily adapt the multi-spout filler with an electric pump for applications where gravity cannot be used to fill bottles because the wine container cannot be raised. The pump is used to feed wine from the container to the filler's holding tank. The pump inlet is simply set up to withdraw wine from the container using a racking tube or by connecting a flexible tube to the spout if the container is so equipped. Attach the pump outlet to the holding tank's inlet using a T-connector with a return tube back to the wine container. This avoids having the pumping action force wine into the tank and overflowing it. When the pump is started, the holding tank fills up and the flow of wine is stopped when the float valve shuts off. The wine will then flow back to the carboy or container. To minimize wine flow back to the container, a variable-speed pump is recommended to match your bottling speed. If the flow of wine back to the container is too aggressive, it will hasten oxidation.

The only inconvenience of the above multi-spout fillers is their low height, which can cause backaches after an hour or so of continuous bottling. Other models, such as the one shown in Figure 9-13, designed with the holding tank well above floor level are easier on the back and provide the same or better bottling efficiency. Unfortunately, these models are pricey and not yet as popular and are therefore hard to find. Some retailers are able to import such specialty equipment on a pre-order basis early in the year for delivery in the summer.

These models, usually equipped with 2 to 8 spouts, consist of a simple holding tank at a height of approximately 3 ft or 5 ft. Wine is fed into the tank by gravity, which can be problematic if you cannot position your wine container higher than the holding tank height. The wine level in the holding tank must also be controlled to avoid overflow. A simple clip on the

Figure 9-13: Bottle filler with a high holding tank

racking tube can be used to control flow of wine into the tank. Spouts have a larger opening and therefore fill bottles at a higher rate than the standard models above. For example, the 3-spout model has a bottling rate of approximately 400 bph.

Upscale models are equipped with a pump at the base of the filler unit to feed wine into the holding tank at the top. This solves the above problem of having to feed wine into the tank by gravity. Some models may also be equipped with a second holding tank for increased bottling throughput.

For serious winemakers with a small-scale winery output, multi-spout fillers with pump and filter are available, albeit very pricey. These allow wine to be filtered and bottled in a single operation.

9.3.5 BOTTLING

Whichever model of bottle filler you choose, you always need to properly sanitize the unit before use.

As a first step, rinse the unit thoroughly with plenty of warm water for approximately 15 minutes. Spoilage microorganisms may have taken up residence in parts of the unit since your last use. Eradicate any organisms by flushing the entire unit with a 1% effective SO_2 sulfite solution for 15–20 minutes, and rinse again with cool water for just a few minutes.

When bottling, leave approximately 2 cm (¾ in) of air space, or ullage, between the wine and the cork to allow for expansion owing to temperature fluctuations. If the ullage is too small, corks can pop out under pressure. If there is too much air space, the ratio of air to wine surface is greatly increased therefore accelerating oxidation.

9.4 CLOSURES FOR STILL-WINE BOTTLES

There are many types of closures now available to home winemakers including agglomerated, synthetic, hybrid, plastic-top and natural corks, shown in Figure 9-14, as well as screw caps, and crown caps. Corks are still the most popular because of the wider availability of bottles that accept corks. Screw cap bottles are still not widely available and therefore screw caps are not as popular yet. Similarly, crown caps can only be used with special bottles, such as sparkling wine bottles, and therefore are not as popular but make a practical and efficient alternative if you can source the bottles.

9.4.1 CORKS

Natural corks are still the most common closure for wine bottles, and are manufactured from natural oak bark with a wide spectrum

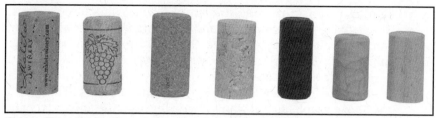

Figure 9-14: Corks (from left) - natural, agglomerated, hybrid, twin-disc agglomerated, and three variations of synthetic corks

of quality. The density of natural corks is lower than for agglomerated, synthetic or hybrid corks, and therefore, less compression is required to insert natural corks into bottles. The more supple material also provides a better airtight seal once inserted. Being a natural product, these corks generally will not be of consistent quality, particularly at lower quality levels, and may have different degrees of porosity. This should not cause any problems if the corks are not defective. A defective cork is easily detected by visible cracks along its length. Natural corks can be used for bottle aging but, in general, it is recommended that you choose a higher grade of cork for longer aging periods.

Agglomerated corks are manufactured from leftover material once the high-quality corks have been punched out from the bark of oak trees, and consequently cost less than natural corks. The material is ground into cork particles and held together with special glue. They are then molded and compressed into shape using one of various molding techniques resulting in less porous and higher density corks compared to 100% natural corks. However, the lower quality of material used coupled with the manufacturing process increase the probability of 2,4,6-trichloroanisole (TCA) contamination (see sections 2.6.2 and 14.17) in agglomerated corks. The same applies to colmated corks – essentially lower-quality, natural or agglomerated corks with cork dust applied on their entire surface with an adhesive to plug pores (surface imperfections).

A variation of the agglomerated cork is the multi-piece cork, such as the twin-disc cork, which replicates the design of Champagne corks using a very dense, agglomerated body sandwiched between top and lower natural cork discs. The advantages of multi-piece corks are that they cost less than natural corks while having natural cork material come into contact with the bottled wine, i.e., TCA taint risks are reduced.

Synthetic corks are manufactured from synthetic polymers and, as the name implies (although the word "cork" is a misnomer), does not contain natural oak material. Unlike older synthetic corks that were plagued by problems, e.g., they impart "plastic" off-flavors and provided a poor seal causing leakage and oxidation, newer synthetic corks do not seem to compromise the quality of the wine, specifically not from TCA, and because they are inert, they do not react with the wine.

Synthetic corks are believed to provide a better, tighter seal although natural cork advocates counter that theirs allow wine to age gracefully because of micro-oxidation effects, i.e., minute air-flow occurs between the cork and the bottle, arguing that synthetic corks unduly retard the development of wine. Only time will prove or disprove these claims. One benefit of synthetic corks is that they do not crumble when uncorked, and also come in various cool colors. In addition, bottles with synthetic corks need not rest on their side during aging as the cork will not (nor does it need to) expand or contract.

Hybrid corks, also known as composite corks, are manufactured using natural and synthetic materials, attempting to provide the best of both worlds. Specifically, the lignin (the woody cell walls of the cork wood) is removed from the bark stock and only the suberin (a fatty substance but the noblest part of raw cork) is used, which is then combined under high pressure with a synthetic cellular material to produce a cork with an excellent seal resistant to diseases and TCA taint.

Plastic-top (T-top) corks are also available for early-drinking wines not intended for aging, such as non-vintage style Port or Sherry wines, or other types of alcoholic drinks not prone to oxidation effects, such as liqueurs, due to the shorter length of the cork material. TCA taint risks of plastic-top corks depend on the cork physiology, i.e., natural vs. agglomerated.

Corks for standard 750-mL bottles with an 18.5-mm inside mouth diameter are available in two standard lengths: short (38 mm, 1½ in) and long (45 mm, 1¾ in). Commercial wineries often use 54–mm (2–in) corks for their best wines. These very long corks are very difficult to find in home winemaking shops. Short corks are adequate for early-drinking wines or wines to be aged up to 18–24 months. Use long, premium quality corks for wines to be aged for longer than 24 months.

Corks are also available in several diameters. Table 9-1 gives the diameter of the most popular cork sizes. A No. 9 cork is the recommended size for standard 750-mL bottles; the other sizes are for smaller or bigger bottles with non-standard mouth diameter.

Corks are also available with or without chamfered edges. Although chamfered-edge corks ease the corking operation, these are not recommended for extended bottle aging as the total effective length of the corks is reduced by more than 10%. Corks without chamfered edges are recommended since there is no reduction in effective length.

Table 9-1
Dimensions for popular cork sizes

Size number	Diameter (mm)
7	20
8	21
8½	22
9	24
10	25

Important Tip #1

Stand bottles upright for at least 24 hours once corked, or 3–5 days if using natural corks, to also allow the corks to re-expand to their original shape and to allow pressure in bottles to equalize. This avoids potential leakage problems from corks not having had a chance to re-expand properly or from corks that are being forced out of the bottle from internal pressure. After the bottles have stood upright for the required duration, they can be flipped upside down in cases for storage or laid horizontally on wine racks.

Important Tip #2

If your bottled wine does not smell or taste like it did before bottling, you are experiencing what is known as "bottle shock", a condition caused by all the handling and processing activities associated with bottling that can mute aromas and flavors. For the same reason, it is recommended not to shake bottles prior to serving and not to cellar bottles in an area where there is a lot of vibration. Bottle shock can last a few days to a few weeks. Test a bottle as needed to determine when the wine has returned to its initial, pre-bottling "quality".

9.4.2 SCREW CAPS

Screw caps found on liquor bottles and now on many wine bottles are quite unfortunately at a disadvantage in terms of consumer acceptance, tradition notwithstanding, even more so than synthetic corks in spite of their longer history. Consumers have become

Should I sanitize corks?

There is a lot of confusion on whether corks need to be rinsed, soaked, or sanitized prior to corking. The first thing to do when buying natural, agglomerated, or hybrid corks is to ask your supplier how the corks were packaged. Nowadays, many manufacturers ship corks in plastic bags injected with sulfur dioxide. Corks are therefore well protected against potential spoilage organisms that could find their way into those tiny pores, and do not require any sanitizing prior to corking. If in doubt or if the bag of corks was not used up in one corking session, i.e., corks are left in an opened bag, then, as a precaution, you should sanitize them in a 1% sulfite solution for 10–15 minutes, no more, prior to corking. Shake off any excess solution before insertion into the bottle. Do not soak corks in boiling water and do not soak them in sulfite solution for more than the recommended time; otherwise, the cork may crumble when uncorked. Also, don't be tempted to soak corks in water to facilitate insertion into the bottle; you may end up contaminating a whole batch of corks from one TCA-tainted cork. Insertion with a good corker should be relatively easy without any soaking.

Any unused corks can be stored for up to 3 months in a clean, tightly sealed plastic bag with, ideally, a little dose of sulfur gas by burning a piece of sulfur stick as outlined in section 8.6. Store the bag of corks in a cool, dry and well-ventilated location; the cellar area is typically too humid. To avoid any problems, only buy the required amount of corks at the time of bottling, and use immediately and completely.

As for synthetic corks, you can sanitize them without worry of damaging the corks. Synthetic corks also do not need any water soaking prior to insertion because they have already been treated with silicone or other lubricants that ease insertion. Because of their higher density, you will need a good floor corker though.

increasingly more sophisticated about wine appreciation and generally associate screw cap wine with an inferior product. Yet, screw caps eliminate any risk of TCA taint because they are lined with an inert polyvinyl material, which also provides a perfect airtight seal therefore eliminating any risk of leakage (screw cap bottles need not rest on their side), and are very easy to apply on bottles and to unscrew. No more fumbling with the corkscrew! The only disadvantage of screw caps to home winemakers is sourcing enough used bottles for larger productions. For the time being, there is a much smaller volume of screw cap bottles available compared to standard wine bottles, unless you use jug wine containers.

When reusing screw caps, always rinse and sanitize them before applying to other bottles of wine.

Figure 9-15: Floor model and hand corkers

9.4.3 CROWN CAPS

Crown caps provide the same type of seal and risk protection as screw caps but need to be inserted using a crimping tool, such as the one used in beer making; however, they can only be used on sparkling wine bottles and cannot be applied on standard wine bottles.

Crown-cap bottles are not commonly used in winemaking, except for sparkling wine, and make this alternative not attractive unless, well, you go against tradition and can source sufficient sparkling wine bottles. Using sparkling wine bottles may prove to be a headache and not worth the trouble if you source used bottles from various places. Specifically, European and American sparkling wine bottles are manufactured with different standards requiring different diameter crown caps and a different crimping head.

When using crown caps, always rinse and sanitize them before applying to bottles of wine.

9.5 CORKER

There are two main types of corkers for still-wine bottles; the floor-model corker and the hand corker, depicted in Figure 9-15.

The floor-model corker is the most convenient and most practical for corking a large quantity of standard- and magnum-size bottles. The hand corker can be used for corking bottle sizes that the floor-model corker cannot. To use a floor corker for small quantities of half-bottles, a block of wood roughly the size of a brick can be inserted on the platform, and then the bottle can be placed on the wood for the bottling operation. You should be careful though, as this is not a secure way to bottle a large quantity of half-bottles.

The floor-model corker has an adjustable corking rod to set the depth of the cork in the bottle. Adjust the rod so that the cork is level with the bottle opening once inserted. The corker is conveniently designed with an auto-locking mechanism to hold the bottle firmly in position and to facilitate insertion of the cork.

As with all winemaking equipment, sanitize the retractable brass jaws in the corking mechanism to avoid contaminating corks as the jaws will come into contact with the corks.

When inserting the cork, hold the corker lever down for several seconds to allow excess pressure to escape from the bottle and to prevent the cork from popping out.

9.6 CAPSULES

Capsules are used to retard mold formation on corks by protecting them from excess humidity, and to give bottles a cleaner look. Capsules are available in a plethora of designs and colors such as red, burgundy red, white, yellow, gold, green and black.

Heat shrink PVC capsules are the most practical type that, when fitted over the mouth of bottles, can be shrunk with boiling water, steam or hot air. These capsules can be used on both regular still- and Port-wine bottles corked with regular and stopper -type corks, respectively. Standard-size heat shrink PVC capsules will fit snugly over standard 750-ml bottles as well as standard half-bottles and magnums (1.5 L) except for the wider-lip Chianti-type magnums. For the latter, larger capsules are available.

Some capsules also have a tear-off tab to remove the top portion of the capsule and expose the cork for removal with a corkscrew. Those without a tear-off tab require a foil cutter to remove the top portion.

There are various methods of applying heat to shrink PVC capsules for fitting onto bottles: Hot water bath, steam, stove-top burner, general-purpose heat gun, or a heat shrink applicator specifically designed for winemaking. Choose the method that best suits your needs, skills, budget and annual production.

The hot–water bath method is cheap, simple, quick and very effective for small batches. To shrink a capsule, hold the capsule with one hand so that it does not fall off, invert the bottle with the other hand, and then immerse the capsule in boiling water in a pan over a stove. The capsule will immediately start shrinking and will stay in place firmly. At that point, you can remove the hand holding the capsule while continuing to fully immerse the capsule using the other hand. Remove the bottle when the capsule has completely shrunk. Keep the water boiling at medium heat throughout this operation and keep the exhaust fan running to vent vapor outdoor. Be sure to keep your hands away from the boiling water.

The drawback of this method is that excessive water can infiltrate, if not careful, and get trapped between the capsule and cork, causing mold to form on the cork top over time. There is little risk of bottle contamination but the sight of mold might be less appealing to your guests. Some capsules have one or two holes on the top disc designed to ease fitting them over bottles, and therefore, the hot water bath method should not be used with these capsules.

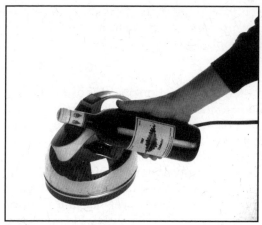

Figure 9-16: Shrinking a PVC capsule using steam

The steam method, shown in Figure 9-16, is simple and effective and can be used for larger productions. There is really no limit to the quantity of capsules that can be shrunk with this method; however, the humidity level in your house may rise beyond an acceptable comfort level.

The method uses a continuous-boil, electric kettle, i.e., the type without an automatic shut-off switch. Fill it with water and fit all bottles with a capsule while waiting for the water to boil. When ready, take a bottle and hold the capsule portion over the steam. The capsule will shrink to a perfect fit within seconds. For best results, penetrate the steam with the capsule and bottle in such a fashion as to shrink the capsule from top to bottom. If the bottom of the capsule is shrunk first, the top will not fit snugly. Remove the capsule and bottle from the steam once the capsule has completely shrunk. Be sure to keep your fingers away from the steam as it can scald your fingers. Also, when shrinking more than 25 bottles in a continuous fashion, perform this in an area with no overhead ceiling made of non-waterproof drywall, wood or other non-waterproof material to avoid mold formation or other more serious damage.

A hot stovetop burner can also be used in a similar fashion as the kettle method, but without problems associated with steam.

A general-purpose 1000- or 1500-Watt heat gun, the type used for drying glue, stripping paint, or bending plastics, and available at hardware stores, is another effective method for larger productions. The limit only depends on your stamina as heat guns can run continuously (check the manufacturer's instructions to ensure that your model can run continuously).

To shrink capsules using a general-purpose heat gun, insert the narrow nozzle attachment on the heat gun (if your model is equipped with one), and point it down from the top of the capsule when applying heat to get a good fit and minimize creasing. When the occasional crease forms, rotate the bottle while applying heat; this should shrink the crease away. With some practice, you should be able to shrink a capsule in a few seconds, but be careful not to apply excessive heat to avoid damaging the capsule or the tear-off tab.

Figure 9-17: Hand-held heat shrink applicators (or heat tunnels) without a blower (left) and with a blower (right)

Hand-held heat shrink applicators, such as the ones shown in Figure 9-17, often called heat tunnels, specifically designed for winemaking are the most time-efficient tools. These are well worth the investment if you make several hundreds of bottles annually. They consist of a coiled heating element that surrounds the capsule for a uniform shrinking. The blower model shown in Figure 9-17 also includes a fan that further increases shrink speed and efficiency.

To shrink a capsule using a hand-held heat tunnel, position it over the capsule for just a couple of seconds, then move on to the next bottle. You can easily capsule 500 bottles in less than 30 minutes if your stamina and back hold up that long. It works very quickly and makes for a nice finish. Do not use excessive heat to avoid damaging the capsule or tear-off tab.

9.7 LABELS

Labels provide the finishing touch on wine bottles and are used to convey information on the bottle's content, as well as to display the winemaker's pride. Labels should indicate the wine style, including varietal(s), alcohol content and date of production or bottling. Pre-printed labels with some of this information are available from local winemaking supply shops.

Pre-printed labels have the advantage of having water-soluble glue on the backing making them very easy to remove. Gummed labels can be removed by immersing the bottle under running hot water. The label will quickly peel off. The only disadvantage with water-soluble glue-backed labels is that they peel when immersed in a bucket of cold water and ice when chilling wine. The alternative is to use water-resistant glue; however, peeling labels will be time-consuming. These will need to be scraped off with a sharp knife.

You can also customize and personalize labels with the use of a personal computer and a good-quality printer. You can produce and print labels in batches on gummed paper available from a good print shop.

The easiest method to apply labels on bottles is by using a water-soaked sponge. Simply moisten the label backing and apply to the bottle.

Note: Labels printed on an ink-jet printer are not recommended as cellar humidity or water from an ice bucket (when chilling wine) will cause the ink to run off.

10
MAKING PINOT NOIR

Sales and consumption of Pinot Noir wine have soared since the 2004 box-office hit *Sideways*, the story of two soul-searching friends on a trip to the Santa Ynez Valley, north of Santa Barbara, in search of the perfect Pinot Noir. The *Sideways* effect aside, the growing popularity – if not obsession – with Pinot Noir is that these wines provide sheer drinking pleasure and can be built for the long run when the best grapes are used. The wines are sublime, exhibiting hedonistic raspberry and cherry aromas, with many layers of fruit flavors and a soft, silky mouthfeel.

The world over has been trying to emulate the great Pinot Noir-based Burgundian wines. Even Robert M. Parker, Jr., the well-known wine critic and Burgundian wine lover, has joined in the Pinot Noir craze by establishing the Beaux Frères Vineyard and Winery in Oregon to focus solely on this variety.

However, Pinot Noir is both capricious in the vineyard and difficult to vinify in the winery – a double challenge for anyone growing this grape and trying to make outstanding wines. Pinot Noir is best suited for cool climate regions; however, it is prone to spring frost and viruses because of its thin skin. Weather changes can also cause timing of harvest to swing greatly forcing wineries to make quick decisions to harvest and vinify. As such, Pinot Noir may not always be harvested with the right balance of sugar, acidity and aromas, translating the challenge to the winemaker. He/she must then determine what set of techniques and technologies to use to extract the optimal amount of aromas and phenolic compounds. For example, specific emphasis on color extraction may be required owing to the lighter color of grapes. Or, sugar and/or acidity corrections may be required for balance. This is always tricky if not forbidden in some winemaking regions of the world. No wonder Pinot Noir is indeed the heartbreak grape!

The following sections outline the meticulous process of making premium Pinot Noir wine. Use the flowchart in Figure 1-11 on page 59 as a reference.

10.1 PREPARATION

Pinot Noir is a thin-skinned grape, which means that wines will tend to be relatively lighter in color and body and with lower tannin concentration compared to their big-muscle red counterparts such as Cabernet Sauvignon and Syrah (Shiraz). So it can be a challenge to make a full-bodied Pinot Noir built for aging. The instructions below will help you optimize phenolic (color, tannin and flavor) extraction for crafting full-bodied, age-worthy Pinot Noir wines from grapes.

First and foremost, you will have to search out the best grapes possible. If you know the vineyard owner, inquire about the yield rate – an indication of the concentration of phenolics in grapes, i.e., the lower the yield, the higher the concentration and therefore, potentially, the higher the quality of the wine. The best wines are made from low-yield vines; however, expect to pay a high premium for such grapes. Most often, these are sold to premium wineries that have a supply agreement with growers. Seek out the lowest possible yield you are able to get (or afford) in your area. A good yield for making great Pinot Noir should not exceed 50 hL/ha or 3 tons/acre, assuming an approximate yield of 650 L per ton (1 ton = 2,000 lbs).

Grapes should look completely healthy with no visible sign of damage from pests, rot or vineyard diseases. Sort grape bunches and berries, and remove any that are unhealthy or not ideal, specifically removing those that are shriveled, moldy, or that lack color intensity.

The sugar level should be between 24.0–26.0 B° (SG between 1.101–1.110) to produce a dry wine with alcohol content between 12.5–13.5% alc./vol. TA should be in the 6.0–8.0 g/L range and the pH should not exceed 3.5. Remember: A higher pH will result in a lighter-colored wine, reduced aging potential, and being more prone to microbial spoilage.

Have all your equipment cleaned, sanitized and ready for when the grapes arrive. As soon as the grapes arrive at your home winery, sort, crush and destem the grapes into an open-top fermentor. Destemming is recommended to avoid imparting harsh tannins to the wine. Immediately run off approximately 10% of juice to concentrate phenolic extraction in the remaining volume of wine, or let the grapes and juice macerate for a couple of hours or more to make a light rosé wine from the free-run juice. Vinify the free-run juice separately using white-winemaking techniques.

Immediately sulfite the crushed grapes to approximately 10 mg/L, as the wine will be malolactic fermented, and slightly more, up to 15–20 mg/L, if the grapes are less than perfect. Using the yield assumptions above, you will need to add approximately 0.7 g of potassium metabisulfite per 100 kg (220 lbs) of grapes to add 10 mg/L of free SO_2.

Measure Brix (SG), TA and pH, and adjust as desired. Ideally, if you have sound grapes, you should not need to chaptalize to correct the sugar level. If you do, add dextrose (corn sugar) or sucrose (beet or cane sugar) at the rate of 17 g/L for each 1% increment in desired potential alcohol. And add tartaric acid if you need to adjust TA.

10.2 PHENOLIC EXTRACTION

To maximize color extraction from the thin-skinned grapes, cold macerate the crushed grapes and juice for up to one week if you have the ability to perform this pre-fermentation cold soak, and add macerating enzymes, such as Lallzyme EX or Scottzyme Color Pro, at crushing. If you are not equipped for cold soak maceration and your grapes are shipped in a refrigerated truck, the grapes will be sufficiently cold to provide up to two or three days of cold soaking by keeping your winemaking area as cold as possible. Be sure to stir and adequately protect the must during cold soaking. Be sure to cover the open-top fermentor with a heavy tarpaulin to keep spoilage-causing fruit flies out of the must. Refer to section 4.3.2 for detailed instructions on cold soak maceration and the use of macerating enzymes.

10.3 ALCOHOLIC FERMENTATION

Following cold soak maceration, bring the temperature of the must up to at least 18° C (65° F) by increasing the surrounding temperature (remember to remove all frozen jugs from the crushed grapes, if used for cold maceration). If possible, try and get the temperature of the must up to close to 30° C (86° F) until fermentation starts and then immediately drop the temperature back down to no less than 18° C (65° F). Use a large floating thermometer to monitor the temperature of the must. Keep in mind that once fermentation becomes vigorously active, temperature will shoot up on its own accord. The idea is to get a quick and hot fermentation, but not so hot as to jeopardize the fermentation and survival of the yeast, and therefore you will need to control the surrounding temperature. Fermentation above 30° C (86° F) can also reduce the positive effects of phenolic extraction in addition to a sluggish or stuck fermentation.

Before fermentation, as you are increasing the temperature of the must, add a yeast nutrient supplement, such as GO-FERM or Superfood, to ensure a good fermentation and to minimize the production of hydrogen sulfide (H_2S) associated with low-nutrient grapes. Refer to section 4.7.1 on page 195 for more information on the use of yeast nutrients, and follow the manufacturer's recommended rate of addition.

Inoculate the must with a cultured yeast strain specifically recommended for full-bodied, dry red wines where full tannin extraction and color stabilization are desired. Lalvin RC 212, RED STAR Pasteur Red, Wyeast Pasteur Red, or White Labs Merlot Red Wine Yeast are specifically recommended for Pinot Noir-based wines.

Fermentation should start within 24–36 hours. Remember to keep the fermentation area as cool as possible during fermentation to avoid having the fermenting wine exceed 30° C (86° F). With a plunger tool, punch down the grape solids and mix the juice thoroughly to avoid the must becoming spoiled. Be sure to replace the tarpaulin over the must to protect it from microbial spoilage and fruit flies.

As fermentation progresses and becomes vigorous, punch down the cap at least three times a day to optimize phenolic extraction and minimize the risk of microbial spoilage. Stir the grape solids and wine thoroughly to dissipate heat created by fermentation.

Monitor fermentation using a hydrometer to ensure it progresses normally. Fermentation is nearing completion when the cap starts falling, usually 5–7 days after the onset of fermentation. Immediately rack the (free-run) wine off the grape solids and transfer it to oak barrels. Transfer the grape solids to the press to extract the (press-run) wine, and transfer it to different oak barrels. Vinify free- and press-run wines separately and then blend them back together prior to bottling, if desired and if the quality of the wines are complementary.

Inoculate all barrels with a malolactic bacteria (MLB) culture to ensure a trouble-free malolactic fermentation (MLF). Remember to secure each barrel with a fermentation lock. Monitor MLF progression using paper chromatography. Gently stir the lees once a week to enhance the flavor profile. Avoid over-stirring which could otherwise inhibit the oxygen-sensitive MLB and result in a stuck MLF. When MLF is complete, measure TA, pH and free SO_2. TA should have decreased while pH should have increased. Sulfite each barrel to obtain an adequate level of protection based on your wine's pH. For example, if the pH is 3.3 and the free SO_2 is 5 mg/L, you will need to add sulfite to increase the free SO_2 by 25 mg/L to approximately 30 mg/L. Refer to section 3.4 for more information on measuring and adjusting free SO_2, and use the Sulfite Calculator at www.winemakermag.com to guide your sulfite additions.

10.4 AGING, FINING AND BOTTLING

Age the wine up to 18 months depending on your desired style, type of oak and toast level of your barrels, and age of the barrels. Taste each barrel at least once a month and determine when the wine needs to be transferred out of the barrels. Remember to top up barrels regularly at the same time. During aging, rack the wine off its lees every 3 months. A positive-displacement pump greatly eases racking from one barrel to another.

At the end of the barrel-aging period (when the desired style is achieved), rack the wine to glass containers or tanks and fine using egg white. Egg white fining is a traditional method of clarifying oak-aged Pinot Noir wines and is ideal for softening the wine's astringency. Add egg white at a rate of 5–10 g/hL of wine, or the white of 1–2 eggs per 100 L. Remember to first separate the egg white from the yolk. Next, prepare a saline solution by dissolving a pinch of salt in 10 mL of water for each egg used, and stir **gently** into the egg white. Salt is added to prevent the solution from getting cloudy. Add the saline egg-white solution directly into the wine and stir thoroughly. Rack the wine within 1–2 weeks, no later.

If the wine was aged in a cool cellar at 13° C (55° F) or less, you do not need to cold stabilize the wine; otherwise, cold stabilization is highly recommended to avoid tartrate crystals from forming in the bottle.

Maintain the free SO_2 at the recommended level according to the pH of the wine through bulk aging and right until bottling.

Conduct extensive taste tests to assess mouthfeel, structure, balance and overall quality, and determine what corrective actions, such as blending or minor TA adjustments, if any, are required to achieve the desired results. At this point, you should expect to only make minor adjustments, assuming that any parameter that required major adjustment was corrected when first discovered. Depending on the amount of phenols extracted, you may need to reduce acidity to get improved mouthfeel and balance. Perform bench trials with samples with reduced TA. For example, if your final TA is 7.0 g/L, prepare two samples by deacidifying using potassium bicarbonate, one at 6.5 g/L and the second at 6.0 g/L. Test both samples, compare with the control sample of 7.0 g/L, and decide which you prefer best. Perhaps, if 6.5 g/L is still too high but 6.0 g/L is too low, you can repeat the trial with samples at 6.4 and 6.2 g/L, for example, until you are happy with the final TA.

Also, compare the overall quality of the free-run and press-run wines to determine if they should be blended. If you find the press-run wine to be of inferior quality or if it seems more austere, do not blend it with the free-run wine. Age each wine or the blended wine in bulk in glass containers or tanks for up to 6 months, or alternatively, bottle the wine and age it in the bottle. Depending on the quality of the vintage, the wine may further improve over the next 6–12 months. Open a bottle every 3 months or so to monitor the wine's evolution and to see how a wine can change so much over its life.

11
MAKING SPARKLING WINE

Sparkling wine, or bubbly, is the wine par excellence to raise a toast or to celebrate a special occasion. The magic of sparkling wine, such as Champagne, always brings a festive mood to any occasion. This is why this type of wine has gained popularity; however, it should not be limited to celebrations. It will make an excellent aperitif, especially with hors d'oeuvres, or with a seafood entrée, or enjoyed with dessert if the wine is sweet.

Sparkling wine is produced mainly as white or rosé although there have been many attempts to commercialize sparkling red wines. As with still wine, sparkling wine is also classified according to the amount of residual sugar (RS). Different countries have different designations and requirements relative to residual sugar content. For example, Brut (medium dry, demi-sec) and Extra Brut (dry, sec) sparkling wines may have a maximum allowable RS of 15 g/L and 6 g/L, respectively. For some producers, the Brut is their driest sparkling wine, which has very little *dosage* (a small volume of wine, called *cuvée*, to which a little sugar is added), while others also offer a sparkling wine called Brut Extra, Brut Ultra or Brut Nature, denoting no dosage or with no perceptible residual sugar.

Sparkling wine is usually labeled as either vintage or non-vintage. A vintage sparkling wine is produced strictly from blended or unblended wines from a single vintage. Non-vintage (the term multi-vintage is also often used) wine is produced using the same process except that wines from different vintages are used in the final blended wine.

Sparkling wine is produced from still wine (referred to as the base wine or *cuvée* in Champagne) by conducting a second alcoholic fermentation by one of two methods to produce the carbon dioxide gas bubbles, or by a variation of these.

The best-known method in the production of premium sparkling wine is to conduct the second alcoholic fermentation in the bottle. Known as *prise de mousse* in French, this bottle-fermentation technique is key in the traditional *méthode champenoise* process for Champagne production. It is also used in the production of premium Californian and Italian sparkling wines as well as Spanish *cava*.

Commercial sparkling wine can only be labeled "Champagne" if it is produced in France's northeastern region of Champagne according to the *méthode champenoise*. In fact, even the use of the descriptor *méthode champenoise* is now legally restricted to wines of that region. Non-Champagne sparkling wines can use such terms as Traditional Method, or *méthode traditionelle*, or Classical Method, or *méthode classique*, for example.

In this method, the sparkling wine is kept in the same bottle throughout the second fermentation during the extended period of aging on the lees, often referred to as *tirage*, when the yeast undergoes autolysis to give Champagne its distinctive and complex aromas and flavors. The yeast deposit (lees) from the long and cool fermentation is collected in a special cap by inverting the bottle. The bottle is inverted from a horizontal to a vertical position in systematic and progressive fashion – a process known as riddling, or *remuage* in French. The neck of the bottle is then frozen to remove the cap and frozen deposit without disturbing the clarity of the wine. This bottle-clarification process is known as disgorgement. Lastly, the dosage is added to each bottle to sweeten the wine to obtain a desired style. In Champagne, the practice of adding dosage is required to balance the high acidity of the base wine resulting from grapes grown in a very cool climate. Cool-climate grapes do not achieve full maturity and, therefore, the sugar level is low and acidity is high.

This method is labor-intensive and requires much experience to achieve a good quality sparkling wine, judged on both the size

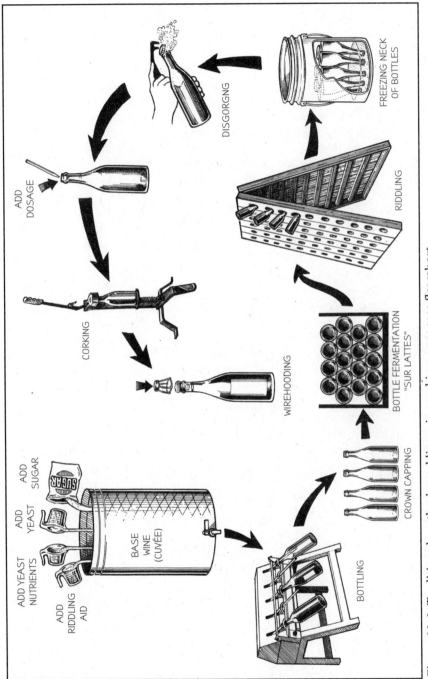

ADD YEAST NUTRIENTS

ADD YEAST

ADD SUGAR

ADD RIDDLING AID

BASE WINE (CUVÉE)

BOTTLING

CROWN CAPPING

BOTTLE FERMENTATION "SUR LATTES"

WIREHOODING

CORKING

ADD DOSAGE

DISGORGNG

FREEZING NECK OF BOTTLES

RIDDLING

Figure 11-1: Traditional method sparkling winemaking – process flowchart

and the amount of bubbles. Endless, tiny rapid-forming and long-lasting bubbles characterize the best-quality sparkling wines.

Sections 11.1 to 11.4 and the flowchart in Figure 11-1 describe the traditional method of making sparkling wine, adapted here for home winemaking.

Another popular method consists in conducting a bulk second fermentation in a stainless steel pressure-resistant tank. This method, known as the *cuve close* (tank fermentation) or Charmat process, bypasses the need for bottle fermentation, riddling and disgorgement. The sparkling wine is then refrigerated for bottling under pressure to minimize gas loss. The only disadvantage with the Charmat process in home winemaking is that the second fermentation produces sediment at the bottom of the tank that needs to be separated by racking, which will cause some loss of gas. The Charmat process for sparkling wine production is a less costly method compared to the *méthode champenoise*, and is commonly used in commercial winemaking. Asti Spumante, the popular low-alcohol (approximately 8% alc./vol.) sweet sparkling wine from Piedmont (Italy) is produced using a variation of the tank fermentation process.

Figure 11-2: 10-week sparkling wine kit

For home winemaking, there are three simple and inexpensive alternatives to produce early-drinking sparkling wines: using a sparkling wine kit, using dialysis tubing or by carbonation.

Ten-week sparkling wine kits, such as the one shown in Figure 11-2, include the concentrate, all necessary ingredients (bentonite, sugar, yeast, etc.), stoppers, wirehoods, capsules and labels. These kits use a variation of the traditional method; they still ferment in the bottle but the sediment is not disgorged. The final wine requires careful pouring from the bottle when serving so as not to disturb the sediment at the bottom.

The dialysis tubing method is a clever way of making traditional method sparkling wine without the need to riddle and disgorge. It is an amazingly simple alternative that produces excellent results. The method involves packaging yeast in dialysis tubing to initiate bottle fermentation, unlike the traditional method where a sugar/yeast solution is pitched directly into the base wine. Once bottle fermentation has completed, the dialysis tubing with the spent yeast is simply removed, and *voilà*, a clear sparkling wine. This method is described in section 11.5.

Carbonation is the process used in soft-drink production where a beverage is injected with carbon dioxide gas. This method produces very good sparkling wine with much less effort and risk, but with fewer and larger bubbles that fade quickly compared to premium sparkling wines. Section 11.6 describes the method for producing sparkling wines by carbonation.

Warning: Sparkling wine production requires the handling of high-pressure containers and bottles. Follow safety precautions to avoid potential accidents and wear protective eyewear at all times.

11.1 PREPARATION

Refer to Figure 11-1 in the following description of the traditional method of making sparkling wine for home winemaking.

Start with a well-balanced still base wine (cuvée), ideally made from whole-bunch pressed grapes to minimize phenolic extraction, with an alcoholic content between 10.0–11.0% alc./vol. to make a good sparkling wine. The cuvée should not exceed 11.0% alc./vol. as bottle fermentation will produce additional alcohol, approximately 1.2–1.5% alc./vol. A good-quality sparkling wine should not exceed 12.5% alc./vol.; otherwise, it will be unbalanced. The sparkling wine produced using the method described in this section will be sweetened with a dosage, therefore, the cuvée should have a TA high in the recommended range (refer to Table 3-2 on page 122).

Table 1-1 and Table 1-2 on pages 50 to 53 list some recommended grape varieties suitable for sparkling wine. In making Champagne, the cuvée is typically a dry-style white wine blend from Chardonnay, Pinot Meunier and Pinot Noir. *Blanc de Blancs* sparkling wine is produced from Chardonnay only while *Blanc de Noirs* is made using non-macerated white juice from red grapes such as Pinot Meunier or Pinot Noir. You can also use other non-Champagne grape varieties, such as Chenin Blanc, Muscat or Riesling, for making excellent sparkling wines.

The cuvée should be cellar-aged for at least 6 months, and should be clarified and cold stabilized to avoid tartrate precipitation during the time when the sparkling wine is placed in cold storage. It should have a free SO_2 level of 15 mg/L or less to ensure successful bottle fermentation. MLF should also be completed, if desired, and stabilized before making sparkling wine.

Warning: The cuvée should not be preserved with a high level of sulfite or be stabilized with potassium sorbate as these will prevent the wine from sparkling.

Prepare a small dosage volume by siphoning between 2–4 % of the cuvée into a glass container and adding an equal volume of sweetener-conditioner. Properly seal the container to protect the wine from oxidation, and place it in cold storage at a temperature between 4°–8° C (39°–46° F).

11.2 BOTTLE FERMENTATION

For bottle fermentation, you will need to prepare a yeast starter culture and to acclimatize it in an alcoholic environment before inoculating the cuvée. Choose a strong fermenting yeast strain that has good tolerance to alcohol, that can ferment at colder temperatures and that can withstand the high pressure created in the bottle during fermentation. Good examples are yeast strains specifically developed for sparkling wine applications, such as Lalvin EC-1118, RED STAR Premier Cuvée, White Labs Champagne and Wyeast Pasteur Champagne strains.

The following protocol[1] for preparing the starter culture produces approximately 2.5 L of starter culture that can be used to inoculate 50 L of cuvée. The volumes can be scaled accordingly for your volume of cuvée to be inoculated. Prepare the starter culture 3–5 days in advance of inoculating the cuvée.

Rehydrate **two (2)** 5-g packet of active dry yeast in 50 mL of water as per the manufacturer's instructions or as described in section 4.7.1. Prepare a 50% sugar solution by dissolving 250 g of sugar in 250 mL of water, stir thoroughly, and then add water to bring the volume to exactly 500 mL. Add 37.5 mL of sugar solution to the rehydrated yeast suspension, 62.5 mL of water, and lastly, 2.5 g of yeast nutrients. Let the yeast suspension acclimatize and ferment at 20° C (68° F) for approximately 24 hours or until the Brix (SG) reaches 0.0 (1.000).

Then, prepare the starter by adding the 150 mL of suspension and 200 mL of 50% sugar solution to 2.15 L of cuvée. Stir thoroughly and let ferment at 20° C (68° F) for 2–4 days until the Brix (SG) reaches 0.0 (1.000). Stir the starter culture at least once a day during fermentation. Slowly lower the temperature down to 13° C (55° F) and let the Brix (SG) reach –1.3 (0.995).

Allow the cuvée to reach a temperature between 18°–21° C (65°–70° F) to make dissolving sugar easier and to favor yeast fermentation. Add 20–25 g of fermentable sugar – dextrose or sucrose

---

[1]Based on Lallemand's Lalvin EC-1118 Technical Information and <u>Protocol for the Preparation of a Starter Culture for a Secondary Bottle Fermentation using Active Dry Wine Yeast.</u>

– per liter of wine and dissolve thoroughly. This will produce an additional 1.2%–1.5% alc./vol. in the finished sparkling wine, and produce approximately 6 bars (approximately 90 psi) of pressure at 20° C (68° F), the equivalent of three times the pressure in car tires.

*Note: Do **not** exceed the prescribed maximum amount of sugar to produce more bubbles; otherwise, excessive pressure will build up in bottles that could cause them to explode.*

During bottle fermentation, sediment will deposit on the bottle walls and will need to be shaken, by riddling, for later removal when disgorging. To ease this operation, add a riddling aid, such as tannins, to the cuvée at the rate of 20 g/hL. Dissolve the tannins in a small amount of wine and then add this to the remainder of the cuvée. You can also use bentonite or other proprietary formulations as riddling aids.

When ready to bottle the inoculated cuvée, sanitize and rinse the required number of sparkling wine bottles. Fill each bottle to within 7 cm (2¾ in) of the top using your bottling device of choice making sure to stir the cuvée regularly during bottling to set the yeast in suspension to ensure good bottle fermentation.

In commercial sparkling wine production using the traditional method, the technique of lees collection is accomplished using special crown caps – similar to the ones used to stopper beer bottles – equipped with a *bidule*. The bidule is a special holder designed to collect the settling lees and facilitate disgorgement. Two types of crown caps/bidules are available: integrated and separate, shown in Figure 11-3. In the integrated type, the bidule is

Figure 11-3: Bidules – integrated and separate

part of the crown cap. In the separate type, the small plastic container (bidule) is inserted into the bottle opening and the cork-lined crown cap is placed over it to provide a perfect seal on the bottle. The only drawback of the separate bidule is that occasionally it remains stuck in the bottle, even under the high pressure of the sparkling wine, when the sediment is frozen during disgorgement. Crown caps on bidules are available in a metal alloy, stainless steel or tinned iron, although the latter is not recommended as it tends to rust and leave a stain on bottle lips. Stainless steel crown caps may also be magnetized, making them handy during the capping operation.

387

Figure 11-4: Crown cappers – amateur model and professional model

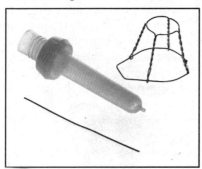

Figure 11-5: The vintrap

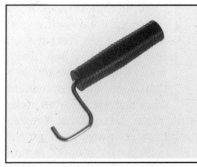

Figure 11-6: Tool for securing wirehood on sparkling wine bottles

The crown cap for both types of bidules is fastened to the bottle opening using a home winemaking crown capper or a professional model, such as the ones shown in Figure 11-4. Crown caps are pressure-resistant and will maintain all carbon dioxide gas produced during bottle fermentation.

Note: Bidules come in different sizes to fit either US or European bottles. Europeans bottles have a slightly wider opening and require 29 mm bidules. Crown cappers are usually equipped with different size attachments for capping US and European bottles.

Note: The techniques of crown-capping and disgorging sparkling wine bottles require extensive experience and are not recommended for novice winemakers. Crown-capped bottles will need disgorging, which involves "decrowning" sparkling wine bottles under very high pressure. Only experienced winemakers should attempt this operation. Refer to section 11.4 for more details and instructions on how to prepare fake "sparkling" wine for the purpose of practicing disgorging.

As an alternative to using bidules, you can use a vintrap, shown in Figure 11-5, a special plastic bottle-fermentation stopper that greatly simplifies lees collection and disgorgement, although it has unfortunately become very difficult to find. The vintrap is similar to a regular sparkling wine bottle stopper, but it has an elongated container to col-

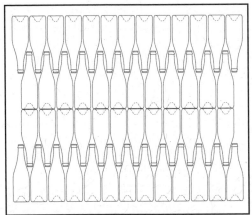

Figure 11-7: Stacking sparkling wine bottles *sur lattes* (top view)

Figure 11-8: Sparkling wine bottles stacked *sur pointes* (top bin) and *sur lattes* (bottom bin)

lect sediment from bottle fermentation as the bottle is inverted. It is simply placed by hand in the bottle and then secured with a wirehood. The wirehood is held in place by twisting the wire 5½ revolutions using the tool shown in Figure 11-6.

Once all the bottles have been filled and capped, transfer all bottles to a wine cellar for a long and slow, cool bottle fermentation at a temperature of approximately 13° C (55° F). The cellar temperature should not be lower than the yeast's optimum fermentation temperature range recommended by the manufacturer. Lay and stack bottles on their sides on wine racks or bins, or *sur lattes* as in the traditional method shown in Figures 11-7 and 11-8, for 12–18 months depending on the desired extent of lees contact.

It is highly recommended that you monitor fermentation progress using a special pressure gauge, known as an aphrometer, shown in Figure 11-9, which is mounted on the crown cap of a bottle. The aphrometer[2] consists of three parts:

- The top part (a screw needle holder) is made up of a manometer, a manual tightening ring, an endless screw that slips into the middle

[2] As defined by the Office International de la Vigne et du Vin's Resolution OENO 21/2003.

part, and a needle that pierces through the capsule. The needle has a lateral hole that transmits pressure to the manometer.

- The middle part (or the nut) enables the top part to be properly centered. It is screwed into the lower part, which holds strongly onto the bottle.
- The lower part (the clamp) is equipped with a spur that slips under the ring of the bottle in order to hold the aphrometer and bottle together. There are rings adaptable to every kind of bottle.

Figure 11-9: An aphrometer

Some models may also include a pressure relief valve.

Mount the aphrometer as per the manufacturer's instructions; there should be no loss of pressure if mounted properly. Shake the bottle several times until the manometer reading remains constant and no longer increases. During fermentation, the pressure will increase, and it will remain constant at its maximum when fermentation has completed. To remove the aphrometer, gently unscrew it until the needle is out of the bottle; if it is equipped with a relief valve, first open the valve to reduce the possibility of foaming.

During fermentation, lees will deposit along the length of the bottle by forming over a large surface area exposed to wine, which will impart the distinctive yeasty aromas and flavors found in sparkling wines aged on the lees.

11.3 RIDDLING

At the end of fermentation and the lees aging period, you will need to invert each bottle to allow all sediment to deposit in the bidule or vintrap in preparation for disgorging to remove the sediment for a crystal clear wine. In the traditional method, a technique known as riddling, known as a *remuage* in French, is used to let the sediment fall and collect in the bidule by sharply rotating and tilting each bottle progressively on a riddling rack, known as a *pupitre* in French and shown in Figure 11-10, over a 21-day period until fully inverted.

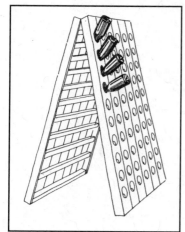

Figure 11-10: A riddling rack

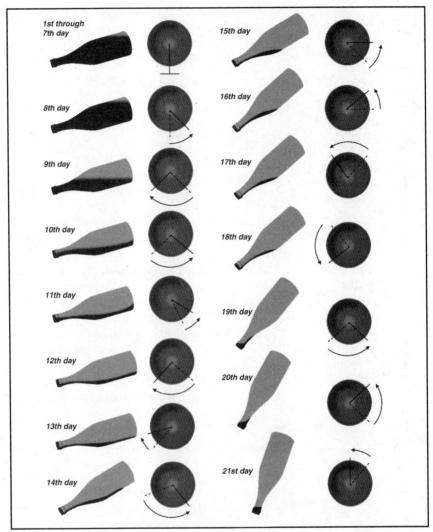

Figure 11-11: Standard riddling program

Figure 11-11 illustrates a typical standard riddling program used in the traditional method. In this program, each bottle is rotated sharply according to Figure 11-11 over a 21-day period to dislodge the sediment. During the rotation of each bottle, each is also progressively tilted upwards to move each bottle from a horizontal position to an almost vertical position by the time the program is completed. In Figure 11-11, the shaded portion of the bottle represents the sediment, and illustrates how it travels to the bidule during riddling. The bottom of the bottle also illustrates the start and end positions of the bottle when riddled, using a dotted

391

Figure 11-12: A *remueur* riddling Champagne bottles

and solid line, respectively. Mark the bottom of each bottle with a short, white line using enamel paint where the inverted T-line is indicated on the first bottle (1st through 7th day) in Figure 11-11. This greatly simplifies keeping track of bottle positions throughout the riddling period.

A *remueur*, depicted in Figure 11-12, can manually riddle thousands of bottles in a single day, some as much as ten or even twenty thousand bottles per day. In modern sparkling winemaking, manual riddling has been replaced by the use of automated riddling machines known as gyropalettes.

When riddling is completed, the sediment in each bottle will be collected in the bidule (or vintrap), ready for disgorgement, as shown in Figure 11-13. At this point, there should be no sediment on the inside wall of bottles and wine should be crystal clear.

Riddling has the advantage of disturbing the sediment minimally while depositing them in the bidule or vintrap (by gravity), therefore maintaining clarity in the wine. The disadvantage is that

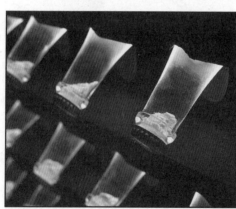

Figure 11-13: Sediment collected in bidules

this process requires more work to tilt each bottle, but it's fun! The alternative is to separate the sediment from the wine by racking or decanting each bottle. This is still a tedious procedure yielding less-than-satisfactory results as there will always be some sediment getting into the finished wine.

At the end of the 21st day, you can proceed with disgorging, or place the riddled bottles vertically upside-down in carton wine cases, or *sur pointes*, as is known in the traditional method pictured in Figures 11-8 and 11-14, for several weeks or months for further aging.

If you do not have a riddling rack, you can simply place bottles vertically upside-down in carton wine cases and then simply twist each bottle partially clockwise and counterclockwise by holding the bottle by its bottom. Repeat this every day until all the sediment is collected in the bidule or vintrap.

11.4 DISGORGEMENT, DOSAGE AND BOTTLING

Before proceeding with disgorgement, ensure that bottle fermentation is complete; use an aphrometer if available to monitor fermentation progression and completion. Fermentation will complete within several months if carried out in a cool cellar at 13° C (55° F). If fermentation is not allowed to complete, it can restart after corking resulting in more sediment in the bottle and an unstable wine.

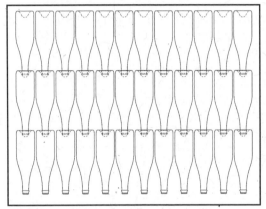

Figure 11-14: Stacking sparkling wine bottles *sur pointes* (lateral view)

Caution: Handle bottles with great care and with safety gloves and a protective face guard during the following bottle handling operations as bottles are under high pressure.

Disgorgement (vintrap)
There are two methods you can use to disgorge sparkling wine made using vintraps.

In the first method with the bottle still in the inverted position, fold the elongated portion of the vintrap above the sediment level. You can use the short metal wire (refer to Figure 11-5) provided with the vintrap to secure the fold to prevent the sediment from dropping back in the wine. The use of this short wire is optional if you will be freezing the sediment in the stopper before removal. It does, however, serve as an additional safeguard against sediment dropping back in the wine. Flip the bottle right side up, remove the wirehood, and pull out the vintrap.

In the second method, transfer the inverted and riddled bottles of sparkling wine to a deep freezer at a temperature between –7° and –4° C (20° and 25° F). When ice crystals start to form – this can take up to 3 hours – retrieve one bottle at a time, remove the wirehood, and pull out the vintrap to disgorge the sediment. As the sediment has frozen inside the vintrap, it can be removed without leaving any deposit in the wine. Almost no gas will escape since, at this near-freezing temperature, most of the precious carbon dioxide will remain dissolved in the wine.

Figure 11-15: Disgorging

Disgorgement (bidule)

Disgorging sparkling wine bottles with bidules, shown in Figure 11-15, is a tricky proposition, which requires a lot of practice. This is not for novice winemakers. You can practice on fake sparkling wine as outlined further down in this section.

When disgorging, the crown cap, bidule and frozen sediment will fly off. To prevent any injury and to avoid making a mess, use a large container to collect the flying debris. Champenois disgorgers often use an old oak barrel, in the upright position, having a large cutout in the center approximately 0.5 m × 0.5 m (18 in × 18 in) in size.

Disgorgement is performed using a disgorging key – also known as a decrowner and shown in Figure 11-16 – a tool that operates on the same principle as the old soda or beer bottle openers. The only difference is that the key pulls the crown cap using a downward instead of an upward motion. Conventional bottle openers will not do the job; they will not work since the upward motion will interfere with flying debris.

You will need a large and shallow container, such as a 20-L pail, which can hold up to ten or more bottles in the inverted position in a brine solution used to freeze the sediment. The number of bottles and size of the container depend on how quickly you can disgorge. The rate of disgorgement will also depend on how quickly the brine solution can freeze the neck of the bottles. The method described below will freeze the sediment in 5–10 minutes. Start out with a few bottles and adjust accordingly based on skill.

Figure 11-16: Disgorging key or decrowner

The brine solution should freeze approximately 2.5–3.0 cm (1–1¼ in) of the neck portion of the bottle, or just above the sediment level. The wine should not be frozen too high above the sediment level, which would otherwise make disgorgement more difficult.

Prepare the brine solution using ice, or snow if you live in a snowy region, and plain coarse salt. If possible, work in a cool cellar to give you more time before the ice starts melting. Crush the ice and place it in the container

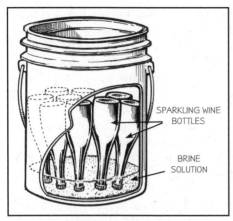

SPARKLING WINE
BOTTLES

BRINE
SOLUTION

Figure 11-17: Freezing bottle necks in a brine solution

in a thin layer just enough to be slightly higher than the sediment level. Spread the salt evenly over the ice; you will need approximately a quarter to a third of the ice volume. This brine solution for freezing the bottlenecks works fast; however, it can be accelerated by substituting plain salt with hydrated calcium chloride, available from a supplier of chemicals. Hydrated calcium chloride lowers the freezing point of water considerably more than plain salt – approximately –55° C (–67° F) versus –20° C (–4° F), respectively.

Before transferring bottles to the container, chill the bottles outdoors if you live in a cold climate area and if you are disgorging in the winter months, or in a refrigerator, to minimize the loss of precious carbon dioxide gas during disgorgement. If the wine is too warm, it will gush out uncontrollably when the crown cap is pulled causing the loss of precious gas and wine.

Transfer bottles to the container with the neck down into the brine solution, as shown in Figure 11-17. Monitor how long it takes for the sediment to freeze. Remember: You don't want the wine to freeze, which will otherwise make disgorging difficult. Once the sediment freezes, you are ready for disgorging.

Warning: Do not attempt to disgorge "à la volée" (on the fly), i.e., without freezing the sediment. This is very difficult and will result in considerable wine loss unless you become an expert disgorger.

Refer to Figure 11-18 for the sequence of disgorgement steps explained below.

Take one bottle from the container and rinse the brine solution from the neck of the bottle by dipping it in a small bucket of water. With the left hand, bring the bottle to an almost but not quite horizontal position and hold it firmly with the bottom resting against your left leg. The air bubble in the bottle should be at the bottom of the bottle, i.e., just over the punt. With the right hand, place the disgorging key in position over the crown cap, and while pulling the cap with a downward motion towards you, rotate the bottle upwards slightly while completely removing the cap. When timed correctly, you should be able to remove the crown cap as the air bubble in the bottle reaches the neck portion; the air bubble

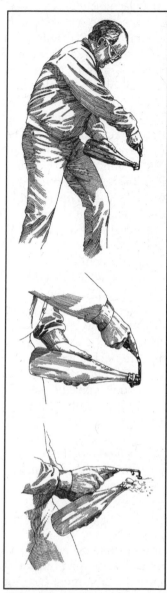

and pressure is what makes the sediment expel. Wine will start gushing out and the sediment will fly out. There will be pressure loss – not much more than 1 bar if done properly – and some wine loss that will need to be replaced at dosage time. Remember to point the bottle and flying ice plug into a container to avoid any accident or mess.

If too much wine is lost, usually due to the wine not being cold enough, hold the bottle by the neck so that your left thumb can reach over and block the mouth as you remove the crown cap. Remove your thumb very slowly to release pressure – you will hear a hissing sound. With a lot of practice and dexterity, you will be able to perform this operation without too much pressure loss and with less than 20 mL of wine loss. This will be replaced with the dosage prior to corking.

At Maleta Winery, we disgorge *à la volée* without chilling bottles using a compressed-air disgorger, the TDD-Grilliat DLV1 Disgorging Machine shown in Figure 11-19, that completely automates the disgorging procedure. The disgorging mechanism is actuated as soon as a bottle is seated (in the horizontal position) in the mechanism. The bottle is automatically rotated upwards and the crown cap is removed and the lees fly out. A stopper with gasket quickly seals the bottle, emulating the operation of the thumb, to stop the foaming and control pressure in the bottle. The bottle is then simply removed and the next one inserted.

Figure 11-18 (top to bottom): Disgorgement – get the bottle and key into position, start pulling the bottle to a horizontal position, and remove the crown cap

Dosage and bottling

The last critical step, adding the dosage, involves adding a small volume of cuvée to which a little sugar is added to balance the wine's acidity and to achieve the desired style, from bone dry to sweet. The French refer to this cuvée solution as the *liqueur d'expédition*, and often contains a distilled spirit such as Cognac. In Ontario, Canada,

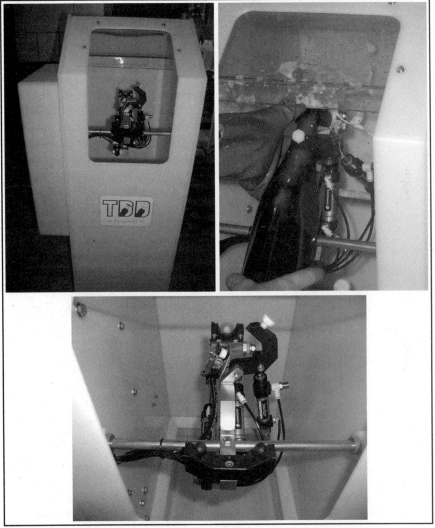

Figure 11-19 (clockwise from top left): TDD-Grilliat DLV1 disgorging machine, disgorging in action and close-up of disgorging mechanism

the technique of adding Icewine as dosage is becoming increasingly popular. Refer to chapter 13 for more information on Icewine.

Table 11-1 provides guidelines for the amount of RS in common styles of sparkling wines from around the world. Countries have different designations and requirements relative to RS that can make such terminology quite confusing.

Add a small amount of dosage (prepared earlier and described in section 11.2) using a syringe to each bottle to obtain the desired

397

Table 11-1
Residual sugar (RS) guidelines for common
styles of sparkling wines from around the world

Style	RS (g/L)	Also known as (see note)
Extra Brut	0–6	Brut de Brut (F) Brut Nature (F) Non Dosage (F) Bone Dry (US)
Brut	0–15	Bone Dry (US)
Extra Dry	12–20	Extra Sec (F) Extra Trocken (G)
Dry	17–35	Sec (F) Trocken (G) Secco (I)
Off-Dry (Semi-Dry)	35–50	Demi Sec (F) Doux (F) Halbtrocken (G) Abboccato (I) Medium Sweet (US)
Sweet	50 & over	Doux (F) Dolce (I)

Note: F=France, G=Germany, I=Italy, US=United States

sweetness level and top up each bottle with good-quality still wine so that a 2-cm (¾-in) ullage is left between the wine and the stopper. It is recommended to add the dosage to bottles while the wine is cold to minimize foaming. Adding the dosage to warm wine will result in excessive gushing and wine loss. If using the latter, be sure to work in an area that can be cleaned easily, and use your thumb to control gushing and wine loss. At Maleta Winery, we use the traditional dosage machine used in Champagne, shown in Figure 11-20, to accurately add dosage and to top up each bottle.

Optionally, you can add a small amount of sulfite to achieve a free SO_2 concentration of no more than 35 mg/L at this stage for extra protection along with some metatartaric acid (10 g/hL) in case the wine was not previously cold stabilized. Use dilute 10% sulfite and 10% metatartaric acid solutions and add at a rate of 0.5 mL and 0.8 mL per bottle, respectively, using a small 1-mL syringe; otherwise, prepare 1% solutions and multiply the required volumes by 10, i.e., 5 mL and 8 mL.

Figure 11-20: Traditional dosage machine

Figure 11-21 (left to right): Champcork 30×48 mm Agglo 2 disc Grade 1 for Euro bottles, cork becomes mushroom-shaped once uncorked from bottle, a wirehood used to secure the cork

To get finer bubbles when the sparkling wine is poured in glasses and to increase persistence of *perlage*, you can add 0.5–5 mL/L of 20% gum arabic solution. Colloidal action from gum arabic reduces dispersion of the tiny carbon dioxide bubbles. Perform bench tests to determine the optimum rate of addition.

Both sulfite and gum arabic can be dissolved in the *liqueur d'expédition*.

The bottles are now ready to be corked. The closure of choice is the traditional sparkling wine cork, such as the Champcork, 30×48 mm Agglo 2 disc Grade 1 for Euro bottles shown in Figure 11-21, better recognized as the mushroom-shaped cork, which must be secured with a wirehood using the wirehooding tool shown in Figure 11-6. The final product, i.e., cork and wirehood, should look like Figure 11-22.

Sparkling wine corks are very difficult to insert because of their

Figure 11-22: Sparkling wine bottle with cork and wirehood

high density and large diameter (30 mm, 1⅗₆-in). Use a floor corker specifically designed for inserting this type of cork, such as the Amez-Droz Rapid 49 corker shown in Figure 11-23. The Rapid 49 corker is specifically designed for corking sparkling wine bottles and comes equipped with an integrated wirehooder. You can insert corks dry if they have been properly stored in their original sulfited bag; otherwise, you can briefly soak the corks in a sulfite solution. Insert the non-tapered end of the cork first, and only

399

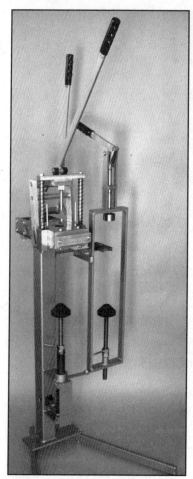

Figure 11-23: Amez-Droz Rapid 49 corker for sparkling wine corks

Figure 11-24: Plastic mushroom-shaped stoppers for North American and European sparkling wine bottles

partially so that the wirehood can be properly secured under the lip of the bottle. This is very important to avoid corks popping out of bottles. Using a 48-mm (approximately 1⅞-in) cork, insert the cork in the bottle at a depth of between 22–26 mm (approximately ⅞–1-in). The wirehooder attachment on the Rapid 49 corker will compress the exposed portion of the cork to its proper shape and to allow the wirehood to seat in place under the bottle lip.

Alternatively, you can use plastic mushroom-shaped stoppers specifically designed for sparkling wine bottles. Two types of stoppers, shown in Figure 11-24, are available depending on the type of bottles used. Sparkling wine bottles manufactured in North America have a slightly smaller opening than those from Europe. Make sure you know what type of bottles you are working with so that you use the proper closure.

Sanitize plastic stoppers in a sulfite solution, insert them by hand by applying a downward pressure until the stopper comes to rest on the bottle opening, and secure with a wirehood.

Rotate each bottle gently but thoroughly, from a horizontal to vertical position by rotating your forearm upward, to mix the dosage with the wine, and then transfer all bottles to a wine cellar. Store bottles horizontally if you are using traditional corks. The sparkling wine will further benefit from 6 months of cellar aging.

Foil capsules are also available to dress sparkling-wine bottles. These are available in such colors as white, black, pink and gold. Simply fit a foil capsule over the stopper and bottleneck, and squeeze the capsule with your hand for a nice finish.

Making fake "sparkling" wine for practicing disgorgement
The traditional method of making sparkling wine can be very difficult. To practice the technique, you can concoct a fake sparkling wine by fermenting a sweet solution. Dissolve 5 mL (1 tsp) of fermentable sugar – dextrose or sucrose – in 500 mL of water with 15 mL (1 tbsp) of lemon juice in a standard sparkling wine bottle, and then inoculate with a yeast strain, such as Lalvin EC-1118. Top up each bottle with water to 750 mL and seal with a crown cap/bidule. Make as many bottles as you need to practice.

11.5 DIALYSIS TUBING METHOD

Another very interesting, simple and fun method for making traditional method sparkling wine is using dialysis tubing. The method, quite simply, involves packaging yeast in dialysis tubing to initiate bottle fermentation, unlike the traditional method where a sugar/yeast solution is pitched directly into the base wine, and also eliminates the riddling and disgorging steps.

Specifically, the dialysis tubing containing the yeast inoculum is inserted into each bottle for the second fermentation. The tubing has microscopic pores that allow the sweetened wine to interact with the yeast through the pores and ferment, but the larger spent lees particles are restricted inside the tubing. At the end of fermentation and aging, each bottle is uncapped and the tubing with spent lees is retrieved, leaving the wine crystal clear. No riddling, no neck freezing, no disgorging required!

The greatest advantage of the dialysis tubing method is that you only make as many bottles as you desire. That means that you can easily experiment with one or a few bottles or produce 27 bottles from your 20-L (5-gal) batch.

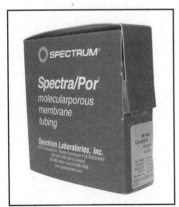

Figure 11-25: SPECTRA/POR 4 dialysis tubing (Item 3787D20)

11.5.1 PREPARATION

The first thing you will need before you get started is 25-mm (0.975-inch) dialysis tubing, more specifically called molecular porous membrane tubing, available from suppliers of scientific materials in packages of 25 feet, sufficient for 30+ bottles of wine. One such type of dialysis tubing is SPECTRA/POR 4 Item 3787D20, shown in Figure 11-25.

The evening before inoculating the cuvée, prepare a yeast starter using a strong fermentor yeast, such Lalvin EC-1118 or RED STAR Premier Cuvée by first rehydrating the yeast in water according to the

401

manufacturer's instructions. At the end of the rehydration period, usually 15 minutes, add 50 mL of water to the yeast starter, and then add 2 tbsp of sugar, $\frac{1}{8}$ tsp of tartaric acid and $\frac{1}{8}$ tsp of yeast nutrients, stir thoroughly and then cover, and let stand overnight.

Ensure that you have a sufficient supply of sparkling wine bottles on hand.

11.5.2 INOCULATION

The next morning, sanitize a sufficient number of 20- to 25-cm strips of dialysis tubing (one strip per bottle of wine to be produced) by immersing them in boiling water for half an hour. Then rinse the strips under running warm water and immerse them in clean warm water in another pan. Keep the strips in the water while you are getting ready.

Dissolve the total amount of sugar in the wine; for a 20-L (5-gal) batch, you will need 40 tbsp or 500 g of sugar.

Assemble all the sanitized bottles. Stir the yeast starter thoroughly. Take one strip of dialysis tubing and tie a knot at one end and open the other end. Using a syringe or pipette, add 10 mL of yeast starter into the tubing. Close this end with a knot while trying to remove as much air as possible out of the tubing. Rinse the tube with lukewarm water to remove any yeast spilled on the outside of the tubing.

Place one such tubing in each bottle and fill the bottles with the sweetened wine to within 2 cm from the top of the bottle. Crown cap all bottles, let stand at room temperature for a day to ensure that fermentation starts without any problems. Then place the bottles away, standing up, in a cool cellar for the long fermentation.

11.5.3 AGING AND DOSAGE

The fermentation period depends mainly on your cellar temperature. You can expect it to take several months in a cellar at 13° C (55° F). Once a week, shake the yeast by rotating the bottle down and up to keep the fermentation going. A gas bubble should form inside the tubing and should grow over the fermentation period; this confirms that fermentation is active.

Caution: Always wear safety glasses and gloves when handling sparkling wine bottles. Bottles are under very high pressure that can inflict serious injury if one were to explode.

Fermentation is more vigorous initially with approximately an average 0.2 bar (3 psi) of pressure forming per day and then subsiding to 0.1 bar (1.5 psi) per week until the end of fermentation, at which point pressure should be between 5–6 bars (70–90 psi).

As dialysis tubing retards autolysis, a longer aging period is required than direct lees contact with the wine to obtain similar results as in the traditional method. A minimum of one year aging is recommended before popping open a bottle of crackling.

To "disgorge", simply remove the crown cap with a beer-bottle opener and remove the floating dialysis tubing. To minimize loss of precious gas, it is highly recommended to chill bottles in a freezer for 20 minutes prior to uncrowning. If the tubing has expanded and cannot be easily removed, pierce a hole with a sharp knife and remove the tubing.

Add the required amount of dosage for the desired wine style, and stabilize the wine by adding 25 mg/L of sulfite. The best method to do this is to prepare a 10% sulfite solution and drawing 0.3 mL using a 1-ml syringe. Add sulfite to each bottle and then crown cap or stopper with plastic sparkling wine stoppers and secure all bottles with a wirehood. Lastly, rotate down and up each bottle to mix the dosage well with the wine, and then cellar for at least 12 months.

11.6 CARBONATION METHOD

Carbonation is the process of injecting soluble gas into a liquid, in this case, CO_2 in wine. The result is a sparkling wine without the need for bottle fermentation, riddling, disgorging and dosage. It's a very practical method for making quick and inexpensive sparkling wine. Another advantage is that there is no need to monitor or control the alcohol level since there is no bottle fermentation.

Making sparkling wine by carbonation is a relatively simple procedure with the right equipment, basically a counter-pressure bottler. Many wine supply shops offer wine carbonation as a service. Figure 11-26 illustrates the set-up for producing sparkling wine using the carbonation method using a MELVICO counter-pressure bottler.

The carbonation method[3] requires a stainless steel pressure-resistant container or keg, such as the widely available 19-L Cornelius soda keg rated at 9 bars (130 psi) purposely designed for carbonating drinks, a carbon dioxide tank equipped with a regulator, and a counter-pressure bottler equipped with a pressure gauge, such as the MELVICO counter-pressure bottler.

The Cornelius keg is equipped with an IN port for gassing and an OUT port to draw wine out and into a bottle. The OUT port is connected to a feed tube that extends to the bottom of the keg. The

[3]This method is based on instructions provided with the MELVICO counter-pressure bottler, and it is used here with the permission of MELVICO INC. Although the MELVICO bottler is no longer disributed, it is the most practical if you can find one; otherwise, use one of the alternative, albeit less sophisticated, counter-pressure bottlers available on the market.

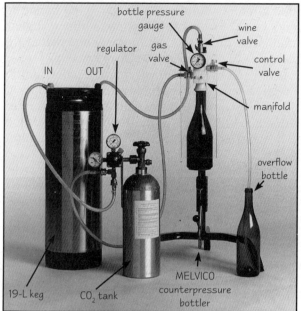

Figure 11-26: Sparkling wine production by carbonation using a MELVICO counter-pressure bottler

carbon dioxide tank is equipped with a regulator to monitor and control bottle pressure. Equal volumes of wine and carbon dioxide will be required.

Note: **GRAY** *adapters connect to* **IN** *ports on Cornelius kegs while* **BLACK** *adapters connect to* **OUT** *ports.*

The MELVICO counter-pressure bottler consists of a bottle stand apparatus with a 3-valve assembly (the newer model has a 4-valve assembly – the control valve consists of 2 separate valves) and pressure gauge mounted on a manifold. The left-hand valve, referred to as the gas valve, is connected to the carbon dioxide tank and regulates its flow. Similarly, the upper valve, referred to as the wine valve, is connected to the OUT port on the keg. This valve regulates the flow of wine into the bottle. The right-hand valve, referred to as the control valve, regulates the bottle pressure. The unit also includes an overflow tube from the control valve to collect any wine (in a bottle) that may overflow during bottling. The 3-valve manifold assembly is also equipped with a rubber seal to provide an airtight seal during bottling.

To clean the keg and MELVICO counter-pressure bottler apparatus, first rinse the keg with water and then fill it halfway with a sulfite solution. Set up the equipment as shown in Figure 11-26 making sure that the carbon dioxide tank is connected to the IN port on the keg. Open the control valve completely. With a bottle properly seated under the manifold, open the wine valve to let the sulfite solution flow through the overflow tube, and collect the solution in a large container. Lastly, rinse the keg with water and repeat the cleaning operation with water instead of the sulfite solution.

To carbonate wine, start with a dry or sweet, cold stabilized wine at a desired alcohol level – this will not be altered with this method – and a total acidity balanced with the residual sugar content. The wine must be sweetened before the gassing operation. With this method, the wine can be fined and preserved with isinglass and sulfite, respectively, as the wine will not undergo another fermentation.

Pour the wine into the keg and place it in a freezer until it reaches a temperature of approximately of 0° C (32° F). Do not allow the wine to freeze. When ready to carbonate the wine, set up the equipment as shown in Figure 11-26, except for the wine valve tube to the OUT port on the keg. All valves, including the main control knob on the gas tank, should be in the CLOSED position.

Invert the keg and open the main control knob on the gas tank valve. Adjust the gas tank pressure until it is between 2.75–3.5 bars (40 –50 psi). Take care not to exceed the recommended maximum pressure; otherwise, bottles may explode. Shake the keg until you can no longer hear the hissing sound from the gas and then flip it back to the upright position. This procedure will saturate the wine with carbon dioxide gas and should take approximately 8–10 minutes for a 19-L keg. Connect the wine valve tube to the OUT port on the keg, and insert the overflow tube (2 tubes in the newer model) from the control valve in the overflow bottle.

You are now ready to bottle. Assemble 25 sanitized sparkling wine bottles, specifically designed to withstand pressure of sparkling wine.

Place one bottle on the stand and seat it properly against the manifold seal; the bottle should be airtight. Open the gas valve to let pressure build up inside the bottle. Open the wine valve and close the gas valve. Wine will not flow until the control valve is opened since the pressure in the bottle and the keg are equal. Slowly open the control valve to lower the pressure inside the bottle and to allow wine into the bottle. Foam will build up in the bottle if you open the control valve too much or too quickly. Fill the bottle to allow a gap of approximately 2 cm when the plastic bottle stopper is inserted. Turn the wine valve to the CLOSED position and let the pressure drop to 0.7 bar (10 psi). On the 4-valve MELVI-CO bottler model, the second control valve can be opened at this point to let the pressure drop to zero, and then re-closed. Allow effervescence in the bottle to stabilize before removing it from the counter-pressure bottler apparatus.

Once the control valve is adjusted correctly with the first bottle, it will require no further adjustment for the duration of the bottling operation, as long as same-size bottles are used.

Remove the bottle, immediately insert a plastic stopper, and secure with a wirehood. Repeat this procedure for the whole batch of wine.

Drink carbonated sparkling wines soon after bottling as aging the wine any further will not improve it. Carbonation does not alter flavors or aromas of the wine (as in the case of bottle fermentation).

12
MAKING PORT WINE

Port is a type of age-worthy fortified wine, originating in Portugal, or more precisely from the city of Oporto in the Douro Valley. Port, or *Porto* as it is known in Portugal, is made from either red or white grapes (although red is by far the most popular) and is fairly sweet with a high alcohol content, typically around 20% alc./vol. Port wine is made by adding alcohol to fermenting wine therefore stopping fermentation and yielding a high residual sugar content. Red Port wines have gained a wide market appeal and are therefore very high in demand compared to white Port wines. This chapter discusses red Port wines.

There are many different Port-wine styles depending on the maturation and aging methods and durations. These methods will alter the "chemical" structure of the wine thereby requiring different fining and/or filtration techniques. Different styles of Port wine are also possible by blending different varietals, from the same or different vintages. The most popular Port-wine styles are Ruby, Tawny, Vintage and Late-Bottled Vintage (LBV).

Ruby Port is a very young wine, most often a blend of a number of varietals from one or more vintages, which can be matured for a short duration in oak barrels or aged in bottles. Being a young wine, Ruby Port will have a very fruity aroma and a deep ruby color. Ruby Port is filtered before bottling to minimize sediment and therefore does not require decanting – the practice of slowly pouring wine in a glass container or decanter to separate the wine from the sediment. It is a style suitable for quick commercialization and for early drinking.

Tawny Port is vinified much like a Ruby Port; however, it is matured for a much longer time in oak barrels, typically 5–7 years. Tawny Port wine will therefore have a predominantly oaky character and will not be as fruity as a Ruby Port. The extended maturation period will also cause the wine to become lighter and acquire a tawny-brown color due to the fining action of tannins from oak barrels. Due to the long sojourn in wood and the controlled interaction with oxygen, the wine will show more complex organoleptic qualities.

Vintage Port is unquestionably the choice of Port wine aficionados due its high quality, richness, and sheer drinking pleasure. This Port style is produced from a blend of the best grapes from multiple vineyards from a single vintage. Vintage Port is only "declared" (produced) in years yielding the best-quality grapes. Port wine that is not "declared" (i.e., it does not meet vintage Port requirements) is declassified and is then vinified differently according to the desired style. Vintage Port requires a short two-year maturation period followed by a very long bottle-aging period of 10, 20, 30 or more years. The wine is bottled unfiltered and will therefore be very deep in color and will produce a heavy sediment requiring decanting. As it ages, the color becomes lighter.

Late-Bottled Vintage (LBV) Port is a Port-style wine from a single vintage bottled after four to six years following the harvest. LBV Port is produced from grapes in a vintage not worthy of being "declared". This wine style may be filtered and therefore will not require decanting. LBV Port, unlike Vintage Port, is meant for early consumption once available on the market.

This chapter describes the process for making a Tawny Port-style wine from red-juice concentrate. Fermentation is carried out to dryness with the residual sugar content obtained by adding a portion of the syrupy concentrate to the wine at the end of fermentation. The desired amount of alcohol is then added for fortification. The added alcohol also prevents refermentation as yeast is inhibited at high alcohol content. The oak maturation process is replaced by the addition of oak extract.

The process described here has been adapted from Wine-Art's Port Wine instructions[1] using 5 L (1¼ gal) of concentrate to give 19 L (5 gal) of "base" Port wine. The Port wine will then be fortified with brandy to achieve a desired final alcohol level. Any grape variety concentrate can be used although it is recommended to use a good-quality Port-wine concentrate. Organoleptic qualities of the wine will be more typical of a Port wine produced using traditional methods.

Alternatively, you can use one of the many Port-style wine kits now available.

12.1 MUST PREPARATION

Pour 1 L (¼ gal) of the concentrate into a sanitized bottle. Seal the bottle with a cork and place it in a freezer for later use. Pour the remaining 4 L (1 gal) of concentrate into a sanitized 23-L (6-gal) open fermentor, such as a plastic pail. Add 5 L (1¼ gal) of warm water to the concentrate and stir thoroughly. Then add the following ingredients to the concentrate:

- 500 g (17½ oz) of glucose solids
- 2.2 kg (4 lbs 13 oz) of corn sugar
- 10 mL (2 tsp) of yeast nutrients
- 15 mL (3 tsp) of grape tannins

Stir the must thoroughly to completely dissolve all solids, and then, add the following ingredients to the must:

- 140 g (5 oz) of dried elderberries
- 57 g (2 oz) of banana flakes or 1.4 kg (3 lbs) of fresh bananas

Note: Place the elderberries in a nylon bag and tie it up for easier removal later.

Lastly, add 10 L (2½ gal) of cold water to bring the must to a total volume of 19 L (5 gal). The actual volume will be higher because of dissolved solids; however, after rackings and filtration, there will be some loss of volume and the final yield will be approximately 19 L.

Measure Brix (SG) and total acidity (TA). These should be approximately 26.5 B° (1.113) and 4.6 g/L, respectively.

12.2 ALCOHOLIC FERMENTATION

Inoculate the must with two packets of a strong fermenting, alcohol-tolerant yeast strain, such as Lalvin EC-1118 or K1V-1116

[1]Used with permission of Wine-Art Inc.

strains, RED STAR Premier Cuvée or Pasteur Red strains, White Labs Merlot Red or French Red strains, or Wyeast Portwine or Zinfandel strains.

Cover the fermentor with a protective plastic sheet or lid. Stir the must at least once daily during fermentation. Allow the alcoholic fermentation to proceed until the Brix (SG) drops to 7.5 B° (1.030) or less, at a temperature between 17°–20° C (63°–68° F). At that point, chaptalize the wine progressively with corn sugar. Be sure that fermentation is active, i.e., not sluggish, before adding any sugar. Progressive chaptalization allows the yeast to transform the sugar into alcohol without causing a sluggish or stuck fermentation.

To chaptalize, first withdraw 1 L (¼ gal) of the fermenting wine and pour into a clean stainless steel saucepan. Heat the wine slowly while adding and dissolving 3 cups (approximately 750 mL) of corn sugar. When the corn sugar is completely dissolved, let the wine cool down just a little so as not to shock the resident yeast population in the fermentor, and then add it to the rest of the fermenting wine in the fermentor. Stir the wine thoroughly and cover the fermentor.

Let the wine ferment for 3 more days while stirring at least once daily, and then add 3 more cups of corn sugar as described above. Again let the wine ferment for another 3 days while stirring at least once daily, add 5 more cups (approximately 1250 mL) of corn sugar as described above, and remove the elderberries before replacing the cover or lid on the fermentor.

Let the wine ferment for 3 more days without stirring. Then, rack the wine into a clean and sanitized glass carboy and allow the wine to splash against the bottom of the carboy. Top up the carboy and secure it with a bung and fermentation lock. Complete fermentation at a temperature of approximately 18° C (64° F) until all yeast activity ceases – this can last up to 4 weeks.

When fermentation is complete, rack the wine into a sanitized carboy. Retrieve the 1 L reserved concentrate and let it thaw completely and then add it to the wine. Then, add the following ingredients to the wine and stir in thoroughly:

- 120 mL (8 tbsp) of glycerol
- 50 mL (10 tsp) of Sinatin 17 liquid oak extract
- 10 mL (2 tsp) of potassium sorbate
- 2.5 mL (½ tsp) sulfite powder

Secure the carboy with a bung and fermentation lock and age the wine for 6 months. Following the aging period, coarse filter the wine, or optionally, rack the wine without filtering and sulfite, if required, to achieve a maximum free SO_2 level of approximately 35 mg/L.

12.3 ALCOHOL FORTIFICATION

At this point, the wine will have an alcohol content of approximately 17%–18% alc./vol. The desired final alcohol content should be between 18%–20% alc./vol. for a Port wine. This is achieved by adding the required volume of brandy, typically with an alcohol content of 40% alc./vol. Brandy will add body to the final wine and will also further clarify the wine. It is therefore recommended to age the wine for an additional 2–4 months before bottling.

Calculate the volume of brandy required to achieve your desired alcohol content according to the blending formula presented in section 7.3 or using the Pearson Square in section 7.4. Assuming a 40% alc./vol. brandy is used and that an alcohol content of 20% alc./vol. is desired, the required volume of brandy (denoted by E) for 19 L of 17%-alc./vol. Port wine is calculated as follows:

$$\frac{(17 \times 19) + (40 \times E)}{(19 + E)} = 20\% \text{ alc./vol.}$$

$$E = 2.85 \text{ L}$$

Therefore, 2.85 L (¾ gal or 97 fl oz) of 40% alc./vol. brandy is required to bring 19 L of a 17% alc./vol. Port wine to 20%.

Following the aging period, bottle the Port wine in Port-style bottles and cork using 19-mm (¾-in) stopper-type corks, shown in Figure 12-1. Simply drive the cork in by hand.

You can cork Port and other fortified-wine bottles using a regular cork; however, the traditional closure for these types of bottles is a cork with a plastic stopper, commonly referred to as a stopper-type cork, or T-top cork. Aficionados insist on using this type of closure for fortified-wine bottles in keeping with tradition.

Figure 12-1: Plastic T-top cork closure for fortified wine bottles

411

13
MAKING ICEWINE

Icewine[1], also known as *Eiswein* of German fame, is an impeccably well-balanced, high-acidity sweet dessert wine, either white or red, produced from grapes naturally frozen on the vines. The most common aromas include peach, apricot and litchi, as well as nutty flavors in older Icewines.

And now, there is also sparkling Icewine, which combines the freshness of a bubbly with the balanced sweetness of Icewine to make for a deliciously refreshing wine with oodles of tropical fruit flavors and aromas that linger on and on.

[1]The production of Icewine in Ontario (Canada) is governed by Vintners Quality Alliance (VQA) regulations set out under the VQA Act and administered by VQA Ontario. The VQA Act and associated regulations comprise an appellation system – akin to the *Appellation d'Origine Contrôlée (AOC)* system in France – designed to regulate viticultural, winemaking and marketing practices. British Columbia (Canada) has also adopted VQA rules and regulations. These explicitly state that commercial Icewine can only be labeled as such if grapes are naturally frozen on the vines, and not artificially frozen (cryoextraction), and cannot be chaptalized. Grapes (only specific Ontario- and British Columbia-grown grapes are allowed) can only be harvested with a minimum sugar level of 35 B° and at a minimum temperature of –8° C (18° F).

The most common grape variety for making white Icewine is Vidal, a hybrid of *V. vinifera* and *V. riparia* species, as it can weather the required harsh cold climate better owing to its thick skin. Riesling and Gewürztraminer Icewines are also highly sought after as these *V. vinifera* varieties are more nuanced resulting in much more complex aromas and flavors. In reds, Cabernet Franc has become a very popular variety for making red Icewine. All these varieties have very fruity aromas, and can achieve high sugar and high acidity contents, both essential for age-worthy wines.

Where weather conditions do not allow for the freezing of grapes on the vines or if the grapes cannot attain optimal sugar and acidity levels, grapes can be artificially frozen in temperature-controlled containers before vinification. This controversial process, called cryoextraction, is commonly practiced nowadays by reputable wineries in sweet wine production although certain countries, such as Canada and Germany, do not allow such wines to be labeled Icewine or *Eiswein*. A common name found on commercially produced Icewine-style wine is *vin de glace*.

To make true Icewine, grapes are allowed to freeze on the vines (see Figure 13-1) and are then harvested at night at subfreezing temperatures, typically around –10° C (14° F). These conditions allow the water content in grape berries to freeze and therefore concentrate sugars, acids and flavor compounds. Whole-cluster

grapes are pressed outdoors immediately following harvesting, still at subfreezing temperatures, to extract the sugar-rich syrup from the marble-hard berries and to discard the frozen water content. The syrup is allowed to warm up before being inoculated for fermentation – a process that will take considerably longer than fermentation in dry wines, often up to 3 months or more depending on sugar content in the juice.

Fermenting the syrup yields a very sweet wine with superb acidity, intense flavors and sublime complexity. The high price of Icewine is due to high viticulture management costs, but more important, due

Figure 13-1: Frozen Vidal grapes on vine

Table 13-1: Typical ranges for key Icewine
enological parameters

Parameter	Range
Starting Brix (SG)	37–42 B° (1.165–1.192)
Alcohol	9–11% alc./vol.
Residual Sugar (RS)	150–250 g/L (15–25% w/v)
Total Acidity (TA)	9–12 g/L
Volatile Acidity (VA)	<2.0 g/L
pH	3.1–3.3

to the low grape yields. Since more than 70% of grape juice is actually water, significant juice volume is lost when pressing frozen grapes.

Analytically, Table 13-1 lists typical enological parameter ranges for Icewine. As a significant amount of tartaric acid would have precipitated as potassium bitartrate while grapes were freezing on the vines, TA in Icewine juice comprises a high percentage of malic acid, in the order of 65–75%, and varies with the pH of the juice. During fermentation, malic acid concentration decreases but TA increases due to acetic acid production resulting from yeast fermenting under stressful conditions and due to succinic acid production from yeast fermentation. Acetic acid, which will be relatively higher than in other types of wines, contributes to higher volatile acidity (VA) and is actually beneficial at low levels in Icewine by contributing to aroma and flavor development. Succinic acid enhances flavors by contributing a salty and bitter taste.

Now, be forewarned! Making Icewine at home is a challenge, even more so for making sparkling Icewine. If you want to make Icewine the simple way, there are now kits for making Icewine-style wine from concentrate in as little as 6 weeks.

Alternatively, you can buy fresh Icewine juice, albeit at a high premium; however, it will be difficult to find a supplier and you will need to be ready to receive the juice on a moment's notice. The juice will also need to be pre-processed for stability; it will need to be protein-stabilized (see section 6.1.2) and filtered successively through coarse, clarifying, fine and membrane filter media.

A more expedient option for making Icewine-style wine at home is by cryoextraction of fresh grape juice and a stepwise fermentation procedure to minimize risks of a stuck fermentation.

The cryoextraction process consists of freezing the grape juice in a deep freezer to extract the sugar-rich syrup and leave the water content behind. The syrup is then fermented in gradually increasing quantities so the yeast can acclimatize to the sugar-rich environment without being overwhelmed. Fermentation is stopped by deep cooling when the desired balance among alcohol level, RS and TA is achieved. Lastly, the wine is stabilize filtered to remove any active yeast still present after fermentation is stopped and then aged a minimum of 6 months.

Warning: Do NOT be tempted to freeze grapes in a deep freezer. Trying to press frozen grapes using your home winepress is asking for trouble; it does not exert sufficient pressure to extract syrup from frozen grapes.

13.1 MAKING ICEWINE FROM FRESH JUICE

This specific process uses 23 liters (6 gallons) of fresh Riesling, Gewürztraminer, Muscat or Palomino grape juice to produce approximately 9 L (2½ gal) or 24 half-bottles (375 mL) of finished Icewine-style wine. The volume, alcohol content and RS of the wine will depend on the volume of syrup extracted.

13.1.1 MUST PREPARATION

Transfer the juice to two separate 20-L (5-gal) pails to allow for expansion of water as it freezes once placed in a deep freezer. Stir the juice thoroughly in each pail and then place both pails in a deep freezer for approximately one week to allow the water content to freeze completely – the syrup will not freeze.

Once the water has frozen, retrieve the pails from the freezer and hang each one by the handle in the cellar at a cool temperature so the bottom of each pail is above floor level. Place an empty pail under each hanging pail to collect the syrup to be extracted. To extract the syrup, drill three 25-mm (1-in) holes on the bottom of each (hanging) pail – the syrup will start flowing out. Extract syrup until you get your desired Brix (SG). This will take several hours or less in a warmer cellar. Constantly monitor Brix (SG) with a high-density hydrometer (most measure up to 39 B° only) or a high-range refractometer before the ice starts melting, which will otherwise dilute the syrup. The syrup should have an initial sugar concentration between 37–42 B° (1.165–1.192). Remember though – the higher the starting sugar concentration, the higher the risks of a stuck fermentation. If a high-density hydrometer or high-range refractometer is not available, you can still measure the sugar concentration using your regular hydrometer. Dilute a test sample of the syrup in water at a rate of 50% until you get a reading between 18.5–21 B° (1.076–1.088).

Adjust the TA to a minimum of 9.0 g/L by adding tartaric or malic acid, or a blend of both, if necessary, so that acidity and RS in the finished wine will be well balanced.

13.1.2 ALCOHOLIC FERMENTATION

As the syrup is very rich in sugar content, you will need to carry out the fermentation progressively in increasing amounts of syrup.

First, transfer 500 mL (approximately 2 cups) of syrup to a 4-L (1-gal) glass container and reserve the remainder in cool (not cold) storage so it does not start fermenting on its own. Prepare a strong yeast strain, such as Lalvin EC-1118, RED STAR Premier Cuvée, White Labs Champagne or Wyeast Rüdesheimer, and add to the 500 mL of syrup. Alternatively, use Lalvin 71B-1122 or RED STAR Côte des Blancs strain as these are more temperature-sensitive therefore making the stopping of fermentation by cooling easier to accomplish. Add yeast nutrients at the maximum rate of 20 g/hL and stir in well. Attach a fermentation lock to the glass container.

Fermentation should start within 24 hours. When good foam forms, add 500 mL (17 fl oz) of the reserved syrup to the fermenting wine and re-attach the fermentation lock. Within 12–24 hours, good foam will form again. Again, add 1 L of the reserved syrup to the fermenting wine and re-attach the fermentation lock. Repeat this process again by adding 2 L of syrup, then 4 L and finally the remainder of the syrup. This progressive addition of syrup to the fermenting must will ensure a successful fermentation. Ferment the wine for a few days, or longer depending on the temperature in your fermentation area, until the sugar concentration reaches between 18.5–22 B° (1.076–1.092). Take a daily Brix (SG) reading, as the fermentation can become vigorous very rapidly.

13.1.3 STOPPING ALCOHOLIC FERMENTATION

When the fermenting must has reached a sugar concentration slightly above the desired Brix (SG) and is deemed well balanced with TA and alcohol, add 50 mg/L of sulfite, without racking, to halt fermentation. Then place the container in cold storage at a temperature between 2°–8° C (36°–46° F) for approximately 1 week. Fermentation cannot be halted spontaneously; therefore, there will be a further reduction in sugar content. Duration of fermentation following the sulfite addition depends mainly on the cold storage temperature.

Rack the wine and coarse filter using No. AF1 pads, for example, and then place the container once again in cold storage for approximately 2 weeks.

After this period, rack the wine, medium filter using No. AF2 pads, for example, add 50 mg/L of sulfite, and then place the container once again in cold storage for 2 more weeks.

After this period, the wine must be stabilized microbiologically by stabilizing filtration as outlined in section 6.2.5 to ensure that any yeast still present is removed, or alternatively, you can flash-pasteurize the wine to annihilate the yeast. Sulfiting and cold storage may not have completely annihilated all yeast cells and so it may still contain a significant amount of inactive yeast cells that may cause fermentation to restart if cellar conditions become favorable for renewed yeast activity. In home winemaking, flash-pasteurization cannot be performed practically with large volumes of wine. For small volumes of 10 L (2½ gal) or less, you can flash-pasteurize by heating the wine for 3–4 minutes at approximately 60° C (140° F) or for a few seconds at 100° C (212° F). Do not exceed these durations so as to avoid the risk of imparting a "cooked" flavor to the wine.

Allow the wine to cool down to room temperature before racking and medium filtering using No. AF3 pads. Place the wine again in cold storage for 2 more weeks.

Perform one last racking before fine filtering the wine using No. AF4 pads. This step can be repeated using No. AF5 pads after 2 weeks of cold storage if the presence of yeast is still suspected. It is also recommended to add potassium sorbate at a rate of 10–20 g/hL to prevent a renewed fermented.

Lastly, age the wine up to 6 months and add sulfite, if necessary, to achieve a free SO_2 level of 50 mg/L before bottling.

This cooling, sulfiting and filtering regimen will produce a wine that will last over 5 years easily. The disadvantage is that the color is lighter. You can reduce the number of filtering operations down to one or two using No. AF2 and/or No. AF3 pads to produce a wine with a more intense color and which will be drunk within 12–18 months.

13.2 MAKING SPARKLING ICEWINE FROM CONCENTRATE[2,3]

Making sparkling Icewine is fun albeit very challenging as it not only involves the formidable task of fermenting Icewine but doing so

[2]Reference: Derek Kontkanen, Debra L. Inglis, Gary J. Pickering, and Andrew Reynolds. **Effect of Yeast Inoculation Rate, Acclimatization, and Nutrient Addition on Icewine Fermentation**. American Journal of Enology and Viticulture. 2004 55: 363-370.

[3]The process described in this section is in part based on consultation with Sue-Ann Staff, and David Sheppard, Head Winemaker at Coyote's Run Estate Winery, previously responsible for sparkling Icewine winemaking at Pillitteri Estates Winery and Inniskillin Wines in Niagara, Ontario (Canada), respectively. The process reflects the pioneering work in Icewine production of now-retired Inniskillin winemaker and co-founder Karl Kaiser.

under extremely difficult fermentation conditions. Specifically, the process involves fermenting Icewine using the Charmat method (see chapter 11) where the final 1.5% alc./vol. in wine will ferment in a pressure-resistant tank to keep the almost 6 bars (90 psi) of carbon dioxide (CO_2) gas dissolved in the wine. The high-sugar content "combined with the death sentence of CO_2 pressure," as Sigrid Gertsen-Briand of Lallemand so aptly described the challenge, "will cause the yeast to stop growing before time; 0.5 bar will negatively impact the growth of the yeast, and 3.0 bars will effectively stop the growth of yeast (but should not stop the fermentation)."

The following sections outline the process for making sparkling Icewine at home using concentrate from a kit, now widely available at winemaking shops in 12-L (3.2-gal) format to make 32 half-bottles (375 mL). The choice of a concentrate here is ideal since it avoids the need of all the pre-filtrations required with freshly-pressed juice, the starting Brix (SG) is usually in the ideal range of 35–37 B° (1.155–1.165), perhaps lower. Anything above this range is asking for trouble as it would greatly increase the risk of stuck fermentation.

Table 13-2 lists enological parameters for sparkling Icewine that will be used as an illustrative example in this section. Refer to Table B-1 in Appendix B to convert between SG, Brix, % sugar and alcohol.

Table 13-2: Example values for key
enological parameters for
sparkling Icewine

Parameter	Values (example)
Starting Brix (SG)	36.0 B° (1.160)
Alcohol	11% alc./vol.
Residual Sugar (RS)	170 g/L
Total Acidity (TA)	11.0 g/L
pH	3.2

Assuming that the starting Brix (SG) of your Icewine concentrate is 36.0 B° (1.160), or 418 g/L of sugar, this represents 19.2% **potential** alcohol. Therefore, to get an **actual** alcohol content of 11.0%, the concentrate will need to ferment down to 16.0 B° (1.065), which represents a **potential** alcohol of approximately 8.2%, and leaving 170 g/L of RS.

Now the tricky part!

You will need to ferment the Icewine as usual in a carboy with a fermentation lock but then you will need to ferment the final 1.5% alc./vol. in a closed tank or keg to keep the CO_2 dissolved in the wine and to get a sparkling Icewine. Therefore, in the example, the fermenting Icewine will need to be transferred to the keg when the Brix (SG) reaches approximately 18.8 B° (1.078), or 9.7% **potential** alcohol. Fermentation will stop on its own when the alcohol reaches approximately 11%; the Brix (SG) should be around 16.0 B° (1.065). Brix (SG) cannot be actively monitored for the final phase of fermentation once the wine is kegged as you should not open the lid while the wine is fermenting. For this purpose, you will need to monitor pressure inside the keg, and fermentation will be deemed to be over when pressure reaches its maximum and remains stable at that pressure.

Caution: To reduce the risk of failure owing to the very difficult fermentation environment and to eliminate any potential danger while handling fermenting wine, strictly follow instructions, particularly with respect to the timing of wine transfer into the keg.

In commercial sparkling Icewine production, the wine is both filtered and bottled under pressure so as not to lose precious bubbles. In home winemaking, filtering under pressure is not possible, or at least not easily done, while bottling under pressure can be achieved using a counter-pressure bottler, such as the MELVICO model discussed in section 11.6.

13.2.1 PREPARATION

Start with 12 L (3.2 gal) of concentrate from a kit specifically designed for making Icewine-style (still) wine. You can either start from a varietal such as Riesling or Vidal if you can find them, or alternatively, you can use a blended concentrate. Make sure the concentrate is at room temperature; otherwise, a cooler temperature will most probably inhibit yeast and fermentation.

Clean and sanitize a 20-L (5-gal) carboy and pour in the concentrate. Do not rinse the bag of concentrate with water; this would change the starting volume and Brix, and alter the balance of the must. Stir the must thoroughly and withdraw a small sample to measure the starting Brix (SG) using your hydrometer and record the measurement.

If the Brix (SG) of your concentrate is lower than the desired starting level, add the required amount of sugar. For example, if the Brix (SG) of the concentrate is 34.0 B° (1.150) and you need 36.0 B° (1.160), then, using Table B-1 in Appendix B, you will need to add 418–390=28 g/L of sugar, or 28×12=336 g (just under ¾ lb) for the total volume of concentrate. Confirm the addition and starting Brix (SG) by taking another hydrometer measurement, and adjust the must if required. Measure and record TA, and adjust to the desired range by adding tartaric or malic acid, or a blend of both.

If the kit came with a packet of bentonite, prepare a bentonite solution as per instructions in section 5.2.1; otherwise, prepare a solution using a rate of addition of 100–200 g/hL, or 12–24 g for the 12-L batch. The bentonite (counterfining) treatment is required to ensure that the wine is protein stable. Add the bentonite solution to the concentrate, stir thoroughly, let stand for a couple of days or until the bentonite has completely settled and the juice is clear, and then rack the wine into another carboy. Note that this treatment is recommended to be done before yeast inoculation and fermentation to minimize bentonite and yeast interaction that could otherwise impact the difficult fermentation even further; therefore, do NOT use the instructions provided with the kit for bentonite addition, which call for sprinkling the bentonite over the surface of the concentrate.

At least three (3) hours ahead of inoculating the concentrate, you will need to prepare and acclimatize a yeast culture using a stepwise procedure. THIS IS VERY IMPORTANT!

Rehydrate **two** (2) 5-g packets of active dry yeast in 100 mL of water as per the manufacturer's instructions or as described in section 4.7.1, which will provide an inoculum rate of addition of just under 1 g/L (a minimum of 0.5 g/L is required). Choose a strong fermenting yeast with low nutrient requirements specifically recommended for Icewine production, such as Lalvin K1V-1116, or alternatively, one of the strong yeast strains listed in section 13.1.2 or the one supplied by the kit manufacturer (which should be one from the list above).

At the same time as when adding the yeast to the water, also add natural yeast rehydration nutrients, such as GO-FERM, at a rate of 30 g/hL, or 3.6 g for the 12-L volume of concentrate, or as directed by the manufacturer of the yeast nutrient.

Note: The use of yeast nutrients increases the rate of fermentation (and also decreases the amount of acetic acid produced) but will ferment to a lower alcohol level than without nutrients; therefore, be sure to keep your starting Brix (SG) as low as possible in the desired range and not to set too high a value for alcohol.

Dilute 50 mL (approximately 1¾ fl oz) of concentrate in an equal volume of water, **both at room temperature**. After the inoculum's rehydration period (15 minutes), add the 100 mL (3½ fl oz) of diluted sample to the rehydrated yeast, hold for 60 minutes and stir the sample gently every 30 minutes. At this point, the sample should be at approximately one-quarter of the starting Brix of concentrate; in our example, that would be 9.0 B° (1.036).

Now add 100 mL (approximately 3½ fl oz) of concentrate to the starter culture, hold for 120 minutes and stir the sample gently every 30 minutes. At this point, the sample should be at approximately one-half of the starting Brix of concentrate; in our example, that would be 18.0 B° (1.074). The reading will be higher owing to the presence of suspended yeast and nutrients.

Lastly, inoculate the concentrate with the acclimatized starter culture, add 20 g/hL of yeast nutrients (DAP) as a water solution, or 2.4 g in the 12-L batch, and stir thoroughly. Place a bung and fermentation lock on the carboy and set the carboy in an area at room temperature, ideally between 20°–25° C (68°–77° F), to promote a favorable environment for the yeast. Fermentation should start very quickly and will be noticeably vigorous within a couple of hours.

Figure 13-2: : An 11.4-L (3-gal) keg for making sparkling Icewine

For the final phase of fermentation where CO_2 gas will get trapped in the pressure-resistant tank and remain dissolved in the wine to make it bubbly, you will need a keg – the type used for soft-drinks and beer – with a small modification. The keg should be rated for a minimum of 9 bars (130 psi) and it should hold the exact amount of wine with very little headspace to ensure that CO_2 gas produced during keg fermentation remains dissolved in the wine. In our example, an 11.4-L (3-gal) keg, such as the one shown in Figure 13-2, will work well.

Important: It is absolutely critical that wine almost completely fills the keg to the top with very little headspace; otherwise, not all CO_2 gas produced will remain dissolved in the wine.

You will need to make a small modification to the keg, specifically to the tube protruding from the OUT port to the bottom of the keg, to allow transfer of wine from the keg to bottles when ready to bottle without drawing sediment from fermentation. Disassemble the OUT port hardware from the keg to remove the tube, cut off approximately 2.5 cm (1 in) of the tube using a hacksaw, and then reassemble the tube and hardware.

Alternatively, instead of sawing off the tube, you can simply bend it from inside the keg until it is positioned sufficiently high to clear sediment that will form.

You will also need to mount a simple gauge on a port quick-connect with a short piece of reinforced PVC tube rated for 9 bars (130 psi), and then mount this on the IN port of the keg, as shown in Figure 13-2, to monitor pressure inside the keg during the final phase of fermentation when trapping the CO_2 gas.

13.2.2 ALCOHOLIC FERMENTATION

During alcoholic fermentation, measure and record the Brix (SG) every day, and stir the fermenting wine twice a day to get the yeast back into suspension.

Let the wine ferment until the Brix (SG) drops down to 18.8 B° (1.078) or as per your calculations. This can take as little as 4–5 days or as much as 2–3 weeks or more depending on your fermentation environment, namely temperature and use of yeast nutrients, as well as your starting Brix (SG) – the higher the sugar concentration, the slower the fermentation. It is also recommended to transfer the wine at a slightly higher Brix (SG) to ensure that sufficient gas is produced from fermentation to give wine enough bubbles. Therefore, in our example, the wine can be transferred when the Brix (SG) reaches approximately 20.0 B° (1.083) – it will be easy to release some pressure if it gets too high, whereas it will be very difficult to get gas back in.

When the wine has reached the Brix (SG) point to start trapping CO_2, you are ready to transfer it from the carboy to the keg. First, stir the wine thoroughly to get the nutrient-rich sediment back into suspension.

Clean and sanitize the keg, and then transfer the wine from the carboy to the keg, filling it to just under the IN port with a little headspace; otherwise, the fermenting wine will flow into the pressure gauge attachment. Replace the lid on the keg making sure that it provides a perfect seal and that the **relief valve is closed**.

As wine continues to ferment, CO_2 gas will remain dissolved in the wine. Read and record the pressure to monitor fermentation. Let the wine ferment until the pressure maxes out – typically around 4.5–5.5 bars (65–80 psi) – and remains at that level for at least 2 weeks. If pressure starts exceeding 6 bars (90 psi), slowly open the relief valve to release some pressure to keep it at or below that level, and repeat until fermentation stops. Then immediately transfer the keg to cold storage (the colder the temperature, the better, but do not freeze) and let stand for a few days to chill and stabilize the wine.

Figure 13-3: Anti-foam AF-72 Liquid

Optionally, while still cold, slowly open the relief valve, remove the lid, and add an antifoaming agent, such as Antifoam AF-72 Liquid shown in Figure 13-3, a food-grade silicone oil emulsion, to reduce foaming when bottling the wine, particularly if the wine cannot be chilled. Add the antifoaming agent at a rate of 1 mL/hL, or, using a good eyedropper, approximately 2 drops in the 12-L batch. Stir the wine VERY GENTLY.

Leave the keg in cold storage for a minimum of 4 weeks to let all the sediment drop to the bottom to get a clear wine. The wine will not be fined or filtered and so it is advisable to be patient and let the natural sedimentation process take its course.

13.2.3 BOTTLING

Clean and sanitize 32 375-mL, pressure-resistant bottles specifically designed for sparkling wine, such as the one depicted in Figure 13-4.

To each bottle, you will need to add sulfite to achieve a free SO_2 level of 45 mg/L and add 20 g/hL potassium sorbate to stabilize the wine and protect it against renewed fermentation. Prepare a 10% sulfite solution and, using a 1-mL syringe, dispense 0.3 mL into each 375-mL bottle. Then dissolve 2.4 g of potassium sorbate in 32 mL of water and, using a 1-mL syringe, dispense 1.0 mL into each bottle.

Figure 13-4: A typical bottle used for sparkling Icewine

Prepare and setup your counter-pressure bottler and proceed to bottle the sparkling Icewine under pressure. Remember that the keg and wine must be chilled as much as possible. Refer to section 11.6 if using a MELVICO unit to bottle under pressure. Do not shake or disturb the keg during the bottling operation to avoid getting sediment back into suspension.

Secure each bottle with a cork or plastic stopper and wirehood.

When you pour sparkling Icewine in a sparkling wine flute, bubbles will seem less intense and less persistent than other bubbly wines, and that's because sparkling Icewine is very sweet with a fairly thick consistency. However, as you drink the wine, you should definitely feel the intensity and persistence in the mouth, assuming that you were able to generate and trap sufficient CO_2 in the wine.

14
TROUBLESHOOTING
WINEMAKING PROBLEMS

Premium wine production at home can be a relatively easy task, free of any problems if great care is exercised during the various winemaking and vinification phases. Problems, however, can sometimes occur and winemakers have to be able to recover from them to protect their investment. A good knowledge of how to circumvent such problems will prove very useful in those rare occasions.

Table 14-1 on pages 426 to 431 summarizes this chapter to help you quickly troubleshoot common problems encountered in home winemaking.

In trying to zero in on a probable cause, first identify the symptom or the nature of the problem. Identify the possible causes, try to narrow it down to one most likely cause using a process of elimination, assess the root cause of the problem, and then take corrective action. Not all problems can be corrected; in some cases, the only course of action is to discard the wine down the sewer, and therefore, prevention is the best cure.

This section also includes problems arising from the use of oak barrels in making wine; problems related to the physical aspect of oak barrels are described in section 8.7.

Table 14-1
Troubleshooting common winemaking problems

Symptom (section)	Possible Causes	Corrective Actions, if any	Reference Sections
Alcoholic fermentation is stuck or sluggish (14.1)	a) Fermentation temperature is too low or too high	a) Adjust temperature	a-l) 4.7
	b) Sugar concentration is too high	b) Conduct a progressive fermentation	
	c) Alcohol content is too high	c) Re-inoculate with a strong fermenting yeast strain	
	d) Poorly prepared yeast starter	d) Re-inoculate with fresh yeast	
	e) Lack of oxygen available to the yeast	e) Aerate must/wine by stirring or racking	
	f) Lack of nutrients	f) Prepare a fresh inoculum and add yeast nutrients	
	g) pH is too low	g) Deacidify and re-inoculate with fresh yeast	g) 3.2.3, 3.3.3
	h) Volatile acidity (VA) is too high	h) Reduce VA and re-inoculate with fresh yeast	h) 3.2.5
	i) Free SO₂ content is too high	i) Aerate must/wine by stirring or racking	
	j) Elevated amount of LAB present in the grapes or juice	j) Treat must/wine with lysozyme	
	k) Elevated amount of mold in the grapes	k) Add yeast nutrients and treat with lysozyme	k) 6.2.4
	l) Low yeast count	l) Re-inoculate with fresh yeast	

Table 14-1, *continued*

Symptom (section)	Possible Causes	Corrective Actions, if any	Reference Sections
Malolactic fermentation (MLF) is stuck or sluggish (14.2)	a) Fermentation temperature is too low or too high	a) Adjust temperature	a-i) 4.8
	b) Oxygen (air) has inhibited MLB	b) Re-inoculate with fresh MLB and protect from air	
	c) SO₂ content is too high	c) Re-inoculate with fresh MLB that has high tolerance to SO₂	
	d) pH is too low	d) Lower TA or increase pH	d) 3.2, 3.3
	e) Alcohol content is too high	e) Re-inoculate with a strong MLB strain	
	f) MLB have insufficient nutrients	f) Stir the lees or add yeast/MLB nutrients	
	g) High levels of inhibitory polyphenols	g) Treat with OptiRED and add fresh MLB	g) 4.7.1
	h) Lysozyme concentration is too high	h) Treat must/wine with bentonite	h) 6.2.4
	i) Low MLB count	i) Re-inoculate with fresh MLB	
Color is too light (14.3)	a) Light whites: Excessive fining and/or filtration	a) & b) Blend with one or more other wines	4.3
	b) Light reds: Excessive fining and/or filtration, poor vintage, poor viticultural practices, grape variety, or too short of a maceration. Also due from aging young, richly-colored wine with little tannin content.	b) Add grape skin powder for reds, or treat pre-fermentation with natural yeast derivative nutrients in conjunction with macerating enzymes.	4.7.1 5.2 5.3

427

Table 14-1, *continued*

Symptom (section)	Possible Causes	Corrective Actions, if any	Reference Sections
Wine is browning and/or smells like Sherry (14.4)	Oxidation due to defective or poor use of winemaking equipment, excessive exposure to air during processing or storage, or insufficient sulfite.	Lightly oxidized: Treat lightly browned whites with casein, PVPP or OptiWHITE; leave reds alone. If no change, try treating with activated carbon. Heavily oxidized: Discard wine	3.4 4.7.1 5.2.2 5.2.8
Wine smells vinegary or of nail polish remover, and/or has formed a white film (14.5)	Wine has been exposed to air causing an interaction with *Acetobacter* spoilage organisms and/or wine has not been sufficiently sulfited.	• For mild cases, drink wine if tolerable • For more serious cases, dump the wine	3.2.5 3.4 6.2.3
Wine smells of sulfur (14.6)	Overuse of sulfite and/or yeast stressed during fermentation.	• Aerate must/wine by stirring/racking, or • Treat must/wine with dilute 3% H_2O_2 solution	3.4

Table 14-1, *continued*

Symptom (section)	Possible Causes	Corrective Actions, if any	Reference Sections
Wine smells of rotten eggs or burnt rubber (14.7)	a) Elemental sulfur on grapes b) Excessive use of sulfite c) Wine in contact with sulfur deposits in oak barrels d) Nutrient deficiency e) Extended contact with gross lees f) Extreme fermentation temperatures g) Yeast strain known to produce high levels of H_2S	• For mild cases, rack wine and aerate abundantly • For more serious cases, do **not** aerate wine; treat wine with dilute 1% $CuSO_4$ solution, with Bocksin, or OptiRED for reds. If no change, try treating with activated carbon.	3.4 4.7
Wine smells yeasty (14.8)	Wine has been in contact for too long with the lees (autolysis)	No corrective action. Drink/dump wine.	4.7
Wine is cloudy (14.9)	a) Incomplete alcoholic fermentation b) Improper racking/clarification c) Wine is not protein stable d) High pectin content e) Excessive aeration in high-iron content wine (ferric casse)	a) Let fermentation complete b) Let wine settle until clear and rack carefully; fine/filter as required c) Treat with bentonite d) Treat with pectic enzymes e) Fine/filter, and add ascorbic acid	a) 4.7 b) 5.1, 5.2, 5.3 c) 6.1.2 d) 5.2.7 e) 6.2.4

429

Table 14-1, *continued*

Symptom (section)	Possible Causes	Corrective Actions, if any	Reference Sections
Wine throws tartrate crystal deposits (14.10)	Wine has not been cold stabilized.	• Rack and cold stabilize wine, or • Rack wine and add metatartaric acid	6.1.1
Wine is fizzy or carbonated (14.11)	a) Residual CO_2 gas still present in wine b) Incomplete alcoholic or malolactic fermentation	a) Degas wine by racking, stirring or using a vacuum pump b) Let alcoholic or malolactic fermentation complete	b) 4.7, 4.8, 14.1, 14.2
Wine is too sweet (14.12)	a) Incomplete alcoholic fermentation b) Wine is not balanced	a) Let alcoholic fermentation complete b) Increase TA to achieve balance, or blend with another wine	a) 4.7, 14.1 b) 3.2, 7
TA and/or pH is too low or too high (14.13)	Poor vintage, grape variety, soil conditions or vinification techniques.	• Check expiry date of NaOH solution; redo test with fresh solution if required • For high TA/low pH or low TA/high pH, adjust TA and/or pH • For high TA/high pH, treat with phosphoric acid, or blend wine • For low TA/low pH, blend wine	3.2 3.3

Table 14-1, *continued*

Symptom (section)	Possible Causes	Corrective Actions, if any	Reference Sections
Wine tastes overly bitter (14.14)	a) Extraction of "bad" tannins from stems and seeds b) Over-extraction of "good" tannins from maceration or barrel aging c) Wine is not balanced	a) & b) Fine with egg whites, PVPP or gelatin, or treat with OptiRED c) Reduce TA	a) 4.7.1, 5.2 b) 4.3, 8.4 c) 3.2, 7.1
Wine is hot and heady (14.15)	High sugar content in must was fermented extensively	Blend wine with low-alcohol wine	7
Wine has an unpleasant smell of geraniums (14.16)	Due to addition of potassium sorbate to a malolactic fermented wine	No corrective action	4.8 6.2.4
Wine smells moldy or musty (14.17)	The result of a chemical reaction between phenolic compounds in oak wood & wines, and mold or chlorine that produces TCA	No corrective action	2.6.2
Wine has a strong barnyard smell (14.18)	*Brettanomyces* yeast infection	• In wine: Sulfite and stabilize filter • In barrel: Discard barrel if odor is strong	6.2.2 6.2.5
Wine has an unpleasant sour-milk taste (14.19)	*Lactobacillus* or *Pediococcus* bacterial infection	If wine is drinkable, sulfite and stabilize filter; otherwise, dump the wine	6.2.3 6.2.5

14.1 ALCOHOLIC FERMENTATION IS STUCK OR SLUGGISH

A stuck alcoholic fermentation is a condition where there is no yeast activity, whether it never started or has ceased, and yeast can no longer convert sugar into alcohol. A sluggish fermentation occurs when yeast is struggling to ferment, and it could potentially stop fermenting altogether and become stuck. For alcoholic fermentation to become and remain active, yeast requires a favorable environment until all the sugar has been converted into alcohol. As there are several factors or causes that can impact yeast activity, a stuck or sluggish alcoholic fermentation is not an uncommon occurrence, even in commercial winemaking, but fortunately, in most cases, fermentation can be successfully restarted.

Assuming that you have determined the desired style of wine, assessed the environmental conditions, and selected an appropriate yeast strain accordingly, possible causes of stuck alcoholic fermentation include:

a) Fermentation temperature is too low or too high,
b) Sugar concentration is too high,
c) Alcohol content is too high,
d) Poorly prepared yeast starter,
e) Lack of oxygen available to the yeast,
f) Lack of nutrients,
g) pH is too low,
h) Volatile acidity (VA) is too high,
i) Free SO_2 content is too high,
j) Elevated amount of lactic acid bacteria (LAB) in the grapes or juice,
k) Elevated amount of mold in the grapes, or
l) Low yeast count.

Generally, white wines are fermented cool and red wines are fermented relatively hot. Most yeast strains have a fairly wide fermentation temperature range but may not ferment outside the range or may become stuck or sluggish at the low and high ends. If your fermentation area's temperature is too low or too high, increase or decrease temperature accordingly to get the must or wine within the recommended range. Stir the must or wine thoroughly to distribute temperature evenly and to get the yeast back into suspension. Fermentation should (re)start within 24–36 hours.

Yeast feeds on sugar, but if there is too much sugar in must or wine, the yeast might actually become overwhelmed and be inhibited. If the sugar concentration is high, (where the potential alcohol is beyond the yeast's alcohol tolerance threshold), the recommended method to (re)start fermentation is to conduct a progressive fermentation by incrementing the must volume. Inoculate a small volume of must – 2.5% of the total volume diluted with an equal volume of water – at 18°–20° C (64°–68° F) with a strong fermenting yeast strain, such as Lalvin EC-1118, RED STAR Premier Cuvée, White Labs Cabernet Red, or Wyeast Zinfandel, at a rate of 25 g/hL (1 g per 4 L or gallon), and add an equal amount of complex nutrients. Reserve the remaining volume of must in a sealed container and place it in a fridge or cold cellar. Once yeast activity starts and fermentation is vigorous, double the must volume by adding an equal amount of reserved must that is warmed up to within a few degrees of the temperature of the yeast starter. Fermentation will slow down for a short time but should become vigorous once again. Double the must volume repeatedly in this manner until the whole batch is fermenting. If fermentation seems to become vigorous shortly after each volume addition of must, you may combine the entire volume at approximately the halfway point. If you are adding sugar to must to increase the alcohol content, avoid over-chaptalizing to prevent a stuck fermentation; use the progressive fermentation method and chaptalize in stages.

Yeast can also become inhibited at high alcohol, typically at around 15–16% alc./vol. If yeast activity has ceased and the alcohol content has exceeded the recommended level for the selected yeast type, re-inoculate the wine with a stronger, alcohol-tolerant yeast strain, such as those recommended above for high sugar musts, and add yeast nutrients. First prepare a yeast starter by inoculating a 5% volume of must. When this volume of must is fermenting vigorously, add it to the remaining must; the whole batch should start refermenting.

Yeast that has not been correctly rehydrated according to manufacturer's instructions, e.g., too low of a temperature or too short of a rehydration time, or a yeast starter that has not been adequately prepared are common causes of stuck fermentation, particularly with novices who may tend to rush through the process. Rehydration and inoculation are simple and trouble free procedures, and should never be the cause of a stuck fermentation, all other parameters being favorable. If you suspect that your inoculum was not prepared properly, prepare some fresh yeast culture and re-inoculate.

Oxygen (air) negatively impacts the quality of wine; however, during active fermentation the fermenting must is protected against oxidation by the yeast as the yeast will quickly scavenge the oxygen. At the onset of active fermentation the yeast will benefit from a small amount of oxygen. If yeast is deprived of air, it could be inhibited and not complete the fermentation. At the beginning

433

of active fermentation, stir or rack the must and leave some head-space to provide oxygen to the yeast. If fermentation is sluggish, try stirring the must vigorously, by racking or by pumping over in conjunction with other corrective actions as required to stimulate fermentation.

Although not required, fermentation will always benefit from the addition of nutrients. If you suspect that your must is nutrient-deficient, add yeast nutrients pre-fermentation. Likewise, if your fermentation is sluggish or stuck because of a lack of nutrients, prepare a fresh inoculum and add yeast nutrients. Also, read the manufacturer's notes; some yeast strains specifically require nutrients during rehydration or during fermentation to ferment properly.

Yeast can also become inhibited in juice or wine with a pH that is too low. First confirm that the problem is not due to high volatile acidity (VA). Measure the TA and pH of the must or wine and deacidify until they are within the desired ranges (refer to Table 3-2 on page 122). Then, re-inoculate with fresh yeast. If fermentation is stuck and the problem is determined that VA is too high (see also section 14.5), there may not be much hope depending on the extent of the problem. Try to reduce VA according to instructions in section 3.2.5, and then re-inoculate with fresh yeast.

A high free SO_2 concentration is another factor that can inhibit yeast. If fermentation is stuck and free SO_2 is high, stir, aerate or pump over the must to try and reduce the free SO_2 concentration as much as possible. Refer to section 14.6 for additional corrective actions.

A high concentration of lactic acid bacteria (LAB), good or bad, can start feeding on sugar and produce excessive volatile acidity (VA), which will inhibit yeast. If LAB concentration is high, treat the must or wine with lysozyme at a rate of 250–300 mg/L and re-inoculate with fresh yeast to restart a sluggish or stuck fermentation.

Moldy grapes can also deprive yeast of much needed nutrients. Add yeast nutrients at the maximum recommended rate when first inoculating the must or to restart a sluggish or stuck fermentation if grapes are moldy. The must or wine will also benefit from a lysozyme treatment. The best way to prevent this problem is to do a severe triage (pre-selection), discarding any moldy bunches before crushing.

If any corrective actions above fail to start or restart fermentation, or in addition to these, re-inoculate the must or wine with fresh yeast, preferably a strong fermenting strain. To improve chances of success, prepare a yeast starter or, alternatively, use a 5% volume of actively fermenting wine as inoculum, supplement with more yeast nutrients, and ferment progressively. And if you counterfine wine with bentonite before the start of fermentation, first rack the wine and supplement with a complex nutrient, such as Fermaid K or Superfood, to replace micronutrients as bentonite will cause yeast to sediment, strip essential vitamins and therefore hamper fermentation.

14.2 MALOLACTIC FERMENTATION (MLF) IS STUCK OR SLUGGISH

A stuck malolactic fermentation (MLF) is a condition where malo-lactic bacteria (MLB) – good LAB – are no longer able to convert malic acid into lactic acid because of adverse or unfavorable environmental conditions. A sluggish MLF occurs when MLB are struggling to ferment, and it could potentially stop fermenting altogether and become stuck. As there are several factors or causes that can impact MLB activity, stuck MLF is a common occurrence if not managed closely. In fact, you should take extra care during MLF as the required environmental conditions also favor growth of spoilage organisms.

Assuming that you have determined the desired style of wine, assessed the environmental conditions, selected an appropriate MLB culture, and confirmed the presence of malic acid by paper chromatography, possible causes of stuck MLF include:

a) Fermentation temperature is too low or too high,
b) Oxygen (air) has inhibited MLB,
c) SO_2 content is too high,
d) pH is too low,
e) Alcohol content is too high,
f) MLB have insufficient nutrients,
g) High levels of inhibitory polyphenols,
h) Lysozyme concentration is too high, or
i) Low MLB count.

MLB are typically inhibited at temperatures below 18° C (60° F), or as specified by the MLB culture manufacturer. If your fermentation area's temperature is too low or too high, increase or decrease temperature accordingly to get the must or wine within the recommended range, and **very gently** stir the MLB culture back into suspension. Do not introduce too much air as most home winemaking MLB strains are anaerobic and therefore sensitive to oxygen.

If you suspect that MLB was overly exposed to air and caused MLF to become stuck, re-inoculate the must or wine with a fresh MLB culture, stir **very gently**, and ensure that the container is properly topped up and protected from air using a fermentation lock. Avoid any oxidation-promoting operations, such as racking and stirring, during MLF.

MLB are very sensitive to SO_2. For MLF to be successful the SO_2 levels should be low enough to allow the bacteria culture to function successfully. Different MLB cultures have different tolerances to SO_2 so use a bacteria culture that has a high SO_2 tolerance in high SO_2 wines.

MLB can also become inhibited in low-pH musts or wines. The typical minimum pH value is 3.2 although different MLB strains can have slightly different requirements. Lower total acidity (TA) or increase pH by one of several methods described in sections 3.2.3 and 3.3.3, respectively, and re-inoculate with a fresh MLB culture, if required.

Most MLB strains can tolerate alcohol contents of up to 14.0% alc./vol. If your strain has a lower tolerance or if your wine contains a relatively high level of alcohol, there may not be much you can do except try re-inoculating with a high-alcohol-tolerant MLB strain. If you expect to ferment to a high alcohol level or if you intend to use a weaker MLB strain, inoculate the wine concurrently with the alcoholic fermentation, a technique known as co-inoculation. The MLB will adapt to the higher alcohol levels as they increase and have a much better chance of completing MLF.

MLB also need nutrients to properly convert malic acid into lactic acid. Carry out the MLF on the nutrient-rich fine lees. If MLF is stuck even in the presence of fine lees, **gently** stir the lees back into suspension. Do not stir vigorously; otherwise MLB can become inhibited from excessive exposure to air. Add yeast nutrients, or preferably MLB nutrients, such as OPTI'MALO PLUS, in addition to stirring the lees, or if there are no lees to provide nutrients.

Red wine with high levels of inhibitory polyphenols can also cause MLF to be inhibited or become sluggish. If you suspect that your wine has an unusually high level of polyphenols, add natural yeast derivative nutrients, such as OptiRED, post fermentation at a rate of 30 g/hL, and then re-inoculate with a fresh MLB culture.

If you treated the must or wine with lysozyme, MLB have most probably been inhibited. You can correct this problem by "deactivating" the lysozyme using bentonite and reconditioning the must or wine for a favorable MLF. Prepare a bentonite solution, as per instructions in section 5.2.1, and add to the must or wine at a rate of 5–20 g/hL. Wait 6–12 hours, rack off the bentonite and then re-inoculate the must or wine with a fresh MLB culture, ensuring that all other MLF environmental conditions are appropriate.

All of the above corrective actions will benefit from the addition of a fresh MLB culture and nutrients, such as OPTI'MALO

PLUS, and, for more difficult conditions, you can first condition the MLB inoculum using commercial apple juice. The use of OPTI'MALO PLUS and the conditioning of MLB inoculum are both described in section 4.8.3. In addition, for the alcoholic fermentation, choose a yeast strain that favors MLF; some yeast strains are known to inhibit MLB.

Musts from grapes or fresh juice may already contain MLB for MLF to start on its own accord if all conditions are favorable. You should still add a MLB culture to these types of musts to avoid complications.

Concentrates and reconstituted juices are not malolactic-compatible since MLB have been eradicated during the concentration or sterilization procedures. These musts have also been tartrate-stabilized during their production and thus contain a very high proportion of malic acid, which would be converted to lactic acid. The wine would have very little acid, and a pH above 3.8 making it very susceptible to bacterial infections. Therefore, MLF should not be attempted in these types of musts.

14.3 COLOR IS TOO LIGHT

Color should always be typical for the type or style of wine being made. For example, a lightly colored, oak-aged Cabernet Sauvignon would certainly be atypical.

An almost-colorless white wine is the result of excessive clarification. The same is true of lightly colored reds although the main cause is either insufficient color development in grape skins, because of a poor vintage or poor viticultural practices, or too short of a maceration period. Some grape varieties have inherently low pigmentation, and no amount of maceration can produce a deeply colored wine.

The recommended corrective action is to blend wines, if possible, until you get the desired color for your style of wine, a practice most often used in red winemaking. Although different wines are usually blended to achieve a specific flavor profile, blending is also used to improve color. Varieties, such as Alicante Bouschet, are often used specifically to add color to light-colored reds. The drawback of blending is that it requires stocking different wines – not always possible in home winemaking – and may require a considerable volume to achieve significant color changes.

Another effective method to improve color in reds is to add natural (dehydrated) grape skin powder; it does not affect the taste of wine. Add the powder to the wine, **before fining or filtering** to avoid bottle sedimentation, at a rate of 5 g/hL by first dissolving it in a little volume of wine. Repeat until you get the desired color.

The use of unorthodox, color-enhancing methods, such as food-coloring addition, is not effective and is not recommended.

If you expect reduced color extraction from your reds, you can add natural yeast derivative nutrients, such as OptiRED, in conjunction with macerating enzymes at the start of red wine fermentation to help stabilize color. Refer to section 4.7.1 for more information on the use of these enological products.

Note that wine will also change color as it ages, more so in reds, as the little amount of oxygen will cause tannins and color pigments (anthocyanins) to combine. The extent of color change depends on tannin and anthocyanin concentrations. For example, you would expect that a richly-colored, young wine with little tannins, such as a young stainless steel (no oak aging) Cabernet, would become lighter. In contrast, tannic wine with little anthocyanins, such as a full-bodied Pinot Noir, which is inherently light-colored, would become redder and darker.

As wine continues to age, browning in bottled wine happens naturally, albeit very slowly, and manifests itself as a deeper color in whites (think of an old Sauternes) or a brownish color, especially at the rim, in reds (think of an old Barolo). In the types of wines where some browning is expected, it is perfectly acceptable although you should not let the wine age too long after this as it will start losing freshness, fruit and subtle aromas, and it will start deteriorating.

14.4 WINE IS BROWNING AND/OR SMELLS LIKE SHERRY

If wine starts browning unexpectedly and prematurely, particularly if it is still in bulk, this points to a more serious problem – oxidation, or oxygen converting ethanol into acetaldehyde. Depending on the extent of oxidation, the wine will also take on nutty aromas and flavors, akin to Sherry wine. These symptoms are precursor to acetic spoilage and mycoderma, discussed below in section 14.5.

The root cause of oxidation can be defective or poor use of winemaking equipment, excessive exposure to air during processing or storage, or insufficient sulfite. Browning is very difficult to correct in oxidized wine, and the smell cannot be corrected.

For reds, it is best to leave the wine alone. Deeply browned white wines may unfortunately have to go the way of the sewer.

To improve color in whites affected by slight oxidation, treat the wine with casein at a rate of 50–100 g/hL. Start at the lower end, or perform some bench trials, as casein tends to strip wine of some aromas. Dissolve the powder in cold water and add quickly to the wine while stirring thoroughly. Follow this with a bentonite treatment at a rate of 25–100 g/hL. If your bench trials conclude that casein strips out too much aromas, try using PVPP at a rate of 25–75 g/hL. Alternatively, add OptiWHITE, a specific inactivated yeast with high antioxidant properties that protects against oxidation of phenols and aromas, to improve color in whites affected by slight oxidation. Add OptiWHITE at a rate of 20–30 g/hL by first performing bench trials.

As an absolute last resort only and when other treatments are not effective, you can try "improving" color by removing brown coloration using activated carbon, available in black powder format. Add activated carbon at a rate of up to 5 g/hL directly to the wine and stir thoroughly; never add more than the maximum because activated carbon will strip color excessively and leave a carbon-like off-flavor. You should always perform bench tests on a sample before treating a whole batch. Add bentonite immediately after the activated carbon treatment, rack after a few days, and filter the wine before bottling.

14.5 WINE SMELLS VINEGARY OR OF NAIL POLISH REMOVER, AND/OR HAS FORMED A WHITE FILM

When a wine smells vinegary, the root cause is acetic spoilage – a condition where wine has been overly exposed to air allowing harmful acetic acid bacteria, known as *Acetobacter aceti* (*A. aceti*), or more commonly known as *Acetobacter*, to feed on alcohol in the presence of air to produce acetic acid and VA.

Depending on the extent of the problem, acetic spoilage will first manifest itself as a vinegary smell and sour taste and then as an off-putting aroma of nail polish remover at higher concentrations. In the worst case, a white film forms on the wine's surface – a condition referred to as mycoderma – as shown in Figure 3-16 on page 148.

These symptoms are usually the result of poor or defective winemaking equipment, such as poor seal from bungs or dry fermentation locks, excessive manipulation of wine during transfers or other cellar operations, a pH that is too high or TA that is too low, or simply, careless winemaking, such as a poor topping regimen. The risks of these symptoms developing are always greater if wine is not adequately protected with the recommended minimum amount of sulfite. MLF will also increase the amount of acetic acid by transforming any citric acid present. For this reason, wines to be malolactic-fermented should have a low citric acid component.

Wine affected by advanced acetic spoilage cannot be cured and is best destined to the sewer. If it is slightly affected, there is still a chance to treat the wine and minimize the symptoms. Filter the wine through double cheesecloth to remove any white film that may have formed on the surface, then sulfite to the maximum level below the detectable threshold of 2.0 mg/L of molecular SO₂ (refer to Figure 3-18 on page 152), and bottle immediately. Drink the wine as soon as possible.

Refer to section 3.2.5 for a list of tips and best practices in avoiding high VA and *Acetobacter* spoilage in wine.

14.6 WINE SMELLS OF SULFUR

When the smell of sulfur is detectable in wine, it is considered a fault and can actually become overpowering and irritating to the nose at high concentrations, and points to over-processing with sulfite and/or yeast being stressed during fermentation (see also section 14.7). It can be easily detected by its distinctive pungent burnt-match smell.

If you detect a sulfur smell in the fermentor, try aerating the wine by successive vigorous rackings. If you detect a sulfur smell in the bottle, aerate the wine by decanting and/or by letting the bottle stand open upright for several hours.

Alternatively, for musts or wines with very high levels of free SO₂, up to 100 mg/L, you can treat these effectively with a dilute 3% hydrogen peroxide (H_2O_2) solution. H_2O_2 is an effective agent in reducing free SO₂. Add the solution at a rate of 18 mL/hL of wine to reduce the free SO₂ content by 10 mg/L (free SO₂ is actually being oxidized into bound SO₂). For example, to reduce free SO₂ content by 25 mg/L in a 20-L (5-gal) batch, add $18 \times 20/100 \times 25/10 = 9$ mL of 3% H_2O_2 solution. Use a syringe to measure the required amount carefully, and run bench trials on a small sample before adding H_2O_2 to the whole batch. If free SO₂ is well beyond 100 mg/L, there might not be any hope to salvage the wine as bound SO₂ would become too high to be considered safe.

Warning: The use of hydrogen peroxide (H_2O_2) requires chemistry laboratory experience and is therefore only recommended for experienced home winemakers. Excessive addition of H_2O_2 can actually oxidize wine quickly, making it undrinkable.

To prevent sulfur smell, avoid stressing the yeast during fermentation and only add the recommended amount of sulfite based on the wine's pH to achieve the desired free SO₂ level at a molecular SO₂ level of 0.8 mg/L. Refer to section 3.4 on page 146 for more details on free SO₂ analysis and control.

14.7 WINE SMELLS OF ROTTEN EGGS OR BURNT RUBBER

A stinky smell of rotten eggs or burnt rubber is the result of the production or presence of sulfide compounds in must or wine.

Specifically, hydrogen sulfide (H_2S) is the culprit for the stinky, rotten-egg or rotten-sewer smell while mercaptans are responsible for the burnt-rubber or rotten-cabbage smell. Volatile sulfur compounds such as H_2S and mercaptans usually arise from the yeast being stressed by one or more of the following factors:

a) Elemental sulfur on grapes,
b) Excessive use of sulfite,
c) Wine in contact with sulfur deposits in oak barrels,
d) Nutrient deficiency,
e) Extended contact with gross lees,
f) Extreme fermentation temperatures, or
g) Yeast strain known to produce high levels of H_2S.

Elemental sulfur on grapes is a common cause resulting from vinification using grapes that have been over-treated, or treated too close to harvest, with sulfur-based vineyard mildew and fungus inhibitors. Red winemaking is more prone to H_2S problems as the juice has more prolonged contact with the grape solids that are prone to develop volatile sulfur compounds. In white winemaking, the settling of particles before yeast inoculation and alcoholic fermentation allows for the separation of the juice from many of the sulfur-contaminated particles.

Excessive use of sulfite prior to fermentation can cause similar problems as well as prolonged contact of wine with sulfur deposits in oak barrels – arising from burnt sulfur dropped inside the barrel during barrel maintenance.

H_2S can also form during fermentation where yeast is deprived of key nutrients, for example, the juice being nitrogen deficient as a result of grapes not having ripened adequately. Other sources of this problem may result from wine, particularly white wine, left on the gross lees for too long a period, or too high of a fermentation temperature.

Yeast also produces some small amount of H_2S during fermentation, some strains more than others, so be sure to consult the manufacturer's specifications on yeast strains to get a sense of what to expect. For example, the Montrachet strain is known to produce high levels of H_2S. This may not necessarily be a problem, although H_2S may mask key fruit aromas; however, if other unfavorable conditions exist, particularly low nutrients, then the rotten-egg smell will become more obvious.

The success of any corrective action depends on the intensity of the smell (i.e., concentration of H_2S).

If H_2S is barely detectable, there is a good chance that it can be reduced, and possibly eliminated, by aerating the wine, such as by racking. This has the drawback of accelerating oxidation and has to be assessed against the severity of the H_2S problem.

If H_2S is quite noticeable, you should **immediately** treat the wine with a dilute 1% copper sulfate ($CuSO_4$) solution – prepared by dissolving 1 g of the blue-colored copper sulfate crystals in water to bring the volume to 100 mL. You need to measure the required amount of $CuSO_4$ solution very carefully because you will need a very small volume for even the smallest correction.

Add the 1% $CuSO_4$ solution at a rate of 0.05 mg/L of wine once fermentation has completed. That would then be 0.5 mL of solution, or approximately 10 drops using a good eyedropper, to 100 L (25 gal) of wine.

Copper sulfate reacts with hydrogen sulfide to form and precipitate copper sulfide. Before treating the wine, run extensive bench tests to establish if copper sulfate does in fact correct the fault and to determine the minimum rate of addition to correct the problem. Strictly use the minimum – no more. This is **VERY IMPORTANT** as copper is toxic to humans at higher levels. In the US, the legal limit is 0.5 mg/L as copper. *WineMaker* magazine's Wine Wizard (a.k.a. Alison Crowe) outlines the following procedure as a bench trial.

"Label two wine glasses, one as *control* and one as *copper*. Measure about 50 mL of the wine in question into the wine glasses. Measure out 1 mL of 1% copper sulfate solution into the *copper* glass. Swirl each glass, let them sit for about five minutes, then smell each (do **NOT** taste as this is quite a bit of copper for 50 mL of wine).

If the *copper* glass still has the stinky smell, it goes to follow that copper sulfate will not help out your wine.

If you do find that the 1 mL of 1% copper sulfate solution does help your wine, you can hone in on the amount you should use."[1]

Start with the minimum rate of addition to a 1-L sample of wine. Swirl the glass, let it sit for about five minutes, then smell and taste the wine. If the stinky smell is still noticeable, increase the amount of 1% $CuSO_4$ solution and repeat the process until the stinky smell disappear **BUT** do **NOT** exceed the maximum rate of addition. Once you have determined the amount of solution required to neutralize the stinky smell in the 1-L sample of wine, scale up the addition for the entire batch.

A safer alternative solution outlined by Tim Vandergrift, a contributing author to *WineMaker* and Technical Services Manager at Winexpert, Inc., uses Bocksin, a German-made product "related to the fining agent silicon dioxide (kieselsol). It immediately bonds to

[1]Crowe, A. 2005. Copper Sulfate Solutions. *WineMaker December 2004 – January 2005* 7(6): 11.

H_2S and removes the aroma. Because it's formulated like silicon dioxide, it acts like a fining agent, bonding to proteins in the wine, settling out and leaving sediment."[2] Add Bocksin at a rate of 1 mL/L of wine. Stir in gently but thoroughly and then rack the wine once the sediment has settled at the bottom. Optionally, you can filter the wine.

Another safer alternative for reds is to add natural yeast derivative nutrients, such as OptiRED, at a rate of 30 g/hL as outlined in section 4.7.1.

If the stinky smell was quite noticeable, you should **not** aerate the wine; otherwise, this can further compound the problem and make it irreversible. Similarly, you should treat H_2S immediately as soon as detected. Oxygen will transform H_2S into what is known as mercaptans and disulfides – foul-smelling compounds that cause wine to spoil. Wine afflicted with mercaptans and disulfides is best dumped down the sewer. Clearly, the best cure for H_2S is prevention.

As an absolute last resort only and when other treatments are not effective, you can try reducing bad odors or flavors using activated carbon, available in black powder format. Add activated carbon at a rate of up to 25 g/hL **directly** to the wine and stir thoroughly. You should always perform bench tests on a sample before treating a whole batch to determine if the treatment will work and to determine the rate of addition. Too much activated carbon will strip color excessively and leave a carbon-like off-flavor. Add bentonite immediately after the activated carbon treatment, rack after a few days, and filter the wine before bottling.

14.8 WINE SMELLS YEASTY

A yeasty smell in wine is the result of a reaction between wine and dead yeast cells, or lees, known as autolysis. In some wines, namely sparkling wines and Chardonnay, autolysis is actually desirable to give wine more flavor complexity and mouthfeel. However, the smell can become unpleasant if the wine is left in contact with the lees, particularly the gross lees, for too long and develop into H_2S and mercaptans.

Unfortunately, there is no corrective action for autolysis. To prevent it, rack wine from its lees according to the recommended schedule in section 5.1.1, and avoid leaving the wine on its lees for more than 18 months.

14.9 WINE IS CLOUDY

There can be several different causes of cloudiness in wine.

[2]Vandergrift, T. 2003. Kit First Aid. *WineMaker December 2002 – January 2003* 5(6): 34.

A common cause amongst beginners is an incomplete alcoholic fermentation. Although there may seem to be no yeast activity, yeast might still be fermenting quietly, and that will cause the wine to be cloudy until fermentation completes and lees fall to the bottom. So be sure to monitor fermentation with your hydrometer and proceed to racking, clarification and stabilization only when fermentation is complete.

The most common cause though is improper racking or clarification, either fining or filtration, where particles go back into suspension in the wine. Let the wine settle until the wine becomes clear again, then carefully rack without disturbing the sediment, and fine and/or filter again as desired. Always fine using the recommended rate of addition and wait period before racking. And if filtering, be sure to filter progressively with finer pads, i.e., do not attempt to filter an unclear wine using fine pads without first doing a coarse filtration, then a clarifying filtration, and finally a fine filtration.

A perfectly crystal clear wine can also suddenly turn cloudy if it is protein/heat unstable, i.e., it has a high protein content that can cause cloudiness if the wine is subjected to high temperatures. If the wine was properly racked, fined and/or filtered, and then it turned cloudy, test the wine for protein/heat stability as outlined in section 6.1.2. If the test is positive, treat the wine with bentonite.

Another cause of cloudiness is high-pectin content, usually a more common occurrence in fruit and country wines. If the wine was properly racked, fined and/or filtered, and then it turned cloudy, test the wine for the presence of pectin as outlined in section 5.2.7. If the test is positive, treat the wine with pectic enzymes.

A lesser-known cause is a condition known as ferric casse that occurs from excessive aeration, particularly in high-iron content wine. If the wine was properly clarified and heat stabilized, and then it turned cloudy, first fine and/or filter the wine again until it becomes clear, then add ascorbic acid just prior to bottling, as outlined in section 6.2.4. To prevent ferric casse in wine known to have a high-iron content, add gum arabic as outlined in section 6.2.4.

14.10 WINE THROWS TARTRATE CRYSTAL DEPOSITS

Tartrate crystal deposits, mainly considered as a minor aesthetic fault, are the result of wine being subjected to cold temperatures for an extended period of time causing tartaric acid to crystallize, i.e., the wine was not properly cold stabilized.

Tartrate crystals are easily separated from wine in containers by racking. If they form in bottles, simply decant or pour the wine carefully.

To prevent tartrate crystals from forming in the bottle, cold stabilize the wine by chilling or by adding metatartaric acid as outlined in section 6.1.1. Be sure to re-measure TA and pH as these will have changed, and make any necessary adjustments.

14.11 WINE IS FIZZY OR CARBONATED

A fizzy or carbonated wine points to the presence of dissolved carbon dioxide (CO_2) gas.

In the simplest case, a slightly fizzy wine may be the result of rushed winemaking or insufficient degassing, conditions often seen in wine that is produced and bottled too quickly.

A fizzy wine can also be the result of incomplete alcoholic or malolactic fermentations, often because of rushed winemaking or poor monitoring. A more serious situation is when wine starts refermenting, either alcoholic or malolactic, particularly if the wine is already bottled, which can cause bottles to explode.

Corrective actions will depend on the chemistry of the wine, and if it is still in bulk containers or if it has already been bottled.

If in bulk, first assess by hydrometry and paper chromatography whether the wine has completed alcoholic and malolactic fermentations. If the wine has not completed alcoholic fermentation, let fermentation run its course; if it is sluggish or stuck, take appropriate corrective actions. If the wine has not completed MLF, where it is desired, let it run its course; if it is sluggish or stuck, take appropriate corrective actions. Where MLF is not desired, even though it may have started, take immediate corrective actions to inhibit MLB. When all fermentation is complete, there will still be some CO_2 gas dissolved in the wine but it will dissipate over time, and so be sure to keep a fermentation lock on the container. Stabilize the wine as required.

If you want to bottle the wine quickly – and only after you are absolutely certain that all fermentation is complete – you will need to degas the wine. You can degas by racking and/or by stirring the finished wine vigorously 2 or 3 times per day until there is no perceptible gas. Do not overdo it to avoid accelerating oxidation, and be sure to properly stabilize the wine prior to degassing. An alternative method of degassing wine is by using an electric vacuum pump. Connect the pump and tubing to a carboy being sure it is properly sealed to effectively operate under vacuum. Leave some headspace in the carboy as you will need to shake the carboy vigorously. Start the pump and shake the carboy to dissipate CO_2 gas as much as possible, and continue for several minutes until there is no more bubbling from the wine.

If CO_2 gas is detected in bottled wine (hopefully before bottles start exploding), you will need to pour all bottles from that batch into a large container, then follow the instructions above for completing either or both fermentations.

14.12 WINE IS TOO SWEET

The most common cause of a wine being undesirably too sweet is high residual sugar (RS) as a result of an incomplete alcoholic fermentation, either because the fermentation became stuck or the must had an unusually high Brix (SG) level and it could not ferment completely.

If the wine's unusually high RS is acceptable and is well balanced with the acidity, simply stabilize it and add potassium sorbate to turn it into a good dessert wine. If there is some residual sugar but you wish to reduce the perception of sweetness, perform some bench trials by adding varying amounts of tartaric acid until the right balance is achieved. The amount needed to balance the wine depends on your taste, RS and TA. Be sure to cold stabilize the wine and re-adjust TA if needed. Note that increasing TA reduces the "perception" of sweetness; it does not change the actual sugar concentration.

If on the other hand you want a totally dry wine, you will need to restart fermentation by adding fresh yeast and nutrients.

If a wine is too dry, i.e., RS is too low, you can always add table sugar or a sweetener-conditioner until you achieve the desired balance with acidity.

An alternative to adjusting sweetness and acidity levels by adding sugar and tartaric acid is by blending. If available, try blending sweet wine with a dry, fresh wine, in varying proportions until the desired balance is achieved.

In all cases where there is residual sugar in wine, you need to stabilize it with potassium sorbate or by stabilizating filtration.

14.13 TA AND/OR PH IS TOO LOW OR TOO HIGH

Unusually low or high total acidity (TA) and/or pH can be the result of the vintage (sunshine, rain, cold, etc.), grape variety, soil conditions or vinification techniques. The specific conditions of low TA/high pH and high TA/low pH can be corrected by adjusting TA and pH using one of several methods outlined in sections 3.2.3 and 3.3.3, respectively.

The more complex problems of either high TA/high pH or low TA/low pH pose a much greater challenge to home winemakers. Commercial wineries make use of special chemicals and processes not readily available to home winemakers. Acidification and deacidification cannot be used, as these will correct one parameter at the expense of the other. You can however use phosphoric acid to reduce the pH in a high pH/high TA wine although it will affect both the taste and texture of the wine. Refer to section 3.3.3 for more information.

The best solution is to blend wines that improve both TA and pH levels. For example, a high TA/high pH wine can be corrected by blending it with a wine of normal TA and pH or low TA/low pH. The drawback of this method is that it requires stocking TA- and pH-unbalanced wines. Such wines cannot be stored for an extended time as they are prone to bacterial infection or other spoilage problems.

Before blending, first determine the root cause of the problem with the high TA/high pH or low TA/low pH wine. If the root cause points to a serious wine fault, do not blend the problem wine with a healthy wine; this could spoil a perfectly good batch of wine. If the root cause points to a chemical imbalance from grape components, for example, you can safely blend the wine.

A word of caution! A common reason for a seemingly low TA is the use of old sodium hydroxide (NaOH) titrate solution that has lost its strength, i.e., its Normality is no longer 0.1N or 0.2N, when measuring TA. There may be nothing wrong with the actual TA except for a false measurement that must be compensated for the weaker titrate solution. Refer to section 3.2.2 for a description of how to determine the actual strength of NaOH solution and how to compensate the TA measurement.

If TA and pH numbers are as desired but the wine is lacking mouthfeel, try adding gum arabic as outlined in section 6.2.4 to improve mouthfeel and overall taste balance.

14.14 WINE TASTES OVERLY BITTER

A wine that tastes overly bitter or astringent is most often a result of too much tannins and may be the result of extraction of "bad" tannins from green stems and/or grape seeds from crushing, maceration or pressing, over-extraction of "good" tannins from maceration or from oak barrel aging, or simply poor balance between wine components. Good tannins will soften over time, although it could take a very long time, and will reduce astringency.

An effective way to reduce tannins is to perform a fining with egg white, PVPP or gelatin, or using gum arabic. Maceration with OptiRED as a corrective treatment is also very effective for helping to integrate green or aggressive tannins. Alternatively, you can blend a highly tannic wine with a softer wine.

A wine may also be bitter or astringent because of an imbalance in the wine components. Specifically, high acidity or high alcohol will reinforce bitterness and astringency. Typically, you will not want to alter the alcohol content, but you can reduce TA. This will make the wine much more balanced even if the alcohol content is relatively high, although considered normal for the type of wine.

14.15 WINE IS HOT AND HEADY

Hot and heady are terms used to describe a wine that is high in alcohol, particularly in a very tannic wine where the burning sensation is further amplified. High alcohol is simply the result of high Brix (SG) in juice that was successfully fermented extensively.

Commercial wineries that produce huge quantities of wine and that can afford and justify the investment of very expensive equipment use reverse osmosis (RO) technology to remove alcohol from wine. In home winemaking, the only practical solution is to blend a high-alcohol wine with a low-alcohol wine. Alternatively, you can add water to the wine but this has the drawback of diluting everything else in the wine, namely color, aromas, flavors, acidity and mouthfeel. Maceration with natural yeast derivative nutrients, such as Lallemand's BoosterRouge, as a corrective treatment is also very effective for helping to integrate high-burning alcohol characters.

Surprisingly, quite often, a hot or heady wine is the result of over-chaptalization, i.e., the wine was a tad too low in potential alcohol and then too much sugar was added. So go easy when chaptalizing. Double-check your sugar addition calculations, add sugar progressively, taking a hydrometer reading after each addition, and determine your new potential alcohol and make sure it matches your calculations.

14.16 WINE HAS AN UNPLEASANT SMELL OF GERANIUMS

An unpleasant smell of geraniums in wine is the result of a reaction between sorbic acid, found in potassium sorbate, and lactic acid bacteria used for MLF. The reaction produces hexadienol, otherwise known as geraniol, which produces the strong and disagreeable odor of rotting geraniums – a highly undesirable outcome that cannot be fixed. Potassium sorbate is an ingredient used to stabilize wines by inhibiting the growth of yeast and mold. Malolactic-fermented wines may still have lactic acid bacteria present unless adequately inhibited with sulfite.

This condition, for which there is no cure, is best avoided by eliminating the use of potassium sorbate, especially in totally dry wines, unless it is required to stabilize a sweet wine, in which case you should not malo the wine. Refer to sections 4.8 and 6.2.4 for more information on MLF and the use of potassium sorbate, respectively.

14.17 WINE SMELLS MOLDY OR MUSTY

A moldy or musty smell in wine is a serious fault likely due to 2,4,6-trichloroanisole, more commonly known as TCA, the culprit in so-called corked wines, which can also devoid wine of its complex flavors and aromas that we seek out so much. Although not a common occurrence in home winemaking, the nasty effects of TCA can be devastating if not prevented, and prevention is the only cure. There is no corrective action but to dump the wine if the smell is overwhelming. Refer to section 2.6.2 for more information on TCA and how to avoid it.

14.18 WINE HAS A STRONG BARNYARD SMELL

If wine has acquired a strong barnyard smell, beyond what would be acceptable, the culprit is indigenous *Brettanomyces* yeast. Brett, as it is commonly known, can also impart medicinal, sweaty, "Band-Aid" and rancid aromas to wine, and is very difficult to eradicate.

Your only recourse to eliminate or reduce Brett in finished wine is by stabilizing filtration, discussed in section 6.2.5, or by blending with another wine if the smell is faint. For more information on *Brettanomyces*, refer to section 6.2.2.

If a strong Brett odor has developed in an oak barrel, your only option is to discard the barrel. It is nearly impossible to eradicate Brett from barrels.

14.19 WINE HAS AN UNPLEASANT SOUR-MILK TASTE

If wine has acquired an unpleasant sour-milk taste, the culprit is lactic taint – a *Lactobacillus* or *Pediococcus* bacterial infection – originating from a number of sources including previously contaminated equipment, possibly from contact with spoiled and contaminated wine, or damaged grapes. The bacteria can multiply easily in wine under favorable environmental conditions and, at high levels, they will compromise the quality of the wine. Bacteria can also nestle in nooks and crannies of equipment that are difficult to clean, such as pumps, hoses and barrels, as well as in poorly sanitized equipment, such as carboys and tanks. Lactic taint is often accompanied by a vinegary smell as acetic acid bacteria (*Acetobacter*) are a by-product of the bacterial infection.

If the taste and smell are tolerable, sulfite and stabilize filter the wine, and drink as soon as possible; otherwise, if the taint is pronounced, the wine may need to be dumped.

For more information on *Acetobacter*, *Lactobacillus* and *Pediococcus* bacterial infections, refer to section 6.2.3.

15
BUILDING A COOL WINE CELLAR

Once wine is completed and matured in bulk, or it is bottled for storage or further aging, it will still evolve – some slower than others. The rate of evolution and flavor development greatly depends on quality of the vintage, varietals, viticultural practices, and vinification techniques; however, the storage and aging environment is as important and can accelerate development undesirably, mute flavor development, or cause a wine to decline or even spoil if conditions are not ideal.

The ideal cellar for storage and aging of wine should provide the following environmental characteristics:

a) A constant temperature in the 12–15° C (54–59° F) range,
b) A constant relative humidity (RH) in the 55–75% range,
c) Free of any smell that might penetrate corks and into bottles,
d) Free of any vibration that affects the stability of wine, and
e) Total darkness, or protection from strong light sources, particularly sunshine.

In this chapter, we will look at how to build the ideal cellar that also doubles as the winemaking area equipped with electrical outlets, water service, etc.

15.1 PLANNING CELLAR CONSTRUCTION

Maintaining a constant cool temperature and a relatively high humidity are the most important environmental conditions to respect when building a cellar. It should be free of vibrations and light sources that would otherwise accelerate the wine's aging process. Therefore, avoid heavy-traffic locations such as a garage or under stairs, and store wine away from strong light sources, particularly from damaging UV sunrays. That's why most bottles of commercial wine are tinted. And when painting or varnishing cellar walls, avoid products with strong odors, which could otherwise penetrate bottles through and around the cork and negatively affect the wine's taste and flavors.

Temperature and humidity are most difficult to control because of the various sources of heat and cold around a cellar enclosure. The interaction between temperature and humidity as well as the changing seasons further complicate matters. Careful planning of temperature and humidity control will be critical in building an efficient cellar.

The ideal cellar temperature should be in the 12–15° C (54–59° F) range and it must be kept constant throughout the year to ensure wine evolves slowly over time to develop subtle flavors and aromas. As temperature increases, wine ages at a faster rate and must therefore be drunk earlier (not always a problem). If the temperature is too cold, then the wine is stifled and cannot evolve. Therefore, refrigerators or un-insulated cold rooms are not recommended for wine storage except for chilling bottles to be drunk within a few hours.

If you cannot maintain temperature in the recommended range, try not to exceed 21° C (70° F) and avoid large rapid swings, which would otherwise negatively impact wine quality. A constant higher temperature is preferable than letting it swing, for example, from 13° C (55° F) to 21° C (70° F) in the same day. The same swing over several weeks or months would be less damaging although not ideal.

The cellar enclosure should face as northerly as possible to minimize temperature variations from the sun. A cellar with below-grade walls will improve temperature-control efficiency since heat transfer between the cellar and its surrounding is minimized.

A cellar is more tolerant to RH, compared to temperature, although you should avoid extremes. Ideally, RH should be in the

55–75 % range. If it drops well below the minimum, corks may start to leak because they may tend to shrink under drier air conditions – another reason why refrigerators are not appropriate. Barrel wood will also shrink causing stave joints to widen and barrels to leak. Bottle or barrel leakage can easily cause mold to form and spoil wine. If RH gets too high, the excess moisture in the air can cause mildew to form on corks and barrels, and contaminate and spoil wine.

Mount a thermometer and hygrometer, or a digital hygro-thermometer capable of recording minimum and maximum temperatures and RH, on a wall in the center of the cellar to monitor temperature and RH.

Next, determine your electrical power requirements based on your design. Consult a qualified electrical contractor to help you determine your needs and to perform all electrical work according to code.

At a minimum, you will need a separate 120V/15A circuit for lighting and outlets to operate pumps and other electrical equipment. This circuit should be equipped with a GFCI (Ground Fault Circuit Interrupter) to protect against accidents or electrical malfunction, for example, if water is accidentally splashed in the outlet. It's easy to recognize a GFCI circuit in your house; it's the outlet with TEST and RESET buttons, usually black and red, respectively. For lighting, 40W bulbs provide a good compromise between sufficient lighting and minimum heat production. In larger cellars requiring more than one light bulb, use light fixtures with built-in switches to turn bulbs on/off individually in each work area. A good rule of thumb is to plan for one 40W light bulb per 5.5–7.5 m^2 (60–80 sq ft) of cellar area.

If your cellar design will require hot- and cold-temperature control, you will need to plan separate circuits for your cooling and heating units. You will need either 120V/15A or 240V/15A circuits depending on the type of units chosen.

Plan for both hot and cold water taps as well as a 2-inch drain (minimum) because you will be cleaning and rinsing many carboys, demijohns, stainless tanks and oak barrels. Having access to water and drainage right in the cellar will avoid having to carry equipment to another location for cleaning and rinsing. Buy a heat-resistant hose sufficiently long to reach all corners of the cellar. Ordinary garden hoses will not withstand hot water when sanitizing equipment or swelling barrels. A portable four-legged sink is a good idea for rinsing bottles and cleaning equipment. Simply connect a discharge pipe that can be easily hooked to the floor drain when using the sink. When no longer needed, you can simply store the sink away in a corner.

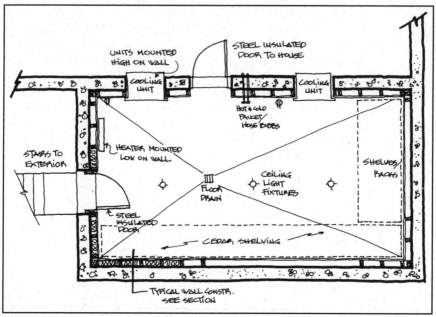

Figure 15-1: Example of a small home winery floor plan

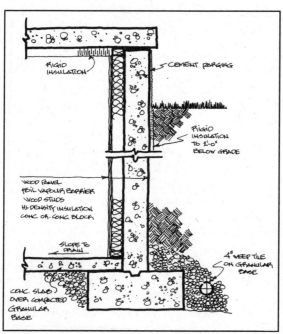

Figure 15-2: Example of a cross-section of a home winery enclosure

Lastly, plan for some convenient access to the cellar from both the exterior as well as from inside the house. There will be a lot of traffic in and out of your cellar; carrying carboys and demijohns from the garage into the cellar, taking pressed skins out to the compost, etc. Install 32-inch doors or wider; you want to make sure you will be able to fit that large fermentation tank that you will buy in a couple of years.

Figures 15-1 and 15-2 illustrate a typical layout and building construction of a cellar doubling as a small home winery.

15.2 TEMPERATURE AND HUMIDITY CONTROL

Let's take a closer look at temperature and humidity control as these pose the greatest challenge in cellar and winery design.

Temperature control is not easy because of the many sources of heat or cold that need to be monitored and accounted for. And if you live in a region with large temperature differences from one season to another, you need to implement solutions for controlling both low and high temperatures. The first thing you need to do is understand the temperature profile – seasonal highs and lows – of the enclosure by monitoring and recording temperature readings throughout the year. Wide seasonal temperature swings are okay if they are gradual over several weeks or months; however, spontaneous fluctuations will hamper a wine's ability to evolve and mature into a complex wine, and will accelerate aging.

The best solution to control temperature is to install one or more cooling units specifically designed for wine cellars to operate at low temperatures and maintain the ambient RH. Conventional room air conditioners for use in a cellar are not recommended; these are not designed to operate continuously, especially at high humidity levels, and remove too much moisture in the air, reducing much-needed humidity in the cellar. Borrowing cold/warm air from a central house system has the same disadvantages, and will never be able to meet the temperature needs of the cellar because the thermostat is set to control house temperature.

Cellar cooling units, such as Vintage Keeper's chillR PLUS shown in Figure 15-3, are favorites amongst wine aficionados because of their "plug-and-play" feature. They are specifically designed for low-temperature cellar applications, maintaining the temperature within one degree and RH in the range 40–80%. RH can be easily maintained in the 55–75 % with proper cellar construction. Note that cellar cooling units are designed to remove warm air from a cellar and ventilate to an adjacent interior space; they should **never** be installed on an exterior wall for venting to the outdoors. Exposing a cooling unit to the elements will cause damage and void the warranty.

Several models are available to match different cellar capacities (volume) and are rated in BTUs (British Thermal Units) – a measure of thermal energy. Manufacturers provide a chart listing volume and BTU for each model. To determine what model you need, calculate the volume of your cellar by multiply-

Figure 15-3: chillR PLUS cellar cooling unit

455

ing its length, width and height, and adjusting for any lost space from a bay area, for example. Then simply match the result to the appropriate model. For example, if your cellar is 12 ft long by 10 ft wide by 7 ft high, or 840 cu ft (23.8 m³), then you will need a chillR PLUS model rated for up to 900 cu ft (25.5 m³) or 3,000 BTUs. If your capacity exceeds the highest rated model, you can add a second unit. For example, if your cellar volume is 2,000 cu ft (56.6 m³), you will need a chillR unit and an 1800 unit providing a total of 7,400 BTUs.

Breezaire is another manufacturer of cellar cooling units including a split system that allows installation of the condenser up to 100 ft away from the cellar, similar to home central air conditioning units. A split system is ideal where the cooling unit cannot be installed directly on a cellar wall because of venting limitations.

Cellar cooling units described above all operate on 120V/15A circuits. Plan for a separate circuit for each unit when installing two or more.

If you need to heat your cellar during the winter months, you will need to install a heater. Space heaters can do the job in small cellars but they are not designed for continuous operation. Another disadvantage is that the heating element and forced air consume moisture in the air thus reducing RH. Warm air is also not distributed evenly throughout the cellar and creates uneven "pockets" of cold and warm air.

Convection-type heaters are the best solution because they distribute warm air evenly, they operate quietly because they do not have any fans, and their slim design greatly improves on cellar space. Your local renovation center should carry these types of heaters.

Convection-type heaters, such as the one in Figure 15-4, require a 240V/15A circuit and are rated in Watts. Use approximately 1000W per 100 sq ft (9.3 m²) to determine your needs. For example, for a 12×10 ft cellar, you will need a 1200W unit. Be sure to install the heater closest to the source of cold air, such as next to the exterior door.

Figure 15-4: Convection-type heater

15.3 INSULATION

Temperature-control units achieve maximum cooling or heating performance in a properly insulated enclosure. This means that you need to adequately insulate all walls, ceiling and doors, and eliminate any source of air infiltration that could greatly compromise temperature control performance.

All walls, ceiling and doors must be insulated to a minimum of R-20 (R-30 is best). The R-value is a measure of the resistance to conductive heat flow through a material: The higher the R-value, the greater the insulating efficiency. For example, a one-inch material with a value of R-10 provides twice the insulating efficiency of an R-5 material. Walls should be framed using 2×4 ft studs (2×6 ft is best for exterior walls) spaced at 16 or 24 inches for installing the insulating material.

There are several choices of insulating materials depending on your cellar needs and budget. In order of increasing cost, they are: fiberglass or mineral wool thermal batts, polystyrene foam boards, urethane/isocyanurate foam or boards, or sprayed polyurethane foam. Material and installation costs vary widely as they are geographically sensitive. Visit your local renovation center and consult contractors to obtain material and work estimates.

Thermal batts, such as PINK fiberglass insulation, are widely available at renovation centers. They are the lowest-cost solution and are very easy to install although their low R-value, in the R-3 to R-4 range, would require 6 to 9.5 inches of insulation material. That would result in very thick walls cutting down on precious cellar space. Batts are placed between wall studs and should be properly protected with a vapor barrier, such as polyethylene, on the inside wall (warm) surface to prevent condensation problems.

Extruded polystyrene foam insulation, such as BLUE STYRO-FOAM rigid boards, is rated at R-5 per inch, and is the alternative to thermal batts because of their higher insulation efficiency per inch. They also provide more resistance to moisture. For R-20 and R-30 insulating efficiency, you would need a foam thickness of 4 and 6 inches, respectively. Install 2×8 ft or 4×8 ft boards right against the wall to be insulated.

Urethane and isocyanurate insulation, rated between R-7 and R-8, provides higher efficiency for temperature and moisture control. Approximately 5 inches of foam is required to achieve R-30 insulating efficiency (an extra inch has been added to compensate for the drop in R-value due to material aging). Install 4×8 ft foil-faced foam boards (the aluminum foil on each side of the insulating material acts as the vapor barrier) up against the wall and fasten tightly as they tend to buckle.

Alternatively, you can opt for sprayed polyurethane foam; the material used in commercial walk-in refrigerators and refrigerated transport trucks. The foam is applied by spraying it directly on the wall. It quickly expands to fill cavities, and then hardens into a very dense and rigid material adding structural strength. It also acts as an excellent vapor barrier while providing good soundproofing. You will need to call upon the services of a contractor for this work, making this the costliest solution.

Where possible, insulate the exterior face of outside walls (i.e., exposed to the elements) to improve temperature and humidity control in the cellar, especially in areas with wide seasonal temperature variations. For example, you can install one-inch thick 2×8 ft polystyrene foam boards below grade around the exterior perimeter of the cellar walls to keep low ground-frost temperatures away. Foundation walls should already be protected with a layer of tar to prevent water infiltration.

As for the cellar floor, a concrete slab is most practical, and does not require any insulation if the floor is below grade; if it is above grade, you will need R-20 or R-30 insulation. Make a provision to install a water drain on waterproof flooring as you will be using a lot of water.

Consult a building contractor who can advise you on design and material required for your specific cellar requirements that also meet building regulations in your area. Most of the materials listed above must be covered with an approved fire-retardant material, such as gypsum boards.

Interior walls can be finished using moisture-resistant panels, such as cedar or redwood, or water-retardant gypsum boards (the ones with green paper on the faces). Use an odorless, non-water-based latex paint; the water content in paint will cause mildew to form on walls under high RH in the cellar.

Exterior doors should be steel insulated with R-20 minimum protection and adequate weather-strips around the exterior perimeter to minimize air infiltration that would otherwise compromise temperature-control efficiency. Install a hydraulic door closer to ensure that the door is not accidentally left open. A doorstopper will be handy to hold the door open when carrying things in and out of the cellar.

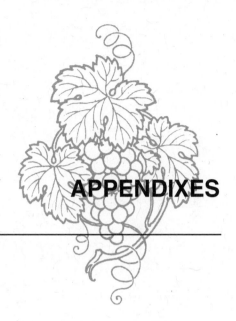

APPENDIXES

A CONVERSION FACTORS BETWEEN METRIC, IMPERIAL AND U.S. SYSTEMS

B SUGAR CONCENTRATION AND ALCOHOL LEVEL CONVERSIONS

C WINEMAKING LOG CHART

D USAGE GUIDELINES FOR COMMON CHEMICALS, FINING AGENTS, ADDITIVES AND MORE

E BIBLIOGRAPHY

APPENDIX A—CONVERSION FACTORS BETWEEN METRIC, IMPERIAL
AND U.S. SYSTEMS

Table A-1 provides a list of abbreviations for systems and units of measure used in this book.

Table A-1: List of abbreviations for systems and units of measure

Unit of measure	Abbreviation	Unit of measure	Abbreviation
acre	acre	micrometer	micron *or* µm
atmosphere	atm	milligram	mg
bar	bar	milliliter	cc *or* mL
Brix degrees	B°	millimeter	mm
centimeter	cm	ounce	oz
cup	cup	parts per million	ppm
degrees Celsius	°C	parts per trillion	ppt
degrees Fahrenheit	°F	pound(s)	lb(s)
fluid ounce	fl oz	pounds per square inch	psi
foot (feet)	ft	psi differential	psid
gallon	gal	Specific Gravity	SG
gram	g	square feet	sq ft *or* ft2
hectare	ha	square inches	sq in *or* in2
hectoliter	hL	square yards	sq yd *or* yd2
Imperial	Imp	tablespoon	tbsp
inch	in	teaspoon	tsp
kilogram	kg	ton	ton
kiloPascal	kPa	United States	U.S.
liter	L	volume	vol *or* v
meter	m	weight	wt *or* w
metric ton (tonne)	MT	yard	yd

Length
1 micrometer (micron *or* µm) = 1×10^{-6} m
1 cm = 10 mm = 0.39 in
1 in = 2.54 cm
1 m = 39.37 in = 3.28 ft = 1.09 yd
1 ft = 0.30 m
1 yd = 3 ft = 0.91 m

Mass and Weight
1 g = 0.035 oz
1 kg = 2.2 lbs
1 lb = 16 oz = 454 g
1 oz = 28.35 g
1 U.S. ton = 2,000 lbs = 0.91 MT
1 MT = 1,000 kg = 2,200 lbs = 1.1 U.S. ton

Volume
1 L = 0.26 U.S. gal = 0.22 Imp gal
20 L = 5.2 U.S. gal = 4.4 Imp gal
100 L = 1 hL = 26 U.S. gal = 22 Imp gal
1 U.S. gal = 128 U.S. fl oz = 0.83 Imp gal = 3.79 L
1 Imp gal = 160 Imp fl oz = 1.2 U.S. gal = 4.55 L
1 mL = 0.034 U.S. fl oz = 0.035 Imp fl oz
1 U.S. fl oz = 29.57 mL
1 Imp fl oz = 28.41 mL
1 tsp = 5 mL
1 tbsp = 3 tsp = 15 mL
1 cup = 8 U.S. fl oz = 237 mL

Concentration and Density
1 ppm = 1 mg/L (based on a density of 1 g per mL)
1000 ppm = 0.01 lb/gal (based on a density of 1¼ oz per U.S. fl oz)

Temperature
$°F = 9/5 \times (°C) + 32$
$°C = 5/9 \times [(°F) - 32]$

Pressure
1 kPa = 0.145 psi = 0.01 bar = 0.00987 atm = 0.0102 kg/cm^2
1 psi = 0.0689 bar = 0.0680 atm = 6.89 kPa = 0.0703 kg/cm^2
1 bar = 100 kPa

Acreage
1 acre = 4840 sq yd (yd^2) = 0.405 ha
1 ha = 10,000 m^2 = 2.471 acres

NOTE: All equivalents are approximate due to rounding.

Appendix B—Sugar concentration and alcohol level conversions

Use Table B-1 when required to convert between Specific Gravity, Brix degrees, sugar as a percentage of weight to volume, and potential alcohol (PA) level as a percentage of volume to volume (% alc. vol/vol).

These measurements are approximate given the hydrometer's limitations and inaccuracy, specifically in the presence of other solubles and/or alcohol. The margin of error on the measured alcohol content will be less than 0.5% alc./vol., which is quite acceptable.

The following conversions are valid at a temperature of 15.5° C (60° F).

Use Tables B-2 and B-3 to correct readings to compensate for temperature differences when using hydrometers calibrated at 20° C (68° F) and 15.5° C (60° F), respectively.

Table B-1: Conversions between SG, Brix, % sugar (w/v) and Potential Alcohol (PA) % alc./vol.

SG	Brix	% sugar (w/v)	PA	SG	Brix	% sugar (w/v)	PA	SG	Brix	% sugar (w/v)	PA	SG	Brix	% sugar (w/v)	PA
0.990	−2.6	−2.6	0.0	1.015	3.9	3.9	1.5	1.032	8.1	8.4	3.8	1.049	12.2	12.8	6.1
0.995	−1.3	−1.3	0.0	1.016	4.1	4.2	1.6	1.033	8.3	8.6	4.0	1.050	12.4	13.1	6.2
1.000	0.0	0.0	0.0	1.017	4.4	4.4	1.8	1.034	8.6	8.9	4.1	1.051	12.7	13.3	6.3
1.001	0.3	0.3	0.0	1.018	4.6	4.7	1.9	1.035	8.8	9.1	4.2	1.052	12.9	13.6	6.5
1.002	0.5	0.5	0.0	1.019	4.9	5.0	2.0	1.036	9.1	9.4	4.4	1.053	13.2	13.8	6.6
1.003	0.8	0.8	0.0	1.020	5.1	5.2	2.2	1.037	9.3	9.7	4.5	1.054	13.4	14.1	6.7
1.004	1.0	1.0	0.0	1.021	5.4	5.5	2.3	1.038	9.6	9.9	4.6	1.055	13.6	14.4	6.9
1.005	1.3	1.3	0.1	1.022	5.6	5.7	2.5	1.039	9.8	10.2	4.8	1.056	13.9	14.6	7.0
1.006	1.6	1.6	0.2	1.023	5.9	6.0	2.6	1.040	10.0	10.5	4.9	1.057	14.1	14.9	7.1
1.007	1.8	1.8	0.4	1.024	6.1	6.3	2.7	1.041	10.3	10.7	5.0	1.058	14.3	15.2	7.2
1.008	2.1	2.1	0.5	1.025	6.4	6.5	2.9	1.042	10.5	11.0	5.2	1.059	14.6	15.4	7.4
1.009	2.3	2.4	0.7	1.026	6.6	6.8	3.0	1.043	10.8	11.2	5.3	1.060	14.8	15.7	7.5
1.010	2.6	2.6	0.8	1.027	6.9	7.1	3.1	1.044	11.0	11.5	5.4	1.061	15.0	15.9	7.6
1.011	2.8	2.9	0.9	1.028	7.1	7.3	3.3	1.045	11.3	11.8	5.6	1.062	15.3	16.2	7.8
1.012	3.1	3.1	1.1	1.029	7.4	7.6	3.4	1.046	11.5	12.0	5.7	1.063	15.5	16.5	7.9
1.013	3.4	3.4	1.2	1.030	7.6	7.8	3.6	1.047	11.7	12.3	5.8	1.064	15.7	16.7	8.0
1.014	3.6	3.7	1.4	1.031	7.9	8.1	3.7	1.048	12.0	12.5	6.0	1.065	15.9	17.0	8.1

Table B-1, *continued*

SG	Brix	% sugar (w/v)	PA	SG	Brix	% sugar (w/v)	PA	SG	Brix	% sugar (w/v)	PA	SG	Brix	% sugar (w/v)	PA
1.066	16.2	17.2	8.3	1.083	20.0	21.7	10.4	1.100	23.8	26.1	12.4	1.117	27.4	30.6	14.4
1.067	16.4	17.5	8.4	1.084	20.2	21.9	10.5	1.101	24.0	26.4	12.6	1.118	27.6	30.8	14.5
1.068	16.6	17.8	8.5	1.085	20.5	22.2	10.6	1.102	24.2	26.7	12.7	1.119	27.8	31.1	14.7
1.069	16.9	18.0	8.6	1.086	20.7	22.5	10.8	1.103	24.4	26.9	12.8	1.120	28.0	31.4	14.8
1.070	17.1	18.3	8.8	1.087	20.9	22.7	10.9	1.104	24.6	27.2	12.9	1.121	28.2	31.6	14.9
1.071	17.3	18.6	8.9	1.088	21.1	23.0	11.0	1.105	24.8	27.4	13.0	1.122	28.4	31.9	15.0
1.072	17.5	18.8	9.0	1.089	21.4	23.3	11.1	1.106	25.0	27.7	13.1	1.123	28.6	32.1	15.1
1.073	17.8	19.1	9.1	1.090	21.6	23.5	11.2	1.107	25.3	28.0	13.3	1.124	28.8	32.4	15.2
1.074	18.0	19.3	9.3	1.091	21.8	23.8	11.4	1.108	25.5	28.2	13.4	1.125	29.0	32.7	15.3
1.075	18.2	19.6	9.4	1.092	22.0	24.0	11.5	1.109	25.7	28.5	13.5	1.126	29.2	32.9	15.5
1.076	18.5	19.9	9.5	1.093	22.2	24.3	11.6	1.110	25.9	28.7	13.6	1.127	29.4	33.2	15.6
1.077	18.7	20.1	9.6	1.094	22.5	24.6	11.7	1.111	26.1	29.0	13.7	1.128	29.7	33.4	15.7
1.078	18.9	20.4	9.8	1.095	22.7	24.8	11.8	1.112	26.3	29.3	13.8	1.129	29.9	33.7	15.8
1.079	19.1	20.6	9.9	1.096	22.9	25.1	12.0	1.113	26.5	29.5	14.0	1.130	30.1	34.0	15.9
1.080	19.4	20.9	10.0	1.097	23.1	25.3	12.1	1.114	26.7	29.8	14.1	1.131	30.3	34.2	16.0
1.081	19.6	21.2	10.1	1.098	23.3	25.6	12.2	1.115	27.0	30.0	14.2	1.132	30.5	34.5	16.1
1.082	19.8	21.4	10.3	1.099	23.5	25.9	12.3	1.116	27.2	30.3	14.3	1.133	30.7	34.8	16.2

Table B-1, *continued*

SG	Brix	% sugar (w/v)	PA	SG	Brix	% sugar (w/v)	PA	SG	Brix	% sugar (w/v)	PA	SG	Brix	% sugar (w/v)	PA
1.134	30.9	35.0	16.4	1.151	34.3	39.5	18.2	1.168	37.6	43.9	20.0	1.185	40.8	48.3	21.8
1.135	31.1	35.3	16.5	1.152	34.5	39.7	18.3	1.169	37.8	44.2	20.1	1.186	41.0	48.6	21.9
1.136	31.3	35.5	16.6	1.153	34.7	40.0	18.4	1.170	38.0	44.4	20.3	1.187	41.2	48.9	22.0
1.137	31.5	35.8	16.7	1.154	34.9	40.2	18.5	1.171	38.2	44.7	20.4	1.188	41.4	49.1	22.1
1.138	31.7	36.1	16.8	1.155	35.1	40.5	18.7	1.172	38.3	44.9	20.5	1.189	41.5	49.4	22.2
1.139	31.9	36.3	16.9	1.156	35.3	40.8	18.8	1.173	38.5	45.2	20.6	1.190	41.7	49.6	22.3
1.140	32.1	36.6	17.0	1.157	35.5	41.0	18.9	1.174	38.7	45.5	20.7	1.191	41.9	49.9	22.4
1.141	32.3	36.8	17.1	1.158	35.7	41.3	19.0	1.175	38.9	45.7	20.8	1.192	42.1	50.2	22.5
1.142	32.5	37.1	17.2	1.159	35.8	41.5	19.1	1.176	39.1	46.0	20.9	1.193	42.3	50.4	22.6
1.143	32.7	37.4	17.4	1.160	36.0	41.8	19.2	1.177	39.3	46.3	21.0	1.194	42.5	50.7	22.7
1.144	32.9	37.6	17.5	1.161	36.2	42.1	19.3	1.178	39.5	46.5	21.1	1.195	42.6	51.0	22.8
1.145	33.1	37.9	17.6	1.162	36.4	42.3	19.4	1.179	39.7	46.8	21.2	1.196	42.8	51.2	22.9
1.146	33.3	38.1	17.7	1.163	36.6	42.6	19.5	1.180	39.9	47.0	21.3	1.197	43.0	51.5	23.0
1.147	33.5	38.4	17.8	1.164	36.8	42.9	19.6	1.181	40.0	47.3	21.4	1.198	43.2	51.7	23.1
1.148	33.7	38.7	17.9	1.165	37.0	43.1	19.7	1.182	40.2	47.6	21.5	1.199	43.4	52.0	23.2
1.149	33.9	38.9	18.0	1.166	37.2	43.4	19.8	1.183	40.4	47.8	21.6	1.200	43.5	52.3	23.3
1.150	34.1	39.2	18.1	1.167	37.4	43.6	19.9	1.184	40.6	48.1	21.7	1.201	43.7	52.5	23.4

Table B-1, *continued*

SG	Brix	% sugar (w/v)	PA
1.202	43.9	52.8	23.5
1.203	44.1	53.0	23.6
1.204	44.3	53.3	23.7
1.205	44.5	53.6	23.8
1.206	44.6	53.8	23.9
1.207	44.8	54.1	24.0
1.208	45.0	54.4	24.1
1.209	45.2	54.6	24.2
1.210	45.3	54.9	24.3
1.211	45.5	55.1	24.4
1.212	45.7	55.4	24.5
1.213	45.9	55.7	24.6
1.214	46.1	55.9	24.7
1.215	46.2	56.2	24.8
1.216	46.4	56.4	24.9
1.217	46.6	56.7	25.0
1.218	46.8	57.0	25.1
1.219	46.9	57.2	25.2
1.220	47.1	57.5	25.3
1.221	47.3	57.7	25.4
1.222	47.5	58.0	25.5
1.223	47.6	58.3	25.6
1.224	47.8	58.5	25.7
1.225	48.0	58.8	25.8
1.226	48.2	59.1	25.9
1.227	48.3	59.3	26.0
1.228	48.5	59.6	26.1
1.229	48.7	59.8	26.1
1.230	48.9	60.1	26.2
1.231	49.0	60.4	26.3
1.232	49.2	60.6	26.4
1.233	49.4	60.9	26.5
1.234	49.5	61.1	26.6
1.235	49.7	61.4	26.7
1.236	49.9	61.7	26.8
1.237	50.1	61.9	26.9
1.238	50.2	62.2	27.0
1.239	50.4	62.5	27.1
1.240	50.6	62.7	27.2
1.241	50.7	63.0	27.3
1.242	50.9	63.2	27.4
1.243	51.1	63.5	27.5
1.244	51.3	63.8	27.6
1.245	51.4	64.0	27.7
1.246	51.6	64.3	27.7
1.247	51.8	64.5	27.8
1.248	51.9	64.8	27.9
1.249	52.1	65.1	28.0
1.250	52.3	65.3	28.1
1.251	52.4	65.6	28.2
1.252	52.6	65.8	28.3
1.253	52.8	66.1	28.4
1.254	52.9	66.4	28.5
1.255	53.1	66.6	28.6
1.256	53.3	66.9	28.7
1.257	53.4	67.2	28.8
1.258	53.6	67.4	28.8
1.259	53.8	67.7	28.9
1.260	53.9	67.9	29.0
1.261	54.1	68.2	29.1
1.262	54.2	68.5	29.2
1.263	54.4	68.7	29.3
1.264	54.6	69.0	29.4
1.265	54.7	69.2	29.5
1.266	54.9	69.5	29.6
1.267	55.1	69.8	29.7
1.268	55.2	70.0	29.7
1.269	55.4	70.3	29.8

Table B-2
Approximate Brix/SG corrections for hydrometers calibrated at 20° C (68° F)

T (°C)	T (°F)	Brix	SG	T (°C)	T (°F)	Brix	SG
10	50.0	−0.6	−0.001	20	68.0	0.0	0.000
11	51.8	−0.5	−0.001	21	69.8	+0.1	0.000
12	53.6	−0.5	−0.001	22	71.6	+0.1	0.000
13	55.4	−0.4	−0.001	23	73.4	+0.2	+0.001
14	57.2	−0.4	−0.001	24	75.2	+0.3	+0.001
15	59.0	−0.3	−0.001	25	77.0	+0.4	+0.001
16	60.8	−0.2	−0.001	26	78.8	+0.4	+0.001
17	62.6	−0.2	0.000	27	80.6	+0.5	+0.001
18	64.4	−0.1	0.000	28	82.4	+0.6	+0.002
19	66.2	−0.1	0.000	29	84.2	+0.6	+0.002
20	68.0	0.0	0.000	30	86.0	+0.7	+0.002

Example
Brix reading of 20.0 at 25° C should be corrected to 20.0+0.4=20.4 B°.

Table B-3

Approximate SG/Brix corrections for hydrometers calibrated at 60° F (15.56° C)

T(°F)	T(°C)	SG	Brix	T(°F)	T(°C)	SG	Brix	T(°F)	T(°C)	SG	Brix
50	10.0	-0.001	-0.2	62	16.7	0.000	+0.1	74	23.3	+0.001	+0.4
51	10.6	-0.001	-0.2	63	17.2	0.000	+0.1	75	23.9	+0.001	+0.5
52	11.1	0.000	-0.2	64	17.8	0.000	+0.1	76	24.4	+0.002	+0.5
53	11.7	0.000	-0.2	65	18.3	0.000	+0.2	77	25.0	+0.002	+0.5
54	12.2	0.000	-0.2	66	18.9	0.000	+0.2	78	25.6	+0.002	+0.6
55	12.8	0.000	-0.1	67	19.4	+0.001	+0.2	79	26.1	+0.002	+0.6
56	13.3	0.000	-0.1	68	20.0	+0.001	+0.2	80	26.7	+0.002	+0.6
57	13.9	0.000	-0.1	69	20.6	+0.001	+0.3	81	27.2	+0.002	+0.7
58	14.4	0.000	-0.1	70	21.1	+0.001	+0.3	82	27.8	+0.002	+0.7
59	15.0	0.000	-0.1	71	21.7	+0.001	+0.3	83	28.3	+0.002	+0.7
60	15.6	0.000	0.0	72	22.2	+0.001	+0.4	84	28.9	+0.003	+0.8
61	16.1	0.000	+0.1	73	22.8	+0.001	+0.4	85	29.4	+0.003	+0.8

Example

SG reading of 1.083 at 77° F should be corrected to 1.083+0.002=1.085.

Appendix C—Winemaking log chart

Keeping records of all vinification and winemaking measurements and operations is essential in the production of premium quality wines. By quantitatively following the evolution of wine and its many components, critical elements – temperature, sugar concentration, alcohol content, total acidity (TA), pH, and free SO_2 – can be adjusted to maintain the required balance favoring successful winemaking. This data will also prove useful for future reference when wanting to duplicate specific results or when needing to identify the root-cause of a winemaking problem.

Measurements should be recorded as per the recommended frequency for each element. Frequency will be a function of the winemaking phase.

In addition to the above elements, the type of operation, and ingredients and quantities added should also be recorded. Type of operation will include procedures such as crushing, destemming, maceration, pressing, alcoholic fermentation, malolactic fermentation, racking, fining, filtration, microbial and cold stabilization, blending, oak-aging, and bottling.

Notice: The winemaking log chart on the opposite page can be photocopied with enlargement to fit an 8½×11-inch page or otherwise reproduced for the purpose of maintaining winemaking records. Alternatively, a full-page template of this log chart can be downloaded from the following web site: http://www.vehiculepress.com.

Batch ID No. _____

Vintage _____

Date Started _____

Grape Variety _____

Quantity _____

Price _____

Juice Volume

Free-run _____

Press-run _____

Date	Type of Operation	Ingredient Added	Quantity Added	Temp. (°C)	Brix (B°)	Potential % alc./vol.	TA (g/L)	pH	Free SO$_2$ (mg/L)	Remarks & Observations

Appendix D— Usage guidelines for common chemicals, fining agents, additives and more

Chemical / Ingredient	Usage	Recommended concentration	Comments
Acid blend	Increase TA	1 g/L	To increase TA by approx. 1 g/L (check ratio of each acid component)
Activated carbon	Remove brown coloration	1–5 g/hL	Dissolve directly in wine & treat with bentonite
	Remove bad odors and flavors	5–25 g/hL	
Antifoaming agent	Reduce foaming in sparkling wine	1 mL/hL	
Ascorbic acid	Antioxidant	2–3 g/hL	Dissolve in water; only use with sulfite
	Prevent ferric casse		
Bentonite	Fine white and red wines	25–100 g/hL	Dissolve in water
	Fine sparkling wines	25–50 g/hL	
Bocksin	Reduce hydrogen sulfide (H_2S)	1 mL/L	Dissolve in water
Casein	Fine or improve color in whites	50–100 g/hL	Dissolve in warm water
Citric acid	Increase effectiveness of sulfite solution for sanitizing equipment	Equal parts as sulfite	
Conditioner	Sweeten a finished wine	12–25 mL/L	Add just prior to bottling
Copper sulfate	Reduce hydrogen sulfide (H_2S)	0.5–1.0 mL of a 1%-solution per hL	Never exceed 5.0 mL/hL
Egg whites	Fining reds and high-tannin whites	5–10 g/hL	Combine with a salted water solution
Gelatin	Fining red & high-tannin or high-pectin white wines	1–5 g/hL	Dissolve in water; increase up to 25 g/hL for high-pectin wines
Grape tannins	Increase tannin content	10–30 g/hL	Dissolve in warm water; increase to 50 g/hL when fining high-pectin wines with gelatin

Chemical / Ingredient	Usage	Recommended concentration	Comments
Gum arabic	Enhance action of metatartaric acid; prevent turbidity & precipitation in bottled wine; improve aromatic intensity & complexity, & taste balance; prevent ferric casse in high-iron wines; enhance "perlage" or bubbling in sparkling wine	0.5–5 mL of a 20%-solution per L	Dissolve directly into wine
Hydrogen peroxide	Reduce free SO_2 content	18 mL of a 3%-solution per hL	For each 10 mg/L of free SO_2 to be reduced
Isinglass	Fining white wines	Liquid: 1 mL/L Powder: 1–3 g/hL	Liquid: dilute in wine Powder: dissolve in water
Kieselsol	Fining white and red wines	25–50 mL/hL	Add directly to wine
Lysozyme	Protect against microbial spoilage	100–300 mg/L	Add as a 5%-solution
Metatartaric acid	Prevent precipitation of tartrate crystals	Up to 10 g/hL	Dissolve in cold water Store powder in refrigerator
Oak chips	Add oak aromas and flavors to wines	Whites: 1–2 g/L Reds: 2–4 g/L	
Pectic enzymes	Fining wines	Whites: 1–2 g/hL Reds: 2–4 g/hL	Dissolve in water
Pectolytic enzymes	Enhance varietal aromas	2–3 g/hL	Dissolve in 10× its weight of wine
Phosphoric acid	Reduce pH in high-pH/high-TA wines	1–2 drops of a 30%-solution per L	
Polyvinylpolypyrrolidone (PVPP)	Reduce tannin content	25–75 g/hL	Add directly to wine
Potassium bicarbonate	Reduce TA or increase pH	1 g/L	To reduce TA by 1 g/L or increase pH by 0.1 unit
Potassium bitartrate	Help tartrate crystallization during cold stabilization by chilling	50–100 g/hL	

Chemical / Ingredient	Usage	Recommended concentration	Comments
Potassium metabisulfite	Sanitize equipment Preserve wine	Sanitizing: 1–10 g/L Preserving: Typically to achieve up to 35 mg/L of free SO_2	Sanitizing: Add equal parts of citric acid to increase effectiveness Preserving: Additions should be based on pH of wine
Potassium sorbate	Prevent refermentation of bottled wines	10–20 g/hL	Do not use in ML-fermented wines
Sodium carbonate (soda ash)	Clean plastic equipment Dissolve tartrate crystals Neutralize acetic acid	8–12 g/L of water	Dissolve in hot water Rinse with a sulfur-citric solution
Sodium hypochlorite (chlorinated pink powder)	Clean and sanitize glass containers	1 g/L of water	Do not use on plastic or s/s equipment or oak barrels
Sodium percarbonate	Clean winemaking equipment Treat oak barrel spoilage problems	1–3 g/L of water	Dissolve in hot water Store solution tightly sealed
Sodium metabisulfite	Sanitize equipment	1–10 g/L	Dissolve in warm water
Sparkolloid	Fining white and red wines	10–40 g/hL	Dissolve in water
Sugar (table/corn)	Increase potential alcohol level	17 g/L	To increase potential alcohol by 1%
Tartaric acid	Increase TA or reduce pH	1 g/L or more if wine to be cold stabilized	Increase TA by 1 g/L or reduce pH by 0.1 unit
Yeast (active dried)	Alcoholic fermentation	20 g/hL	Rehydrate as per manufacturer's instructions
Yeast nutrients (DAP) & rehy-dration/derivative nutrients	Enhance fermentation capability of yeast	10–20 g/hL	Dissolve in warm water

Appendix E—Bibliography

1. American Wine Society, The. THE COMPLETE HANDBOOK OF WINEMAKING. Ann Arbor: G.W. Kent, Inc. 1993.

This handbook is a collection of technical articles from renowned authorities from the wine trade and academia as well as from avid home winemakers. This reference textbook will prove most useful to advanced winemakers as the contents tend to be too technical for beginners. It assumes that readers have a good knowledge of winemaking techniques and processes. Wine analysis is discussed in details although discussions on the use of different types of wine yeasts and clarification agents and filtration techniques are cursory. A chapter on sparkling wine production presents the true *méthode champenoise* procedure for practical home winemaking use. In addition to winemaking, this book describes the elements (visual, olfactory, and gustatory) of wine tasting and how to organize and conduct wine tastings.

2. Barrel Builders, Inc. BARREL MAINTENANCE AND REPAIR MANUAL. St. Helena: Barrel Builders, Inc. 1995.

This concise, 33-page manual is an excellent reference on how to prepare, treat and maintain both used and new oak barrels. This manual was written by experienced coopers who have been serving the California wine industry for over 20 years; their advice on barrel maintenance has stood the test of time. Although the section on barrel repairs is beyond the woodworking abilities of most winemakers, it does provide interesting reading.

3. Bettiga, Larry J., Golino, D.A., McGourty, G., Smith, R.J., Verdegaal, P.S. Weber, E.. WINE GRAPE VARIETIES IN CALIFORNIA. California: University of California, Division of Agriculture and Natural Resources, Publication 3419. 2003.

This book is nicely illustrated along with superb photographs of grape varieties grown in California. Photographs along with morphology information for each variety make this resource invaluable. It also includes other useful information such as ripening periods and ripening dates by growing district. A must-have resource if your winemaking includes grapes sourced from California.

4. Boulton, R.B., V.L. Singleton, L.F. Bisson, and R.E. Kunkee. PRINCIPLES AND PRACTICES OF WINEMAKING. New York: Chapman & Hall (International Thomson Publishing). 1996.

Anyone considering a professional career in enology should read this textbook, authored by viticulture and enology professors from the University of California at Davis. It provides highly technical and in-depth discussions of modern winemaking practices and equipment. The book is structured for use as a teaching aid and is geared to professional winemaking. It assumes a solid technical background in pure and applied sciences, namely, chemistry, biochemistry and microbiology. Advanced home winemakers wanting to further their technical knowledge of winemaking will find this book indispensable.

5. Clarke, Oz. OZ CLARKE'S ENCYCLOPEDIA OF GRAPES: A COMPREHENSIVE GUIDE TO VARIETIES AND FLAVORS. New York: Harcourt, Inc. 2001.

Oz Clarke is one of the world's leading wine experts and writers. This 320-page book, covering varieties from Albariño to Zinfandel, is an excellent complement to a similar work, VINES, GRAPES & WINES, by Jancis Robinson. It is well presented with beautiful photographs and illustrations along with very useful "consumer information" for varieties, such as the best producers and recommended wines. An important and useful aspect of this book is the description of differences of varieties from various winemaking regions throughout the world.

6. Fugelsang, K.C., Edwards, C.G., WINE MICROBIOLOGY: PRACTICAL APPLICATIONS AND PROCEDURES – SECOND EDITION. Berlin, Germany: Springer (Springer Science+Business Media). 2006.

This technical textbook on wine microbiology complements PRINCIPLES AND PRACTICES OF WINEMAKING. Also geared to professional winemaking, this book provides in-depth descriptions of various bacteria, yeasts and molds, and their role in winemaking. This textbook is very technical and requires a good knowledge of microbiology.

7. Goode, Jamie. THE SCIENCE OF WINE: FROM VINE TO GLASS. Berkeley: University of California Press. 2005.

This engaging book is laid out in three major sections covering the hotly-debated issues in the fields of science of viticulture, winemaking and human interaction with wine. It covers scientific, technological and often controversial innovations from precision viticulture and genetically-modified grape vines, to reverse osmosis, spinning cones, evaporators and screwcaps, to wine flavor chemistry and health. A fun and interesting read!

8. Iland, Patrick, Ewart, A., Sitters, J., Markides, A., and Nick Bruer. TECHNIQUES FOR CHEMICAL ANALYSIS AND QUALITY MONITORING DURING WINEMAKING. South Australia: Patrick Iland Wine Promotions. 2004.

This updated edition is a must-have in every winery's library. It covers the plethora of laboratory procedures, each described in step-by-step instructions along with pertinent chemical concepts. The spiral-bound, laminated, hard paperback format is ideal for the laboratory environment.

9. Jackisch, Philip. MODERN WINEMAKING. Ithaca: Cornell University Press. 1985.

This complete handbook is an excellent reference for serious winemakers. It offers one of the most complete lists of winemaking problems, and how to prevent and correct these problems. The author, a research chemist, shares his wealth of winemaking knowledge from his years of experience as winemaker, wine consultant, wine competition judge, and teacher. Readers should have a good technical background. Those interested in submitting their homemade wines into wine competitions will find a short but useful section on competition rules and judging procedures.

10. Jackson, David, and Danny Schuster. THE PRODUCTION OF GRAPES & WINE IN COOL CLIMATES. New Zealand: Gypsum Press and Daphne Brasell Associates Ltd. 2001.

Whether you make wine in Burgundy, New Zealand, Niagara or the Finger Lakes region, this book provides valuable information on cool-climate grape growing and winemaking. Agronomical information such as ideal soil type, vigor, pruning methods, disease susceptibility, effect of wet weather, rootstocks, and expected yields will prove very useful in identifying and selecting grapes. It covers the major V. vinifera varieties but also lesser known and obscure cool-climate varieties such as Blaufrankischer, St. Macaire, and Zweigeltrebe.

11. Johnson, Hugh and James Halliday. THE VINTNER'S ART: HOW GREAT WINES ARE MADE. New York: Simon and Schuster. 1992.

Hugh Johnson is a world-renowned and authoritative wine writer. James Halliday is a wine writer and also the owner and winemaker of a small Australian winery. Together, they have authored an excellent book geared to those interested in acquiring a general knowledge of wine production without all the intricate technical details. The book is logically sequenced in three sections describing wine production from vineyard to winery to bottle. First, the effects of terroir, climate, grape variety, harvesting techniques and other viticultural factors on wine quality are described. Second, production processes for different types and styles of wine – from light-bodied white wines to full-bodied red wines and fortified wines – are outlined and explained in very simple language. Third, the chemistry and analysis of wine are briefly, but effectively, treated. Stunning photographs and superb illustrations enhance the visual dimension of this fascinating book.

12. Margalit, Phd., Yair. WINERY TECHNOLOGY & OPERATIONS: A HANDBOOK FOR SMALL WINERIES. San Francisco: The Wine Appreciation Guild. 1996.

This handbook should belong in every serious home winemaker's library. Although quite technical in nature – the author has an academic background in chemistry and physical chemistry in addition to his experience in small-winery winemaking – the book is very concise and offers practical advice on all winemaking procedures. It is a truly practical handbook. For example, procedures for basic analysis of must and wine are detailed. Margalit has also authored two other excellent books for anyone considering a career in enology and winemaking, both published by The Wine Appreciation Guild: CONCEPTS IN WINE CHEMISTRY (2004) and CONCEPTS IN WINE TECHNOLOGY (2004).

13. Olney, Richard. ROMANÉE-CONTI: THE WORLD'S MOST FABLED WINE. New York: Rizzoli International Publications, Inc. 1995.

Richard Olney is a food writer with a seemingly keen interest in top-rate wineries and their highly-acclaimed legendary wines. This book recounts the fascinating history and winemaking practices of Le Domaine de La Romanée-Conti (DRC), unquestionably the most famous Burgundian winery located in the Côte d'Or. It describes the winemaking philosophy and practices in the production of such premium DRC wines as La Tâche, Grands Echézeaux, Richebourg, and, of course, Romanée-Conti. Home winemakers can now get an appreciation of how these great Burgundian wines are made and the extent to which such wineries will go to achieve the highest quality standards possible.

14. Olney, Richard. YQUEM. Suisse: Flammarion. 1985.

Richard Olney recounts the fascinating history and winemaking practices of Château d'Yquem, the producer of the legendary Premier Grand Cru Classé Sauternes wine. Written with the same purpose and style as his book on Le Domaine de La Romanée-Conti, YQUEM, however, is supplemented with superb glossy photographs such as the 32 vintage bottles ranging from 1858 to 1944.

15. Ough, C.S. and M.A. Amerine. METHODS FOR ANALYSIS OF MUSTS AND WINES. New York: John Wiley & Sons, Inc. 1988.

Ough and Amerine have been two of the most influential enologists in American winemaking. Researchers, professors and writers, they have laid much of the initial groundwork in California in the post-Prohibition era to revive the winemaking industry. This book is strictly geared for those pursuing a career in professional winemaking, or more specifically, in wine analysis. The contents are highly technical and require extensive knowledge in various branches of chemistry. It does, however, provide very detailed descriptions of analytical procedures that are otherwise very difficult to find in other textbooks.

16. Peynaud, Émile. KNOWING AND MAKING WINE. Spencer, Alan F., tr. New York: John Wiley & Sons, Inc. 1984.

Émile Peynaud has been unquestionably the leading authoritative research enologist and teacher of modern winemaking. In spite of its very technical content, this scholarly book is still indispensable and should be part of any winemaker's library. It is one of the most complete practical textbooks on winemaking. The many lists of advantages and disadvantages of various equipment, winemaking and vinification procedures will prove very helpful when deciding which to use.

17. Peynaud, Émile. THE TASTE OF WINE: THE ART AND SCIENCE OF WINE APPRECIATION. Schuster, Michael, tr. London: Macdonald & Co. (Publishers) Ltd. 1987.

Making wine is half the fun! The other half is tasting wine. And once again, Émile Peynaud has done a scholarly job of describing the science and practice of wine tasting. Specifically, it describes how to assess the visual, olfactory and gustatory aspects of wine, and outlines tasting techniques. Assessing and describing a wine requires a very rich and descriptive vocabulary. Émile Peynaud provides a comprehensive vocabulary with accurate definitions used in wine tasting. One's ability to accurately describe a wine depends on mastery of this vocabulary.

18. Ribéreau-Gayon, P., Dubourdieu, D., Donèche, B., and A. Lonvaud. HANDBOOK OF ENOLOGY: VOLUME 1 – THE MICROBIOLOGY OF WINE AND VINIFICATIONS. Branco, Jeffrey M., tr. Chichester: John Wiley & Sons Ltd. 2000.

Pascal Ribéreau-Gayon, director of the Institut d'Œnologie de Bordeaux and son of Jean Ribéreau-Gayon, the "father of modern enology" and Émile Peynaud's mentor, has teamed up with other Bordeaux scholars to produce this authoritative textbook on the microbiology of wine. This book is intended for those having a chemistry background and wanting to pursue a career in commercial winemaking, research in enology, or wine analysis. This first volume focuses on the role of yeasts, bacteria and sulfur dioxide in red and white wine vinifications.

19. Ribéreau-Gayon, P., Glories, Y., Maujean, A., and D. Dubourdieu. HANDBOOK OF ENOLOGY: VOLUME 2 – THE CHEMISTRY OF WINE, STABILIZATION AND TREATMENTS. Aquitrad Traduction, tr. Chichester: John Wiley & Sons Ltd. 2000.

In this second volume, Pascal Ribéreau-Gayon and his co-authors focus on the chemistry of wines – alcohols, carbohydrates, phenolic compounds, aromas, etc. – as a prelude to detailed discussions on stabilization procedures and treatments of wine including fining, filtration, and aging. In spite of the highly technical nature of this text, as well as Volume 1, the authors provide valuable practical advice, recommended additive concentrations and limits imposed by the European Community, and much more.

20. Robinson, Jancis, ed. THE OXFORD COMPANION TO WINE – THIRD EDITION. Oxford: Oxford University Press. 2006.

Jancis Robinson, a Master of Wine, writer and leading authority in enology, is the editor of this beautiful and updated masterpiece. This heavy, encyclopedia-style book contains 3900 entries from *abboccato* to *zymase*. Over 160 Masters of Wine, writers, researchers, professors, enologists, wine consultants and others have contributed to this work. Each entry is concise and yet thorough and informative.

This reference textbook is sprinkled with superb photographs, illustrations, and maps of wine-producing regions. A must-have in every library.

21. Robinson, Jancis. VINES, GRAPES & WINES. New York: Mitchell Beazley Publishers. 1986.

Ever wondered what Auxerrois or Valdepeñas are? Or what are the differences between the various Muscat grape varieties? These grape variety entries and over 800 more can be found in this reference book with detailed descriptions of origin, characteristics, and the type of wines they produce. Illustrations of grape bunches are useful in learning about grape physiology. A very useful comprehensive list of synonyms for each grape variety is also provided. If a grape variety cannot be found in this textbook, it probably does not exist! Although there is considerable overlap with Robinson's OXFORD COMPANION TO WINE, this book still offers a lot more details.

22. Zoecklein, Bruce W., Fugelsang, K.C., Gump B.H., and F.S. Nury. WINE ANALYSIS AND PRODUCTION. Gaithersburg: Aspen Publishers, Inc. 1999.

Zoecklein is a world-renowned researcher in the field of wine science and technology. He is a professor at the Department of Food Science and Technology at the Virginia Polytechnic Institute & State University. He has teamed up with other experts from California State University at Fresno to deliver an outstanding book that every serious winemaker should own and have read thoroughly. This book is very technical in nature, yet well organized and very easy to read. It is one of the most practical and useful book on wine analysis and production, with an extensive section on laboratory procedures.

CREDITS – IMAGES AND TRADEMARKS

Some of the copyright material has previously appeared in another form in *WineMaker* magazine or winemakermag.com. The publisher has granted its reuse by the author here in this book.

Note: Every effort possible was made to contact copyright owners to obtain their permission to use copyrighted material, and extensive trademark searches were executed to ensure the accuracy of trademark acknowledgments. The author and publisher would be happy to correct any errors or omissions in a future edition of this book.

IMAGES

The author and publisher wish to thank the following organizations and individuals for their kind permission to reproduce the images and other material in this book.

Accuvin, LLC, Figures 3-6, 3-11, 3-12, 3-15 and 6-5.
American Wine Society, Figure 1-8. Reproduced from American Wine Society, THE COMPLETE HANDBOOK OF WINEMAKING. Ann Arbor: G.W. Kent, Inc. 1993. For further information on The American Wine Society, please contact (716) 225-7613.

American Wine Society, Figures 11-10 and 11-18. Reproduced from Manual #16, "Sparkling Wine" by Jim Gifford. AWS, 3006 Latta Road, Rochester, NY 14612. Illustrations by William Benson.

Amez-Droz SA, Figure 11-23.

Barnant Company (Thermo Fisher Scientific Inc.), Figure 5-9.

Battenkill Communications, LLP, Figure 4-5.

Better Bottle Div. High-Q, Inc., Figures 2-8 and 5-2.

Buon Vino Manufacturing Inc., Figures 9-9 and 9-10.

Charles Plant, Table 3-5. Adapted from Plant, Charles. "The Use of Sulphur Dioxide (SO2) in Winemaking." VAWA - Using Sulphur Dioxide To Protect Wine, http://www.bcwine.com/vawa/usingso2.htm/. 1997.

CHEMetrics, Inc., Figure 3-21.

Comité Interprofessionnel du Vin de Champagne (CIVC) Photothèque, Figures 11-12 (Photo ROHRSCHEID Collection CIVC) and 11-15.

Cryo Clean, Inc. (dba Barrel Blasting), Figures 8-5, 8-9, 8-10, 8-11 and 8-12.

Enotecnica di Pillan R.L.I. snc, Figures 2-4, 5-10, 5-14, 5-15 and 9-12.

Fermentis – Division of S.I. Lesaffre, Figure 4-8, and Table 4-3, adapted from Lesaffre Yeast Corporation (RED STAR) product documentation.

Fisher Scientific (Thermo Fisher Scientific Inc.), Figure 3-2 (middle).

Gary Crowe, Figure 8-17.

Ghidi divisione INOX, Figure 2-11 (top).

LAINOX s.r.l., Figure 2-12.

Lallemand, Inc., Figures 4-3 (left), 4-7, 4-11, 4-12, 4-13, 4-17, 4-19 and 4-21; and Tables 4-2, 4-6 and 4-8, adapted from Lallemand product documentation.

Meissner Filtration Products, Inc., Figures 6-8 and 6-9.

Mick Rock/Image Network Inc., Figure 11-13.

MoreWine! (MoreFlavor!, Inc.), Figures 2-2 (bottom) and 4-4.

Ohaus Corporation, Figure 2-26.

Piazza & Associates/LMI Lithographers Ltd., Figures 2-6 and 2-7.

Research & Development Glass Products & Equipment, Inc., Figures 3-13 and 3-23.

Scott Laboratories, Inc., Figure 4-20. Adapted from Scott Laboratories, Inc. FERMENTATION HANDBOOK 07. 2007. p. 41.

Spagni snc, Figure 9-13.

Spectre, Figures 3-25 and 11-11. Reproduced from Jens Priewe, WINE: FROM GRAPE TO GLASS. New York: Abbeville Press. 1999. Used with permission of Verlag Zabert Sandmann. GmbH, Munich.

St. Patrick's of Texas, Figure 2-14.

Tenco s.r.l. unipersonale, Figure 9-11.

ToolKing.com, Figure 2-25.
Vinquiry, Inc., Figure 4-18.
Vintage Keeper Inc., a division of Drobot Inc., Figure 15-3.
White Labs Inc., Figures 4-16 and 6-3, and Table 4-4, adapted from White Labs product documentation.
Wyeast Laboratories, Inc., Figures 4-10 and 4-16 (left), and Table 4-5, adapted from Wyeast Laboratories product documentation.

PHOTOGRAPHERS:

Paul Labelle Photographe Inc., Figures 2-1, 2-2 (top), 2-3, 2-5, 2-9, 2-15, 2-17, 2-18, 2-19, 2-21, 2-22, 2-23, 3-1, 3-2 (top), 3-14, 5-7, 8-1, 9-1, 9-3, 9-6, 9-8, 9-15, 11-5, 11-6, 11-24, 11-26 and 12-1.
Daniel Pambianchi, Figures 1-1, 1-5, 1-6, 1-7, 2-10, 2-13, 2-16, 2-20, 2-24, 2-27, 3-5, 3-7, 3-8, 3-9, 3-10, 3-16, 3-19, 3-20, 3-22, 4-1, 4-2, 4-3 (right), 4-6, 4-9, 4-14, 4-15, 4-16 (right), 4-22, 5-1, 5-3, 5-4 (top), 5-5, 5-6, 5-8, 5-11, 5-12, 5-13, 5-17, 6-1, 6-2, 6-4, 6-6, 6-7, 6-10, 8-2, 8-3, 8-4, 8-6, 8-8, 8-13, 8-14, 8-15, 8-16, 8-18, 9-4, 9-5, 9-7, 9-14, 9-16, 9-17, 11-2, 11-3, 11-4, 11-8, 11-9, 11-16, 11-19, 11-20, 11-21, 11-22, 11-25, 13-1, 13-2, 13-3, 13-4, and 15-4.

ILLUSTRATORS:

Don Martin, Figures 1-2, 1-3 and 1-4 (adapted from reference 3 [Bettiga et al.]), and 1-9, 1-10, 1-11, 1-12, 1-13, 1-14, 1-15, 2-11 (bottom), 3-4, 4-5 (owned by Battenkill Communications, LLP), 5-4 (bottom), 5-16, 6-11, 6-12, 8-7, 9-2, 11-1 and 11-17.
Daniel Pambianchi, Figures 1-10, 1-11, 1-12, 1-13, 1-14, 1-15, 3-2 (bottom), 3-3, 3-17, 3-18, 3-24, 4-23, 4-24, 11-1, 11-7, and 11-14.
Mauro Pambianchi, Figures 15-1 and 15-2.

TRADEMARKS

This section acknowledges trademarks registered in various countries worldwide with the United States Patent and Trademark Office (USPTO), the Canadian Intellectual Property Office (CIPO), the World Intellectual Property Organization (WIPO), and the German Patent and Trade Mark Office (DPMA) for products and/or services cited in this book.

ACIDEX is a registered trademark of Erbslöh Geisenheim AG.

ACTIVATOR, VINTNER'S CHOICE, 4021–Pasteur Champagne, 4028–Chateau Red, 4242–Chablis, 4244–Chianti, 4267–Bordeaux, 4767–Port Wine, 4783–Rudisheimer, 4946–Zinfandel are trademarks of Wyeast Laboratories, Inc.

ARABINOL is a registered trademark AEB S.p.A.

BESTBUNG is a trademark of Make-It Manufacturing Inc.

BETTER BOTTLE is a registered trademark of Gibbs, Erich L. (High-Q, Inc.) and Dry Trap is a trademark of High-Q, Inc.

BREATHING BUNG is a trademark of Ferm-Rite, Inc.

CHILLR and CHILLR PLUS are trademarks of Vintage Keeper Inc., a division of Drobot Inc.

CLARO K.C. is a registered trademark of Wine Art Company Ltd., now Wine Kitz (World Vintners Inc.).

CLINITEST is a registered trademark of Siemens Medical Solutions, a division of Siemens AG.

EFFERBAKTOL is a trademark of Martin Vialatte Œnologie.

ENOLMATIC and ENOLMASTER are trademarks of Tenco s.r.l. unipersonale.

FILL JET, MINI JET and SUPER JET are registered trademarks of Buon Vino Manufacturing, Inc.

LALVIN and LALVIN 31, 71B, BOURGOBLANC CY3079, CROSS EVOLUTION, BM45, BM4X4, EC-1118, ICV-D254, ICV-D80, QA23, RC 212, RHÔNE 2056, and V1116, ENOFERM BDX and L2226, GO-FERM, LALLZYME, OPTI'MALO, OPTIRED, OPTIWHITE, FERMAID, MBR, and UVAFERM 43 are registered trademarks of Lallemand, Inc. and/or its subsidiary, Danstar Ferment AG. BOOSTERROUGE and LYSO-EASY are trademarks of Lallemand, Inc.

MELVICO is a trademark of Melvico, Inc.

MICROQIT is a trademark of Prahl Biolab ApS (now distributed by White Labs Inc.)

OENOSTERYL is a registered trademark of Laffort Oenologie.

ONE STEP is a trademark of Logic, Inc.

PASTEUR RED and SUPERFOOD and are registered trademarks of Dr. Lisa Van de Water (dba The Wine Lab).

POLYCLAR is a registered trademark of International Speciality Products (ISP).

PRODESSERT is a registered trademark of Proenol - Indústria Biotecnológica, Lda.

PROXYCLEAN is a trademark of Barrel Builders, Inc.

QUICK TESTS is a registered trademark of ACCUVIN, LLC.

RAPIDASE is a registered trademark of DSM IP ASSETS B.V.

RED STAR is a registered trademark of Lesaffre Yeast Corporation.

SCOUT is a registered trademark of Ohaus Corporation.

SIHA is a registered trademark of E. Begerow GmbH & Co. SIHADEX is a trademark of E. Begerow GmbH & Co.

SINATIN 17 is a trademark of Winemakeri Inc.

SPARKOLLOID and COLD MIX SPARKOLLOID are registered trademarks of Scott Laboratories, Inc.

SPECTRA POR is a registered trademark of Spectrum Medical Industries, Inc.

STAVIN is a registered trademark of StaVin Incorporated.

STYROFOAM is a registered trademark of The Dow Chemical Company.

SULFACOR and Dr. Stührk'sche Titrierlösung are registered trademarks of Richard Wagner GmbH + Co. KG.

TANNISOL is a trademark of Esseco Group s.r.l.

THE V VESSEL SYSTEM and Design are registered trademarks of Piazza & Associates Ltd.

TIGERFLEX is a registered trademark Tigers Polymer Corporation.

TITRETS is a registered trademark of CHEMetrics Inc. TITRETTOR is a trademark of CHEMetrics Inc.

INDEX

Page numbers in **bold** type indicate important and most relevant references.

NOTES